# Clean Hydrogen for Decarbonisation

Aliaksei Patonia • Rahmatallah Poudineh

# Clean Hydrogen for Decarbonisation

## Beyond the 'Next Oil' Narrative

palgrave
macmillan

Aliaksei Patonia
The Oxford Institute for Energy Studies
Oxford, UK

Rahmatallah Poudineh
The Oxford Institute for Energy Studies
Oxford, UK

ISBN 978-3-032-19441-1 ISBN 978-3-032-19442-8 (eBook)
https://doi.org/10.1007/978-3-032-19442-8



This Palgrave Macmillan imprint is published by the registered company Springer Nature Switzerland AG
The registered company address is: Gewerbestrasse 11, 6330 Cham, Switzerland

# Foreword

*When you come to a fork in the road, take it*
—Yogi Berra

The global conversation on low-emission hydrogen and its role in the energy transition began gaining momentum around 2019, including at the United Nations. Hydrogen emerged from technical obscurity to political prominence, heralded by some as the holy grail of decarbonisation, and dismissed by others as a costly distraction. Between these extremes lies a more complex reality that this book investigates with clarity and scientific rigour.

The book is timely and needed. Lately, the debate on hydrogen has become less fact-based and rather polarized, increasingly revolving around beliefs rather than facts. With its future direction uncertain, today's discourse on hydrogen stands at a fork in the road.

*Clean Hydrogen for Decarbonisation: Beyond the 'Next Oil' Narrative* reframes hydrogen's role in the energy transition. Rather than taking side in the debate, Aliaksei Patonia and Rahmatallah Poudineh chose to chart a middle course: hydrogen is neither a cure-all nor a mere fluke. Its value as an energy carrier could only be assessed on a case-by-case basis and in a broader context of technology, infrastructure, policy and market interplay.

The book's strength lies in its systemic approach. Patonia and Poudineh do not try to convince us that hydrogen is a priori 'good', 'bad', 'green', or 'blue''. Instead, they ask more meaningful questions: *Why and where does hydrogen matter? Under what conditions? At what scale? In what situations? At what cost?* Each chapter contributes a critical piece of this puzzle, from production to transport, trade, storage, and end-use applications.

Yet the book is far more than a joyride along the value chain. Its message is clear: hydrogen will not be the oil of the twenty-first century, nor will it become the universal energy carrier on the scale the hydrocarbons are today. Its future will be more modest, more fragmented, and more context-dependent. But within those constraints lies a profound strategic significance.

For the hard-to-abate sectors that still underpin the global economy—steel, chemicals, long-distance transport and shipping—low-emission hydrogen with its derivatives is not a luxury but a serious alternative. Its importance will grow as renewable energy penetration deepens and as the limits of electrification of everything become more visible. The challenge, the book argues, is not to further fuel the hydrogen's hype but to understand its proper place within a future decarbonised world.

*Branko Milicevic, Secretary, UNECE Hydrogen Task Force*[1]

Geneva, Switzerland Branko Milicevic

[1] The views expressed herein are those of the author and do not necessarily reflect the views of the United Nations.

# Preface

This book grew out of our shared journey since 2019, during which we have worked—sometimes together, sometimes independently—on different parts of the hydrogen value chain. From electrolysers and transport infrastructure to long-distance shipping, storage, and support mechanisms such as Contracts for Difference, our research at the Oxford Institute for Energy Studies has gradually converged around one central question: *where, when, and how does hydrogen truly matter?*

As researchers in energy and industrial policy, we have combined our perspectives to bridge the gap between what is technologically possible and what is economically viable. The result is a book that aims to ground a fast-moving debate in evidence rather than aspiration. At a time when governments publish hydrogen strategies, investors announce multi-billion projects, and expectations run high, there is a pressing need for clarity—about costs, infrastructure realities, and hydrogen's true comparative advantage within both the energy system and the wider economy.

Our central argument is simple: clean hydrogen will not be the 'next oil', but it will remain indispensable in those parts of the economy where no other option can deliver deep decarbonisation. The book is written for policymakers, industry leaders, investors, researchers, and students who seek a rigorous yet accessible guide to the economics, technologies, and governance of hydrogen.

We are grateful to the Oxford Institute for Energy Studies for its research support, to our colleagues who reviewed drafts and offered invaluable feedback, and to our families for their patience and encouragement throughout this long project.

We hope this book cuts through the noise and provides a solid foundation for the critical decisions that lie ahead.

Oxford, UK
November 2025

Aliaksei Patonia
Rahmatallah Poudineh

*Competing Interests* The authors have no competing interests to declare that are relevant to the content of this manuscript.

# Contents

# Abbreviations

| | |
|---|---|
| ABS | American Bureau of Shipping |
| ACCR | Australasian Centre for Corporate Responsibility |
| ATAG | Air Transport Action Group |
| BF-BOF | Blast Furnace-Basic Oxygen Furnace |
| BMWK | Bundesministerium für Wirtschaft und Klimaschutz (German Federal Ministry for Economic Affairs and Climate Action) |
| CCfD | Carbon Contract for Difference |
| CCS / CCUS | Carbon Capture and Storage / Carbon Capture, Utilisation and Storage |
| CBAM | Carbon Border Adjustment Mechanism |
| CfD | Contract for Difference |
| $CGH_2$ | Compressed Gaseous Hydrogen |
| CORSIA | Carbon Offsetting and Reduction Scheme for International Aviation |
| CSTEP | Center for Study of Science, Technology and Policy |
| DRI | Direct Reduced Iron |
| EAF | Electric Arc Furnace |
| EEA | European Environment Agency |
| EHB | European Hydrogen Backbone |
| EMSA | European Maritime Safety Agency |
| ETS | Emissions Trading System |
| EU | European Union |

| | |
|---|---|
| FAA | Federal Aviation Administration (United States) |
| GHG | Greenhouse Gas |
| GW / MW / kW | Gigawatt / Megawatt / Kilowatt |
| HEFA | Hydroprocessed Esters and Fatty Acids |
| HYBRIT | Hydrogen Breakthrough Ironmaking Technology (Sweden) |
| $H_2$-ICE | Hydrogen Internal Combustion Engine |
| $H_2$-DRI | Hydrogen-based Direct Reduced Iron |
| $H_2$FLY | Hydrogen-electric flight company (Germany) |
| $H_2$GLASS | EU Hydrogen for Glass project |
| $H_2$Global | German Hydrogen Import and Trading Initiative |
| IATA | International Air Transport Association |
| ICAO | International Civil Aviation Organization |
| IEA | International Energy Agency |
| IEEFA | Institute for Energy Economics and Financial Analysis |
| IRENA | International Renewable Energy Agency |
| IPCC | Intergovernmental Panel on Climate Change |
| IPHE | International Partnership for Hydrogen and Fuel Cells in the Economy |
| IRA | Inflation Reduction Act (United States, 2022) |
| $LH_2$ | Liquid Hydrogen |
| LOHC | Liquid Organic Hydrogen Carrier |
| MOF | Metal–Organic Framework |
| NG | Natural Gas |
| NGO | Non-Governmental Organisation |
| NOx | Nitrogen Oxides |
| OECD | Organisation for Economic Co-operation and Development |
| PEM / PEMFC | Proton Exchange Membrane / Proton Exchange Membrane Fuel Cell |
| PtL | Power-to-Liquid |
| RED II / RED III | Renewable Energy Directive II / III (European Union) |
| SAF | Sustainable Aviation Fuel |
| SMR | Steam Methane Reforming |

| | |
|---|---|
| SOFC | Solid Oxide Fuel Cell |
| TRL | Technology Readiness Level |
| UN / UNECE / UNEP | United Nations / United Nations Economic Commission for Europe / United Nations Environment Programme |
| USD / EUR | United States Dollar / Euro |
| WEF | World Economic Forum |
| WWF | World Wide Fund for Nature |
| ZEROe | Airbus Hydrogen Aircraft Programme |

## Units and symbols

| | |
|---|---|
| °C | Degrees Celsius |
| $CO_2$ | Carbon Dioxide |
| $H_2$ | Hydrogen |
| $tCO_2$ | tonnes of Carbon Dioxide Equivalent |

# List of Figures

# List of Tables

CHAPTER 1

# Introduction

The urgency with which the world must decarbonise is no longer abstract. The latest assessments of the emissions gap show that even today's commitments leave us far short of what is needed to keep warming to 1.5 °C (UNEP, 2024). In many countries, energy systems are stuck in a 'low-hanging fruit' phase like switching from coal to natural gas, rolling out renewables and improving efficiency but still emitting hundreds of megatons of carbon dioxide ($CO_2$) annually. The window for deep transformation is closing: to meet the Paris goals, global energy $CO_2$ emissions must reach net zero by 2050 (IEA, 2023). Meeting this challenge requires reshaping energy generation, infrastructure, and consumption patterns from the ground up.

A key insight from energy transitions is that non-trivial residual emissions remain even in highly electrified, efficient energy systems. Some sectors and processes resist decarbonisation by standard pathways. Heavy industries such as steel, cement, and chemicals alone contribute roughly 6 Gt $CO_2$ per year (about 70% of industrial $CO_2$ emissions), and it is difficult to decarbonise because of high-temperature requirements and process emissions (IEA, 2022; Cretech, 2024). Meanwhile, long-distance transport modes like shipping and aviation demand energy densities and ranges that challenge battery or electric solutions. This means, to reach net zero, we must confront what are often called 'hard-to-abate' sectors—where



A. Patonia, R. Poudineh, *Clean Hydrogen for Decarbonisation*,
https://doi.org/10.1007/978-3-032-19442-8_1

efficiency, renewables, and electrification are necessary but may not be sufficient.

The magnitude of this challenge becomes clearer when one reflects on the scale of transformation required. The World Economic Forum's 'Net-Zero Industry Tracker' (2024) estimates that seven industries alone already account for near 30% of global greenhouse gas emissions and must converge sharply towards zero by mid-century (Net Zero Professional, 2023; WEF, 2024) (see Fig. 1.1). If these sectors lag, all the gains from decarbonising power and buildings will be overwhelmed. In effect, the decarbonisation imperative is not just about 'what to decarbonise first', but also about how to decarbonise everything in a way that is systemic, cross-sectoral, and interdependent.

Within that context, hydrogen is re-emerging from decades of scientific curiosity and sporadic deployment to take a role in the narrative of decarbonisation. Hydrogen is not new to industry or energy systems; it already powers refining, fertilizer manufacture, and numerous chemical processes around the world. The modern revival of hydrogen is however different: it is built on a recognition that there are emission sources which are hard to abate and cannot simply be electrified. This turn in the hydrogen story is also underpinned by converging stresses in energy systems: the accelerating penetration of variable renewable generation, rising needs for

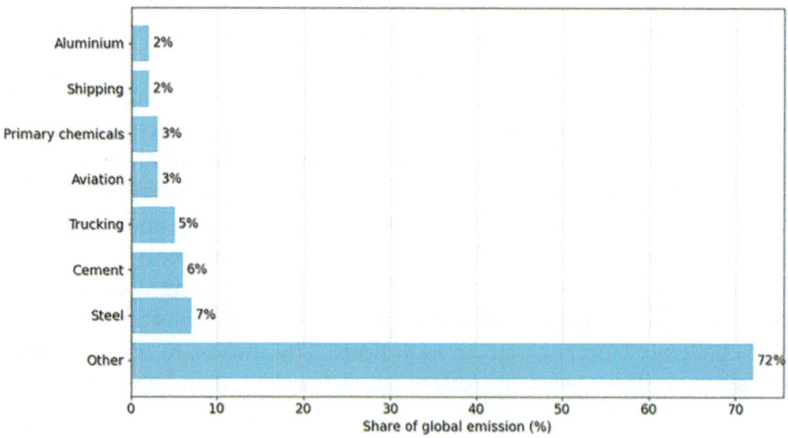


**Fig. 1.1** Global share of greenhouse gas emissions by sector. (Source: WEF (2024))

long-duration storage, and geopolitical volatility in fossil fuel markets. Renewable electricity, once constrained by intermittent supply, is creating surplus periods, and hydrogen can offer a pathway to absorb and store that surplus for later use. At the same time, under right conditions, hydrogen can provide the dispatchable, seasonal, or high-temperature energy that batteries, transmission, or heat pumps struggle to deliver at this stage of technological development. In short, hydrogen can potentially serve as the molecular 'glue' that connects decarbonised grids to decarbonised end uses.

From a technical perspective, hydrogen is unique among energy carriers in that it straddles two modes: production from primary energy, and conversion or utilisation in multiple downstream forms. On the upstream side, hydrogen can be derived via a spectrum of chemical and electrochemical technologies from steam methane reforming (SMR) with or without carbon capture to water electrolysis (alkaline, proton exchange membrane, aneon exchange membrane, and solid oxide) to emerging paths such as biomass gasification, thermochemical/solar splitting, and plasma/pyrolysis (Abubakr et al., 2024). Each pathway has distinct cost, energy, emissions, and maturity characteristics. What unites them is the chemical product $H_2$, but the differences in how we get there constrain where and how hydrogen can play in decarbonisation.

Once produced, hydrogen must be stored, transported, blended, or converted before reaching its end uses. Midstream options include compressed gas, liquefaction, chemical carriers such as ammonia, synthetic hydrocarbons or hydrogen carriers like LOHCs (liquid organic hydrogen carriers), and pipeline or shipping logistics. In many proposed hydrogen economies, derivative molecules (e.g., ammonia, e-methanol, synthetic fuels) act as the tradeable forms rather than pure hydrogen, especially for long-distance or international transport. In areas where geology allows, bulk storage in salt caverns or depleted gas fields offers seasonal flexibility; elsewhere, hydrogen may circulate as part of local networks or hubs.

The end-use side is where hydrogen's many faces appear most vividly—as a feedstock (e.g., in ammonia, methanol, refining), a chemical reductant (e.g., in steel making through direct reduction of iron), a high-heat fuel (for cement, glass, chemicals), a transportation fuel (fuel-cell trucks, ships, aircraft via e-fuels), and as a flexible energy carrier in power or heating (fuel cells, turbines, hydrogen boilers, blending). For hydrogen to play a role in decarbonisation, its demand must expand from conventional sectors like refining and chemicals into novel uses in heavy industry, long-distance transport, and seasonal storage.

Yet, this vision carries a caveat. Hydrogen has always lived in tension with performance realities: the costs are steep, the efficiency losses are substantial, its footprint has been almost entirely 'grey' until recently (i.e., produced from fossil fuels without carbon capture), and scaling low-carbon hydrogen infrastructure is a massive undertaking. In earlier cycles, hydrogen was hailed prematurely as the 'new oil' or 'fuel of the future', only to recede when costs and engineering complexity proved too stubborn. The current resurgence is more cautious but the stakes are higher. Today, governments, corporations, and investors are committing hundreds of billions to hydrogen strategies. The International Energy Agency in 2025 reports that more than 200 committed low-emissions hydrogen production projects exist globally, but adoption remains uneven, and uncertainties about cost, infrastructure, and regulation loom large (IEA, 2025). The comeback has begun, but it must pass a far sterner test than earlier iterations.

Indeed, history is littered with hydrogen optimism that failed to bear fruit. In the early 2000s, hydrogen fuel cells were presented as the inevitable successor to gasoline engines (Romm, 2004), but battery-electric technology matured faster, and infrastructure costs for hydrogen never scaled. Similarly, in periods of elevated fossil fuel interest, hydrogen has resurfaced as a bridging narrative only to recede when markets shifted. Critics caution that the current wave resembles earlier cycles—a flurry of announcements, ambitious roadmaps, speculative trades—but still lacking firm evidence of cost, demand, or logistical feasibility (Gaster, 2024). The challenge then is to move beyond romanticism to rigorous evaluation: which parts of the hype are viable, and which are misdirection?

That tension between promise and practicality gives rise to the hard questions that frame this book. When is hydrogen truly indispensable rather than marginal? Under what cost, infrastructure, and policy conditions can hydrogen compete? How will hydrogen move, trade, and be stored at scale? How does hydrogen integrate into energy systems dominated by electrons? Which policy levers reliably mobilize investment? And finally, what environmental and social guardrails can ensure that hydrogen widens climate ambition rather than erodes it? Only by confronting these kinds of questions we might be able to separate the durable from the speculative.

Hydrogen's climate profile also requires explicit attention to emissions beyond $CO_2$: in addition to upstream methane control for blue hydrogen, hydrogen leakage itself matters. Hydrogen is not a direct greenhouse gas, but when emitted it can exert an indirect warming influence through atmospheric chemistry, and the sector still lacks mature, low-cost monitoring-reporting-verification approaches at scale. We therefore treat leakage not only as a safety and cost issue, but also as a climate-governance constraint that shapes acceptable pathways.

Crucially, the hard questions are not independent; they are deeply interlinked. Whether hydrogen is used in particular sectors depends on cost trajectories, which, in their turn, depend on policy and infrastructure. Infrastructure design depends on production pathways, which depend on support policies and lifecycle emissions considerations. Energy system integration feeds into sectoral deployment choices, and environmental/social safeguards impose limits on acceptable pathways. The seven foundational questions introduced earlier constitute a tightly interwoven logic: resolving one often requires engaging with several others. So the task of this book is not to treat hydrogen silos (production, transport, policy) in isolation, but to trace how they entangle across systems and sectors.[1]

Hydrogen's return to the centre of the decarbonisation debate reflects both technological progress and political aspiration. Yet the excitement surrounding it sometimes masks the physical and economic constraints that remain stubbornly in place. Producing hydrogen requires significant energy, and converting it back into useful work—whether through combustion or fuel cells—inevitably involves significant efficiency losses across the full cycle. Infrastructure development poses another hurdle: transporting and storing hydrogen safely and economically demands new materials, dedicated (or repurposed) pipelines, and high capital investment. Moreover, the water required for large-scale electrolysis, and the methane control necessary for blue hydrogen, introduce resource and environmental dependencies that must be tightly managed. These constraints remind

[1] While hydrogen markets and value chains are global, this book draws much of its policy-detail and institutional analysis from Europe—particularly the EU and the United Kingdom—where policy documentation is richest and where the authors' empirical engagement is deepest. This creates an inevitable Eurocentric tilt. To reduce the risk of over-generalising from European experience, we flag (where relevant) major developments and contrasting conditions in other key regions (e.g., China, India, North America, Japan/Korea), even when we do not provide full country case studies.

us that hydrogen's value lies not in ubiquity but in precision—it should be used where it makes sense, not where alternatives already perform better.

However, dismissing hydrogen on the grounds of these challenges would be equally misguided. If we use the history of previous energy transitions as guide, we can see that they rarely unfolded through one dominant technology but through a mosaic of complementary solutions. Hydrogen can provide the missing links between sectors where electricity alone cannot deliver the necessary energy density or process conditions. The task, therefore, is not to ask whether hydrogen has a role at all, but to define where it adds unique value within a broader portfolio of decarbonisation options.

The pragmatic path forward lies between those extremes of technoptimism and scepticism. It requires evidence-based assessment of hydrogen's comparative advantage across regions and sectors, and policies that reward real emissions reduction rather than symbolic deployment. Governments and industries must learn from the experience of renewables: rapid cost declines came not from hype but from technological advances, consistent policy signals, standardisation, and scale. Likewise, a rational hydrogen transition will depend on carefully targeted support, credible certification, and rigorous lifecycle accounting. This book proceeds in that spirit—neither as advocacy nor as doubt, but as an inquiry into how hydrogen, deployed wisely and within its limits, can contribute meaningfully to the global decarbonisation effort.

The book unfolds as a journey from fundamentals to frontiers—from the core technologies that produce hydrogen to the intricate web of infrastructure, policies, and end uses that determine its ultimate value in a decarbonised world. It is not a linear story but a systems narrative: each chapter contributes a piece to the overarching questions introduced earlier—when, where, and how hydrogen truly matters. The sequence of chapters is designed to move from how hydrogen is made, to how it moves and is stored, and finally to how it is and could be used across sectors that resist straightforward electrification. Throughout, the book weaves technical, economic, and policy perspectives into a single analytic fabric, emphasising cross-sector linkages and trade-offs rather than siloed discussions.

The first three chapters establish the technological and policy foundations. Chapter 2 (Key Technologies and Costs of Hydrogen Production) provides a transparent, evidence-based assessment of hydrogen production pathways and their economics—setting the baseline for every subsequent discussion. Chapter 3 (Low-Carbon Hydrogen Production Support Schemes) examines the policy instruments that can bridge the cost gap between clean and fossil-based hydrogen, focusing on the limits and potential of Contracts for Difference and complementary tools. Chapter 4 (Hydrogen Transportation and Trade) extends the analysis to the midstream, comparing pipelines, carriers, and shipping routes, and highlighting the emerging geography of hydrogen as a traded commodity. Together, these chapters answer the first two foundational questions of the book: which production pathways are viable, and under what infrastructure and policy conditions can they scale?

Building on that foundation, the next two chapters explore the enabling infrastructure that anchors hydrogen within energy systems. Chapter 5 (Hydrogen Storage Technologies) analyses options from compressed and liquefied storage to underground caverns, showing how storage underpins both flexibility and energy security. Chapter 6 (Hydrogen in the Power Sector) then investigates hydrogen's role in long-duration energy storage, particularly during periods of renewable shortfall. These chapters collectively speak to the book's questions about system integration—where hydrogen fits within power grids, and what technical and economic boundaries define its value as a resilience tool.

The following sequence—Chaps. 7, 8, 9, 10, and 11—shifts from infrastructure to sectoral applications, tracing hydrogen's selective but critical role in end-use decarbonisation. Chapter 7 (Hydrogen in Road and Rail Transport), Chap. 8 (Hydrogen for Maritime Transport), and Chap. 9 (Hydrogen in Aviation) dissect the transport sector, revealing where hydrogen and its derivatives could complement or compete with electrification and sustainable fuels. Chapter 10 (Hydrogen for Steel Production) provides one of the book's analytical centrepieces: an in-depth look at hydrogen-based direct reduction of iron and the industrial transformation it implies. Chapter 11 (Hydrogen for Cement Production) follows, showing that even where hydrogen can reduce fuel-related emissions, carbon capture and process innovation remain indispensable. Across these chapters, hydrogen appears not as a universal fuel but as a specialised enabler in specific contexts—a precision tool in a larger decarbonisation kit.

The industrial focus deepens in Chaps. 12 and 13, which examine the chemical sector and high-heat processes. Chapter 12 (Hydrogen for the Chemical Industry) discusses hydrogen's role as both an energy carrier and feedstock, assessing pathways for ammonia, methanol, and olefin production. Chapter 13 (Hydrogen for High-Heat Processes) broadens the scope to refining, glass, and ceramics, analysing where hydrogen combustion is advantageous and where electrification or CCUS will dominate. These chapters collectively illuminate how hydrogen interacts with industrial processes – answering the questions of where it can substitute, where it must complement, and where it cannot compete. They reinforce a central theme of the book: that the hydrogen transition is not uniform but profoundly sector- and context-dependent.[2]

The final Conclusions chapter returns to the seven guiding questions introduced in the opening section, synthesising insights across all domains—technological, economic, infrastructural, and social. The analysis indicates that hydrogen's progress will emerge from the interplay of cost declines, policy refinement, and integrated action among industries, rather than from any single game-changing discovery. The concluding message is one of measured caution: clean hydrogen will unlikely become 'the new oil' or 'fuel of the future'. Instead, hydrogen can play an important role in the decarbonisation process, but only if deployed judiciously—in the right places, at the right scales, and with the right governance. The book thus closes where it began: navigating between promise and pragmatism.

## References

Abubakr, M., Shahid, S., & Arman, I. (2024). *A review on hydrogen production technologies and its future demand* [Online]. Retrieved October 8, 2025, from https://arxiv.org/abs/2410.08154.

Cretech. (2024). *MIT-backed fund aims to tackle the toughest climate challenges* [Online]. Retrieved November 29, 2025, from https://www.cretech.com/news/mit-backed-fund-aims-to-tackle-the-toughest-climate-challenges/.

Gaster, R. (2024). *A realist approach to hydrogen. Washington, DC: Information Technology & Innovation Foundation (ITIF)* [Online]. Retrieved October 8, 2025, from https://itif.org/publications/2024/01/17/a-realist-approach-to-hydrogen/.

IEA. (2022). *Achieving net-zero heavy industry sectors in G7 members.* International Energy Agency (IEA).

[2] Chapters 7, 8, 9, 10, 11, 12, and 13 follow a common analytical template (technology → infrastructure → economics → policy → pilots) to allow comparison across sectors; where elements of the hydrogen supply chain would otherwise repeat, we cross-refer back to Chaps. 4, 5, and 6 and keep later chapters focused on sector-specific constraints.

IEA. (2023). *Net-zero by 2050: A roadmap for the global energy sector.* International Energy Agency (IEA).

IEA. (2025). *Global hydrogen review 2025.* International Energy Agency (IEA).

Net Zero Professional. (2023). *Chemicals industry must transform to avoid 4 °C rise* [Online]. Retrieved November 29, 2025, from https://netzeroprofessional.com/chemicals-industry-must-transform-to-avoid-4%E2%81%B0c-rise/

Romm, J. J. (2004). The hype about hydrogen. *Issues in Science and Technology, 20* (3) [Online]. Retrieved October 8, 2025, from https://issues.org/romm-hydrogen-clean-energy/.

UNEP. (2024). *Emissions gap report 2024: No more hot air ... please! With a massive gap between rhetoric and reality, countries draft new climate commitments.* United Nations Environment Programme (UNEP).

WEF. (2024). *Net-zero industry tracker 2024.* World Economic Forum (WEF).

CHAPTER 2

# Key Technologies and Costs of Hydrogen Production

## Introduction

Leading international organisations have positioned clean hydrogen—i.e., $H_2$ produced with minimum or no carbon emissions—as a cornerstone of the global energy transition. In this connection, roadmaps from the International Energy Agency (IEA), the International Renewable Energy Agency (IRENA), the Hydrogen Council, and BloombergNEF (BNEF) project that hydrogen could account for 10–15% of global final energy demand by 2050 (IEA, 2022; IRENA, 2022; Hydrogen Council, 2021; BloombergNEF, 2023). These scenarios assume hydrogen will complement electrification by decarbonising or helping to decabonise hard-to-abate sectors such as steel, cement, chemicals, aviation, and shipping.

These ambitious outlooks become clearer when placed against the backdrop of hydrogen's historical evolution. First produced commercially in the late nineteenth century, hydrogen's large-scale use grew throughout the twentieth century, primarily for ammonia fertiliser production and refining. For decades, the production cost trajectory was heavily influenced by the price of fossil feedstocks, with steam methane reforming (SMR) establishing itself as the dominant, lowest-cost method. The idea of 'clean hydrogen' and its colour-based classification system is relatively new, having taken shape in the twenty-first century as part of broader climate-mitigation agendas.



A. Patonia, R. Poudineh, *Clean Hydrogen for Decarbonisation*,
https://doi.org/10.1007/978-3-032-19442-8_2

Yet these projections are highly contingent upon rapid declines in the levelised cost of hydrogen (LCOH) and the parallel rollout of infrastructure, among other factors. In particular, according to most common estimates, green hydrogen average costs currently range from USD 3–8 per kg in most real projects, with lowest estimates going below USD 3 per kg being restricted to regions with abundant cheap renewables, such as Saudi Arabia's NEOM project or Spain's HyDeal initiative (BloombergNEF, 2023; H2-Diplo, 2023). Blue hydrogen, in turn, is often assumed to offer a lower-cost transition pathway, with recent studies suggesting USD 1.2–3/kg under favourable natural gas and carbon capture conditions (Massarweh et al., 2023; Li et al., 2025; Patonia, 2025). However, it remains exposed to volatile gas prices and concerns over methane leakage (Howarth & Jacobson, 2021). Finally, although so far confirmed in only one small field in Mali, white hydrogen—naturally occurring and geologically sourced $H_2$—has been claimed by pilot developers and start-ups to cost below 1 USD per kg, though its scalability and environmental impacts are highly uncertain (Patonia et al., 2024).

The gap between modelled costs in global scenarios and achieved costs in real projects therefore raises critical questions about hydrogen's true role in decarbonisation. This chapter examines the key hydrogen production technologies as well as their actual and estimated costs drawing on peer-reviewed evidence, project data, and industry analyses. It assesses how cost trajectories shape the feasibility of hydrogen as a large-scale decarbonisation pathway. Together, these insights form the technical basis for understanding hydrogen's real cost drivers and clarify why, despite enthusiasm, hydrogen's economics remain highly context-specific.

The chapter is structured as follows. Section "Current Technologies of Hydrogen Production" begins with a comprehensive review of production technologies. Section "Current and Projected Costs of Hydrogen Production" details the LCOH methodology and analyses current costs associated with each of the key production pathways. Next, Section "Roadmap Assumptions vs. Real Costs" critically compares roadmap assumptions with real-world data. Finally, Section "A Future Forged by Pragmatism" concludes with a realistic outlook on hydrogen's future.

## Current Technologies of Hydrogen Production

The expansion of hydrogen's role in the energy transition depends not only on policy and demand but also on the maturity, scalability, and environmental profile of its production technologies. At present, hydrogen is produced predominantly from fossil fuels, but low-carbon and renewable pathways are gaining traction. To ensure a comprehensive overview, this section begins with a brief review of all key production routes before delving into deeper analysis of the most prominent clean hydrogen pathways.

### *Conventional Production from Fossil Fuels*

The vast majority of hydrogen today is manufactured through steam methane reforming (SMR) of natural gas (Fig. 2.1). In this well-established process, methane reacts with water steam at high temperature to produce synthesis gas, which is then shifted and purified to yield hydrogen (Patonia & Poudineh, 2020; IEA, 2022). Plant capacities normally range from small refinery units producing tens of tonnes per day to very large complexes often integrated with ammonia or methanol production, supplying several hundred tonnes daily (Pan et al., 2025). It is not surprising that the economics of SMR are largely determined by natural gas feedstock prices, while the process itself is energy-intensive and highly

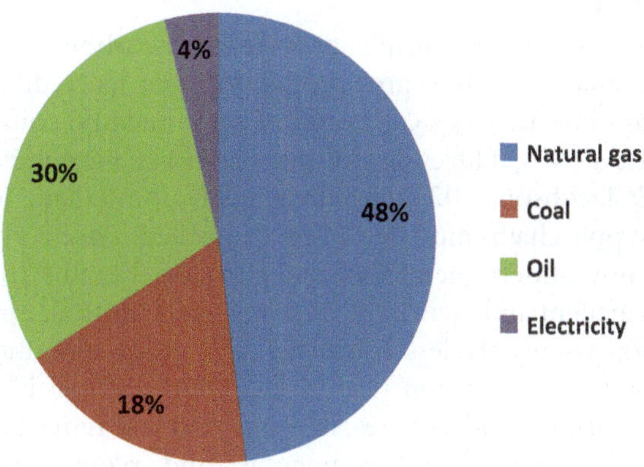


**Fig. 2.1** Global hydrogen production by source. (Source: Adapted from Le et al. (2023))

carbon-emitting—i.e., normally producing at least 10 kg of carbon dioxide per each kg of hydrogen (Table 2.1).

Coal gasification remains another important route, particularly in countries with abundant coal resources such as China and India, where it has historically supplied significant shares of hydrogen primarily for fertilisers and chemicals (IEA, 2022). Oil-derived hydrogen, mainly for refining processes like hydrocracking and desulphurisation, adds further (rather stable) demand, as this process is highly integrated into the mechanism of oil refining itself. Together, these pathways provide scale and reliability but are associated with very high carbon intensities, which make them incompatible with long-term decarbonisation targets without additional mitigation (Pan et al., 2025).

### *Fossil-Based Hydrogen with Carbon Management*

- **Conventional hydrogen production and CCS**

One of the most widely discussed decarbonisation strategies for conventional hydrogen production is coupling reforming processes with carbon capture. When combined with storage, the product is commonly referred to as blue hydrogen. Carbon capture can be applied at different points in SMR or autothermal reforming systems, and cluster projects such as H2H Saltend in the United Kingdom illustrate efforts to integrate reformers with $CO_2$ transport and storage infrastructure at scale (Equinor, 2024).

Blue hydrogen can, in principle, provide lower-carbon hydrogen at volumes comparable to existing grey production, but its credibility depends on several conditions. First, $CO_2$ capture rates must be consistently very high, well above 90%, if lifecycle emissions are to be meaningfully reduced (Howarth & Jacobson, 2021). Second, upstream methane leakage from natural gas supply chains must be tightly controlled, since even small losses can significantly undermine climate benefits (Patel et al., 2024). Finally, access to permanent and secure $CO_2$ storage sites is critical; carbon capture and utilisation routes are less robust because many utilisation pathways ultimately re-emit the carbon (Pan et al., 2025). While blue hydrogen could offer transitional advantages, its long-term role remains uncertain in light of these technical, environmental, and regulatory challenges, among others.

**Table 2.1** Key hydrogen generation processes, their estimated carbon intensity, and levelised cost of production

| *Origin* | *Feedstock/source* | *H2 production technology/ mechanism* | *CO2 abatement/ elimination technology* | *Example of main chemical reaction(s)* | *Estimated carbon intensity (kg-CO2e/ kg-H2)* | *Estimated levelised cost of production (USD/kg)a* |
|---|---|---|---|---|---|---|
| Manufactured | Natural gas | Steam methane reforming | n/a | $CH_4 + H_2O \rightarrow CO + 3H_2$ | 10.09–17.21 | 1.03–2.16 |
| | | | CCS | | 2.97–9.16 | 1.22–2.26 |
| | | Methane pyrolysis | CCU | $CH_4 \rightarrow 2H_2 + C$ | 1.9–9.14 | 1.36–2.45 |
| | Biomass | Biomass gasification | n/a | $C + H_2O \rightarrow CO + H_2$ (steam); | 0.31–8.63 | 1.48–3.00 |
| | | | CCS | $C + CO_2 \rightarrow 2CO$ (carbon) | -11.66–17.55 | 2.27–3.60 |
| | | Biomass pyrolysis | CCU | $C_xH_yO_z \rightarrow xC + y/2\ H_2 + CO + CO_2$ | TBD | 1.21–2.19 |
| | Coal | Coal gasification | n/a | $C + H_2O \rightarrow CO + H_2$ (steam); | 14.4–30.9 | 0.96–1.88 |
| | | | CCS | $CO + H_2O \rightarrow CO_2 + H_2$ | 0.78–10.35 | 1.40–3.60 |
| | Wind & water | Electrolysis of water | n/a | $2H_2O \rightarrow 2H_2 + O_2$ | 0.52–2.2 | 3.56–10.82 |
| | Solar & water | | | | 1.32–7.1 | 3.34–14.87 |
| | Nuclear & water | | | | 0.47–2.13 | 3.29–8.21 |
| | S-I | Thermochemical cycle | CCS or n/a[b] | | 0.41–2.2 | 1.47–2.71 |
| | Cu-Cl | | | | 0.7–1.8 | 1.47–2.70 |

*(continued)*

**Table 2.1** (continued)

| *Origin* | *Feedstock/source* | *H2 production technology/ mechanism* | | *CO2 abatement/ elimination technology* | *Example of main chemical reaction(s)* | *Estimated carbon intensity (kg-CO2e/ kg-H2)* | *Estimated levelised cost of production (USD/kg)a* |
|---|---|---|---|---|---|---|---|
| Naturally occurring | Olivine & water | Serpentinisation | | n/a | $6[(Mg_{1.5}Fe_{0.5})SiO_4] + 7H_2O \rightarrow 3[Mg_3Si_2O_5(OH)_4] + Fe_3O_4 + H_2$ | ~0.4–1.5 | Potentially <1 |
| | Hydrocarbons/ biomass/waste & heat | Deep-seated/thermal decomposition | | n/a or CCS | $CH_4 + 1/2O_2 \rightarrow 2H_2 + CO$ | | |
| | Water & ionising radiation | Radiolysis | | n/a | $2H_2O \rightarrow 2H_2 + O_2$ | | |
| | Organic compound & anaerobic microorganisms | Fermentation | Microbial/ biological | | $C_6H_{12}O_6 + 2H_2O \rightarrow 2CH_3COOH + 2CO_2 + 2H_2$ | | 1.26–10.57 |
| | Photosynthetic bacteria/ cyanobacteria/ algae & light & water | Photosynthesis | | | $2H_2O \rightarrow 2H_2 + O_2$ | | |

Source: Adapted from Patonia et al. (2024)

[a]Range depends on technology assumptions and regional factors

[b]Thermochemical cycles generate hydrogen by splitting water through a chain of high-temperature reactions powered by an external heat source—typically a nuclear reactor or concentrated solar energy—though, in theory, fossil-based heat could also be applied. (Ozcan et al., 2014)

- **Methane pyrolysis**

In addition to applying carbon capture and storage to conventional hydrogen production from natural gas, methane pyrolysis can also be used to generate the so-called turquoise hydrogen. This process decomposes methane (from natural gas or biogas) into solid carbon and hydrogen, using thermal or catalytic methods. The primary advantage is the avoidance of $CO_2$ emissions during production, with the carbon by-product potentially having market value (e.g., as carbon black). However, the technology is at an early demonstration stage, and challenges remain regarding reactor durability, energy intensity, and finding reliable markets for the solid carbon output (Wei et al., 2024).

### *Nuclear-Powered Electrolysis*

Using low-carbon electricity from nuclear power to drive electrolysers is also viewed as a viable pathway for clean ('pink') hydrogen production. Nuclear power provides a high-capacity factor, stable baseload electricity, which is advantageous for electrolyser operation. Advanced concepts also involve using high-temperature heat from advanced reactors for thermochemical water splitting, which promises higher efficiencies but is still in the R&D phase (IEA, 2022). Pilot initiatives confirm that producing hydrogen with nuclear energy is technically viable, but broader rollout is constrained by high capital costs and stringent regulatory processes.

### *Renewables-Derived Hydrogen*

- **Biomass and biogenic routes**

Hydrogen can be produced from biomass via gasification or reforming processes. When biomass systems are paired with carbon capture and storage (BECCS-$H_2$), the resulting hydrogen can achieve net-negative emissions. Nevertheless, while biomass gasification is a proven technology, its scalability is constrained by the sustainable availability of biomass feedstocks, logistical challenges, and competition for land use. The cost and complexity of integrating CCS further add to the challenges, keeping this pathway niche for the foreseeable future (Hosseini et al., 2024).

- **Electrolysis from renewable electricity**

Electrolysis powered by renewables—i.e., the splitting of water into hydrogen and oxygen using electricity coming from renewable power sources—represents the archetype of green hydrogen, which, in turn, is often viewed by many as 'the holy grail of decarbonisation'. Its potential rests on coupling with renewable electricity, enabling near-zero operational emissions (Table 2.1). While the core cost component of green hydrogen is power, electrolysers play crucial role in its production, as they represent the key piece of equipment that enables the manufacturing process (Fig. 2.2). At the moment, several electrolyser technologies exist, at different stages of maturity, each with distinct characteristics.

**Alkaline electrolysers** are the most established, with decades of industrial use in chemical production. They are mechanically robust and cost-effective at scale, but have lower current densities and limited flexibility in responding to rapid changes in power supply (Patonia & Poudineh, 2022; Wei et al., 2024). This, in general, makes them more suited to steady operation with baseload renewables or grid electricity (ibid.). In addition, apart from being the most technologically mature and powerful type of electrolysers, they are also currently typically the cheapest option available on the market (Table 2.2). Typical stack lifetimes are in the range of 60,000–90,000 h, with degradation rates of 0.5–1.5 μV/h (ibid.). A key

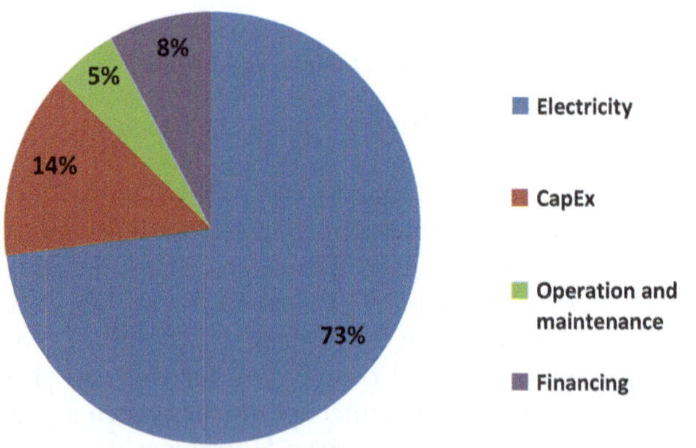


**Fig. 2.2** Main cost drivers (%) for 'green' hydrogen. (Source: Adapted from Patonia and Poudineh (2022))

**Table 2.2** Key characteristics of major electrolyser technologies

| *Technology* | *Current commercial status* | *Efficiency (LHV) (%)* | *Dynamic response* | *Key materials* | *Typical CapEx (USD/kW, 2023–2024)* | *Expected 2030 CapEx (USD/kW)* | *Key advantages* | | *Key challenges* | |
|---|---|---|---|---|---|---|---|---|---|---|
| | | | | | | | *Overall* | *For cost reduction* | *Overall* | *For cost reduction* |
| *Alkaline (AEL)* | Mature, widely deployed | 60–70 | Moderate | Nickel-based electrodes | 500–900 | 300–500 | • Low cost<br>• Proven | • Economies of scale in manufacturing | • Limited flexibility<br>• Large footprint | • Standardisation of BoP |
| *Proton exchange membrane (PEM)* | Commercial, scaling rapidly | 70–80 | Fast ramping | Platinum group metals (Pt, Ir) | 900–1500 | 500–800 | • High purity $H_2$<br>• Flexible operation | • Reduction of PGM loading<br>• Iridium thrifting & recycling | • High catalyst cost<br>• Supply risk | • PGM<br>• Increased manufacturing scale |
| *Anion exchange membrane (AEM)* | Early commercial pilots | 55–65 | Good | Non-precious catalysts (still under development) | 700–1200 | 400–600 | • Potential lower cost than PEM | • Commercialisation of non-precious catalysts | • Durability<br>• Limited lifetime data | • Membrane durability improvements |
| *Solid oxide electrolysis (SOE)* | Demonstration stage | 70–80 (with heat integration) | Slower dynamics | Ceramic oxides (yttria-stabilised zirconia) | 1200–2000 (pilot level) | 800–1200 | • High efficiency<br>• Industrial integration | • Automation of manufacturing for ceramic components | • Thermal stress<br>• Long-term stability | • Solving stack longevity issues |

Source: Adapted from Schmidt et al. (2017), Buttler and Spliethoff (2018), IEA (2022), IRENA (2022), Patonia and Poudineh (2022), Arsad et al. (2023), IEA (2024)

operational cost is the requirement for high-purity water (deionised) and the management of potassium hydroxide electrolyte (ibid.).

**Proton exchange membrane (PEM) electrolysers** are newer but increasingly commercialised. They operate with higher current densities, can ramp rapidly, and produce high-purity hydrogen. These features allow closer integration with variable solar and wind power. However, PEM systems depend on scarce and costly materials such as platinum group metals, which constrain large-scale deployment unless material intensity is reduced (Patonia & Poudineh, 2022). In addition to higher costs, if compared to alkaline options, PEM electrolysers are typically less powerful. At present, for this type of electrolyser, stack lifetimes are generally shorter than those of alkaline electrolysers, despite being expected to be similar or longer, typically around 30,000–60,000 h, with higher degradation rates (1.5–3 μV/h), which can be exacerbated by frequent start-stop cycling (Liu et al., 2024). The critical constraint is the supply of iridium, a rare and expensive catalyst; current R&D focuses on 'thrifting' (reducing loadings) and recycling strategies to mitigate supply chain risks (Patonia & Poudineh, 2022).

**Anion exchange membrane (AEM) electrolysers**, initially created to bridge the gap between alkaline and PEM systems to take the best of 'both worlds', represent a hybrid approach, combining some of the material benefits of alkaline systems with the compactness and flexibility of PEM. Despite having been commercialised a couple of years ago by a German-Italian company Enapter, they are still at a rather earlier stage of commercialisation around the world, with pilot deployments under way but questions about durability and lifetime still mostly not fully resolved (Liu et al., 2024; Enapter, 2025). The key promise is the use of non-precious metal catalysts, but challenges persist with membrane chemical stability and ionic conductivity, which directly impact lifetime and efficiency. Public data on long-term stack durability is still limited.

Looking ahead, **solid oxide electrolysis (SOE)** is expected to become commercially significant in the upcoming years, though, as of 2025, full commercialisation is yet to be achieved. Operating at high temperatures, SOE leverages thermal energy to improve efficiency and is particularly promising for integration with industrial waste heat or concentrated solar power (Wolf et al., 2023). Yet it faces substantial materials and system engineering challenges, especially in ensuring long-term stability under demanding conditions (Patonia & Poudineh, 2022). At the moment, the primary challenges are still slow start-up times and susceptibility to thermal cycling stress, which leads to material degradation (e.g., delamination of ceramic layers) (Wolf et al., 2023). Stack lifetimes are currently the shortest among major technologies, often below 20,000 h, posing a significant barrier to commercialisation.

Regardless of the electrolyser technology, the cost of electricity remains the principal driver of hydrogen's levelised production cost (Fig. 2.2). Electrolyser capital costs, while significant, are secondary to the economics of power supply. This makes the availability of abundant, low-cost renewable energy at high utilisation rates the critical determinant of green hydrogen competitiveness (ibid.). Scaling electrolyser manufacturing and reducing material bottlenecks, particularly for PEM, are also central to bringing down costs.

To provide a forward-looking perspective, it is useful to compare current CapEx with plausible 2030 projections, accounting for learning rates and material constraints (Table 2.2). Electrolyser capital costs currently range from about 750 to 1300 USD per kW for Chinese systems and around 2000 USD per kW for non-Chinese manufacturers (IEA, 2024). For the central case used in this book, a value of 800 USD per kW is adopted as an optimistic 2030 projection.

In the future, alkaline electrolysers are expected to see costs fall from USD 500–900/kW to USD 300–500/kW, driven by economies of scale and standardization. PEM electrolysers, in turn, could decline from USD 900–1500/kW to USD 500–800/kW, contingent on reducing platinum group metal loadings and scaling manufacturing. In principle, AEM systems might also reach USD 400–600/kW from USD 700–1200/kW if membrane durability improves. Finally, solid oxide systems face a longer road, potentially moving from USD 1200–2000/kW to USD 800–1200/kW, dependent on solving stack longevity issues.

### *Natural (Geologic) Hydrogen*

Among the different production pathways, natural hydrogen that is often referred to as 'white' (and sometimes 'gold') has recently attracted growing attention as a potentially disruptive supply option. Unlike green or blue hydrogen, which rely on industrial processes to convert energy carriers into hydrogen, natural hydrogen refers to geologically generated $H_2$ that can, as expected, accumulate in subsurface reservoirs and be extracted in a manner similar to natural gas (Patonia et al., 2024).

**Table 2.3** Comparative characteristics of hydrogen production pathways

| *Production route* | *Technology maturity* | *Typical scale (t/d)* | *Carbon intensity* | *Key challenges* | *Key opportunities* |
|---|---|---|---|---|---|
| *SMR (grey)* | Fully commercial | 100–500 | Very high | • $CO_2$ emissions<br>• Fossil fuel dependence | • Established infrastructure |
| *Coal gasification* | Fully commercial (mainly China, India) | 10–200 | High | • Linked to fossil fuel processing | • Embedded in refineries |
| *Refining (oil-based)* | Fully commercial | 10–200 | High | • Linked to fossil fuel processing | • Embedded in refineries |
| *SMR/ATR + CCS (blue)* | Early commercial | 100–300 | Medium-high (depends on leakage and capture) | • $CO_2$ storage access<br>• Methane leakage | • Potential transitional role |
| *Electrolysis + renewables (green)* | Commercialising | 10–200 | Low | • High CapEx<br>• Renewable intermittency | • Decarbonisation of hard-to-abate sectors |
| *Natural hydrogen (white)* | Very early stage (Hydroma's project in Mali) | <1 | Low (if scalable) | • Geological uncertainty<br>• Regulation | • Potential disruptive low-cost supply |

Source: Adapted from Howarth and Jacobson (2021), Patonia and Poudineh (2022), IEA (2022), IRENA (2022), Equinor (2024), Hosseini et al. (2024), IEA (2024), Vedrtnam et al. (2025)

While modelling studies and geological surveys suggest that significant deposits may, in theory, exist, empirical evidence remains very scarce. To date, the only confirmed commercial case is the Bourakébougou field in Mali, where a small-scale well has produced natural hydrogen since the early 2010s, supplying electricity to a local village (Prinzhofer et al., 2019). Nevertheless, pilot investigations are ongoing in many other regions across the globe, including the United States, Canada, Europe, Australia, and South America, but these remain at the exploration stage with no large-scale production yet demonstrated (Patonia et al., 2024).

Therefore, at the moment, native hydrogen holds primarily theoretical promise due to its low projected production costs—early pilot estimates suggest below USD 1/kg—as well as its minimal carbon footprint (Table 2.1). However, it is critical to state that no scalable, commercial LCOH has been demonstrated. The geological uncertainty is substantial: reservoir size, replenishment rates, accumulation mechanisms, and extraction feasibility, among others, are poorly understood, and current exploration is limited by the absence of established regulatory and market frameworks. Major uncertainties include high exploration risk, complex permitting for a new resource, significant surface handling and safety challenges related to $H_2$ and $O_2$ mixtures, and unknown reservoir replenishment rates. Furthermore, environmental considerations, such as subsurface impacts and interactions with other resources, are largely unexplored. Therefore, in the current conditions, natural hydrogen is a nascent and highly uncertain pathway and it is too early to treat it as a reliable contributor to decarbonisation scenarios, given that its global role is currently confined to a single small-scale case in Mali.

Overall, taken together, current hydrogen production technologies represent a spectrum of trade-offs between maturity, emissions, and scalability (Table 2.3). It is unfortunate for our decarbonisation plans, but fossil-based methods such as SMR and coal gasification that are extremely carbon-intensive (Table 2.1) are still by far the most dominant in today's supply. Adding carbon capture can reduce their footprint, yet challenges around capture efficiency, methane leakage, and storage limit their robustness as a long-term solution. By contrast, electrolysis is technically capable of achieving near-zero emissions when powered by renewables and offers strong synergies with variable power generation, though its expansion is constrained by equipment costs, supply chains, and renewable intermittency. Other pathways like methane pyrolysis and biomass gasification offer niche opportunities but face their own scalability challenges. Natural hydrogen, while potentially disruptive, remains speculative until further geological evidence and operational demonstrations are available. This landscape suggests a transitional role for blue hydrogen in some markets, but with green hydrogen increasingly positioned as the end goal for deep decarbonisation, provided key technological and economic barriers can be overcome.

## Current and Projected Costs of Hydrogen Production

It should be of no surprise that the economic feasibility of hydrogen as a decarbonisation vector is closely tied to the cost of its production, which varies widely by production pathway and regional conditions.

To ensure transparency and credibility, the LCOH estimates presented in this chapter are based on a standard discounted cash flow methodology. The core LCOH formula is the total capital and operating costs over the project life divided by the total hydrogen produced. All costs are in real 2023 US dollars. The key uniform assumptions used for the central estimates in this chapter include a Weighted Average Cost of Capital (WACC) of 6–8%, a project life of 20–30 years, and capacity factors of 40–60% for green hydrogen and 90–95% for blue/grey hydrogen. No by-product credits or carbon price is applied in the central case.

The cost estimates are highly sensitive to these inputs (Table 2.4). For context, a ±20 USD/MWh swing in electricity prices can alter the levelised cost of hydrogen by approximately ±1 USD/kg, assuming ~50 kWh electricity consumption per kg $H_2$ (European Hydrogen Observatory, 2024; IEA, 2019; ICCT, 2024). The capacity factor is also critical; a change from 70% to 30% can move the LCOH from \$2.5/kg to \$4.5/kg (ibid.). Electrolyser CapEx variations between \$500/kW and \$1200/kW result in an LCOH range of about \$3.0/kg to \$4.0/kg, while a WACC shift from 4% to 10% alters the LCOH between \$3.2/kg and \$3.8/kg (ibid.).

In 2023, green hydrogen projects reported levelised costs ranging, on average, from USD 3.5 to 4.5 per kilogram in regions with exceptionally cheap renewable energy (BloombergNEF, 2023; H2-Diplo, 2023). The NEOM Project in Saudi Arabia, for example, leverages abundant solar and wind resources to achieve these figures for green hydrogen production by 2027 (NEOM, 2023). Similarly, Spain's HyDeal España initiative targets an LCOH of approximately USD 3–4 per kg by combining large-scale photovoltaic generation with electrolysis (HyDeal, 2023). By contrast, at the moment, Australian pilot projects demonstrate the upper end of the spectrum, with costs of USD 6–8 per kg, which related primarily to higher electricity prices, smaller project scale, and additional infrastructure costs (BloombergNEF, 2023).

While electrolyser CapEx remains high, currently ranging from USD 500 to 1000 per kilowatt, as mentioned, electricity prices constitute the largest single component of operating expenses (Patonia & Poudineh, 2022; BloombergNEF, 2023). Financing conditions, including interest rates and access to low-cost capital, also materially influence overall project economics. Roadmaps, such as those produced by the IEA and IRENA, assume that costs could decline below USD 2 per kg by 2030, but these projections are contingent on rapid technological improvements, mass production of electrolysers, and sustained low renewable electricity prices, among other factors,—i.e., conditions that have yet to materialise in most real-world projects (IRENA, 2022; IEA, 2022).

Blue hydrogen, produced from natural gas coupled with carbon capture and storage (CCS), is often viewed as a complementary pathway with lower near-term costs, typically between USD 1.5 and 4.7 per kg depending on natural gas prices, capture rates, and methane leakage management (Table 2.5) (Massarweh et al., 2023; Curcio, 2025). While notable projects such as H2H Saltend in the United Kingdom plan to capture over

**Table 2.4** Key parameters and their impact on LCOH (Green)[a]

| *Parameter* | *Base case* | *Low LCOH scenario* | *High LCOH scenario* | *Impact on LCOH (USD/kg)* |
|---|---|---|---|---|
| *Electricity price (USD/MWh)* | 40 | 20 | 80 | ~2.0–3.5 |
| *Capacity factor (%)* | 50 | 70 | 30 | ~2.5–4.5 |
| *Electrolyser CapEx (USD/kW)* | 800 | 500 | 1200 | ~3.0–4.0 |
| *Weighted average cost of capital (%)* | 7 | 4 | 10 | ~3.2–3.8 |

Source: Adapted from Howarth and Jacobson (2021), BloombergNEF (2023), HyDeal (2023), H2-Diplo (2023), Massarweh et al. (2023), NEOM (2023), ACWA Power (2024), Al-Khelaiwi et al. (2024), Patonia et al. (2024), Rystad Energy (2024), Li et al. (2025)

[a]Electricity cost sensitivity is the dominant driver. A ±20 USD/MWh swing changes LCOH by ≈ ±1 USD/kg (assuming ≈50 kWh/kg)

90% of $CO_2$ emissions, apart from very often being unable to deliver the stated level of capture efficiency, they often face delays in final investment decisions and continue to be sensitive to fluctuations in gas markets (S&P Global, 2024). Canadian blue hydrogen initiatives, particularly in Alberta, demonstrate similar sensitivities, with cost competitiveness strongly linked to both gas price volatility and the effectiveness of methane leakage mitigation (Ishaq & Crawford, 2025). Beyond costs, lifecycle emissions remain an open question: if methane leakage is higher than anticipated or CCS capture rates fall short, the carbon intensity of blue hydrogen could undermine its decarbonisation potential (ibid.).

Emerging white hydrogen, produced from naturally occurring geological sources, is viewed as showing promise in terms of low estimated production costs, with the only operating project in Mali suggesting potential LCOH as low as USD 0.5–1/kg (Rystad Energy, 2024). However, at the moment, the scalability of white hydrogen remains uncertain, as does the availability of deposits at the scale required for industrial applications, and all the projections and models viewing its future potential have been created based on the only available data from the Bourakébougou field (ibid. and Patonia et al., 2024). As such, these cost figures should be treated as highly speculative, site-specific pilot quotes rather than demonstrable commercial LCOH. Therefore, the applicability of such models remains very much questionable, as white hydrogen itself has so far been characterised as 'high impact, low probability' matter (ibid.).

When compared to other options, grey hydrogen—the most conventional type of $H_2$ that is produced from natural gas without carbon capture—still remains the dominant and cheapest baseline option at roughly USD 1–1.5 per kg (with low gas prices) but carries high carbon intensity (Table 2.5). Therefore, alternative decarbonisation options (other than clean $H_2$), such as direct electrification of industrial processes, bio-based fuels, or retrofitted CCS, are often considered to be even more cost-effective than hydrogen in certain sectors, particularly where renewable electricity prices are low or infrastructure investment costs are prohibitive. Overall, the current and projected costs of hydrogen production indicate that while large-scale deployment remains technically feasible, economic viability varies substantially by production pathway and geography. Understanding these cost dynamics is essential for evaluating whether hydrogen can achieve the widespread decarbonisation role envisioned in international roadmaps or whether its deployment will remain concentrated in niche applications.

**Table 2.5** Representative estimated LCOH (USD/kg $H_2$) and their key drivers by 'colour' and region

| *Colour* | *Representative project/region (real project of flagship study)* | *Typical observed/ modelled LCOH (USD/kg $H_2$)* | *Key caveats and drivers* |
|---|---|---|---|
| *Green* | NEOM Green Hydrogen (large-scale renewables + electrolysis) | **~1.5–3.0** (project targets, indicative range) | • Very low LCOE location + large scale & low WACC drive down costs<br>• Project targets depend on delivery of very low renewables costs and financing |
| | HyDeal España (lighthouse design/captive PV) | **~1.5–4.0** (targeted techno-economic range, early estimates) | • Optimistic mass-scale assumptions and highly-optimised captive PV<br>• WACC and system integration crucial |
| | Europe 2022–2023 average (grid & dedicated renewables) | **~4.0–12.0** | Wide range driven by:<br>• Higher electricity prices<br>• Higher electrolyser CapEx<br>• Less favourable resource quality |
| *Blue* | H2H Saltend (Equinor/ National Grid NPV/ feasibility) | **~1.5–3.5** | • Highly sensitive to natural gas price, CCS capture rate (%), and methane leakage assumptions<br>• Higher if gas spike or capture is <90% |
| | Alberta blue H2 projects/ Canadian TEAs | **~1.0–3.0** | • Lower costs when gas is cheap and CCS infrastructure available<br>• Variability from fugitive methane assumptions<br>• Peer literature places blue broadly in this band |
| | Global blue hydrogen estimates | **~1.8–4.7** | • BNEF and industry reports show blue can be lower-cost than green in many scenarios but lifecycle carbon depends on methane and capture performance |

(*continued*)

**Table 2.5** (continued)

| *Colour* | *Representative project/region (real project of flagship study)* | *Typical observed/ modelled LCOH (USD/kg $H_2$)* | *Key caveats and drivers* |
|---|---|---|---|
| *White/ natural (pilot evidence)* | Hydroma/Mali | **~0.5–1.0** (very early, site-specific) | • Extremely site-specific<br>• Pilot quotes (company disclosures) claim sub-1$/kg in favourable deposits, but commercial scalability, permitting and resource certainty are uncertain |
| *Grey (SMR without CCS – baseline)* | Industrial SMR/typical refineries | **~1.0–1.5** | • Market baseline<br>• Carbon-intensive and increasingly exposed to carbon prices |

Source: Adapted from Howarth and Jacobson (2021), BloombergNEF (2023), HyDeal (2023), H2-Diplo (2023), Massarweh et al. (2023), NEOM (2023), ACWA Power (2024), Al-Khelaiwi et al. (2024), Patonia et al. (2024), Rystad Energy (2024), Li et al. (2025)

## Roadmap Assumptions Versus Real Costs

Many hydrogen roadmaps assume that by 2030 and further we will see drastic declines not only in hydrogen production costs but in the underlying inputs: electricity prices, electrolyser CapEx, material costs, supply chain stability, and financing. These assumptions are critical because, if they do not materialise, the more optimistic deployment scenarios for hydrogen—from deep decarbonisation of steel, chemicals, high-heat processes to transport—become far less plausible. Indeed, the vast majority of these decarbonisation scenarios rely overwhelmingly on low-carbon hydrogen, with a primary focus on blue and particularly green hydrogen as the core alternatives to replace fossil fuels. This narrow focus means that the success of the entire energy transition could be contingent on the rapid and cost-competitive scaling of these specific production pathways.

### *Cost Decline Assumptions*

A common assumption in hydrogen roadmaps (IEA, IRENA, etc.) is that electrolyser CapEx will fall to below USD 300 per kW, and that electricity input costs will drop to USD 20–30 per MWh, by around 2030 (IEA, 2022; IRENA, 2022). These benchmarks often serve as tipping points in scenario models, making green hydrogen competitive with blue pathways or even fossil fuels subject to carbon pricing. However, real-world data suggest that these assumptions face significant challenges. In particular, the learning curves once expected to apply to electrolysers in a similar way as they did to solar panels do not appear to follow the same pattern.

Specifically, recent reports highlight that electrolyser costs remain substantially higher than previously estimated. For instance, the IEA noted that installed costs for non-Chinese alkaline electrolysis systems have recently been reported at around USD 2000 per kW, and for PEM systems of non-Chinese origin even higher, with only Chinese systems occasionally achieving lower ranges (~USD 750–1300/kW) (IEA, 2024). Similarly, stack-only costs for PEM electrolysers in 2023 remained higher than expected, and although projections suggest these may substantially decline by 2030, such reductions require higher learning rates, material advances, scale, and stable input costs (Krishnan et al., 2023).

In fact, electricity price assumptions also display tension with reality. Renewable electricity prices in many regions remain much higher than what roadmaps assume, particularly when factoring in intermittency, grid connection, balancing and transmission costs. Furthermore, inflation, rising labour, materials and interest rates since around 2021 have pushed up both input and capital costs in many regions (IEA, 2024).

This challenge is significantly compounded within the European Union by the strict application of the additionality principle. The rule requires that hydrogen be produced using newly built renewable capacity, rather than relying on electricity already supplied by the grid (European Commission, 2023). While the intent is to ensure that green hydrogen production genuinely contributes to decarbonisation and does not inadvertently create demand that is met by fossil-fuelled generation, in practice, however, this creates a substantial barrier to rapid deployment. In particular, it currently prohibits electrolyser operators from using cheaper, established renewable sources or from taking advantage of grid electricity during periods of extreme renewable oversupply and low/negative prices (RBN Energy, 2024). Instead, developers are forced to build new, dedicated wind or solar farms, layering on massive upfront capital costs, complex permitting procedures, and lengthy development timelines before a single kilogram of hydrogen can be produced (ibid.).

Furthermore, the global economic landscape has exacerbated these financial hurdles. Inflation, rising labour, materials and interest rates since around 2021 have pushed up both the input and capital costs for these new renewable projects and the electrolysers themselves in many regions (IEA, 2024). Therefore, the additionality principle, while environmentally rigorous in theory, in practice acts as a substantive brake on the scaling of green hydrogen by directly inflating its cost and delaying its market entry, creating a tension between regulatory ideals and on-the-ground economic and deployment realities.

### *Timely and Massive Infrastructure Rollout*

A central premise in most hydrogen roadmaps is the expectation that infrastructure will expand at unprecedented speed, enabling the simultaneous development of production, transport, and storage capacity. Projections from the European Hydrogen Backbone (EHB) initiative, for example, anticipate the construction or repurposing of tens of thousands of kilometres of hydrogen pipelines across the EU by 2040 (European Hydrogen Backbone, 2025). These scenarios assume rapid permitting, seamless cross-border coordination, and sufficient capital flows to finance projects on a continental scale.

However, as it is common with many large-scale ambitious projects, real-world progress has been significantly slower. The EHB itself has faced delays linked to regulatory fragmentation, financing constraints, and uncertainties around demand aggregation (IEA, 2022). At the same time, large-scale storage—considered indispensable for balancing supply and demand—has been constrained by regulatory and technical hurdles. While salt caverns and depleted hydrocarbon fields are recognised as the most suitable storage option for hydrogen, their development faces protracted permitting processes, environmental concerns, and often limited geological availability (IRENA, 2022; Patonia et al., 2025).

This creates a significant material gap between modelled assumptions and present feasibility. As Equinor's H2H Saltend project illustrates, hydrogen clusters can indeed integrate production with localised infrastructure, but scaling this model nationally or internationally has proven challenging (Equinor, 2024). Without coordinated rollout, the sector risks being trapped in a 'chicken-and-egg' dynamic, where insufficient infrastructure depresses demand signals, which in turn undermines the business case for investment in transport and storage facilities.

### *Blue Versus Green Dynamics*

Another assumption in many roadmaps is that blue hydrogen will act as a bridging technology, enabling emissions reduction while green hydrogen scales up; eventually, green becomes the predominant pathway (Dickel, 2020). Implicit in that assumption is that blue hydrogen costs are lower or comparable in the near term, and that policy will support both until green becomes cheaper.

Nevertheless, peer-reviewed comparative techno-economic work suggests that blue hydrogen's competitiveness is highly sensitive to both methane leakage and $CO_2$ capture rate. For instance, Davids et al. (2025) find that if the carbon capture rate is below ~90% or methane leakage exceeds ~1%, blue hydrogen's climate and emissions credentials degrade significantly, reducing its viability in either constrained regulatory environments or under stringent carbon pricing. In many regions, uncertainty about natural gas price, regulatory risk, and $CO_2$ transportation and storage infrastructure means that blue hydrogen's projected low costs may become unreliable.

Simultaneously, green hydrogen pathways face their own uncertainties: supply chain constraints for critical materials (e.g., rare metals for PEM electrolyser catalysts), intermittency of renewables affecting capacity factor, and risk of cost overruns. Projections that green hydrogen will reach cost parity with blue within a decade (or shortly after) assume steady declines in CapEx, high utilisation, and stable regulatory or tariff support. As previously discussed, a quick reality check demonstrates that this is not exactly what we are observing at the moment.

### *Social and Environmental Costs*

Even if costs in dollars per kilogram decline just as models assume, social and environmental trade-offs introduce additional 'real' costs rarely captured fully in roadmaps. In particular, as briefly mentioned, for blue hydrogen, methane leakage is a persistent concern. Specifically, studies show that even relatively small leakage rates of 0.5–1% can undercut the climate benefits of blue hydrogen over short to medium timeframes, especially if upstream and downstream emissions are poorly managed (Davids et al., 2025). This is so because methane is a potent greenhouse gas over 20- to 30-year horizons, emissions from leakage can negate much of the benefit of $CO_2$ capture unless capture rates are very high and leakage very low (Princeton Engineering, 2023).

For green hydrogen, water usage, land use, and local environmental impacts are increasingly recognised as material constraints. Large scale electrolysis requires high-purity water, and in water-scarce regions this can compete with agricultural or human uses (Patonia, 2025). Similarly, land requirements for renewable generation (solar, wind) plus associated infrastructure (transmission, electrolysers) may meet regulatory or community opposition (ibid.). Material sourcing for electrolysers (e.g., iridium, platinum group metals, rare earths) adds both cost risk and environmental/social risk, as markets for these materials are often volatile and politically complex (Patonia & Poudineh, 2022).

In parallel, hydrogen emissions themselves are increasingly recognised as a non-trivial climate concern: while hydrogen combustion does not release $CO_2$, unintended releases can contribute to warming indirectly, and it remains uncertain whether hydrogen emissions can be measured and verified economically across diffuse infrastructure. This strengthens the case for early investment in leak detection, measurement standards, and credible certification regimes.

## A Future Forged by Pragmatism

This chapter has shown that the economics of clean hydrogen remain highly contingent on both technology trajectories and the broader policy and market environment. Current production costs vary widely—green hydrogen still commands a premium compared with fossil-based alternatives, while blue hydrogen's competitiveness is undermined by gas market volatility and methane leakage concerns. Other pathways like turquoise and pink hydrogen remain niche or in development, while natural hydrogen, although theoretically promising, remains confined to one small-scale case in Mali, with its scalability and geological availability yet to be demonstrated. The roadmap assumptions that underpin many national and international strategies—including rapid cost declines in electrolysers and renewable power, and massive infrastructure rollouts in parallel with production—are increasingly challenged by supply chain bottlenecks, high financing costs, and regulatory delays.

Against this backdrop, hydrogen's future will be determined by a set of cross-cutting enablers and barriers. On the enabling side, geopolitical catalysts such as sustained natural gas price volatility and ambitious industrial policy frameworks such as the US Inflation Reduction Act and the EU Green Deal Industrial Plan are expected to create stable demand pools and relative competitiveness for low-carbon hydrogen. Technological breakthroughs, particularly in next-generation electrolysis and hydrogen carrier systems, may shift the cost curve more decisively than incremental improvements in current technologies. Furthermore, the cluster-based model offers a pragmatic pathway for de-risking investment by co-locating production, demand, and infrastructure.

Yet, significant barriers remain. While the efforts to lowering the costs of production remain important, the remaining parts of the clean hydrogen value chain appear to be equally as (if not more) important, as the sector continues to grapple with the persistent 'chicken-and-egg' dilemma, where insufficient demand discourages infrastructure investment, and the lack of infrastructure constrains demand growth. Macroeconomic headwinds—rising interest rates, high capital intensity, and increasing geopolitical trade frictions—further complicate the investment landscape. Public opposition and environmental trade-offs also introduce delays and uncertainty, whether through low social acceptance of infrastructure projects or scrutiny of lifecycle emissions and freshwater use.

Taken together, the credible potential of hydrogen is undeniable, but its role as a ubiquitous energy vector remains a hypothesis rather than a certainty. The most plausible future lies between the two extremes: a world in which hydrogen achieves meaningful scale in specific regions and hard-to-abate sectors, while falling short of the most optimistic forecasts. Progress will likely be uneven—rapid where policies, infrastructure, and clusters align, and slower in jurisdictions lacking such enabling conditions. The strategic imperative, therefore, is to shift the narrative away from hydrogen's inevitability towards its selectivity. Hydrogen's future will ultimately be forged less by technological determinism than by policy and pragmatism: a targeted, sector-specific deployment strategy will offer the most credible pathway for transforming its promise into durable reality.

## References

ACWA Power. (2024). *NEOM Green Hydrogen Project* [Online]. Retrieved September 19, 2025, from https://acwapower.com/en/projects/neom-green-hydrogen-project.

Al-Khelaiwi, M., Al-Masaabi, T. A., Farag, H., & Rehman, S. (2024). Evaluation of green and blue hydrogen production potential in Saudi Arabia. *Energy Conversion and Management: X, 24*(1), 1–12.

Arsad, A. Z., et al. (2023). Hydrogen electrolyser technologies and their modelling for sustainable energy production: A comprehensive review and suggestions. *International Journal of Hydrogen Energy, 48*(72), 27841–27871.

BloombergNEF. (2023). *Hydrogen market outlook* [Online]. Retrieved September 11,2025,fromhttps://euHydrogenweek.eu/wp-content/uploads/2023/12/Adithya-Bhashyam-Associate-—-Hydrogen-BloombergNEF.pdf

Buttler, A., & Spliethoff, H. (2018). Current status of water electrolysis for energy storage, grid balancing and sector coupling via power-to-gas and power-to-liquids: A review. *Renewable and Sustainable Energy Reviews, 82*(3), 2440–2454.

Curcio, E. (2025). Techno-economic analysis of hydrogen production: Costs, policies, and scalability in the transition to net-zero. *International Journal of Hydrogen Energy, 128*(1), 473–487.

Davids, D., et al. (2025). Impact of methane leakage rate and carbon capture rate on blue hydrogen sustainability using combines warming index. *Applied Energy, 394*(1), 1–19.

Dickel, R. (2020). *Blue hydrogen as an enable of green hydrogen: The case of Germany.* Oxford Institute for Energy Studies.

Enapter. (2025). *AEM technology by Enapter* [Online]. Retrieved September 20, 2025, from https://enapter.com/en/aem-by-enapter-electrolysis/.

Equinor. (2024). *H2H Saltend* [Online]. Retrieved September 20, 2025, from https://www.equinor.com/energy/h2h-saltend.

European Commission. (2023). *Commission sets out rules for renewable hydrogen* [Online]. Retrieved September 19, 2025, from https://ec.europa.eu/commission/presscorner/detail/en/ip_23_594.

European Hydrogen Backbone. (2025). *The European Hydrogen Backbone (EHB) initiative* [Online]. Retrieved September 20, 2025, from https://ehb.eu/.

European Hydrogen Observatory. (2024). *Levelised Cost of Hydrogen (LCOH) calculator manual* [Online]. Retrieved November 13, 2025, from https://observatory.clean-hydrogen.europa.eu/sites/default/files/2024-06/Manual%20-%20Levelised%20Cost%20of%20Hydrogen%20%28LCOH%29%20Calculator.pdf.

H2-Diplo. (2023). *Saudi Arabia's key energy export market opportunities in light of climate change mitigation through hydrogen production and use* [Online].

Retrieved September 12, 2025, from https://h2diplo.de/wp-content/uploads/2023/11/H2-Diplo_KSA_Study1_AK_-22-SEP-2023_final.pdf.

Hosseini, T., et al. (2024). Low-emission hydrogen production from gasification of Australian coals – Process simulation and technoeconomic assessment. *International Journal of Hydrogen Energy, 86*(1), 245–260.

Howarth, R. W., & Jacobson, M. Z. (2021). How green is blue hydrogen? *Energy Science & Engineering, 9*(10), 1676–1687.

HyDeal. (2023). *Green hydrogen: Its extraordinary power to substitute to fossil fuels* [Online]. Retrieved September 12, 2025, from https://www.hydeal.com/green-hydrogen-its-extraordinary-power.

Hydrogen Council. (2021). *Hydrogen Insights 2021* [Online]. Retrieved September 11, 2025, from https://hydrogencouncil.com/en/hydrogen-insights-2021/

ICCT. (2024). *The price of green hydrogen: Estimate of future production costs* [Online]. Retrieved September 18, 2025, from https://theicct.org/the-price-of-green-hydrogen-estimate-future-production-costs-may24.

IEA. (2019). *Global levelised cost of hydrogen production by energy source and technology, 2019-2050* [Online]. Retrieved November 12, 2025, from https://www.iea.org/data-and-statistics/charts/global-average-levelised-cost-of-hydrogen-production-by-energy-source-and-technology-2019-and-2050.

IEA. (2022). *Global hydrogen review 2022* [Online]. Retrieved September 11, 2025, from https://iea.blob.core.windows.net/assets/c5bc75b1-9e4d-460d-9056-6e8e626a11c4/GlobalHydrogenReview2022.pdf.

IEA. (2024). *Global hydrogen review 2024* [Online]. Retrieved September 13, 2025, from https://iea.blob.core.windows.net/assets/89c1e382-dc59-46ca-aa47-9f7d41531ab5/GlobalHydrogenReview2024.pdf.

IRENA. (2022). *Global hydrogen trade to meet the 1.5 °C climate goal* [Online]. Retrieved September 11, 2025, from https://india-re-navigator.com/public/uploads/1651644555-IRENA_Global_Trade_Hydrogen_2022.pdf.

Ishaq, H., & Crawford, C. (2025). Towards less carbon-intensive blue hydrogen Integrated natural gas reforming and CO2 capture approach. *Journal of Environmental Chemical Engineering, 13*(2), 1–13.

Krishnan, S., et al. (2023). Present and future cost of alkaline and PEM electrolyser stacks. *International Journal of Hydrogen Energy, 48*(83), 32313–32330.

Le, P. A., et al. (2023). The current status of hydrogen energy: An overview. *RSC Advances, 40*(1), 1–26.

Li, Y., Hao, J. S., & Zhou, Y. (2025). Economic analysis of different hydrogen production routes under a CO2 pricing mechanism – A levelized cost of hydrogen based study. *International Journal of Hydrogen Energy, 128*(1), 47–67.

Liu, L., et al. (2024). Recent advances and challenges in anion exchange membranes development/application for water electrolysis: A review. *Membranes, 14*(4), 1–24.

Massarweh, O., et al. (2023). Blue hydrogen production from natural gas reservoirs: A review of application and feasibility. *Journal of CO2 Utilization, 70*(1), 1–24.

NEOM. (2023). *NEOM Green Hydrogen Company completes financial close at a total investment value of USD 8.4 billion in the world's largest carbon-free green hydrogen plant* [Online]. Retrieved September 12, 2025, from https://www.neom.com/en-us/newsroom/neom-green-hydrogen-investment

Ozcan, H. and Dincer, I. (2014) 'Performance investigation of magnesium-chloride hybrid thermochemical cycle for hydrogen production', *International Journal of Hydrogen Energy*, 39 (1), pp. 76-85.

Pan, X., et al. (2025). Development status and future prospects of hydrogen energy technology: Production, storage, and cost analysis. *Advanced Energy and Sustainability Research, 7*(1), 1–54.

Patel, G. H., et al. (2024). Climate change performance of hydrogen production based on life cycle assessment. *Green Chemistry, 26*(992), 992–106.

Patonia, A. (2025). Green hydrogen and its unspoken challenges for energy justice. *Applied Energy, 377*(C), 1–11.

Patonia, A., Lambert, M., Lin, N., & Shuster, M. (2024). *Natural (geologic) hydrogen and its potential in a net-zero carbon future: Is all that glitters gold?* Oxford Institute for Energy Studies.

Patonia, A., Lambert, M., Lin, N., & Shuster, M. (2025). *Underground storage for decarbonisation: Trade-offs between hydrogen, natural gas, and carbon dioxide.* Oxford Institute for Energy Studies.

Patonia, A., & Poudineh, R. (2020). *Ammonia as a storage solution for future decarbonized energy systems.* Oxford Institute for Energy Studies.

Patonia, A., & Poudineh, R. (2022). *Cost-competitive green hydrogen: How to lower the cost of electrolysers?* Oxford Institute for Energy Studies.

Princeton Engineering. (2023). *Switching to hydrogen fuel could prolong the methane problem* [Online]. Retrieved September 19, 2025, from https://engineering.princeton.edu/news/2023/03/13/switching-hydrogen-fuel-could-prolong-methane-problem

Prinzhofer, A., et al. (2019). Natural hydrogen continuous emission from sedimentary basins: The example of a Brazilian $H_2$-emitting structure. *International Journal of Hydrogen Energy, 44*(12), 5676–5685.

RBN Energy. (2024). *Gimme three steps – Additionality rules throw a monkey wrench into plans for hydrogen scale-up* [Online]. Retrieved September 19, 2025, from https://rbnenergy.com/gimme-three-steps-additionality-rules-throw-a-monkey-wrench-into-plans-for-hydrogen-scale-up.

Rystad Energy. (2024). *The white gold rush and the pursuit of natural hydrogen* [Online]. Retrieved September 12, 2025, from https://www.rystadenergy.com/news/white-gold-rush-pursuit-natural-hydrogen

S&P Global. (2024). *Equinor pushes back target FID on UK blue hydrogen plans amid funding uncertainty* [Online]. Retrieved September 13, 2025, from https://www.spglobal.com/commodity-insights/en/news-research/latest-news/energy-transition/061224-equinor-pushes-back-target-fid-on-uk-blue-hydrogen-plans-amid-funding-uncertainty.

Schmidt, O., et al. (2017). Future cost and performance of water electrolysis: An explicit elicitation study. *International Journal of Hydrogen Energy, 42*(52), 30470–30492.

Vedrtnam, A., Kalauni, K., & Pahwa, R. (2025). A review of water electrolysis technologies with insights into optimization and numerical simulations. *International Journal of Hydrogen Energy, 140*(1), 694–727.

Wei, X., et al. (2024). Comparative life cycle analysis of electrolyzer technologies for hydrogen production: Manufacturing and operations. *Joule, 8*(1), 1–26.

Wolf, S. E., et al. (2023). Solid oxide electrolysis cells – current material development and industrial application. *Journal of Materials Chemistry A, 11*(1), 17977–18028.

CHAPTER 3

# Low-Carbon Hydrogen Production Support Schemes

## Introduction

The interest in low-carbon hydrogen, as an instrument of decarbonisation, has been rising over the last few years. Yet despite policy interest and a large pipeline of announced projects, deployment remains modest relative to climate timelines. A material cost gap persists between low-emission hydrogen and incumbent fossil options, while infrastructure and off-take risks depress bankability. This 'premium plus coordination' problem motivates a closer look at which policy instruments can accelerate scale-up efficiently and fairly.

Experience from other low-carbon technologies suggests that no single instrument is likely to suffice. Economy-wide carbon pricing provides a uniform signal but often arrives at levels or with volatility that are inadequate for first-of-a-kind projects. Capital grants can stimulate announcements but do little to underwrite long-term operating viability. Contracts for Difference (CfDs) and similar revenue support mechanisms can crowd in private finance by de-risking cash flows, while quotas and mandates can create predictable demand where market signals alone are weak. The emerging policy toolkit also includes tax credits, public procurement, and targeted infrastructure support (pipelines, storage, terminals). Each tool addresses a different friction—cost, risk, coordination, or demand—raising the central design question: which combinations deliver the greatest



A. Patonia, R. Poudineh, *Clean Hydrogen for Decarbonisation*,
https://doi.org/10.1007/978-3-032-19442-8_3

climate benefit per unit of public spending, while preserving competition and avoiding windfall gains?

Fairness adds a further layer of complexity. Choices about who receives support (producers vs. consumers), how costs are socialised (bills vs. taxes), and where value chains are located (domestic content, regional clusters) have distributional consequences. Industrial policy aims—jobs, resilience, strategic autonomy—can sit uneasily alongside least-cost decarbonisation, particularly if support inadvertently favours mature options over potentially superior nascent ones. Moreover, communities exposed to local impacts (water use, land, transport) expect participation and safeguards. An effective policy framework must therefore balance static efficiency (least-cost abatement today) with dynamic efficiency (learning, innovation, and future cost reductions), while embedding procedural fairness and just-transition principles.

Technological uncertainty complicates these trade-offs. Competing production routes (electrolysis powered by renewables, nuclear-enabled electrolysis, methane reforming with carbon capture), diverse carriers (compressed or liquefied hydrogen, ammonia, methanol, e-fuels), and competing end-use technologies (direct reduction in steel, refinery applications, fuel cells vs. combustion) are evolving rapidly. Prematurely 'picking winners' risks lock-in, stranded assets, or missed learning opportunities; yet excessive agnosticism can stall investment if developers and financiers lack clear, durable signals. Policy must therefore be both directional and adaptive: directional enough to mobilise capital at scale, adaptive enough to pivot as evidence on cost, performance, and system integration accumulates.

Governance choices also shape international interoperability. Hydrogen and its derivatives will likely be traded across borders, making mutual recognition of standards and certification crucial to avoid green-washing, double counting, or carbon-leakage loopholes. Robust rules for additionality, temporal and geographic correlation of electricity inputs, and lifecycle accounting are needed to ensure that 'clean' claims correspond to real emissions reductions. At the same time, heterogeneous national endowments—renewable resources, $CO_2$ storage, industrial bases—call for frameworks that enable specialisation and trade rather than duplicative, inward-looking subsidies. Aligning domestic incentives with credible certification can lower transaction costs and increase investor confidence.

This chapter is motivated by these overlapping challenges. We ask, first: what policy frameworks—CfDs, quotas, mandates, carbon pricing—are most effective to scale hydrogen in a fair and cost-efficient way? We then ask: how can governments avoid 'picking winners' prematurely under deep technological uncertainty? Answering these questions calls for combining insights from real-world behaviour—seen in auctions, tax incentives, and early CfD schemes—with theoretical work on risk-sharing and market formation, as well as practical lessons from deploying similar tools in wind and solar. As the discussion shows, the success of hydrogen policy support depends on balancing cost-reduction incentives with flexibility. Unlike renewables, where falling capital costs drove predictable learning curves, hydrogen's volatility and input dependency demand a more adaptive framework.

The outline of this chapter is as follows: the next section discusses approaches to incentivise investment in low-carbon hydrogen technologies with a focus on UK CfDs. Section "The Effectiveness of Low Carbon Hydrogen CfD" discusses the challenges of achieving cost reduction and scale for low-carbon hydrogen using a fixed price long-term contract like CfD by comparing it with renewable electricity CfDs. Section "Unintended Consequences" addresses unintended consequences while Section "Conclusions" provides concluding remarks.

## Incentivising Low-Carbon Hydrogen

Carbon pricing, while necessary to internalise externalities and create a uniform decarbonisation signal, is not sufficient to unlock investment in low-emission hydrogen at the scale and speed required. Two strands of evidence underpin this. First, policy makers themselves conclude that carbon-pricing instruments 'are not suited to bring about a significant shift towards renewable and low-carbon fuels in the short and medium term', hence the need for a dedicated regulatory approach (European Union, 2023b). Second, the project-level economics of early hydrogen plants remain reliant on public support: the IEA finds that many planned projects' 'economic feasibility depends on public support', and urges governments to implement necessary support instruments and pair them with regulation to create demand (IEA, 2023). Recent systems analysis in Nature Energy reaches a similar conclusion, showing that even with carbon prices aligned to EU climate targets, additional targeted support is required to close the cost gap and de-risk deployment (Odenweller and Ueckerdt, 2025).

A second body of evidence comes from revealed preference in early auctions and support programmes. In the EU's first Hydrogen Bank pilot auction, seven winning projects required a pay-per-kilogram operating subsidy between €0.37 and €0.48/kg of renewable (RFNBO) hydrogen (European Commission, 2024)—clear, quantitative evidence that carbon pricing alone did not render these projects bankable. Similarly, the United Kingdom's Low Carbon Hydrogen Business Model, which is a revenue support contract similar to a Contracts for Difference (CfD), was created to provide financial assistance. This model is intended to address the gap in operating costs between low-carbon hydrogen and high-carbon fuels, which confirms that governments are bridging a continuous operational expenditure premium rather than a single capital expenditure hurdle (DESNZ, 2025). This persistent cost gap exists despite ambitious roadmap targets, as detailed in Chap. 2 that covered key technologies and costs of hydrogen production.

Third, demand risk remains binding without appropriate instruments. The IEA suggests that support measures, such as financial incentives, should be combined with regulations like quotas or mandates to require the use of low-emission hydrogen in current applications (IEA, 2023). The EU has now institutionalised this logic: in aviation, ReFuelEU imposes rising minimum shares of Sustainable Aviation Fuels and a specific sub-mandate for synthetic (hydrogen-derived) aviation fuels—e.g., 6% SAF in 2030 (with a 1.2% average synthetic share over 2030–2031) rising to 70% SAF with 35% synthetic by 2050 (European Union, 2023a)—which can create bankable off-take for e-kerosene. In maritime, FuelEU sets progressively tighter lifecycle GHG-intensity limits on ship energy (−2% in 2025 to -80% by 2050) (European Union, 2023b), explicitly acknowledging that carbon pricing alone will not trigger the fuel switch in time.

Taken together, the evidence supports a pragmatic policy mix: maintain economy-wide carbon pricing to drive efficiency and long-run substitution, but pair it with targeted, time-bound support that addresses the hydrogen 'premium' (auctions, CfDs, tax credits), and with demand-side mandates that create reliable off-take in hard-to-abate sectors.[1]

[1] Also robust certification standards are essential complements to price signals and subsidies, both to target support efficiently and to avoid green-washing. The EU's RFNBO rules require additionality (new renewable generation coming into operation within 36 months of the electrolyser), temporal correlation (monthly until 2029, hourly from 2030), and geo-

Since contract for differences (CfDs) have emerged as a key instrument to address the low-carbon hydrogen cost gap in many countries, in what follows we analyse this instrument by comparing with counterpart in the electricity sector focusing on the case of United Kingdom as a pioneering market that has adopted this instrument.[2]

### *Long-Term Contracts as an Instrument of Investment Incentives*

Long-duration contracts have traditionally helped reduce renewable electricity costs, largely through their impact on financing charges. Their effectiveness lies in their alignment with the capital-intensive nature of renewable power projects.[3] In technologies such as wind and solar, the bulk of expenditure is concentrated in upfront investments—construction, installation, and commissioning of turbines or photovoltaic panels—while operating costs are comparatively low and the inputs (sunlight and wind) are free. Under such conditions, long-term fixed-price contracts, including Power Purchase Agreements (PPAs), Feed-in Tariffs (FiTs), and Contracts for Difference (CfDs), provide revenue certainty that reduces investment risk and lowers the cost of capital. In turn, this enables developers to optimise capital deployment and deliver lower project costs and falling electricity prices over time.

There is substantial evidence that these instruments have accelerated cost declines across renewable technologies. In Germany, FiTs contributed to a 70% reduction in the installation costs of photovoltaic systems between 2000 and 2007, with average costs falling further from €5/kWp in 2006 to €1.60/kWp by 2014. During the same period, the cost of wind turbines decreased by around 25% (FuturePolicy.org, 2019). In Italy, the Conto Energia FiT scheme facilitated rapid PV deployment, with solar

graphic correlation (same or appropriately interconnected bidding zone), so that grid electricity used for 'renewable hydrogen' actually reflects incremental, local renewable supply (European Union, 2023c).

[2] Not every country adopted CfD. In the United States, the 45V clean-hydrogen credit determines eligibility and credit level by lifecycle emissions rates measured with DOE's 45VH2-GREET model; the final rule provides the top tier credit of $3/kg for hydrogen below 0.45 kg $CO_2e$/kg when prevailing-wage and apprenticeship conditions are met (US Department of Treasury, 2025). These accounting rules directly govern which projects qualify and at what level thereby shaping investment in a different way than a CfD contract.

[3] This alignment between contract incentives and cost structure was fundamental to their success—an alignment largely absent in the hydrogen value chain.

module prices declining by more than 50% between 2000 and 2011 (Ameli and Kammen, 2014). The United Kingdom's experience with CfDs for offshore wind demonstrates the same dynamic: the levelised cost of electricity (LCOE) fell from £140/MWh in 2015 to around £44/MWh (2012 prices) in Allocation Round 5 (2023), largely due to the revenue stability created by CfDs. Beyond Europe, PPAs in the United States have been instrumental in reducing the cost of wind power, while Brazil's renewable expansion has relied on long-term contracts to mitigate regulatory risk and secure stable revenue streams, producing significant cost reductions in wind and hydro (Hochberg and Poudineh, 2018; Genoese et al., 2016). Collectively, these experiences highlight the importance of predictable, long-term price signals in driving cost reductions.

### *Contract for Difference Under the UK Hydrogen Allocation Round*

The United Kingdom's Hydrogen Allocation Round (HAR) is a cornerstone of government policy to accelerate low-carbon hydrogen production, a critical component of its broader decarbonisation agenda (Department for Energy Security and Net Zero, 2023b). First launched in July 2022, HAR1 was specifically designed to support electrolytic hydrogen, aligning with the ambition set out in the British Energy Security Strategy to scale national low-carbon hydrogen capacity to 10 GW by 2030, with at least half of this expected to come from electrolysis. By addressing financing and revenue risks, the scheme seeks to provide the certainty needed for projects to reach Final Investment Decision (FID) and begin construction.

At the heart of HAR is the Hydrogen Production Business Model (HPBM), which offers long-term revenue support, in some cases combined with capital assistance from the Net Zero Hydrogen Fund (NZHF). The mechanism is intended to bridge the gap between the strike price required by producers and the revenues they are able to achieve in early, illiquid hydrogen markets. Support is allocated through a competitive process in which developers bid both their strike price and expected production volumes. This process is designed to identify projects that can deliver hydrogen at the lowest cost while meeting technical and policy criteria.

The resulting agreements resemble the Contracts for Difference (CfDs) used in the renewable electricity sector but have been adapted to reflect the particular challenges of hydrogen. Under each contract, producers are assured a predetermined strike price, designed to cover allowable production costs and provide a fair return, while reference prices serve to estimate hydrogen's market value. If the reference price is lower than the strike price, producers are compensated with a top-up; if it exceeds the strike price, they may need to return the surplus to the counterparty. The reference price is usually benchmarked to natural gas, as the closest fossil fuel substitute, but incorporates adjustments for hydrogen's end-use in power generation, transport, or industrial applications. Importantly, only volumes that meet the Low Carbon Hydrogen Standard and are sold for qualifying purposes are eligible for subsidy support (BEIS, 2022).

Several safeguards are embedded in the design. A floor price mechanism ensures that reference prices cannot fall below a defined threshold (the lower of the strike price or gas benchmark), preventing excessive subsidy outlays in periods of depressed market conditions. Volume adjustments also apply: a sliding-scale top-up supports producers when sales volumes are low, while penalties are imposed if production exceeds 125% of the contracted cap or falls below 75% of expected output. Non-qualifying sales may also trigger repayments if reference prices exceed the strike price, on the logic that such volumes would not have been produced absent government support (BEIS, 2022). Collectively, these features are intended to balance risk between producers, government, and consumers while incentivising market development.

The first allocation round concluded in December 2023, with 11 projects awarded contracts under HAR1 (Department for Energy Security and Net Zero, 2023d). Together, these represent more than 125 MW of low-carbon hydrogen capacity, awarded at a weighted average strike price of £241/MWh (£175/MWh in 2012 prices) (ibid.). The portfolio includes both green hydrogen projects using renewable electricity and blue hydrogen schemes based on natural gas with carbon capture. Geographically, projects are concentrated in industrial regions such as Yorkshire, the North West, and Wales, as well as in Scotland, where abundant renewable potential exists. While some projects are relatively large—such as the 24.5 MW Bradford Low Carbon Hydrogen facility—most remain modest in scale, reflecting a cautious industry approach to early deployment. The successful projects span both major utilities (EDF Renewables, Scottish Power) and smaller developers (HYRO, GeoPura), suggesting a degree of diversity in market participation at this stage.

HAR2, launched in December 2023, marked a significant expansion in ambition, with up to 875 MW of capacity to be supported. In contrast to HAR1, the second round provides revenue support exclusively through the HPBM, with no additional capital support from the NZHF. Projects selected under HAR2 are expected to commission between 2026 and 2029, with results scheduled for announcement in 2024 following the competitive application process.

The hydrogen CfD framework differs from traditional electricity CfDs in three important ways. First, because hydrogen markets remain illiquid, the scheme substitutes proxy reference prices and floor prices for genuine market signals, providing predictability where transparent benchmarks do not yet exist. Second, the scheme focuses on maximising decarbonisation benefits by limiting subsidies to eligible volumes, directing hydrogen to high-impact areas like heavy industry and transport instead of lower-impact applications such as gas grid blending. Third, the scheme incorporates incentives to minimise subsidy expenditure over time, rewarding producers who secure higher sales prices and thereby reducing the government's net payout.

In sum, the hydrogen CfD is deliberately more complex than its electricity predecessor, reflecting the risks of a nascent and uncertain market. It seeks to provide investors with sufficient stability to commit capital while ensuring that public funds are targeted and controlled. Yet the model also faces inherent challenges: the immaturity of hydrogen markets, the diversity of potential applications, and the volatility of input costs mean that its capacity to drive cost reductions and large-scale deployment remains untested. Crucially, unlike in renewable electricity, where CfDs provided robust risk mitigation that catalysed rapid cost declines, the current hydrogen CfD framework offers more limited protection. Whether it can deliver the same transformative impact therefore remains an open question.

## The Effectiveness of Low-Carbon Hydrogen CfD

The central question that now arises is whether long-term fixed-price contracts—so effective in scaling renewable electricity—can be expected to deliver similar benefits for green hydrogen. At first glance, the analogy appears compelling: both renewables and hydrogen face early-stage cost disadvantages, rely heavily on policy support to crowd in private capital, and require credible long-term signals to unlock investment. However, closer examination suggests that the parallel may be misleading. Hydrogen differs from renewable electricity in its cost structure, technological maturity, and market context. These differences raise legitimate doubts about whether the same contractual instruments that accelerated wind and solar cost reductions can be straightforwardly transplanted into the hydrogen sector.

This calls for caution. While fixed-price contracts such as CfDs can reduce financing risk for capital-intensive projects, their ability to drive sustained cost declines and scale in hydrogen is more limited and more complex than in electricity. Unlike solar or wind, where long-term contracts aligned neatly with cost structures dominated by upfront capital expenditure, hydrogen production is shaped by volatile operational inputs (primarily electricity), underdeveloped infrastructure, and uncertain demand. These features fundamentally alter the balance of risks between producers, off-takers, and governments.

In the remainder of this section, we examine the reasons why hydrogen CfDs may not replicate the transformative effect of renewable electricity CfDs. We highlight three interrelated areas of concern: (i) the misalignment between the incentive structure of long-term fixed-price contracts and hydrogen's cost structure; (ii) the challenges of risk allocation, particularly around exposure to volatile input costs and evolving technology trajectories; and (iii) the uncertainty of market demand, which complicates the role of long-term contracts in securing reliable off-take. Taken together, these challenges suggest that while long-term contracts will remain part of the policy toolkit, they will need to be complemented by other instruments if hydrogen is to achieve scale and cost reduction in a sustainable way.

### *Incentive Structure Versus Cost Structure*

Unlike renewable electricity, green hydrogen production is less capital-intensive and more operationally expensive, since its cost structure is dominated by the price of electricity used as a feedstock. As a result, the ongoing cost of production constitutes a significant share of total expenses. Fixed-price contracts for hydrogen, by guaranteeing output prices, may lower financing costs for electrolysers but do not address the variability of electricity input costs. Thus, the effectiveness of these contracts in lowering overall production costs is limited, and the benefits of reduced capital costs may be offset by exposure to volatile electricity markets.[4] Therefore, managing this risk may require complex instruments such as hedging strategies, which diminish the simplicity and effectiveness of long-term fixed-price arrangements.

One theoretical solution would be to pair long-term hydrogen off-take contracts with equally long-term electricity supply contracts, thereby stabilising both revenue and input costs. This could recreate for hydrogen producers the type of predictable environment that long-term contracts created for renewable electricity. In practice, however, such arrangements face major obstacles. Electricity forward markets are relatively illiquid, with contracts typically extending only a few years, far shorter than the 10–15-year horizons needed for hydrogen projects.

In addition, increasing volatility in wholesale electricity prices—driven by fluctuating renewable generation—makes fixed-price electricity contracts both expensive and difficult to negotiate. Policy uncertainty, particularly around the trajectory of carbon pricing and renewable deployment, further complicates the formation of stable long-term electricity agreements. As a result, hydrogen producers remain vulnerable to operational cost variability, which undermines the stabilising function of long-term hydrogen contracts. The challenge is amplified by the fact that long-term electricity contracts often come at a premium, as sellers price in future volatility and policy risk. This premium can erode the business case for green hydrogen, which is already struggling to compete on cost.

Economies of scale represent another point of divergence. Renewable technologies benefitted from large-scale deployment that drove significant cost reductions through standardisation, learning-by-doing, and globalised supply chains. For electrolysers, some economies of scale are possible, but the scale required to make hydrogen competitive is immense and unlikely to be achieved in the near term. China has achieved notable cost reductions in electrolyser manufacturing through government support and industrial scaling, but electrolysis systems are more complex than solar PV modules, limiting opportunities for standardisation and mass production. Furthermore, geopolitical tensions, trade protectionism, and

[4] Hydrogen production cost is highly sensitive to electricity price: a difference of tens of US$/MWh in electricity cost can change the cost of hydrogen by up to US$1/kg or more (ICCT, 2024; IEA, 2019).

overcapacity concerns restrict the prospects for global cost convergence in electrolyser manufacturing.[5]

Finally, renewable electricity technologies were already moving down steep learning curves when long-term contracts were introduced, meaning that instruments like PPAs, FiTs, and CfDs accelerated an ongoing cost-reduction trajectory. By contrast, hydrogen technologies—whether electrolysis-based green hydrogen or blue hydrogen with carbon capture—remain at earlier stages of technological maturity, with limited infrastructure and supply chains. Transport and storage infrastructure, in particular, is underdeveloped, and investment in pipelines or terminals is costly. The relative immaturity of the hydrogen sector therefore limits the effectiveness of long-term contracts in driving down costs in the way they did for renewables.

In sum, the structural mismatch between the cost composition of hydrogen production and the incentive mechanisms embedded in long-term fixed-price contracts suggests that hydrogen is unlikely to experience the same dramatic cost reductions as renewable electricity under such schemes. While long-term contracts can still play a role in reducing financing risk for electrolysers, they do not address the volatility of operational costs that dominate hydrogen production. As such, complementary policy instruments—such as input hedging mechanisms, flexible CfDs, and demand-side mandates—may be necessary to achieve the scale and cost reductions needed for hydrogen to become a cornerstone of a decarbonised energy system.

### *Risk Allocation*

In fixed-price, long-term contracts, risk is distributed asymmetrically: producers are exposed primarily to cost risk, while off-takers assume profit risk. Cost risk refers to the possibility that actual production costs (e.g., raw materials, labour, or financing expenses) turn out higher than expected, eroding project margins. By contrast, profit risk arises when buyers are locked into paying a fixed contract price that turns out to exceed market prices, although this also shields them from sudden price spikes. While these risks have long been familiar in the electricity sector, they take on

[5] As discussed in Chap. 2, electrolyser cost reductions face material and supply chain constraints that differ from the commoditised solar PV supply chain.

added complexity in the case of green hydrogen, where both production cost structures and market dynamics differ substantially.

*Cost Risk*

Electricity sector experience shows how cost escalation can undermine the viability of projects bound by long-term contracts. In offshore wind, developers have been hit hard by inflation since 2021, with reported cost increases ranging between 11% and 20%, and in some cases exceeding 30% (Westwood Global Energy Group, 2023). Rising commodity prices for steel and copper, higher financing costs, and vessel charter rate increases, compounded by global supply chain strains, have forced nearly three-quarters of developers to reassess their project plans. These pressures have led to delays, contract renegotiations, and outright cancellations. Westwood estimates that such cost escalation could add around $280 billion to offshore wind capital expenditures over the next decade—about a 20% increase—implying either higher costs for consumers or increased state support (Westwood Global Energy Group, 2023).

Nuclear power offers another illustration. The Hinkley Point C project in the United Kingdom, developed under a CfD, was initially forecast to cost £18 billion and be operational by 2017. It is now expected to require between £31 and 35 billion, with commissioning delayed until at least 2029, and potentially 2031 under pessimistic scenarios (Carbon Brief, 2024). Drivers include inflation, post-Brexit supply disruptions, COVID-19 delays, and stricter safety requirements. The CfD structure left EDF, the developer, carrying the burden of these rising costs, highlighting how long-term contracts can expose producers to significant financial strain.

Similar challenges have emerged in emerging markets. In India, developers of large-scale solar PV projects contracted through highly competitive auctions agreed to supply at very low tariffs under long-term PPAs. Subsequent increases in solar module prices, safeguard duties on imports, and currency depreciation raised project costs beyond the assumptions made when bidding. Several developers struggled to fulfil their contracts, with many seeking renegotiations or delaying delivery. In 2018, a spike in module prices and import duties forced some developers to formally request PPA revisions (PV Magazine, 2018; IJPIEL, 2022).

For green hydrogen, exposure to cost risk is arguably more acute. Electrolyser-based production depends heavily on electricity as a feedstock, meaning operational expenditure rather than upfront capital dominates the cost profile. This creates ongoing vulnerability to volatile electricity prices. The immaturity of hydrogen supply chains and the absence of large-scale economies of scale compound this risk. While hedging instruments such as futures and options exist for electricity, they typically cover only short horizons.

Electrolyser projects, however, require investment horizons of 15–20 years. Even in Germany, which has one of Europe's most liquid forward electricity markets, trading activity is mostly limited to contracts within two years (ACER, 2022). In the United Kingdom, extensive reliance on government-backed CfDs has also dampened liquidity in forward markets, reducing opportunities for long-term hedging. This lack of long-term hedging instruments means producers are forced to bear the full brunt of electricity price volatility, which can quickly render a project unprofitable even with a CfD in place.

Regulatory conditions, including requirements for geographical and temporal alignment and additionality, add further complexity. While intended to guarantee that hydrogen is produced from genuinely new and clean renewable sources, these rules complicate the establishment of long-term electricity agreements. Under additionality rules, producers cannot simply buy power from existing renewable plants; they must either build their own renewable generation assets or contract with new projects built specifically for their hydrogen facility. This drastically reduces the pool of eligible suppliers, increases power prices, and forces careful coordination of the commissioning dates of both the renewable project and the electrolyser. If one comes online before the other, the electricity supply cannot be counted as 'additional', undermining compliance.

The hourly correlation requirement adds another layer of complexity. Producers can no longer match their electricity consumption to renewable output on a yearly or monthly basis—it must now align on an hourly level. This means an electrolyser powered by solar energy can only operate when the sun is shining unless supported by costly battery storage. To remain compliant, hydrogen producers must either invest in storage systems to shift renewable electricity to non-generation hours or curtail hydrogen production during periods of low renewable output. These constraints lead to higher capital and operating costs, more complex system configurations, and increased risk exposure—all of which make long-term electricity hedging and project financing far more challenging.

Regulatory volatility further constrains the development of long-term electricity contracts. Adjustments to capacity mechanisms, renewable support schemes, or carbon pricing can significantly alter expected price trajectories, deterring market participants from committing to multi-decade agreements. Long-term forward contracts also demand substantial collateral and creditworthiness, excluding many smaller firms. One possible mitigation strategy is co-location of electrolysers with renewable generation, enabling direct access to low-cost electricity. Yet this approach creates new risks: if electrolysers operate mainly during periods of high renewable output, their utilisation rates fall, weakening project economics unless storage or backup capacity is added. Ultimately, hydrogen CfDs cannot be designed in isolation from electricity market structures. The United Kingdom's Review of Electricity Market Arrangements (REMA) aims to reconfigure the market to support decarbonisation and security of supply (DESNZ, 2024), but whether such reforms will sufficiently address hydrogen producers' exposure to cost volatility remains uncertain.

*Profit Risk*

Off-takers, in turn, face profit risk when contracted prices exceed prevailing market levels. This has been observed in the electricity sector. In the United Kingdom, some offshore wind projects locked into CfDs at relatively high strike prices. When wholesale electricity prices collapsed during 2020—falling below £40/MWh due to COVID-19 demand reductions and oversupply—the government, via the Low Carbon Contracts Company, was obliged to pay generators above-market rates, effectively transferring costs onto taxpayers and consumers.

California offers another case. Utilities such as PG&E, SCE, and SDG&E signed long-term PPAs with solar developers in the early 2000s, securing fixed tariffs to de-risk investment. As solar technology costs rapidly declined, however, new projects offered electricity at much lower rates, leaving utilities tied to significantly more expensive legacy contracts. Germany's FiT regime created a similar burden: although PV supplied only 14% of non-hydro renewable electricity in 2010, committed FiT payments amounted to roughly €100 billion over 20 years, with annual FiT obligations exceeding 40% of the EEG's total support budget (Huenteler, Schmidt, and Kanie, 2012). These rising liabilities ultimately forced reforms to reduce FiT levels for new entrants.

For green hydrogen, the likelihood of significant profit risk is higher still. Rapid technological improvements in electrolysis are expected to drive down production costs quickly. Meanwhile, hydrogen markets remain nascent, with little historical price data to inform expectations. The policy framework is also evolving: subsidies, carbon pricing schemes, and electricity market reforms could dramatically reshape future cost trajectories. In this environment, off-takers who commit to long-term hydrogen contracts face a heightened risk of being locked into prices well above future market levels. The combination of technological uncertainty, policy fluidity, and market immaturity makes profit risk a more pressing concern for hydrogen buyers than it has been for electricity off-takers, raising fundamental questions about how such contracts should be structured. This dynamic creates a prisoner's dilemma for early off-takers: committing too early risks being uncompetitive, but waiting too long could leave them without supply or facing higher prices if the market tightens.

*Market Demand*

Unlike electricity, which benefits from a large and established consumer base, the long-term demand trajectory for hydrogen remains highly uncertain. Several structural, technological, and policy-related factors contribute to this unpredictability, making it difficult for investors to rely on stable revenue streams.

A first source of uncertainty stems from the high current cost of producing green hydrogen. Electrolysis-based production depends on renewable electricity and relatively immature electrolyser technology, both of which remain expensive compared with incumbent fossil-based hydrogen. Unless costs fall sharply and predictably, hydrogen may struggle to compete with other energy carriers, constraining the expansion of demand. Furthermore, the potential future scalability of naturally occurring 'white' hydrogen adds another layer of uncertainty to long-term demand projections for manufactured low-carbon hydrogen.

While hydrogen is already used in refining and ammonia production, scaling into new industrial applications such as steelmaking or cement depends critically on its ability to displace existing fuels and feedstocks at acceptable cost. In transport, the picture is equally unsettled. In fact, adoption of hydrogen in transport may be hindered by rival technologies, including road electric vehicles and advanced biofuels for aviation and shipping. Hydrogen's prospective role in power generation or long-duration storage is similarly contingent on technological advances, cost reductions, and the availability of alternative storage solutions.

Competition from other low-carbon technologies could further dampen the role of hydrogen. Widespread electrification and the deployment of cost-effective batteries may reduce hydrogen's attractiveness in end-uses where multiple decarbonisation options exist. Although breakthroughs in hydrogen production, storage, or distribution are possible, the timing and scale of such advances are inherently uncertain. Consequently, the range of possible demand outcomes remains broad, making projections difficult to anchor.

Infrastructure gaps are another major constraint. Large-scale adoption of hydrogen requires substantial investment in production facilities, storage capacity, and transport networks, including pipelines, ports, and distribution hubs. The absence of such infrastructure could slow or even stall demand growth. Integration with existing systems is also uncertain: while blending hydrogen into natural gas networks or repurposing fossil-fuel infrastructure has been proposed, the technical and economic feasibility of such approaches is not yet proven at scale. If infrastructure deployment lags behind production capacity, demand may not materialise at the required pace.

Government policy will be decisive in shaping hydrogen demand. At present, demand creation depends heavily on subsidies, mandates, and regulatory incentives. Shifts in political priorities, fiscal pressures, or changes in leadership could reduce the level of support available, leaving hydrogen markets underdeveloped. Conversely, ambitious regulatory mandates—such as quotas for hydrogen-derived fuels in aviation and shipping—could create significant demand. The inherent political risk means that the scale and stability of future demand cannot be assumed.

This uncertainty has important implications for long-term contracting. In markets where demand is volatile or underdeveloped, fixing a price does not ensure that all contracted volumes will be purchased. If demand falls short of projections, producers may face oversupply, storage bottlenecks, or underutilisation of assets, raising per-unit costs and eroding profitability. In extreme cases, assets tied to long-term contracts risk becoming stranded if market conditions shift before they reach economic maturity. The problem is magnified in fast-evolving markets where newer, cheaper decarbonisation technologies could displace hydrogen, undermining the relevance of projects locked into long-term arrangements.

External shocks—such as swings in global energy prices, geopolitical instability, or major policy changes—could further destabilise hydrogen demand. Compared with renewable electricity, which enjoys a broad set of uses across residential, commercial, and industrial sectors, hydrogen's demand base remains narrow and emerging. This concentration increases vulnerability to sector-specific risks. While long-term contracts can shield investors from price volatility, they do little to protect against the risk of insufficient demand. In hydrogen markets, therefore, the central challenge is not only price uncertainty but also whether adequate demand will exist at all, raising fundamental questions about the suitability of conventional long-term fixed-price contracts in this sector.

## Unintended Consequences

The use of long-term contracts to stimulate investment in emerging energy sectors, such as hydrogen, can generate unintended consequences alongside the intended benefits of stability and scale. By locking in prices, technologies, and actors over long horizons, these instruments risk introducing inefficiencies, inequities, and structural rigidities into the energy system. Lessons from the history of renewable and conventional energy deployment illustrate that, while long-term contracts are powerful tools, their design must be carefully calibrated to avoid adverse side effects.

One potential issue concerns the distribution of financial burdens. When the costs of fixed-price hydrogen contracts are passed through to end-users, consumers who do not directly benefit from hydrogen adoption may nonetheless bear higher energy bills. In a context of uncertain demand and limited storage, overcapacity can amplify these costs by pushing up the unit cost of hydrogen. If the wider public perceives these additional expenses as unfair or disconnected from tangible benefits—such as lower emissions—political resistance may build, jeopardising support for the energy transition. A parallel can be found in Germany's Renewable Energy Act (EEG). Its feed-in tariff (FiT) system, introduced in 2000, financed renewable deployment through surcharges on electricity bills. While it successfully expanded wind and solar, it also increased costs for households and small businesses, generating strong public backlash and eventually forcing reforms (Frondel et al., 2008, 2010).

A second unintended effect is the risk of overcapacity and fiscal unsustainability. If subsidies embedded in long-term contracts are too generous or poorly adjusted to falling technology costs, deployment can accelerate beyond expectations, straining public budgets. Spain's solar PV boom in the late 2000s illustrates this dynamic. High FiT rates, combined with rapidly declining module prices, led to an uncontrolled surge in installations. By 2009, annual subsidies for PV reached €2.6 billion—half of all renewable support costs despite representing only 10% of renewable electricity output (Del Río and Mir-Artigues, 2014). The mismatch between support levels and market realities resulted in mounting tariff deficits, forcing the government to impose retroactive cuts, quotas, and ultimately a moratorium. These measures damaged investor confidence and underscored the dangers of overgenerous, rigid long-term contracts.

A third concern is market concentration and reduced innovation. Fixed-price contracts often favour large incumbents with the financial capacity and scale to compete successfully in auctions or meet stringent eligibility criteria. While this can generate economies of scale, it risks squeezing out smaller firms, which are often more innovative and experimental.

The early years of electricity sector privatisation in the United Kingdom provide an example: after liberalisation in the 1990s, market power became concentrated in a handful of companies with long-term contracts and infrastructure dominance (Green, 2006; Thomas, 2006). Progress in innovation remained slow until later reforms, including the New Electricity Trading Arrangements (NETA) and Electricity Market Reform (EMR), renewed competition and provided targeted support for renewable energy. By analogy, a hydrogen market dominated by a few large players could prioritise optimising existing processes over pursuing breakthrough technologies, reducing the sector's dynamism. This is particularly problematic for hydrogen, where multiple production pathways and technologies are still in development. A CfD scheme that inadvertently favours one technology (e.g., alkaline over PEM electrolysis) or one production route (e.g., blue over green) could stifle the very innovation needed for long-term cost reduction and performance improvement.

The risk of infrastructure lock-in presents a further challenge. Long-term contracts linked to specific production methods—such as blue hydrogen with carbon capture—may discourage switching to cleaner or more efficient technologies as they emerge. The broader energy sector provides cautionary precedents. Large-scale investment in coal-fired power in the United States and China entrenched coal as the backbone of electricity supply for decades, creating sunk costs and political inertia that slowed the transition to renewables (Erickson et al., 2015). Even as environmental concerns intensified, the persistence of coal infrastructure made change costly and contested. Similarly, long-term contracts in hydrogen could tie producers and policymakers to particular technologies, limiting the sector's flexibility to adopt next-generation electrolysers or novel production pathways.

Taken together, these risks highlight a paradox: long-term contracts are essential to mobilise early investment and infrastructure for hydrogen, yet they may simultaneously undermine the sector's adaptability. By socialising costs unevenly, favouring incumbents, and locking in technologies, such instruments can generate political resistance, reduce innovation, and slow technological progress. The key difficulty is finding the right balance between giving investors security and preserving adaptability for future developments. Without careful design, long-term contracts could entrench structural inertia that ultimately hinders the full potential of hydrogen to deliver an inclusive and innovative energy transition.

## Conclusions

This chapter set out to investigate whether long-term fixed-price contracts, particularly Contracts for Difference (CfDs), can deliver for low-carbon hydrogen the same cost reduction and scale-up benefits that they did for renewable electricity. In doing so, it examined the rationale for CfDs as an instrument of risk reduction, compared the cost and risk structures of renewable electricity and hydrogen, and assessed the implications of applying similar mechanisms in a sector still marked by technological immaturity, infrastructural gaps, and uncertain demand.

The evidence suggests that while CfDs were highly effective in renewable—where capital-intensive cost structures aligned with predictable, falling technology costs—the analogy breaks down in the case of hydrogen. Hydrogen production is dominated by variable operational expenditure, primarily electricity input costs, which fixed-price contracts cannot fully stabilise. This limits their ability to trigger steep cost declines of the kind observed in solar and wind, where CfDs accelerated technologies already moving down learning curves.

The analysis also showed that risk allocation under hydrogen CfDs is more problematic than in renewables. Producers remain exposed to volatile electricity markets and immature supply chains, while off-takers risk being locked into uncompetitive prices in a rapidly evolving technological and policy landscape. These asymmetries suggest that rigid, symmetric CfD designs may be poorly suited to hydrogen and that more adaptive, flexible approaches—such as strike prices partially indexed to input costs, or two-part contracts separating capacity and commodity payments—may be needed to share risks more equitably across the value chain.

A further challenge lies in demand uncertainty. Whereas electricity benefited from a broad, established customer base, hydrogen's future markets remain narrow, contested, and policy-dependent. Long-term contracts can guarantee revenue stability only where demand exists; they cannot create it. Without stronger demand-side measures—such as quotas, mandates, and public procurement—CfDs risk underwriting production that lacks adequate off-take, creating oversupply or stranded assets.

In addition, the potential unintended consequences of long-term contracts highlight the need for careful calibration. If poorly designed, they may entrench incumbents, burden consumers with rising costs, or lock in suboptimal technologies, undermining flexibility and innovation in a sector that is still at a formative stage. This paradox—where instruments intended to provide stability risk producing rigidity—underscores the importance of designing contracts with sunset clauses, adaptive mechanisms, and incentives for continuous cost reduction.

The overarching conclusion is that CfDs for hydrogen should not be expected to replicate the transformative role they played in renewables. Instead, they must be positioned as one part of a broader and adaptive policy toolkit. Carbon pricing should continue to provide a long-term decarbonisation signal, targeted subsidies should bridge the operational cost gap, mandates should secure predictable demand, and international certification should underpin market development and trade. CfDs can help reduce financing risk for early projects, but it is this multi-pronged, coordinated, and flexible policy mix that will ultimately determine whether hydrogen can scale up to become a cornerstone of the net-zero transition. Therefore, a 'copy-paste' of the renewable electricity CfD model is unlikely to succeed for hydrogen. The policy must be rethought to fit the unique contours of the hydrogen value chain.

Accordingly, the following chapters extend the analysis beyond production policy to the infrastructure that will determine hydrogen's spatial and economic reach—transport, storage, and trade—and, further, to specific applications of clean hydrogen at the off-take in the context of decarbonisation.

## References

ACER. (2022). *ACER's final assessment of the EU wholesale electricity market design*. Agency for the Cooperation of Energy Regulators (ACER).

Ameli, N., & Kammen, D. (2014). Innovations in financing that drive cost parity for long-term electricity sustainability: An assessment of Italy, Europe's fastest growing solar photovoltaic market. *Energy for Sustainable Development, 19*(1), 130–137.

BEIS. (2022). Low carbon hydrogen production business model heads of terms [Online]. Retrieved November 12, 2025, from https://assets.publishing.service.gov.uk/media/639c470f8fa8f5069707c0fe/

Carbon Brief. (2024). *EDF takes €12.9bn hit after Hinkley Point C delays and cost overruns* [Online]. Retrieved October 08, 2024, from https://www.carbonbrief.org/daily-brief/edf-takes-e12-9bn-hit-after-hinkley-point-c-delays-and-cost-overruns/.

Del Río, P., & Mir-Artigues, P. (2014). *A cautionary tale: Spain's solar PV investment bubble* [Online]. Retrieved September 7, 2024, from https://www.iisd.org/gsi/sites/default/files/rens_ct_spain.pdf.

DESNZ. (2023b). *Government response to market engagement on the second hydrogen allocation round* [Online]. Retrieved November 12, 2025, from https://www.gov.uk/government/publications/hydrogen-allocation-round-2.

DESNZ. (2023d). *Hydrogen production business model: Net zero hydrogen fund – HAR1 successful projects* [Online]. Retrieved September 4, 2024, from https://www.gov.uk/government/publications/hydrogen-production-business-model-net-zero-hydrogen-fund-shortlisted-projects/hydrogen-production-business-model-net-zero-hydrogen-fund-har1-successful-projects.

DESNZ. (2024). *Review of electricity market arrangements (REMA): Second consultation document.* March [Online]. Retrieved November 11, 2025, from https://www.gov.uk/government/consultations/review-of-electricity-market-arrangements-rema-second-consultation.

DESNZ. (2025). *Hydrogen production business model. Department for Energy Security and Net Zero (DESNZ)* (updated 12 February 2025). [Online]. Retrieved August 19, 2025, from https://www.gov.uk/government/publications/hydrogen-production-business-model.

Erickson, P., Kartha, S., Lazarus, M., & Tempest, K. (2015). Assessing carbon lock-in. *Environmental Research Letters, 10*(1), 1–11.

European Commission. (2024). *Report from the Commission to the European Parliament and the Council on the functioning of the European carbon market in 2023.* [Online]. Retrieved August 19, 2025, from https://climate.ec.europa.eu/document/download/92ec0ab3-24cf-4814-ad59-81c15e310bea_en?filename=2024_carbon_market_report_en.pdf.

European Union. (2023a). *Regulation (EU) 2023/2405 of the European Parliament and of the Council of 18 October 2023 on ensuring a level playing field for sustainable air transport (ReFuelEU Aviation). Official Journal of the European Union, 31 Oct 2023.* [Online]. Retrieved August 21, 2025, from https://eur-lex.europa.eu/legal-content/EN/TXT/PDF/?uri=CELEX%3A32023R2405.

European Union. (2023b). *Regulation (EU) 2023/1805 of the European Parliament and of the Council of 13 September 2023 on the use of renewable and low-carbon fuels in maritime transport, and amending Directive 2009/16/EC. Official Journal of the European Union*, September 22 [Online]. Retrieved August 21, 2025, from https://eur-lex.europa.eu/legal-content/EN/TXT/PDF/?uri=CELEX%3A32023R1805

European Union. (2023c). *Commission Delegated Regulation (EU) 2023/1184 of 10 February 2023 supplementing Directive (EU) 2018/2001 of the European Parliament and of the Council by establishing a Union methodology setting out detailed rules for the production of renewable liquid and gaseous transport fuels of non-biological origin. Official Journal of the European Union*, June 20 [Online]. Retrieved August 19, 2025, from https://eur-lex.europa.eu/legal-content/EN/TXT/PDF/?uri=CELEX%3A32023R1184

Frondel, M., Ritter, N., & Schmidt, C. M. (2008). Germany's solar cell promotion: Dark clouds on the horizon. *Energy Policy, 36*(11), 4198–4204.

Frondel, M., Ritter, N., Schmidt, C. M., & Vance, C. (2010). Economic impacts from the promotion of renewable energy technologies: The German experience. *Energy Policy, 38*(8), 4048–4056.

FuturePolicy.org. (2019). *The German Feed-in Tariff* [Online]. Retrieved October 8, 2024, from https://www.futurepolicy.org/climate-stability/renewable-energies/the-german-feed-in-tariff/.

Genoese, F., Drabik, E., & Egenhofer, C. (2016). The EU Power sector needs long-term price signals. *European Economics: Microeconomics & Industrial Organization eJournal.*

Green, R. (2006). Market power mitigation in the UK power market. *Utilities Policy, 14*(1), 76–89.

Huenteler, J., Schmidt, T. S., & Kanie, N. (2012) 'Japan's post-Fukushima challenge: implications from the German experience on renewable energy policy', *Energy Policy,* 45, 6–11.

Hochberg, M., & Poudineh, R. (2018). *Renewable auction design in theory and practice: Lessons from the Experiences of Brazil and Mexico.* Oxford Institute for Energy Studies, EL 28.

ICCT. (2024). *The price of green hydrogen: How and why we estimate future production costs* [Online]. Retrieved November 10, 2025, from https://theicct.org/the-price-of-green-hydrogen-estimate-future-production-costs-may24

IEA. (2019). *Global average levelised cost of hydrogen production by energy source and technology, 2019 and 2050* [Online]. Retrieved November 10, 2025, from https://www.iea.org/data-and-statistics/charts/global-average-levelised-cost-of-hydrogen-production-by-energy-source-and-technology-2019-and-2050?utm

IEA. (2023). *Global hydrogen review 2023.* International Energy Agency.

IJPIEL. (2022). *Analysis of change in law and safeguard duty on solar power projects in India* [Online]. Retrieved October 9, 2024, from https://ijpiel.com/index.php/2022/03/14/analysis-of-change-in-law-and-safeguard-duty-on-solar-power-projects-in-india/

Odenweller, M., & Ueckerdt, F. (2025). The green hydrogen ambition and implementation gap. *Nature Energy, 10*(1), 110–123.

PV magazine. (2018). *India: 25% safeguard duty will threaten ongoing solar PV projects* [Online]. Retrieved October 9, 2024, from https://www.pv-magazine.com/2018/07/18/india-25-safeguard-duty-will-threaten-ongoing-solar-pv-projects/

Thomas, S. (2006). The British model in Britain: Failing slowly. *Energy Policy, 34*(5), 583–600.

US Department of the Treasury. (2025). Credit for production of clean hydrogen and energy credit. *Federal Register*, January 10 [Online]. Retrieved August 21, 2025, from https://www.federalregister.gov/documents/2025/01/10/2024-31513/credit-for-production-of-clean-hydrogen-and-energy-credit

Westwood Global Energy Group. (2023). *Tackling the cost inflation challenge in offshore wind*. June [Online]. Retrieved November 12, 2025, from https://www.westwoodenergy.com/wp-content/uploads/2023/06/Tackling-the-Cost-inflation-Challenge-in-Offshore-Wind.pdf

CHAPTER 4

# Hydrogen Transportation and Trade

## Introduction

The viability of hydrogen as a decarbonisation cornerstone depends not merely on production, but on its ability to be cost-effectively and safely moved from regions of abundant supply to demand centres. While much attention has been given to the cost and scalability of hydrogen production, the question of how hydrogen can be transported and traded at scale remains equally critical. In contrast to fossil fuels, which rely on mature global supply chains, hydrogen presents unique challenges because of its physical and chemical characteristics, prompting key questions about efficient transport from producers to end-users. This challenge is compounded by the persistent cost gap in production, as examined in the previous chapter, making efficient transport even more critical to the overall hydrogen economy.

The geographical distribution of renewable and low-carbon energy resources is uneven. Regions with abundant solar or wind potential may produce hydrogen at relatively low cost, but their domestic demand may be limited, while industrialised or energy-intensive economies may require large imports (IRENA, 2022a). This imbalance implies that significant flows of hydrogen—or hydrogen-based products—may need to occur both within regions and across borders. Understanding which transport modes can underpin such flows, and at what scale, is therefore a prerequisite for any credible vision of a global hydrogen economy.





A. Patonia, R. Poudineh, *Clean Hydrogen for Decarbonisation*,
https://doi.org/10.1007/978-3-032-19442-8_4

Several technical options are under consideration for moving hydrogen across different distances (see Fig. 4.1). Pipelines, whether newly built or converted from natural gas use, trucks, railroad, or even transferring electricity instead through HVDC lines are seen as candidates for regional transport (Patonia et al., 2023). Alternatives include shipping hydrogen in gaseous or liquid form, or transforming it into derivative carriers such as ammonia, methanol, or synthetic fuels (IEA, 2023a). Each pathway involves trade-offs in terms of cost, energy efficiency, infrastructure readiness, and safety. The comparative appeal of these approaches continues to be explored in both research and policy discussions.

Hydrogen's low volumetric energy density makes it more difficult to transport than fossil fuels (Patonia et al., 2023). Compression,

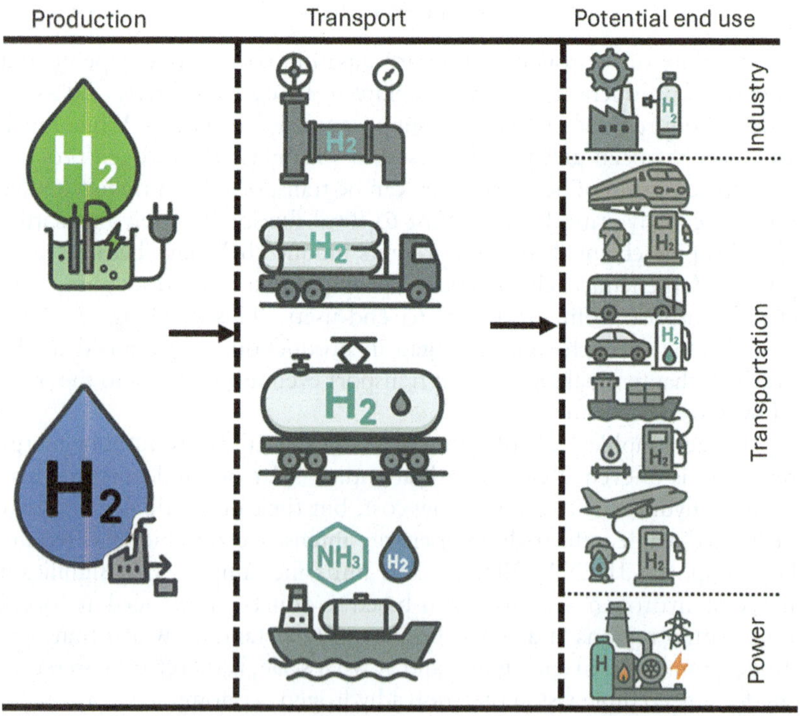


**Fig. 4.1** Different means of hydrogen transportation. (Source: Authors)

liquefaction, or chemical conversion can mitigate this, but each process entails additional capital and energy costs (Patonia & Poudineh, 2022). Questions remain about the extent to which existing natural gas infrastructure can be repurposed, the viability of long-distance liquid hydrogen shipping, and the competitiveness of derivatives in meeting future trade needs. These challenges raise uncertainties not only about the technical feasibility but also about the eventual cost structures of hydrogen trade.

Despite these uncertainties, governments and industry actors are beginning to experiment with different models of hydrogen transport. Pilot projects in Europe, Japan, and Australia have explored shipping liquid hydrogen and trading ammonia, while network development initiatives such as the European Hydrogen Backbone propose large-scale repurposing of pipelines (EHB, 2022; IEA, 2023b). At the same time, hydrogen cluster and hub initiatives in the EU and United States[1] aim to reduce transport requirements in the near term by co-locating production and demand (European Commission, 2020; DOE, 2023). These initiatives suggest multiple pathways are being tested, but it is not yet clear which will dominate.

If hydrogen is to become a widely traded commodity, the choice of transport modes will directly shape the nature of that trade. Pipelines might facilitate intra-regional integration, while shipping of hydrogen or its derivatives could underpin intercontinental flows. Yet the question remains open as to whether hydrogen trade will develop as a bulk commodity akin to natural gas, or whether it will be primarily embedded in chemical carriers and niche applications (IRENA, 2022b). The answer will have implications not only for technology deployment but also for global market design, energy security, and geopolitical dynamics.

These uncertainties highlight the importance of a systematic assessment of hydrogen transport and trade. Central questions arise: What transport modes are most efficient and reliable for hydrogen over short, medium, and long distances? How might these choices shape the scale, form, and direction of hydrogen trade? Addressing these questions requires integrating techno-economic analysis with insights from infrastructure planning, industrial strategy, and international energy policy.

This chapter seeks to provide such an assessment. It surveys the technical, economic, and policy dimensions of hydrogen transport and trade,

[1] More information on the US case can be found here: https://www.energy.gov/oced/regional-clean-hydrogen-hubs-0

drawing on the emerging literature and early project experience. The focus is on transport and trade specifically, while large-scale storage—another critical part of hydrogen system design—is addressed in a separate chapter. By framing the current state of knowledge and highlighting areas of uncertainty, the chapter aims to contribute to an informed discussion on how hydrogen might be moved and traded in support of global decarbonisation goals.

The outline of this chapter is as follows: Section "Hydrogen Transport Infrastructure" examines the physical and technical characteristics of hydrogen that influence its transportation and compares the main infrastructure options, including pipelines, trucking, and shipping. Section "Cost and Technical Comparison of Different Hydrogen Transportation Means" provides a detailed cost and performance comparison of these transport modes, highlighting the economic trade-offs between pipelines, liquid hydrogen, and derivative carriers such as ammonia and methanol. Section "Business Model for Hydrogen Transportation: The Case Study of the UK" analyses the United Kingdom's Hydrogen Transport Business Model (HTBM) as a policy case study for financing and regulating hydrogen networks. Finally, Section "Conclusions" summarises the main insights and policy implications for developing efficient, safe, and economically viable hydrogen transport and trade systems.

## Hydrogen Transport Infrastructure

Hydrogen differs fundamentally from fossil fuels in terms of its physical and chemical properties, and these differences strongly influence its transportation. Hydrogen has about one-third of the volumetric energy density of natural gas and a significantly lower ignition energy, with a much wider flammability range (4–76%) than methane (5–15%) (Martin et al., 2024). As a result, to move the same energy content through a pipeline, hydrogen must flow at higher velocities, and pipeline systems require more compression energy than those designed for fossil gases (Khan et al., 2021). Hydrogen molecules are also the smallest of all gases, which makes them prone to leakage and permeation through seals, welds, and plastic pipes—issues not encountered to the same degree with natural gas or oil (Topolski et al., 2022).

Hydrogen can be transported in several forms depending on distance, scale, and end-use requirements. For small-scale and short distances, gaseous hydrogen is often transported via tube trailers; however, each truck can carry only a limited capacity (e.g., 300–1000 kg), making this mode inefficient for large-scale energy transport (Khan et al., 2022). Liquid hydrogen ($LH_2$) trucks have higher capacity (e.g., 3.6 tonnes per load), but liquefaction consumes a large part of the energy content of hydrogen, making it energy-intensive and costly (Yu et al., 2024). At larger scales and distances, pipelines are the most efficient and cost-competitive solution, while for intercontinental trade, hydrogen is often converted to derivatives such as ammonia or liquid organic hydrogen carriers (LOHCs)[2] (Wolf et al., 2024; IRENA, 2024).

The technological readiness level (TRL) of hydrogen transportation options varies. Hydrogen pipelines have operated for decades in industrial clusters, particularly in the United States and Europe, where the total of about 5000 km of pipelines are already in service (IEA, 2024). These systems operate at steady loads and short distances, connecting refineries and ammonia plants. Liquid hydrogen shipping remains at lower TRL, with significant boil-off and storage challenges (Wolf et al., 2024). Ammonia shipping is more advanced but requires costly conversion and reconversion infrastructure. Trucking of hydrogen, whether gaseous or liquid, is commercially mature, but remains unsuitable for large-scale distribution due to its high cost per unit delivered (Cheng & Cheng, 2023).

Pipelines stand out as the backbone for cost-effective hydrogen transport at scale. Studies show that pipelines can transport hydrogen at less than 1 USD/kg over medium distances when operating at high utilisation rates (Khan et al., 2021; DOE/NETL, 2024). Compared to shipping hydrogen derivatives, pipelines are consistently more economical for distances of up to 2500–4000 km (IRENA, 2022a; JRC, 2022). Moreover, pipelines offer the additional advantage of linepack storage, allowing operators to store hydrogen within the pipeline and balance short-term fluctuations in supply and demand (Hydrogen Council and McKinsey, 2021).

The advantages of pipelines include their scalability, low operational costs once built, and suitability for continuous supply to industry, heating, and power generation. Repurposing natural gas pipelines can cut capital costs by 60–94% compared with building new hydrogen pipelines (Hydrogen Council and McKinsey, 2021; IRENA, 2022a). Pipelines also integrate well with hydrogen hubs and industrial clusters, offering secure

[2] To put this in perspective, a single standard pipeline could transport the equivalent of thousands of tube trailer loads per day, highlighting the scalability limitation of road transport.

and direct connections between producers and users (Project Union, 2022). However, pipelines are capital intensive, requiring billions of dollars in upfront investment and a sufficiently large and predictable demand to ensure economic viability (European Court of Auditors, 2024).

Key challenges in hydrogen pipeline use stem from material compatibility and safety. Hydrogen can cause embrittlement in high-strength steels, particularly at welds, leading to cracks and fatigue failures (DNV, 2023). Leakage risk is higher due to hydrogen's small molecular size, while odorisation methods for leak detection remain underdeveloped (Khan et al., 2021). Pipelines also require more frequent inspection and tailored integrity management to account for the accelerated crack growth rates under hydrogen cycling conditions (DNV, 2023). In addition to safety, leakage has climate relevance: even small loss rates can lower the net climate value of hydrogen pathways via hydrogen's indirect warming effects, which makes robust monitoring and leak-mitigation part of climate governance (not only engineering practice).

The role of repurposing versus new pipelines is central in discussions of hydrogen infrastructure. Repurposing existing natural gas pipelines can reduce costs dramatically and speed up deployment, as demonstrated in the European Hydrogen Backbone plan, where 60% of the proposed network is expected to consist of converted pipelines (European Hydrogen Backbone, 2022). Repurposing is, however, limited by factors such as material grade, weld quality, and original operating conditions. Some pipelines may be unsuitable without costly mitigation, while older pipes may not meet hydrogen-specific standards (DNV, 2023). Therefore, while repurposing is attractive in the short term, new hydrogen-dedicated pipelines might be required for long-distance transmission and export corridors.

Blending hydrogen into natural gas networks has been proposed as a transitional measure. Blends of up to a certain percentage of hydrogen by volume are technically in many low-pressure distribution networks and have already been demonstrated in projects such as HyDeploy in the United Kingdom and Enertrag in Germany[3] (Topolski et al., 2022). However, the energy contribution of technically safe blend is modest—for example 20% by volume corresponds to only ~7% by energy (Martin et al., 2024). Blending also introduces challenges, such as higher leakage rates,

[3] It is reported that HyDeploy has experimented with a hydrogen blend of up to 28.4% and Enertrag up to 70% (Topolski et al., 2022).

end-user equipment compatibility, and the need for expensive separation technologies if pure hydrogen is required downstream (NREL, 2022).

From a policy and regulatory perspective, blending is generally seen as an interim solution rather than a long-term pathway. The EU Gas Package caps hydrogen blending at 2% for cross-border interconnections to avoid inefficiencies and fragmentation (ECA, 2024). In contrast, dedicated pure hydrogen networks are considered the end goal. As a result, while blending may support early decarbonisation and provide flexibility for renewable integration, it is unlikely to play a major role in large-scale hydrogen transport strategies (IEA, 2024).

In summary, hydrogen's unique properties demand tailored transport solutions. Pipelines provide the most efficient means of moving large volumes over land, particularly when repurposed natural gas infrastructure can be utilised. While blending offers short-term benefits, the long-term strategy relies on dedicated hydrogen networks, supported by robust safety standards and regulatory frameworks. The success of this infrastructure build-out will determine whether hydrogen can fulfil its projected role as a key energy carrier in the global net-zero transition.

## Cost and Technical Comparison of Different Hydrogen Transportation Means

Hydrogen can be moved as a gas in pipelines, as liquid hydrogen ($LH_2$), or as derivatives (chiefly ammonia; also LOHCs), and—at small scales—by road. Each pathway has distinct cost structures and technical constraints.

Pipelines (pure $H_2$) are the cost benchmark for continental transport at scale. Europe-focused assessments indicate transport costs of roughly EUR 0.10–0.20 per kg per 1000 km for large, well-utilised lines (JRC, 2022). A Germany import study finds repurposed pipelines at €0.08–0.49/kg and new-build at €0.10–1.34/kg, depending on route length and throughput (Wolf et al., 2024). Engineering cost models for North America show similar scaling, with transport prices on the order of \$0.07/kg per 100 miles (thus ≈\$0.7/kg per 1000 miles) at moderate capacities, falling with greater utilisation and diameter (DOE/NETL, 2024). A national network study for China reports an LCOT range of \$0.13–\$1.81/kg across distances (200–1800 km), capacities (0.25–2 Mt/yr), and design pressures (4–10 MPa), underscoring the sensitivity to volume, pressure, and distance (Yu et al., 2024).

In the case of shipping liquid $H_2$ ($LH_2$), liquefaction and boil-off handling dominate costs. In a 2050-oriented comparison of imports to Germany, $LH_2$ transport totals €1.73–3.40/kg (including liquefaction, storage, shipping, and regasification), making it materially more expensive than pipelines for European-scale routes (Wolf et al., 2024). IRENA's analysis similarly finds $LH_2$ disadvantaged on energy and CapEx intensity versus pipelines at short–medium distances; shipping becomes attractive mainly where pipelines are infeasible (IRENA, 2022b).

Shipping as derivatives such as ammonia or liquid organic hydrogen carriers (LOHCs) is another option. Ammonia offers high volumetric energy density and maritime logistics compatibility, but incurs synthesis and cracking penalties; LOHCs add hydrogenation/dehydrogenation plant CapEx plus carrier costs and losses. To Germany, LOHC routes were estimated at €2.33–7.29/kg, the upper end reflecting carrier cycles and conversion losses (Wolf et al., 2024). IRENA's trade assessments also conclude that derivatives can be justified for intercontinental flows but is hard to compete with pipelines intra-continent (IRENA, 2024).

Road transport (gaseous and liquid) economic dictates specific applications. Tube-trailer (gaseous) delivery is technologically mature but limited in payload, so costs escalate rapidly with distance and station size; it suits early markets and short-haul applications (Transition Accelerator, 2022). Cryogenic $LH_2$ trucking moves larger loads (several tonnes) and is viable at hundreds of kilometres, but liquefaction energy and boil-off dominate delivered cost; compared with pipelines, both trucking modes lose on OpEx and labour/logistics once daily volumes rise beyond a few tonnes per site (Transition Accelerator, 2022).

Repurposing versus new-build pipelines is a central cost lever. Multiple sources find retrofit CapEx will be significantly lower than new dedicated hydrogen lines; indicative unit costs are \$0.6–1.2 m/km (repurpose) versus \$2.2–4.5 m/km (new) (Hydrogen Council and McKinsey, 2021), translating into €0.10–0.20/kg/1000 km transport where throughput is high (JRC, 2022). System studies expect 50–80% of future $H_2$ networks in gas-rich regions to be repurposed, contingent on factors such as steel grade, weld quality, and accessibility for inspection and mitigation (DNV, 2023). Where legacy assets fail material or integrity screens (e.g., high-strength steels prone to embrittlement), new-build becomes necessary.

Cost drivers and uncertainties vary by mode. For pipelines, key drivers are diameter and length, design pressure and compressor spacing, utilisation (load factor), steel and construction costs, route/terrain, and WACC;

uncertainties include standards evolution, material compatibility (embrittlement, fatigue), and permitting timelines. For $LH_2$, electricity price (for liquefaction), plant scale/learning, and boil-off management dominate; for ammonia/LOHC, conversion plant CapEx/efficiency, carrier costs and cycling losses, and cracking (for $NH_3$) or dehydrogenation performance are pivotal. Road logistics hinge on driver and equipment utilisation, fuel/energy prices, and station scale. Scenario ranges in recent studies (e.g., €0.08–1.34/kg for pipelines vs. €1.7–>7/kg for shipped hydrogen/derivatives) reflect these interacting uncertainties, plus geographic risk and financing assumptions (Wolf et al., 2024; IRENA, 2022b).

The bottom line is that with large, steady volumes and continental distances, pure-hydrogen pipelines—especially repurposed assets that pass integrity screens—are the least-cost option and provide valuable linepack flexibility. Derivatives shipping extends reach across oceans at higher cost, suitable where pipelines cannot go. Trucking is indispensable in early roll-outs and last-mile delivery but is out-competed by pipelines as demand densities. The choice is ultimately dictated by distance, volume, asset readiness, electricity prices, and finance, with the biggest open questions lying in standards maturation, compressor and materials performance, and project execution.

### *HVDC Lines Versus Pipelines*

There is an ongoing debate over whether it is more cost-effective to produce green hydrogen close to renewable power sources—such as offshore wind farms—and transport it to demand centres via pipelines, or instead to transmit electricity through high-voltage direct current (HVDC) lines and generate hydrogen closer to the point of use (see Fig. 4.2).

HVDC and hydrogen pipelines represent two central but fundamentally different approaches to long-distance green energy transport. HVDC projects are already widely deployed, with cumulative global capacity exceeding 30 GW by 2020 and the most ambitious single line in China capable of transmitting 12 GW over 3324 km (NS Energy, 2022; Nishioka et al., 2020). By contrast, hydrogen pipelines are less mature: current operational networks amount to just over 5000 km, mainly serving industrial clusters in Europe and North America, though ambitious projects such as the European Hydrogen Backbone envisage over 30,000 km by 2040 (Shell, 2022; Rystad Energy, 2023). This disparity highlights a key difference: HVDC is a mature, scalable transmission technology, whereas

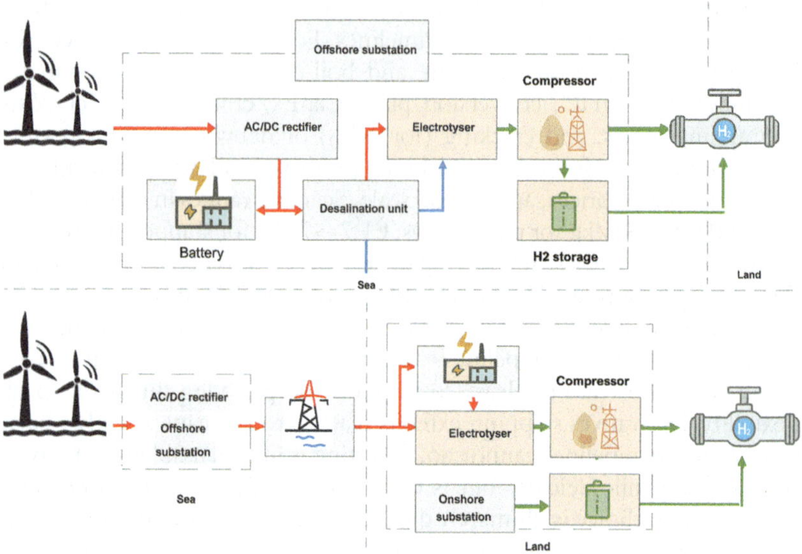


**Fig. 4.2** HVDC lines vs. hydrogen pipelines. (Source: Authors)

hydrogen pipelines remain at an early build-out stage despite their potential to transport larger energy volumes per project.

Technically, HVDC lines excel in transmitting electricity efficiently over long distances due to the absence of reactive power and lower losses compared to HVAC (Reed et al., 2019; Cence Power, 2022). Energy losses are typically around 3% per 1000 km (Patonia et al., 2023). Pipelines, on the other hand, incur lower direct transmission losses—around 1% per 1000 km. However, hydrogen must first be produced via electrolysis, often based on desalinated water, and compressed and with each step introducing conversion losses. These upstream processes can raise overall energy losses in pipeline-based delivery chains to 40% or more, compared to 8–18% for HVDC transmission from offshore wind to consumers (Patonia et al., 2023).

From a cost perspective, both technologies demand high upfront capital investment, but the drivers differ. HVDC projects are dominated by bespoke converter stations, cable manufacturing, and civil works, with average costs ranging from €2.3 to €90/MWh/1000 km depending on conditions (Hagspiel et al., 2014; Purvins et al., 2018; Welder et al.,

2018). Pipelines, in turn, rely heavily on materials, labour, and right-of-way, and cost between €1.1 and €18.2/MWh/1000 km (Timmerberg & Kaltschmitt, 2019; Semeraro, 2021). Repurposing existing natural gas pipelines offers the largest economic advantage: conversion may cost just 10–35% of new construction, reducing expenses by up to four times (DNV, 2022; Rystad Energy, 2023). Yet, hydrogen's physical properties—lower volumetric energy density, higher compression requirements, and embrittlement risks—still raise costs relative to natural gas systems.

In terms of system integration, HVDC provides bi-directional flows that can help balance grids and interconnect networks operating at different voltages or frequencies (Li et al., 2021). Pipelines, in contrast, not only deliver hydrogen but also offer intrinsic storage flexibility through linepack, smoothing seasonal or daily mismatches between production and demand. However, they require stable, large-volume hydrogen flows to operate economically, which is a challenge given the intermittency of renewable generation. As a result, HVDC tends to be the more suitable option for delivering fluctuating renewable electricity directly, while pipelines make more sense when demand is for hydrogen itself, such as in steelmaking, ammonia, or refining sectors.

Risks and environmental impacts also differ. HVDC projects face opposition due to land use, habitat disruption, and visual impacts, alongside potential equipment failure (Wang et al., 2022). Pipelines present risks of leakage, embrittlement, and explosion due to hydrogen's flammability and small molecular size (Bouledroua et al., 2020). Both infrastructures are costly to site underground or subsea, with multiple times more expensive compared with above-ground options (Kaiser, 2017). Both also raise geopolitical and security concerns: cross-border HVDC projects such as Desertec collapsed partly over political tensions (Euractiv, 2013), while the sabotage of Nord Stream highlighted vulnerabilities of pipeline networks (DW, 2022).

In conclusion, neither HVDC nor hydrogen pipelines should be seen as mutually exclusive. HVDC lines offer the more mature and efficient solution for transporting renewable electricity directly, while pipelines are more promising for moving and storing energy in molecular form where end-use requires hydrogen. The optimal choice depends on context: if demand is primarily for electricity, HVDC is superior, but if hydrogen is needed at the point of use, pipelines—especially repurposed natural gas assets—could provide a cost-competitive pathway. Ultimately, both infrastructures are likely to develop in parallel, forming complementary pillars of an integrated green energy system. Therefore, in the end, the choice would not be 'either/or' but would be determined by the final energy form required: electrons for electricity or molecules for feedstock and fuel.

### *Long-Distance Transportation of Hydrogen and the Role of Derivatives*

Long-distance transportation of hydrogen presents another key challenge. Transporting hydrogen directly as liquid hydrogen, over long distanced, is technologically possible but remains extremely challenging because of its cryogenic nature. Liquefaction requires cooling to −253 °C, consuming 30–36% of the hydrogen's own energy content, and boil-off gas (BOG) losses during storage and shipping reduce delivered volumes significantly (Amos, 1999; Garche, 2009). These characteristics make liquid hydrogen one of the most expensive and technically demanding carriers for transoceanic trade (Aziz et al., 2019). Against this background, attention has shifted to derivatives—namely ammonia ($NH_3$), liquid organic hydrogen carriers (LOHCs, particularly methylcyclohexane, MCH), and methanol—as potentially more practical vectors for large-scale maritime hydrogen trade (Papadias et al., 2018).

Ammonia has emerged as a promising derivative, thanks to its high volumetric hydrogen content (about 108 $kgH_2/m^3$, compared with ~71 $kgH_2/m^3$ for liquid hydrogen) and relatively low liquefaction requirements, as it becomes liquid at −33 °C (Kraemer, 2018). Existing infrastructure for global ammonia trade (about 20 Mt/year) provides a ready-made logistical base for scaling hydrogen shipping in this form (IHS Markit, 2022). Moreover, ammonia can be used directly in fertilizer production, shipping fuel, or cracked back into hydrogen at destination. However, challenges remain: ammonia is toxic and corrosive, and cracking it to pure hydrogen requires high temperatures and adds costs. Still, techno-economic modelling suggests ammonia can deliver almost twice as much hydrogen as liquid hydrogen over comparable routes such as Australia-Japan or Morocco-Netherlands[4] (Patonia & Poudineh, 2022; Ishimoto et al., 2020).

[4] It is also important to note that cracking ammonia back into hydrogen using fossil-based energy would significantly undermine its decarbonisation value, highlighting the need for clean cracking process.

LOHCs like methylcyclohexane (MCH) offer different advantages. They are liquids at ambient temperature, avoiding the need for liquefaction or cryogenic storage. MCH can be transported using existing oil infrastructure, and toluene, the parent molecule, is already a major petrochemical feedstock (Papadias & Ahluwalia, 2020). However, LOHCs suffer from low gravimetric hydrogen content (~6 wt%) and high density, meaning transporters carry substantial volumes of the carrier molecule itself, which must then be returned after dehydrogenation, adding costs (Salmon & Bañares-Alcántara, 2021). Case studies indicate that despite infrastructure compatibility, MCH delivers one of the lowest net hydrogen quantities among the hydrogen carriers making it a niche option for contexts where existing petrochemical value chains can absorb the carrier (Wijayanta et al., 2019).

Methanol provides another pathway. It is liquid under ambient conditions, with volumetric hydrogen content (95–99 $kgH_2/m^3$) second only to ammonia, and has a mature international shipping sector. Importantly, methanol can be synthesized as 'e-methanol' from green hydrogen, linking it to broader power-to-x strategies (Bowker, 2019). Methanol can also be used directly as a low-emission marine fuel, and methanol-fuelled vessels are already in commercial service (Offshore Energy, 2020). However, methanol carries inherent carbon emissions: cracking it back to hydrogen releases CO and $CO_2$ unless paired with carbon capture and storage (Kearns et al., 2021). This limits its role as a fully carbon-neutral hydrogen carrier without parallel deployment of CCUS.

When comparing across carriers, ammonia and methanol stand out as the most effective for transporting large hydrogen quantities over intercontinental distances. For example, in the Australia-Japan route, liquid ammonia could deliver 19,000 tonnes of hydrogen, methanol ~15,500 tonnes, compared to ~11000 tonnes for liquid hydrogen and ~8400 tonnes for MCH, using the same tanker capacity (Patonia & Poudineh, 2022). In terms of cost comparisons, ammonia's levelised costs across the value chain are estimated at >\$4.3/$kgH_2$ delivered, methanol >\$2.9/$kgH_2$, while liquid hydrogen exceeds \$8.9/$kgH_2$ and MCH >\$3.2/$kgH_2$ (Patonia & Poudineh, 2022). While these 2022 figures are largely illustrative, the fundamental cost hierarchy is expected to hold, though absolute values will shift with technology learning and energy prices.

In conclusion, derivatives are indispensable for enabling long-distance, transoceanic hydrogen trade. Among them, ammonia appears one of the most scalable and effective, benefiting from high hydrogen density and existing infrastructure, despite safety and cracking challenges. Methanol is another strong candidate, particularly where $CO_2$ capture is viable and shipping fuel co-benefits are attractive. LOHCs like MCH may remain niche, aligned with specific petrochemical markets, while liquid hydrogen itself is likely to play only a limited role in intercontinental trade due to high costs and losses. Ultimately, the choice of derivative will depend not only on thermodynamic and cost considerations but also on regional industrial synergies, safety regulations, and broader decarbonisation strategies.

### *Will Hydrogen Become a Truly Globally Traded Commodity?*

Whether hydrogen will evolve into a globally traded commodity like natural gas is still an open question. Unlike natural gas, which developed a liquid international market relatively quickly once liquefaction and shipping infrastructure matured, hydrogen starts from a much weaker position. Today, production and consumption are largely local, serving industrial clusters through short pipelines or onsite supply. International trade in hydrogen itself is almost non-existent, and the few shipments that have taken place are pilot-scale demonstrations. This suggests that hydrogen, at least in the near term, will remain a regional rather than a global commodity.

That said, the institutional framework for trade is gradually emerging. Governments and international bodies are establishing common rules for infrastructure access, creating registries for emissions accounting, and piloting auction mechanisms to stimulate cross-border flows. Certification schemes and guarantees of origin are beginning to align, which are critical for creating trust between buyers and sellers. These developments echo the early stages of the gas market when contractual arrangements and regulatory reforms laid the foundations for later commoditisation. Yet, while these steps are promising, the market is far from having the kind of transparent benchmarks and deep liquidity that define globally traded commodities.

The nature of hydrogen logistics further complicates the picture. Transporting pure hydrogen over long distances is technically difficult and expensive, so most of the near-term international trade is likely to take place through derivatives such as ammonia or methanol. These carriers are already produced and traded at scale for other purposes, giving them a head start as hydrogen vectors. By contrast, pipelines will play a much larger role regionally, connecting producers and consumers within continents. The result is a bifurcated system: derivatives enabling global trade, pipelines underpinning regional trade.

Taken together, these factors suggest that hydrogen is unlikely to mirror natural gas as a fully global commodity in the foreseeable future. Instead, its market will probably be patchy and hybrid. In some places, hydrogen will move regionally through pipelines; in others, derivatives will be shipped overseas. Over time, as certification standards align, costs come down, and demand deepens, a more integrated trade system may emerge. But rather than becoming 'the new LNG', hydrogen is more likely to settle into a different pattern—part global, part regional, and closely linked to the specific industrial uses and infrastructure choices of importing and exporting countries.

## Business Model for Hydrogen Transportation: The Case Study of the United Kingdom[5]

The UK government initially considered several different approaches to designing a business model for hydrogen transport infrastructure. Options included regulated returns models such as a Regulated Asset Base (RAB) or cap and floor, contractual mechanisms such as Contracts for Difference (CfDs), long-term government capacity booking or availability payments, as well as other approaches including co-investment and merchant models (DESNZ, 2022). Following consultation, the government concluded that most of these options would not provide sufficient revenue certainty or investor confidence during the early stages of hydrogen network development. In particular, stakeholders strongly favoured a RAB model, supplemented by an external subsidy mechanism to avoid costs falling disproportionately on a limited initial user base (DESNZ, 2023a). The government also ruled out introducing interim business models ahead of 2025, on the grounds that these could complicate the enduring framework and risk duplication, noting instead that

[5] This section presents a case study of a country with ambitious climate goals, including the adoption of clean hydrogen as part of its decarbonisation strategy. It examines the issues and options the country faces in the design and implementation of a business model for hydrogen transportation. Readers primarily interested in global trends may wish to skip this section on a first reading. Its purpose is to illustrate, in concrete terms, how transport infrastructure regulation and risk allocation can be designed in a liberalised market, and to highlight lessons that may be transferable to other jurisdictions.

early projects could receive support through existing mechanisms such as the Hydrogen Production Business Model or Ofgem's RIIO framework (DESNZ, 2023a).

The RAB approach was selected because it is a familiar and tested regulatory model in the United Kingdom, used for natural gas, electricity, water, and large infrastructure projects, and is particularly suited to monopolistic, capital-intensive infrastructure. The additional subsidy mechanism, delivered through private law revenue support contracts, was introduced to ensure that charges for early hydrogen users would not be prohibitive while enabling transport providers to recover their allowed revenues (DESNZ, 2023b).

The HTBM is specifically designed to support large-scale onshore hydrogen pipeline infrastructure, rather than road transport, rail, offshore pipelines, or shipping (ibid.). The government prioritised pipelines because they provide the most cost-effective way to transport hydrogen at scale, offer flexibility in serving multiple users and producers, and can integrate with geological storage facilities. This reflects the view that early hydrogen networks must focus on shared regional pipelines to connect production centres, storage, and industrial demand.

In practice, the HTBM consists of two main pillars: a RAB that allows hydrogen transport providers to earn regulated returns, and an external subsidy mechanism to balance charges to consumers while ensuring investment is viable. Ofgem will oversee the RAB component under the Gas Act, while revenue support contracts will be managed by a designated counterparty, following models established in electricity Contracts for Difference (CfD) and CCUS transport and storage business models (ibid.).

Risk allocation under the HTBM follows the principle that risks should be assigned to the party best placed to manage them. Construction and technology risks remain with project developers, who must ensure contingency planning and robust design. Operational risks such as availability and decommissioning are similarly allocated to operators. By contrast, demand risk—stemming from uncertainty about the pace of hydrogen uptake—is largely absorbed by government via the subsidy mechanism, protecting early investors from underutilisation. This allocation was seen as critical for crowding in private finance while maintaining affordability for consumers. This allocation of demand risk to the state also mirrors the challenge identified in Chap. 3, where CfDs also struggle to create demand, which reinforces the need for a separate, robust demand-pull policy.

The HTBM also introduces a strategic allocation process for projects. Initially, the Department for Energy Security and Net Zero (DESNZ) will lead this role, ensuring that transport projects align with hydrogen production and storage developments. Over time, responsibility for strategic planning will shift to National Energy System Operator (NESO) (DESNZ, 2023b). Allocation rounds will prioritise regional, shared pipelines connected to geological hydrogen storage, judged to provide the highest systemic benefits.

Despite its advantages, the HTBM faces challenges. One challenge is ensuring coherence with existing gas regulation, particularly around how repurposed natural gas pipelines should be valued within the RAB. Assessing the residual economic value of pipelines designed for methane but potentially converted to hydrogen raises questions of asset stranding, fair returns, and consumer protection (Ofgem, 2024). If valuations are set too high, consumers may overpay for underutilised assets; if too low, investors may face insufficient incentives. Funding arrangements also remain a challenge, with debate ongoing about whether support will come from government budgets, levy mechanisms such as the Gas Shipper Obligation, or a hybrid model (DESNZ, 2025).

Another set of challenges involves futureproofing. The HTBM is initially limited to large onshore pipelines and excludes smaller-scale, local transport infrastructure and offshore projects, which may still require support in later years. There are also uncertainties around how the HTBM will interact with hydrogen blending into natural gas networks. While blending could create early off-take demand, it risks undermining the economics of dedicated transport infrastructure and complicates billing, safety regulation, and certification frameworks. These issues illustrate the delicate balance between stimulating early demand and ensuring efficient long-term system design.

## Conclusions

This chapter has examined the techno-economic and policy dimensions of hydrogen transportation and trade, highlighting that no single mode of transport can serve as a universal solution. Instead, the viability of different options depends fundamentally on the distance involved, the scale of flows, and the ultimate form in which energy is required. Pipelines clearly dominate for large, steady volumes within and between regions, while derivatives such as ammonia and methanol are better suited for long-distance maritime trade. Road haulage remains an early-market bridge for short-haul deliveries, and high-voltage direct current (HVDC) lines retain an important role where the end-use requires electricity rather than molecules. The future of hydrogen transport, therefore, is a system of complementary options rather than a contest to identify a single winner.

Pipelines stand out as the backbone of regional hydrogen economies. They not only offer the lowest unit transport costs over land but also provide systemic advantages such as linepack storage and the ability to connect multiple producers, consumers, and geological storage facilities. Repurposing natural gas pipelines offers a rapid and comparatively low-cost pathway to early deployment, but its feasibility depends on stringent technical assessments of steel grades, welds, and operating pressures. Where these conditions are not met, new-build hydrogen pipelines will be essential. The practical rule that emerges is to repurpose where possible but build new where necessary, in order to balance cost efficiency with system reliability and safety.

Other options play important transitional or complementary roles. Blending hydrogen into natural gas networks may help stimulate early demand, but its contribution to decarbonisation is modest, and it introduces complications in billing, safety, and downstream separation. Meanwhile, on intercontinental scales, derivative carriers will lead. Ammonia in particular benefits from existing logistics and multi-use applications, while methanol offers synergies with synthetic fuel production. Liquid hydrogen and LOHCs remain technically feasible but less competitive due to cryogenic and efficiency challenges.

These differentiated roles have profound implications for how hydrogen will be traded. Unlike natural gas, which developed into a globally commoditised market via LNG, hydrogen is unlikely to replicate this model in the near to medium term. Instead, trade will be hybrid: regional pipeline networks will underpin pure hydrogen flows within continents, while ammonia and methanol will enable intercontinental trade. Commoditisation will emerge only partially, shaped by certification systems, network codes, and bilateral agreements. Rather than a single global spot market, hydrogen trade is likely to evolve around clusters of industrial demand hubs and dedicated corridors that link production basins with proximate demand centres.

Policy and regulatory frameworks will determine whether these infrastructures are built at the necessary pace. The UK's Hydrogen Transport Business Model (HTBM) illustrates how design choices can address the 'first-mover disadvantage'. By combining a Regulated Asset Base (RAB) framework with revenue support contracts, the HTBM provides stable returns for investors while shielding early users from excessive charges. Crucially, construction, operational, and technology risks remain with developers and operators, while government absorbs demand risk through the subsidy mechanism. Yet significant challenges remain, particularly in valuing repurposed gas assets fairly, ensuring compatibility with existing price controls, and securing durable funding mechanisms.

Taken together, the analysis in this chapter suggests that hydrogen will reshape energy trade geographies and will do so by forging a new, hybrid paradigm of regional molecule networks and global derivative flows, distinct from the fossil fuel era.

## References


Amos, W. (1999). *Costs of storing and transporting hydrogen.* NREL.

Aziz, M., Oda, T., & Kashiwagi, T. (2019). Comparison of liquid hydrogen, methylcyclohexane and ammonia on energy efficiency and economy. *Energy Procedia, 158*, 4086–4091.

Bouledroua, O., Hafsi, Z., Djukic, M. B., & Elaoud, S. (2020). The synergistic effects of hydrogen embrittlement and transient gas glow conditions on integrity assessment of a precracked steel pipeline. *International Journal of Hydrogen Energy, 45*(35), 18010–18020.

Bowker, M. (2019). Methanol synthesis from $CO_2$ hydrogenation. *ChemCatChem, 11*(17), 4238–4246.

Cence Power. (2022). *The benefits of HVDC transmission systems (High-Voltage Direct Current)* [Online]. Retrieved July 10, 2023, from https://www.cencepower.com/blog-posts/hvdc-transmission-systems.

Cheng, W., & Cheng, Y. F. (2023). A techno-economic study of the strategy for hydrogen transport by pipelines in Canada. *Journal of Pipeline Science and Engineering, 5*, 1–12.

DESNZ (2022) *Hydrogen transport and storage infrastructure: Consultation document.* London: UK.

DESNZ. (2023a). *Hydrogen transport and storage infrastructure: Government response to consultation. London: DESNZ* [Online]. Retrieved September 6, 2025, from https://www.gov.uk/government/consultations/proposals-for-hydrogen-transport-and-storage-business-models

DESNZ. (2023b). *Hydrogen transport and storage infrastructure: minded to positions* [Online]. Retrieved September 3, 2025, from https://assets.publishing.service.gov.uk/media/64ca0e6c5c2e6f0013e8d92a/hydrogen-transport-storage-minded-to-positions.pdf

DESNZ. (2025). *Funding mechanism for the hydrogen production business model: Consultation on the proposed Gas Shipper obligation* [Online]. Retrieved September 3, 2025, from https://assets.publishing.service.gov.uk/media/6787cbc3868b2b1923b6467b/proposed-design-gas-shipper-obligation-consultation-document.pdf.

DNV. (2022). Repurposing onshore pipelines for hydrogen: guiding operators through the re-evaluation process [Online]. Retrieved July 13, 2023, from https://www.dnv.com/focus-areas/hydrogen/repurposing-pipelines-for-hydrogen-guiding-operators-through-the-re-evaluation-process.html.

DNV. (2023). *Repurposing onshore pipelines for hydrogen: Guiding operators through the re-evaluation process.* DNV.

DOE (2023) *U.S. Department of Energy Hydrogen Program: 2023 Annual Merit Review and Peer Evaluation Report. DOE/GO-102024-6169.* Golden, CO: NREL.

DOE/NETL. (2024). *FECM/NETL hydrogen pipeline cost model: description and user's manual.* U.S. Department of Energy, National Energy Technology Laboratory.

DW. (2022). *Sweden: Prosecutor confirms Nord Stream 2 sabotage* [Online]. Retrieved September 2, 2023, from https://www.dw.com/en/sweden-prosecutor-confirms-nord-stream-2-sabotage/a-63806519.

Euractiv. (2013). *Desertec abandons Sahara solar power export dream* [Online]. Retrieved September 20, 2023, from https://www.euractiv.com/section/trade-society/news/desertec-abandons-sahara-solar-power-export-dream/

European Commission. (2020). *A hydrogen strategy for a climate-neutral Europe. Communication from the Commission to the European Parliament, the Council, the European Economic and Social Committee and the Committee of the Regions, COM(2020) 301 final.* European Commission.

European Court of Auditors. (2024). *The EU's industrial policy on renewable hydrogen. Special Report 11/2024.* Publications Office of the European Union, Luxembourg.

European Hydrogen Backbone (EHB). (2022). *European Hydrogen Backbone: A European hydrogen infrastructure vision covering 28 countries* [Online]. Retrieved September 2, 2025, from https://ehb.eu/page/publications.

Garche, J. (2009). *Encyclopedia of electrochemical power sources.* Elsevier.

Hagspiel, S., et al. (2014). Cost-optimal power system extension under flow-based market coupling. *Energy, 66*(1), 654–666.

Hydrogen Council and McKinsey. (2021). *Hydrogen Insights 2021.* Hydrogen Council.

IEA. (2023a). *Global hydrogen review 2023*. International Energy Agency. (Revised version: September and December 2023).

IEA. (2023b). *Energy technology perspectives 2023*. International Energy Agency.

IEA. (2024). *Global hydrogen review 2024*. International Energy Agency.

IHS Markit. (2022). *Ammonia fertilizer market and price analysis* [Online]. Retrieved November 12, 2025, from https://ihsmarkit.com/products/fertilizers-ammonia.html.

IRENA. (2022a). *Global hydrogen trade to meet the 1.5°C climate goal: Part I – Trade outlook for 2050 and way forward*. IRENA. ISBN 978-92-9260-430-1.

IRENA. (2022b). *Global hydrogen trade to meet the 1.5°c climate goal: Part II – Technology review of hydrogen carriers*. IRENA.

IRENA. (2024). *Global trade in green hydrogen derivatives: Trends in regulation, standardisation and certification*. IRENA.

Ishimoto, Y., et al. (2020). Large-scale production and transport of hydrogen from Norway to Europe and Japan: Value chain analysis and comparison of liquid hydrogen and ammonia as energy carriers. *International Journal of Hydrogen Energy, 45*(58), 32865–32883.

Joint Research Centre (JRC). (2022). *Ortiz Cebolla, R., Dolci, F. and Weidner-Ronnefeld, J. Assessment of hydrogen delivery options: Feasibility of transport of green hydrogen within Europe*. Publications Office of the European Union.

Kaiser, M. J. (2017). Offshore pipeline construction cost in the US Gulf of Mexico. *Marine Policy, 82*(1), 147–166.

Kearns, D., Liu, H., & Consoli, C. (2021). *Technology readiness and costs of CCS*. Global CCS Institute.

Khan, M. A., MacKinnon, C., Young, C., & Layzell, D. B. (2022). Techno-economics of a new hydrogen value chain supporting heavy duty transport. *Transition Accelerator Reports, 4*(5), 1–52.

Khan, M. A., Young, C., & Layzell, D. B. (2021). The techno-economics of hydrogen pipelines. *Transition Accelerator Technical Briefs, 1*(2), 1–36.

Kraemer, S. (2018, January 9). Missing link for a solar hydrogen is … ammonia? *PhysOrg*.

Li, C., et al. (2021). Flexible control strategy for HVDC transmission system adapted to intermittent new energy delivery. *Global Energy Interconnection, 4*(4), 425–433.

Martin, P., et al. (2024). A review of challenges with using the natural gas system for hydrogen. *Energy Science & Engineering, 12*(11), 3995–4009.

NREL (2022) *Hydrogen Blending into Natural Gas Pipeline Infrastructure: Review of Current Research and Technical Status*. Golden, CO: National Renewable Energy Laboratory.

Nishioka, A., Alvarez, F., & Omori, T. (2020). *Global rise of HVDC and its background. Global Innovation Report*. HITACHI.

NS Energy. (2022). *Changji-Guquan HVDC Transmission Project* [Online]. Retrieved June 3, 2023, from https://www.nsenergybusiness.com/projects/changji-guquan-uhvdc-transmission-project/.

Office of Gas and Electricity Markets (Ofgem). (2024). *RIIO-3 Sector Specific Methodology Decision – Finance Annex* [Online]. Retrieved September 3, 2025, from https://www.ofgem.gov.uk/sites/default/files/2024-07/RIIO-3_SSMD_Finance_Annex.pdf.

Offshore Energy. (2020). *World's 1st methanol-powered commercial ship celebrates 5th birthday* [Online]. Retrieved November 12, 2025, from https://www.offshore-energy.biz/worlds-1st-methanol-powered-commercial-ship-celebrates-5th-birthday/

Papadias, D. D., & Ahluwalia, R. K. (2020). Toluene-MCH as a two-way carrier for hydrogen transmission and storage. *US DOE Hydrogen Program Annual Merit Review*.

Papadias, D. D., Peng, J. K., & Ahluwalia, R.K. (2018, September 11–12). Chemical carrier concepts for hydrogen delivery. *International Hydrogen Infrastructure Workshop*, Boston.

Patonia, A., Lenivova, V., Poudineh, R., & Nolden, C. (2023). Hydrogen pipelines vs. HVDC lines: Should we transfer green molecules or electrons? *OIES Paper ET27*. Oxford, UK: Oxford Institute for Energy Studies.

Patonia, A., & Poudineh, R. (2022). Global trade of hydrogen: what is the best way to transfer hydrogen over long distances? *OIES Paper ET16*. Oxford, UK: Oxford Institute for Energy Studies.

Project Union. (2022). *Project Union executive summary*. National Grid.

Purvins, A., et al. (2018). Submarine power cable between Europe and North America: A techno-economic analysis. *Journal of Cleaner Production, 186*(1), 131–145.

Reed, L., Morgan, M. G., Vaishnav, P., & Armanios, D. E. (2019). Converting existing transmission corridors to HVDC is an overlooked option for increasing transmission capacity. *PNAS, 116*(28), 13879–13884.

Rystad Energy. (2023). *Building the future: Hydrogen pipelines start to materialise in Europe* [Online]. Retrieved May 18, 2025, from https://www.rystadenergy.com/news/building-the-future-hydrogen-pipelines-start-to-materialize-in-europe.

Salmon, N., & Bañares-Alcántara, R. (2021). Green ammonia as a spatial energy vector: A review. *Sustainable Energy and Fuels, 5*(1), 2814–2839.

Semeraro, M. A. (2021). Renewable energy transport via hydrogen pipelines and HVDC transmission lines. *Energy Strategy Reviews, 35*(1), 1–8.

Shell. (2022). *Shell to start building Europe's largest renewable hydrogen plant* [Online]. Retrieved October 25, 2023, from https://www.shell.com/media/news-and-media-releases/2022/shell-to-start-building-europes-largest-renewable-hydrogen-plant.html.

Timmerberg, S., & Kaltschmitt, M. (2019). Hydrogen from renewables: Supply from North Africa to Central Europe as blend in existing pipelines – Potentials and costs. *Applied Energy, 237*(1), 795–809.

Topolski, K., et al. (2022). *Hydrogen blending into natural gas pipeline infrastructure: Review of the state of technology.* National Renewable Energy Laboratory.

Transition Accelerator (2022) *Techno-Economics of a New Hydrogen Value Chain Supporting Heavy Duty Transport.* Transition Accelerator Reports: Volume 4, Issue 5.

Wang, W., Li, G., & Guo, J. (2022). Large-scale renewable energy transmission by HVDC: Challenges and proposals. *Engineering, 19*(1), 252–267.

Welder, L., et al. (2018). Spatio-temporal optimization of a future energy system for power-to-hydrogen applications in Germany. *Energy, 158*(1), 1130–1149.

Wijayanta, A.T. et al (2019) 'Liquid hydrogen, methylcyclohexane, and ammonia as potential hydrogen carriers: Characteristics, application feasibility, and economic performance', International Journal of Hydrogen Energy, 44 (29), pp. 15026–15044

Wolf, N., Kühn, L., & Höck, M. (2024). International supply chains for a hydrogen ramp-up: Techno-economic assessment of hydrogen transport routes to Germany. *Energy Conversion and Management, 23*, 100682.

Yu, C., et al. (2024). Techno-economic analysis of hydrogen pipeline network in China based on levelized cost of transportation. *Energy Conversion and Management, 301*, 118025.

CHAPTER 5

# Hydrogen Storage Technologies

## Introduction

Hydrogen storage is an essential component of hydrogen supply chain. As gas storage made liberalised gas markets workable, hydrogen storage will make a hydrogen economy investable, resilient, and efficient. It is the keystone connecting variable supply to diverse, often peaky, demand. Without it, the chain fragments and decarbonisation costs rise.

Because cost advantages differ across regions, governments and firms are not planning for pure self-sufficiency: they are entering into importing arrangements and piloting long-distance shipments of hydrogen and derivatives (e.g., LOHCs, ammonia) (Landsvirkjun, 2020; RWE, 2021; dw, 2022; Patonia & Poudineh, 2022), making storage the unavoidable link between upstream production and downstream use in a traded market. In such a market, storage hubs at ports and clusters balance arrivals, manage specifications, and buffer maritime and terminal disruptions. By decoupling off-take from berthing windows or cracking availability, storage smooths prices. Where imports arrive as derivatives, capacity on both the derivative and reconverted hydrogen sides coordinates traders and end-users. This stabilises flows and prices, supports bankable contracts, and lowers the cost of capital. In short, storage is the physical market-maker for international hydrogen trade.

Today, most hydrogen is consumed near where it is produced (notably in refining and ammonia), so storage has been limited (IEA, 2019; WHA,



A. Patonia, R. Poudineh, *Clean Hydrogen for Decarbonisation*,
https://doi.org/10.1007/978-3-032-19442-8_5

2021); a broader economy changes this, because mismatches in time and location require buffers only storage can provide. As hydrogen expands into steel (DRI), chemicals, high-temperature heat, power, mobility, and heating, demand profiles diversify and decouple from electrolyser hours. Outages, maintenance, and grid constraints will collide with continuous or time-critical end uses. Storage solves these frictions via short-cycle buffers (linepack, tanks) and long-duration options (salt caverns, depleted fields). It lets plants run steadily on low-carbon hydrogen rather than redesign processes around variable supply, reducing system costs and avoiding oversizing of production or networks.

Storage also lifts renewable utilisation by absorbing surpluses and releasing energy when value is higher. Temporal balancing grows even more important as renewables drive electrolysis: variable wind and solar (including 'Dunkelflaute') decouple generation from consumption (Matsuo et al., 2020), while hydrogen storage cuts curtailment via power-to-X and provides backup/seasonal services that batteries and pumped hydro struggle to deliver at scale (ITM Power, 2022; Guerra et al., 2020). This raises renewable utilisation, bolsters grid stability, and reduces reliance on fossil peakers. It also unlocks remote renewables by turning them into transportable, storable molecules. In planning terms, storage converts variable generation into firm, schedulable service.

Physical realities reinforce the case: hydrogen's low volumetric energy density means gaseous or liquid storage entails significant compression or liquefaction energy and cost (Jensen et al., 2007; US Department of Energy, 2009), strengthening the need for dedicated storage solutions and, where appropriate, alternative vectors (e.g., materials-based carriers) within an integrated strategy. Choosing among high-pressure tanks, cryogenic liquid storage, salt caverns, depleted reservoirs, or carrier-based options involves trade-offs in CapEx, round-trip energy, boil-off, and safety. Portfolios are likely to be needed, if hydrogen economy ever becomes a reality: near-plant tanks for operations, caverns for seasonal shifting, and derivative storage (e.g., ammonia tanks) for trade logistics. Each has distinct siting and permitting needs, shaping regional feasibility and cost.

Storage is also a resilience and security asset. For network operators, hubs and linepack stabilise pressures and flows, improving pipeline efficiency and reducing compression costs. For investors, storage underwrites off-take, enabling bankable models and risk-sharing instruments (PPAs/CfDs, take-or-pay, capacity payments). At import/export nodes, storage supports quality assurance and timing flexibility, lowering demurrage and balancing costs. These features make hydrogen infrastructure behave like mature energy markets, with liquidity and flexibility anchored in physical buffers.

Finally, storage makes sector coupling practical at scale. Transport depots, ports, and airports face spiky refuelling demand for trucks, buses, ships, and e-fuel production; industrial clusters cycle loads; buildings and district heating have diurnal and seasonal peaks. Storage absorbs these fluctuations, ensuring security of supply and efficient asset utilisation. Where permitted, limited blending into gas networks can add buffer capacity while dedicated hydrogen grids emerge.

This chapter analyses the technical, economic, and policy dimensions of hydrogen storage, drawing on emerging literature and early project experience. While it reviews all types of storage, it gives special attention to large-scale underground storage due to its crucial role in enabling the hydrogen economy and achieving broader decarbonisation goals.

The outline of this chapter is as follows: Section "Pathways to Hydrogen Storage" surveys the main hydrogen storage pathways (compressed gas, liquid, material-based carriers, adsorbents, and underground geological options) and explains the techno-economic and TRL differences between them. Section "Energy System and the Role of Underground Hydrogen Storage" explains the role of underground hydrogen storage (UHS) in power-system integration and seasonal balancing, comparing salt caverns, depleted reservoirs, aquifers, and rock caverns and highlighting geomechanical, integrity, and microbial issues. Section "The Costs of Hydrogen Storage Options" provides a cost comparison across storage options, setting out the key drivers of CapEx and OpEx and reporting levelised cost ranges and sensitivities. Section "Hydrogen Storage Business Model: the UK Experience" examines business-model implications with a UK case study, describing the revenue-stabilisation approach and allocation/eligibility issues. Section "Conclusions" draws conclusions and discusses policy implications for coordinating storage with production, transport, and end-use demand.

## Pathways to Hydrogen Storage

Hydrogen storage pathways are commonly grouped into four families: (i) physical storage as compressed gas, cryogenic liquid, or cryo-compressed hydrogen; (ii) material-based storage, which includes reversible metal hydrides, complex/chemical hydrides, liquid organic hydrogen carriers (LOHCs), and related liquid carriers (e.g., ammonia); (iii) adsorptive/porous-materials storage (carbons, zeolites, Metal-Organic Frameworks (MOFs)); and (iv) underground hydrogen storage (UHS) in geological formations for GWh-TWh, seasonal balancing (Fig. 5.1). Each category offers distinct energy densities, operating conditions, safety profiles, and techno-economic maturity, and—crucially—serves different system roles from on-board mobility to intercontinental trade and seasonal grid storage (Eberle et al., 2009; Züttel, 2004; Yang et al., 2023).

For compressed gaseous hydrogen ($CGH_2$), high-pressure vessels are mature for mobility and station applications. Composite tanks routinely operate at up to 700 bar with rapid refuelling (Scottish Enterprise, 2022) but suffer from low volumetric density and cost driven by carbon fibre; linerless concepts remain low-TRL. Typical energy overheads for compression are ~13–18% of the LHV (Usman, 2022), reflecting multi-stage compression and intercooling. Advantages include commercial availability, fast response, and well-developed codes/standards; disadvantages include

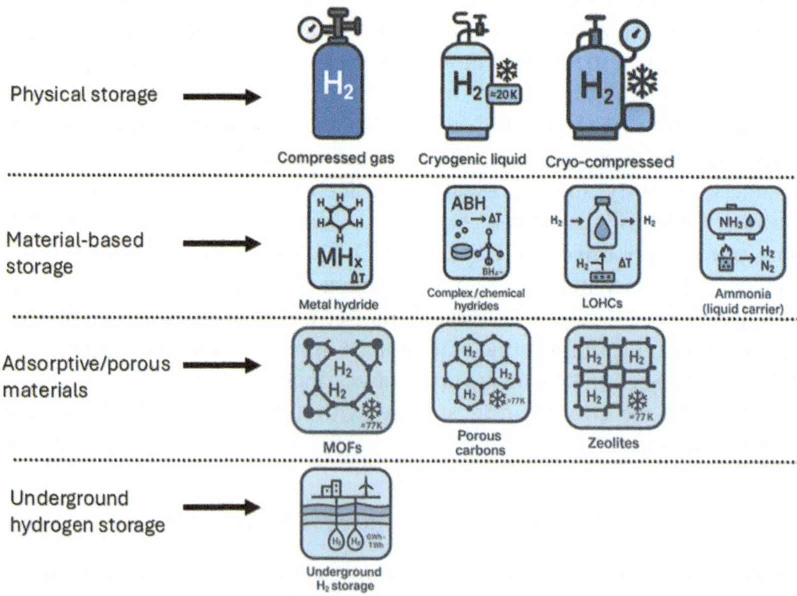


**Fig. 5.1** Key hydrogen storage technologies. (Source: Authors)

high CapEx per kg $H_2$ stored, embrittlement/permeation management, and footprint at depot scale.

Liquid hydrogen ($LH_2$) boosts volumetric density to ~71 kg $H_2$ $m^{-3}$ at ~20 K, enabling aerospace and maritime logistics, but liquefaction is energy-intensive (~30–40% of LHV) and boil-off must be managed; cryo-compressed hydrogen ($CcH_2$) partially mitigates boil-off by combining cryogenics with moderate pressure (~25–35 MPa) to reach ~80 kg $H_2$ $m^{-3}$ (Usman, 2022). Cryogenic systems impose stringent material and sealing demands (embrittlement, fatigue, thermal contraction); despite long heritage in space, lightweight alloys, composites, seals and coatings for aviation-grade $LH_2$ tanks still show major data gaps under 20 K hydrogen and cyclic service (Ghadbeigi et al., 2025). Thus, $LH_2$ is technologically proven but remains capital- and energy-intensive (Usman, 2022); $CcH_2$ is promising yet pre-commercial.

Material-based chemical storage splits into reversible metal hydrides and chemical/complex hydrides. Intermetallic hydrides (e.g., $LaNi_5$, TiFe, Ti-Mn alloys) operate near ambient pressures with fast kinetics and excellent safety but modest gravimetric capacities (≈1–2 wt%); $MgH_2$ offers 7.6 wt% but typically requires ~300 °C for release[1] (Usman, 2022; Sadhasivam et al., 2017). Techno-economically, TiFe/TiFeMn-type systems for stationary storage can approach compressed-gas costs in long-duration duty if material prices fall and waste-heat is integrated; levelized storage costs ~\$0.38–0.45 $kWh^{-1}$ have been modelled for 10 MW/96 h backup scenarios (Wang et al., 2025). Complex hydrides (alanates, borohydrides, amide–imide systems) reach very high theoretical capacities (often 7–18 wt%) but face high desorption temperatures, slow kinetics, by-product management, and poor reversibility—hence are longer-term options (Eberle et al., 2009; Usman, 2022; Nemukula et al., 2025).

Liquid hydrogen carriers include LOHCs (e.g., toluene/methylcyclohexane, dibenzyltoluene, N-ethylcarbazole) and circular carriers like ammonia. LOHCs are liquids at ambient conditions, leverage existing fuel logistics, and improve safety because hydrogen is only released in the presence of heat and catalyst; typical dehydrogenation temperatures are ~200–350 °C, with practical storage capacities around 5–7 wt% $H_2$ (Eberle et al., 2009; Abdin et al., 2021; Cabrera et al., 2024). Techno-economic studies indicate LOHC stations can reduce electrical energy input relative

[1] Recent research focuses on catalysts and nanostructuring to lower this desorption temperature.

to $LH_2$ (hydrogenation is exothermic), but system economics hinge on catalyst turnover, heat integration, and back-transport of the dehydrogenated liquid (Abdin et al., 2021). Ammonia provides 17.6 wt% $H_2$ equivalent (Mekonnin et al., 2025) and a mature shipping base, yet requires high-temperature cracking and $NO_x$ control.

Adsorptive/porous-material storage—in carbons, zeolites, and MOFs—offers fast, reversible uptake via physisorption. Record cryogenic uptakes in advanced MOFs reach ~9–14 wt% at 77 K and up to ~100 bar,[2] but room-temperature capacity is typically <1 wt%, limiting near-term practicality without cooling (Le et al., 2024; Usman, 2022). Engineering 'shaping' (pellets/monoliths) can raise volumetric density and mechanical robustness; for example, pelletised MOF-5 and monolithic carbons markedly improve volumetric storage versus powders while retaining useful porosity (Ren & North, 2014). Overall, adsorptive media are low-TRL for on-board ambient-temperature use, but remain attractive for cryogenic adsorbers and future hybrid systems.

For underground hydrogen storage (UHS), currently, salt caverns are a technology with commercial-scale, cyclic operating experience; they offer very low permeability, self-healing creep, rapid injection/withdrawal, and high purity, with reported storage costs ~\$0.39–2.41 $kg^{-1}$ $H_2$ depending heavily on site specifics, geology, cushion gas requirements, and cycling frequency, among other factors (Qian et al., 2025; Miocic et al., 2022; Crotogino et al., 2010). Depleted hydrocarbon reservoirs and saline aquifers provide TWh-scale potential and lower site CapEx (re-use of wells/infrastructure), but face higher scientific and operational uncertainty: cushion-gas volumes, well and caprock integrity, and microbial reactions that may consume $H_2$ or generate $CH_4/H_2S$ (Miocic et al., 2022; Pan et al., 2021; Raza et al, 2022; Muhammed et al., 2022). Recent field work demonstrated ~84% $H_2$ recovery in a depleted reservoir and in situ geomethanation ($H_2 + CO_2 \rightarrow CH_4$), underscoring both opportunity and complexity for dual-use storage/reactors (Hellerschmied et al., 2024). Thermodynamic modelling for caverns confirms brine 'salting-out' reduces water vapour and gas solubility—useful for dehydration and efficiency predictions (Kiemde et al., 2023).

Technical maturity and roles therefore diverge across options. Near-term, high-TRL solutions: $CGH_2$ (on-board mobility, stations),

[2] These are excess adsorption values, and the deliverable capacity (working capacity) is a more practical metric, which is lower.

salt-cavern UHS (bulk/seasonal), and $LH_2$ for aerospace/shipping; mid-term: LOHCs and ammonia for large-scale liquid logistics, with catalyst/cracking advances; long-term: intermetallic/complex hydrides, and high-capacity porous adsorbents paired with cryogenics or spillover strategies. Across pathways, materials compatibility (embrittlement, seals), thermal management, cushion-gas optimisation and standards remain cross-cutting challenges. As costs fall and data gaps close—e.g., hydride LCOS approaching compressed gas in specific stationary use-cases (Wang et al., 2025) and growing evidence from UHS pilots—these categories will increasingly complement rather than compete, enabling hydrogen to serve mobility, industry, and power sectors at scale when it makes economic sense.

## Energy System and the Role of Underground Hydrogen Storage

As power systems decarbonise and variable renewables scale, countries need multi-week to seasonal flexibility that surface tanks or batteries cannot economically supply; hence the focus turns to underground hydrogen storage (UHS), which can buffer GWh-TWh volumes while drawing on decades of subsurface practice in gas storage and $CO_2$ injection. Yet, unlike methane or supercritical $CO_2$, hydrogen's very low density, viscosity, and high diffusivity alter containment, displacement, and integrity considerations, so site selection and operating envelopes must be tailored to its properties rather than copied from other gases (Liu et al., 2015; Züttel, 2003) (see Fig. 5.2).

Against this backdrop, salt caverns, depleted hydrocarbon reservoirs, deep saline aquifers, and engineered rock caverns emerge as the main options, each with distinct geomechanics, cycling capability, purity outcomes, and monitoring needs that map to different system roles—i.e., from high-frequency balancing to seasonal storage. Because costs, risks, and deliverability vary with geology, design, and market context, economics hinge on leaching volume, materials and sealing requirements, compression and cushion-gas strategies, as well as on policy frameworks that create investable revenue streams for storage capacity (Le Fevre, 2013; DESNZ, 2024b); planning must also account for competition over limited subsurface space as $CO_2$ storage scales (Patonia et al., 2025).

Hydrogen's molecular mass and viscosity being low means diffusivity and buoyancy are high, complicating containment and pressure

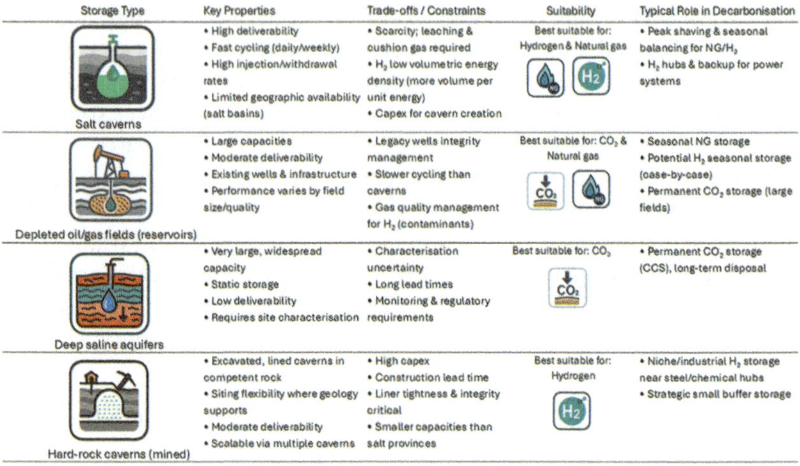


**Fig. 5.2** Underground storage for decarbonisation. (Source: Authors)

management relative to methane; meanwhile, $CO_2$ is typically stored as a dense supercritical fluid (≥7.38 MPa, >31.1 °C) with higher viscosity and much lower diffusivity, easing long-term trapping and lowering leakage risk (Liu et al., 2015; IPCC, 2005; Bachu, 2008). Although hydrogen's low solubility in water is favourable, its high air-diffusion coefficient and low density demand low-permeability formations and robust seals (Bach et al., 2019; Cappellani, 2022). In system terms, UHS is uniquely capable of providing multi-week to seasonal balancing at scale for high-renewables systems, yet choices among formations should reflect physicochemical fit and the desired operating profile.

With that in mind, four geological structures dominate: salt caverns, rock caverns, deep saline aquifers, and depleted hydrocarbon reservoirs. Salt caverns—i.e., solution-mined at roughly 300–1800 m, operated at about 3.5–27 MPa, and sized around $10^5$–$10^6$ $m^3$—offer very low permeability, self-healing creep, and exceptional cycling capability, making them the preferred option for high-frequency hydrogen storage (Patonia et al., 2025). By contrast, rock caverns (~10–1000 m; 0.1–20 MPa; typically $5\times10^4$–$5\times10^5$ $m^3$) suit lower-cycling duties and have higher unit costs; deep aquifers (~400–2300 m; 3–31.5 MPa) and depleted fields (~300–3000 m; 1.5–28.5 MPa) provide very large pore volumes and established trapping, but hydrogen operations must address cushion-gas requirements, geochemical/microbial reactivity, and well/caprock integrity (Patonia et al., 2025).

Extending this comparison, salt caverns are the most technically mature and operationally flexible option for hydrogen, demonstrated at pilot and early commercial scale in Europe and valued for rapid injection/withdrawal, gas-tightness, and high delivered purity (Patonia et al., 2025). Where suitable caverns are scarce, depleted hydrocarbon reservoirs emerge as the leading large-scale alternative; notably, field evidence from Austria shows about 84% hydrogen recovery after seasonal cycling and in-situ geo-methanation ($H_2 + CO_2 \rightarrow CH_4$) by native microbes—useful where grid-compatible methane is desired (Hellerschmied et al., 2024). Aquifers are attractive for very large capacities and prospective seasonal duties but need further de-risking around heterogeneity, microbial effects, and cushion-gas strategies for hydrogen.

From an engineering standpoint, trade-offs are unavoidable. In caverns, hydrogen's high diffusivity and the possibility of hydrate formation necessitate careful operating envelopes, dehydration, and vigilant integrity management. In depleted fields, additional caprock/well qualification, potential $H_2$–hydrocarbon mixing (necessitating purification), and greater monitoring are typical; legacy assets may need replacement to mitigate embrittlement and leakage at valves/flanges. In aquifers, heterogeneity, pressure-management, and long-term monitoring raise both CapEx and OpEx, especially given hydrogen's higher cycling ambitions compared with one-way $CO_2$ injection.

Since subsurface assets are finite and already serve natural gas (dominated by depleted fields) and fast-growing $CO_2$ storage, planning must consider overlaps and opportunity costs; while $CO_2$ will mainly use saline aquifers and large depleted fields, hydrogen and methane may compete for salt caverns and smaller depleted reservoirs in some regions.[3] Consequently, European assessments indicate caverns alone are unlikely to satisfy all hydrogen seasonal needs everywhere (Gas Infrastructure Europe, 2021); additional capacity in depleted fields is expected alongside careful siting, social licence, and cross-border coordination. To avoid underinvestment and shortage or overinvestment and stranded asset, policy frameworks

[3] This competition for limited suitable geological sites, particularly salt caverns, necessitates integrated national energy system planning to avoid conflicts and prioritise based on system value.

should recognise system value—not just levelised costs—when prioritising storage developments across gases.

## The Costs of Hydrogen Storage Options

To make an accurate comparison between costs of different hydrogen storage technologies, a uniform metric is needed. However, the literature report costs on different bases: some give capital intensity per unit of throughput (e.g., '\$ million per tonne-$H_2$ per day'), others give unit CapEx per static capacity (e.g., '\$ per kg-$H_2$ stored'), and several provide levelised costs (either \$/kg-$H_2$ or \$/kWh delivered). With that caveat, the direction of travel is clear. For compressed gaseous hydrogen ($CGH_2$), cost is driven by the pressure vessels and the compression train. Stakeholder evidence from the US DOE 2022 bulk gaseous storage workshop places today's large above-ground tanks capital cost around \$1800–2000 per kg-$H_2$ of storage capacity (with an aspiration to <\$1000/kg), while a frequently cited DOE historical figure for stationary vessels is ~\$700/kg (Abdin et al., 2021; US DOE, 2022). Compressor CapEx scales with throughput ($\approx$ \$0.086 million per t-$H_2$/day in a 500 t $day^{-1}$ reference case), so the electricity price and target pressure dominate OpEx and total cost of service (Abdin et al., 2021; Chen et al., 2025). By contrast, liquid hydrogen ($LH_2$) is plant-intensive: the liquefaction train is the main line item ($\approx$ \$1.87 million per t-$H_2$/day; $\approx$ \$935 million at 500 t $day^{-1}$), while cryogenic tanks are comparatively modest ($\approx$ \$0.035 million per t-$H_2$/day; $\approx$ \$17.5 million at 500 t $day^{-1}$). Power for liquefaction and boil-off management then dominate operating cost.

Within material-based storage, the principal cost driver is the carrier or storage material itself, plus the heat and power needed for (de)hydrogenation or (de)sorption. For LOHCs such as dibenzyltoluene, reactor and tank CapEx intensities are modest ($\approx$ \$0.134 M and \$0.003 M per t-$H_2$/day, respectively), but long-duration cost is dominated by carrier price and attrition ($\approx$ \$5/L, $\approx$ 0.013% loss per cycle, $\approx$ 750 cycles assumed) and by catalyst durability/PGM content; heat integration can offset some energy on the hydrogenation side, whereas dehydrogenation remains the energetic bottleneck (Abdin et al., 2021). Using ammonia ($NH_3$) as a hydrogen carrier, the air separation unit and Haber-Bosch synthesis loop set the capital ($\approx$ \$0.094 M and \$0.219 M per t-$H_2$/day) while $NH_3$ tankage is relatively low ($\approx$ \$0.008 M per t-$H_2$/day); importantly, cracking back to $H_2$ at the point of use is not included in these storage figures and would add both CapEx and OpEx (Abdin et al., 2021). For metal/complex hydrides, system modelling shows LCOS depends most on material $/kg, operating temperature/kinetics (hence electricity/heat use), and waste-heat recovery: intermetallic systems come out around $0.48–1.27/kWh, with an amide-hydride complex case reaching ~$0.38/kWh under favourable assumptions (Wang et al., 2025).

For adsorptive/porous-materials storage (MOFs, high-surface-area carbons/zeolites), the economics are materials-led as well. Chen and co-authors show if material costs are assumed between $5 and 25/kg, it corresponds to roughly $0.08–0.40/kWh for optimized MOF-based systems (Chen et al., 2025). This clearly indicates that storage cost spread largely explained by the adsorbent price and the chosen temperature and pressure operating window that sets compression and any refrigeration loads. In practical systems, shaping/monolithisation and thermal management hardware add cost, but sensitivity analyses consistently show that adsorbent $/kg and usable working capacity dominate the capital side, while electricity price for compression/cooling dominates OpEx—mirroring the pattern seen in compressed gas and liquefaction pathways.

Turning to underground hydrogen storage (UHS), geology and utilization are decisive. Reported levelized costs span wide ranges because the same asset can look cheap or expensive depending on cycling frequency, working-to-cushion gas ratio, and deliverability. A synthesis by Raza et al. reports salt caverns at ~$0.14–14.03/kg-$H_2$ (corresponds to $0.004–0.421/kWh), depleted reservoirs at ≈ $1.42/kg, saline aquifers at ≈ $1.49/kg, and lined hard-rock caverns at $0.36–3.20/kg, with the lower end typically associated with higher utilisation and simpler operations (Raza et al., 2022). Where itemized unit CapEx is available, salt-cavern cost per kg of working gas breaks down into drilling/casing, leaching, mechanical-integrity testing, brine transport/disposal, and compression; site depth and brine logistics explain much of the spread (e.g., brine handling ≈ $13.9 → $5.9/kg as conditions vary), while compressor sizing reflects the target withdrawal rate (Gianni et al., 2024). For porous reservoirs, headline CapEx per unit of working gas can be low (e.g., a depleted-gas field case presented in Gianni et al. ≈ $1.3/kg-$H_2$), but lifecycle cost depends on cushion-gas strategy, gas treatment/purification on withdrawal, and monitoring and integrity management (Gianni et al., 2024).

Across all categories, two cross-cutting drivers explain most cost variance. First, the energy needed to ‘move’ hydrogen—i.e., compressing ($CGH_2$, MOFs), liquefying ($LH_2$), dehydrogenating (LOHC), cracking

($NH_3$), or pressurizing/injecting/withdrawing (UHS)—puts the electricity price (and access to waste heat) at the centre of OpEx and LCOS. Second, the capital element that scales with materials or civil works dominates CapEx: code-qualified vessels and carbon fibre for $CGH_2$; cryogenic machinery for $LH_2$; carrier and catalysts for LOHC; adsorbent or hydride $/kg for solid and porous media; and drilling/leaching/brine handling (plus cushion gas) for UHS.

Taken together, the cost evidence points to a portfolio in which each storage pathway earns a distinct role as the hydrogen economy scales. Above-ground compressed gas remains the practical choice for refuelling depots and short-cycle buffering, but vessel and compression costs keep it best for hours–days rather than seasonal duty. Liquid hydrogen is capital-heavy because of the liquefaction train, so it fits long-distance logistics and aviation/maritime hubs where cheap power and high utilization can amortize plant costs. Liquid carriers—LOHCs and ammonia—shift economics towards the molecule cost and conversion energy, making catalyst durability, cracking efficiency, and heat integration the levers that could open intercontinental trade at scale. Hydrides and porous adsorbents can be competitive on a levelised basis when material $/kg falls and thermal management leverages waste heat, suggesting a future in stationary, behind-the-meter, or hybrid systems rather than near-term mobility. Finally, underground storage is the only option that pencils for GWh-TWh, multi-week/seasonal balancing, with site-specific geology, brine handling, cushion gas, and utilization dictating whether caverns or porous reservoirs deliver the lowest $/kg. Across all pathways, two variables dominate: the price of electricity to 'move' hydrogen (compress, liquefy, dehydrogenate/crack) and the capital element tied to materials or civil works—and progress on those fronts will decide how fast each technology scales from niche to backbone.

## Hydrogen Storage Business Model: The UK Experience[4]

A dedicated business model for hydrogen storage is needed because early markets face classic coordination and investment failures. Storage assets are capital-intensive, long-lived, and sunk, but their revenue is highly

[4] As in Chap. 4, we use the UK here as a contained policy case study to illustrate how market design, revenue stabilisation, and risk allocation can enable early investment in hydrogen enabling infrastructure; the intent is transferable insight rather than UK exceptionalism.

uncertain: producers, pipelines, and end-users will not scale perfectly in step, leaving storage developers exposed to acute volume (utilisation) and price risk. At the same time, storage can deliver system-wide public benefits—security of supply, flexibility for renewables, and resilience during prolonged low-wind periods—that are not fully monetised through bilateral contracts. First-of-a-kind geological projects also carry subsurface appraisal and cushion-gas/initial-fill costs that are difficult to finance without predictable cash flows. Additional complexity arises from the timelines for planning and permitting, requirements for third-party access, and safety regulations. A fit-for-purpose business model therefore has to (i) stabilise revenues enough to be bankable, (ii) preserve incentives to serve real market demand, (iii) allocate risks to the parties best placed to manage them, and (iv) coordinate investment with hydrogen transport and anchor loads so assets are built in the right places and at the right scale. In this section we review the experience of the United Kingdom, on hydrogen storage business model design, because it has articulated a clear, staged pathway from strategy to delivery and tested the trade-offs between regulation and contract-based support.

The UK approaches hydrogen storage as a system enabler—essential to integrate variable renewables, provide security of supply, and unlock hydrogen-to-power and industrial switching at scale. From the UK Hydrogen Strategy onwards, government policy signalled that geological, large-scale, and long-duration storage would be needed alongside regional pipelines as the market grows (BEIS, 2021). This was sharpened by subsequent strategic planning, which concludes that the near-term system needs onshore salt-cavern storage linked by regional pipelines, with an ambition to support initial storage projects by 2030 (DESNZ, 2023c). The 2024 market update then confirms that detailed HSBM design is progressing, with first-round details due in 2025 and up to two large storage projects targeted to be in operation or construction by 2030 (DESNZ, 2024a).

At the core of the HSBM is a revenue-stabilisation contract for storage providers, designed to tackle the specific market failure in early hydrogen systems: volume (utilisation) and price risk arising from uncertain, unevenly timed supply and demand. In its minded-to positions, government set out a minimum revenue floor for eligible storage assets, paired with incentives to maximise market revenues and an upside-sharing mechanism to protect value for money; contracts are envisaged on private-law terms with durations of ≈15 years (DESNZ, 2023a). The government response to consultation confirms this direction and the initial focus on geological storage (e.g., salt caverns) given readiness and scale, while leaving optionality to consider above-ground storage where similar barriers exist (DESNZ, 2023b).

A range of alternative models was examined and, for storage, not adopted at this stage. Stakeholders argued for regulated approaches such as RAB or cap-and-floor to deliver high revenue certainty; others proposed CfD-style constructs or pure availability payments. Government judged that full economic regulation of storage is not appropriate initially—given the nascency of hydrogen markets, the diversity of potential storage technologies, and the desire to retain competitive pressure—and therefore favours private-law contracts that still deliver strong bankability via a floor plus incentives (DESNZ, 2023a, 2023b). Notably, while transport pipelines are steered towards a RAB-style approach (with an external subsidy overlay during the growth phase), storage is deliberately kept outside economic regulation at the outset (DESNZ, 2023a, 2023b).

Funding and allocation arrangements are being staged to match system needs. For the first HSBM round, government signalled bilateral, cohort-based allocation—assessing storage projects alongside transport proposals to ensure pipeline-storage-demand alignment—while funding for storage support (Exchequer and/or levy) remains to be finalised, which creates political and investment uncertainty (DESNZ, 2023b, 2024a).

Detailed market-engagement proposals outline a streamlined process—eligibility screening, scored assessment, cohort assessment to optimise system fit, and bilateral negotiations—aimed at getting the earliest viable projects to FID and COD in the 2028–2032 window (DESNZ, 2023d).

Eligibility and scope crystallise the model's initial focus. The first round prioritises geological storage (new build or suitable conversions) over existing natural-gas storage in routine operation; expects technology maturity (≈TRL ≥7); sets a minimum working-gas scale (e.g., indicative thresholds around tens of GWh); requires evidence on geotechnical risks, cushion-gas plans, and credible third-party access and user engagement; and anchors deliverability with an indicative COD window of 2028–2032 (DESNZ, 2023d). Development expenditure (DevEx) is treated as an allowable cost recoverable through the revenue floor in this first round, recognising FOAK risks and the cost of subsurface appraisal[5] (ibid.).

Risk is allocated to the parties best able to manage it. Under the HSBM, construction, technology performance, and availability risks sit with the storage owner, who must deliver, operate safely, and meet availability/operability standards; demand/volume risk is mitigated by the revenue floor, smoothing cash flows in low-utilisation early years; market/price signals are preserved via sales-maximisation incentives and upside-sharing, so operators still benefit from efficient dispatch and customer development; and planning/community risks remain with developers, incentivised to de-risk through early engagement and consents progress (DESNZ, 2023a, 2023d). Counterparty risk is addressed by statutory powers to designate a contract counterparty, while regulatory oversight focuses on safety and market framework rather than full economic regulation of storage at this stage (DESNZ, 2023b).

Strategic planning is the glue between business models and real assets. Government's Hydrogen Transport and Storage Networks Pathway sets the planning logic and identifies low-regrets early infrastructure, with DESNZ leading initially and the Future (National) Energy System Operator taking on hydrogen strategic planning functions from 2026 (subject to licensing) (DESNZ, 2023c, 2023d). This ensures HSBM allocations target regions with credible production and demand and scarce onshore salt opportunities, and that storage contracts complement HTBM pipeline decisions and power-sector flexibility needs (DESNZ, 2023c).

In policy trajectory terms, the HSBM is deliberately phased and adaptive. The initial cohort—up to two large geological stores by 2030—is intended to prove commercial constructs, supply-chain readiness, and system value (DESNZ, 2023c, 2024a). Over time, government expects support intensity to fall as utilisation rises, competition deepens, and the regulatory/market framework matures—consistent with the design principles of investability, market development, value for money, and simplicity set out in the minded-to package (DESNZ, 2023a).

However, the United Kingdom's HSBM also have problems. Although it settles the core bankability problem, it leaves several economic tensions unresolved. A private-law revenue floor avoids locking storage into full economic regulation, yet investors may still price in higher WACC than

[5] The high initial costs for cushion gas and site appraisal may still pose a financing hurdle despite the revenue floor, potentially requiring targeted capital support.

under a RAB or cap-and-floor, especially while the funding mechanism (levy vs. Exchequer) remains unsettled and politically exposed. Outcomes hinge on how the floor is set and indexed: too low and FOAK projects stall; too high and value-for-money erodes. Revenue support alone may also be insufficient where DevEx, appraisal, and cushion-gas/initial-fill costs dominate early cash needs. Finally, a cohort-based allocation that must mesh with pipeline awards and anchor loads is sensible in theory but creates timing risk in practice; and an early focus on large geological assets, while pragmatic, can sideline smaller or modular options that might accelerate learning and competition.

Technically, the model's near-term dependence on onshore salt-cavern storage concentrates risk in geographies with limited suitable geology and long lead times for permitting, drilling, and cavern conditioning—potentially out of step with early-2030s flexibility needs. Subsurface uncertainties (cavern integrity, cycling limits, cushion-gas volumes) and planning/regulatory frictions—particularly offshore—sit largely outside the contract and can surface late in development. Above all, storage's value is system-contingent: without tightly sequenced pipelines, off-takers and power-system use cases, even well-structured contracts risk under-utilisation. The policy trajectory can mitigate these issues—through transparent floor-setting, targeted capital support for appraisal and initial fill, faster consents for strategic sites, and stronger whole-system planning via the system operator—while broadening scope over time to include diverse resource types that can compete with hydrogen storage projects.

## Conclusions

This chapter has analysed hydrogen storage technologies, examining their technical characteristics, economic drivers, and the policy frameworks necessary for their deployment. It has reviewed the spectrum of storage options, from compressed gas and liquid carriers to material-based and underground storage, assessing their respective roles, costs, and maturity levels. Furthermore, it has explored the critical function of storage within the broader energy system and considered the practical challenges of financing and developing early-stage infrastructure, using the United Kingdom's proposed business model as a case study. Several general conclusions can be inferred from these findings.

Fundamentally, hydrogen storage is a critical infrastructure that decouples variable renewable energy supply from diverse demand profiles, enables efficient international trade by acting as a physical market-maker, and provides the resilience required for bankable investment across the supply chain. Without large-scale, flexible storage solutions, the hydrogen value chain fragments and the overall cost of decarbonisation may rise if hydrogen is to play a role.

From a technological perspective, the evidence clearly indicates that no single hydrogen storage solution is optimal for all applications, necessitating a diversified portfolio. Compressed gas storage is practical for near-term, short-duration roles like mobility refuelling, while liquid hydrogen and carriers such as ammonia and LOHCs are better suited for long-distance logistics. For the essential function of seasonal balancing at the terawatt-hour scale, underground geological storage in salt caverns and depleted reservoirs is currently the only viable option. Each technology presents a distinct set of trade-offs between capital expenditure, energy efficiency, and technological maturity.

Crucially, the economic viability of these pathways is influenced by two universal cost drivers. The first is the price of electricity required for energy-intensive processes like compression, liquefaction, or conversion, which dominates operational expenditures. The second is the capital cost of materials and civil works, such as composite tanks, cryogenic plants, or geological site development. Consequently, future cost reductions will hinge on innovations that reduce these energy penalties and material costs, as well as on strategic siting to maximise asset utilisation.

Given these high capital costs and revenue uncertainties in nascent markets, the analysis of business models reveals that market mechanisms alone are insufficient to trigger investment. Tailored policy support, such as revenue stabilisation mechanisms, is necessary to de-risk early projects and attract private capital. However, as demonstrated by the United Kingdom's experience, such models must be carefully designed to balance bankability with incentives for efficient market operation, avoiding excessive long-term costs to taxpayers or consumers.

Therefore, the successful integration of hydrogen storage into the energy system necessitates more than isolated technological or economic solutions; it demands strategic, holistic planning. The value of any storage asset is entirely contingent on its coordination with hydrogen production, transmission infrastructure, and end-use demand. Furthermore, competition for limited geological resources with carbon sequestration and natural gas storage requires careful prioritisation. Ultimately, unlocking the full potential of hydrogen storage will depend on a coordinated, system-wide approach that addresses these technical, economic, and regulatory challenges in tandem.

## References

Abdin, Z., Tang, C., Liu, Y., & Catchpole, K. (2021). Large-scale stationary hydrogen storage via liquid organic hydrogen carriers. *iScience, 24*(9), 1–11.

Bach, M., Crotogino, F., & Kruckeberg, A. (2019). Underground storage of gases: A review on current technologies and future challenges. *Energy Procedia, 158*, 104–109.

Bachu, S. (2008). Carbon dioxide storage capacity in uneconomic coal beds in Alberta, Canada: Methodology, potential and site identification. *International Journal of Greenhouse Gas Control, 2*(2), 297–308.

BEIS. (2021). *UK hydrogen strategy. CP 475.* London: HM Government. [Online]. Retrieved September 16, 2025, from https://www.gov.uk/government/publications/uk-hydrogen-strategy/uk-hydrogen-strategy-accessible-html-version.

Cabrera, G., et al. (2024). Liquid organic hydrogen carrier concepts and catalysts for hydrogenation and dehydrogenation reactions. *Molecules, 29*(20), 1–11.

Cappellani, C. (2022). *Hydrogen underground storage: Status of technology and perspectives* [Online]. Retrieved December 18, 2024, from https://hydrogen-Portal.com/wp-content/uploads/2022/07/Hydrogen-Portal-Undergound-Storage.pdf.pdf.

Chen, G., et al (2025) 'Review of hydrogen storage in solid-state materials', *Energies*, 18 (2930), pp. 1-22.

Crotogino, F., Donadei, S., Bünger, U., & Landinger, H. (2010). Large-scale hydrogen underground storage for securing future energy supplies. In D. Stolten & T. Grube (Eds.), *18th World Hydrogen Energy Conference 2010 – WHEC 2010, Parallel Sessions Book 4: Storage Systems / Policy Perspectives, Initiatives and Cooperations* (Schriften des Forschungszentrums Jülich / Energy & Environment) (Vol. 78–4, pp. 37–45). Forschungszentrum Jülich GmbH.

DESNZ. (2023a). *Hydrogen transport and storage infrastructure: Minded-to positions.* DESNZ, August [Online]. Retrieved September 9, 2025, from https://assets.publishing.service.gov.uk/media/64ca0e6c5c2e6f0013e8d92a/hydrogen-transport-storage-minded-to-positions.pdf

DESNZ. (2023b). *Hydrogen transport and storage infrastructure: Government response to consultation* [Online]. Retrieved September 9, 2025, from https://assets.publishing.service.gov.uk/media/64c95cbd19f5622669f3c164/hydrogen-transport-storage-consultation-government-response.pdf

DESNZ. (2023c). *Hydrogen transport and storage networks pathway* [Online]. Retrieved September 9, 2025, from https://www.gov.uk/government/publications/hydrogen-transport-and-storage-networks-pathway

DESNZ. (2023d). *Hydrogen storage business model: Market engagement on the first allocation round* [Online]. Retrieved September 9, 2025, from https://www.gov.uk/government/consultations/hydrogen-storage-business-model-market-engagement-on-the-first-allocation-round.

DESNZ. (2024a). *Hydrogen strategy update to the market: December 2024* [Online]. Retrieved September 9, 2025, from https://www.gov.uk/government/publications/hydrogen-strategy-update-to-the-market-december-2024

DESNZ. (2024b). *Hydrogen storage business model: Market engagement on the first allocation round* [Online]. Retrieved April 10, 2025, from www.gov.uk/government/consultations/hydrogen-storage-business-model-market

dw. (2022). Germany and Canada sign hydrogen deal [Online]. Retrieved December 12, 2022, from https://www.dw.com/en/germany-and-canada-sign-hydrogen-deal/a-62899992

Eberle, U., Felderhoff, M., & Schüth, F. (2009). Chemical and physical solutions for hydrogen storage. *Angewandte Chemie International Edition, 48*(36), 6608–6630.

Elberry, A. M., Thakur, J., Santasalo-Aarnio, A., & Larmi, M. (2021). Large-scale compressed hydrogen storage as part of renewable electricity storage systems. *International Journal of Hydrogen Energy, 46*(29), 15671–15690.

Gas Infrastructure Europe. (2021). *Picturing the value of underground gas storage to the European hydrogen system [*Online]. Retrieved October 20, 2024, from https://www.gie.eu/wp-content/uploads/filr/3517/Picturing%20the%20value%20of%20gas%20storage%20to%20the%20European%20hydrogen%20system_FINAL_140621.pdf

Gianni, E., et al. (2024). Underground hydrogen storage: The techno-economic perspective. *Open Research Europe, 4*(17), 1–36.

Ghadbeigi, H., et al (2025) *Cryogenic hydrogen materials. Global research landscape*. Sheffield, UK: The University of Sheffield.

Guerra, O. J., Eichman, J., Kurtz, J., & Hodge, B. M. (2020). The value of seasonal energy storage technologies for the integration of wind and solar power. *Energy & Environmental Science, 7*(1), 1–26.

Hellerschmied, C., et al. (2024). Hydrogen storage and geo-methanation in a depleted underground hydrocarbon reservoir. *Nature Energy, 9*, 333–344. https://doi.org/10.1038/s41560-024-01458-1

IEA. (2019). *The future of hydrogen* [Online]. Retrieved December 13, 2022, from https://www.iea.org/reports/the-future-of-hydrogen

IEA. (2024). Hydrogen production and infrastructure projects database [Online]. Retrieved December 27, 2024, from https://www.iea.org/data-and-statistics/data-product/hydrogen-production-and-infrastructure-projects-database.

Ilyushechkin, A., Schoeman, L., Carter, L., & Hla, S. S. (2023). Material challenges and hydrogen embrittlement assessment for hydrogen utilisation in industrial scale. *Hydrogen, 4*(3), 599–619.

IPCC. (2005). *Carbon dioxide capture and storage. Special Report of the Intergovernmental Panel on Climate Change*. Cambridge University Press.

ITM Power. (2022). *Green hydrogen for grid balancing* [Online]. Retrieved December 14, 2022, from https://itm-power.com/markets/grid-balancing

Jensen, J. O., Vestbø, A. P., & Bjerrum, N. J. (2007). The energy efficiency of onboard hydrogen storage. *Journal of Alloys and Compounds, 446–447*(1), 723–728.

Kiemde, A. F., et al. (2023). Hydrogen and air storage in salt caverns: A thermodynamic model for phase equilibrium calculations. *Science and Technology for Energy Transition, 78*(1), 10–23.

Landsvirkjun. (2020). *An agreement made to explore the possibilities of green hydrogen* [Online]. Retrieved December 12, 2022, from https://www.landsvirkjun.com/news/an-agreement-made-to-explore-the-possibilities-of-green-hydrogen-export-from-iceland-to-rotterdam.

Le Fevre, C. (2013). *Gas storage in Great Britain*. Oxford Institute for Energy Studies.

Le, T. H., Kim, M. P., Park, C. H., & Tran, Q. N. (2024). Recent developments in materials for physical hydrogen storage: A review. *Materials, 17*(3), 666–682.

Liu, Y., Teodoriu, C., & Bello, M. A. (2015). Use of underground space for the storage of selected gases: A review on geological conditions and safety issues. *Journal of Natural Gas Science and Engineering, 27*(1), 1–12.

Matsuo, Y., et al. (2020). Investigating the economics of the power sector under high penetration of variable renewable energies. *Applied Energy, 267*(113956), 1–28.

Mekonnin, A. S., et al. (2025). Hydrogen storage technology, and its challenges: A review. *Catalysts, 15*(3), 260–281.

Miocic, J., et al. (2022). Underground hydrogen storage: A review. *Geological Society, London, Special Publications, 528*, 73–86.

Muhammed, N. S., et al. (2022). A review on underground hydrogen storage: Insight into geological sites, influencing factors and future outlook. *Energy Reports, 8*, 461–499.

Nemukula, E., Mtshali, C. B., & Nemangwele, F. (2025). Metal hydrides for sustainable hydrogen storage: A review. *International Journal of Energy Research, 15*, 1–12.

Pan, B., Yin, X., Ju, Y., & Iglauer, S. (2021). Underground hydrogen storage: Influencing parameters and future outlook. *Advances in Colloid and Interface Science, 294*(1), 11–25.

Patonia, A., Lambert, M., Lin, N., & Shuster, M., (2025). *Underground storage for decarbonisation: Trade-offs between hydrogen, natural gas, and carbon dioxide*. OIES Paper: ET 47. Oxford Institute for Energy Studies, Oxford, UK.

Patonia, A., & Poudineh, R. (2022). *Global trade of hydrogen: What is the best way to transfer hydrogen over long distances?* Oxford Institute for Energy Studies.

Qian, X., et al. (2025). Underground hydrogen storage in salt cavern: A review of advantages, challenges, and prospects. *Sustainability, 17*(13), 5900–5921.

Raza, A., et al (2022) 'A holistic overview of underground hydrogen storage: Influencing factors, current understanding, and outlook', *Fuel*, 330 (1), pp. 1- 20.

Ren, J., & North, B. C. (2014). Shaping porous materials for hydrogen storage applications: A review. *Journal of Technology Innovations in Renewable Energy, 3*(1), 12–20.

RWE. (2021). *Naftogaz and RWE sign memorandum of understanding on hydrogen* [Online]. Retrieved December 12, 2022, from https://www.rwe.com/en/press/rwe-supply-and-trading/2021-08-22-naftogaz-and-rwe-sign-memorandum-of-understanding-on-hydrogen

Sadhasivam, T., et al. (2017). Dimensional effects of nanostructured $Mg/MgH_2$ for hydrogen storage applications: A review. *Renewable and Sustainable Energy Reviews, 72*, 523–534. https://doi.org/10.1016/j.rser.2017.01.107

Scottish Enterprise (2022) *Compression, storage and distribution of gaseous hydrogen.* Glasgow, UK: Scottish Enterprise.

US Department of Energy. (2009). *DOE hydrogen and fuel cells program record: Energy requirements for hydrogen gas compression* [Online]. Retrieved December 17, 2022, from https://www.hydrogen.energy.gov/pdfs/9013_energy_requirements_for_hydrogen_gas_compression.pdf.

US Department of Energy. (2022). *Bulk storage of gaseous hydrogen: Workshop summary report.* U.S. Department of Energy.

US Energy Information Administration. (2022). *Hydrogen explained* [Online]. Retrieved July 04, 2024, from https://www.eia.gov/energyexplained/hydrogen/.

Usman, M. R. (2022). Hydrogen storage methods: Review and current status. *Renewable and Sustainable Energy Reviews, 167*, 11–27.

Wang, X., et al. (2025). Technoeconomic insights into metal hydrides for stationary hydrogen storage. *Advanced Science, 12*, 24–73.

WHA. (2021). *Hydrogen industry applications: Past, present, and future* [Online]. Retrieved December 13, 2022, from https://wha-international.com/hydrogen-in-industry/.

Yang, M., et al. (2023). A review of hydrogen storage and transport technologies. *Clean Energy, 7*(1), 190–216.

Züttel, A. (2003). Hydrogen storage methods: A review on current technologies and future directions. *Naturwissenschaften, 90*(4), 157–172.

Züttel, A. (2004). Hydrogen storage methods. *Naturwissenschaften, 91*(4), 157–172.

CHAPTER 6

# Hydrogen in the Power Sector

## Introduction

Electricity grids with high penetration of intermittent renewable energy sources (IREs) face fundamental stability challenges stemming from their inherent unpredictability. Unlike conventional power plants that can be dispatched on demand, wind and solar generation fluctuate based on weather conditions. These fluctuations occur across multiple timescales—from seconds to seasons—creating persistent imbalances between supply and demand. When renewable output suddenly drops due to passing clouds or decreasing wind speeds, grid frequency can deviate beyond acceptable limits, potentially triggering protective equipment and cascading into wider system failures. Even with advanced forecasting technologies, this uncertainty presents a continuous operational challenge for grid operators.

A critical concern in renewable-heavy grids is the reduced system inertia (Qvist et al., 2023). Conventional power plants provide rotational inertia that naturally resists sudden frequency changes, offering valuable seconds for control systems to respond to disturbances. In contrast, renewables typically connect through power electronic interfaces that don't inherently provide this stabilising effect. This reduces power system's inertia and consequently increases the rate of change of frequency (RoCoF) when an event happens (e.g., loss of a major generation facility) (see Fig. 6.1). Therefore, as synchronous generators are progressively retired and



A. Patonia, R. Poudineh, *Clean Hydrogen for Decarbonisation*,
https://doi.org/10.1007/978-3-032-19442-8_6

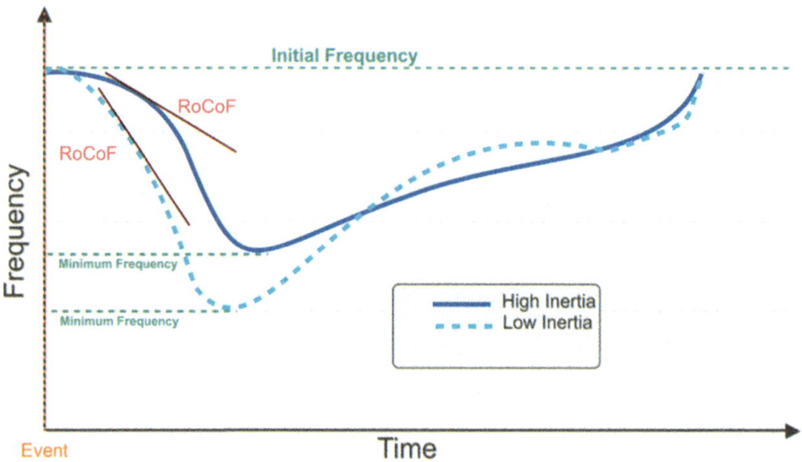


**Fig. 6.1** The effect of inertia on rate of change of frequency (RoCoF). (Source: Authors)

replaced with renewables, the grid becomes more vulnerable to frequency fluctuations, requiring faster and more sophisticated control mechanisms to maintain stability.

Another challenge of weather-dependent power systems is persistent balancing challenge resulting from the temporal mismatch between renewable generation and electricity demand. For example, solar PV generation peaks during midday when residential demand may be relatively low, while dropping to zero during evening consumption peaks. In regions with significant penetration of solar PV resources, this leads to net load fluctuations (load minus supply of variable renewable resources) throughout the day, resembling the shape of a duck (see Fig. 6.2). Over the years, as the share of solar PV in the generation mix increases, this phenomenon becomes even more critical. The duck curve presents operational challenges, including grid stability risks, increased cycling of conventional plants, and higher curtailment of renewable energy (Calero et al., 2022). In a similar way, wind generation may be strongest overnight when demand is minimal. This mismatch extends geographically as well, with optimal renewable resources often located far from population centres and industrial loads. This is specifically a challenge where there are transmission constraints. Grid operators must continuously manage these temporal

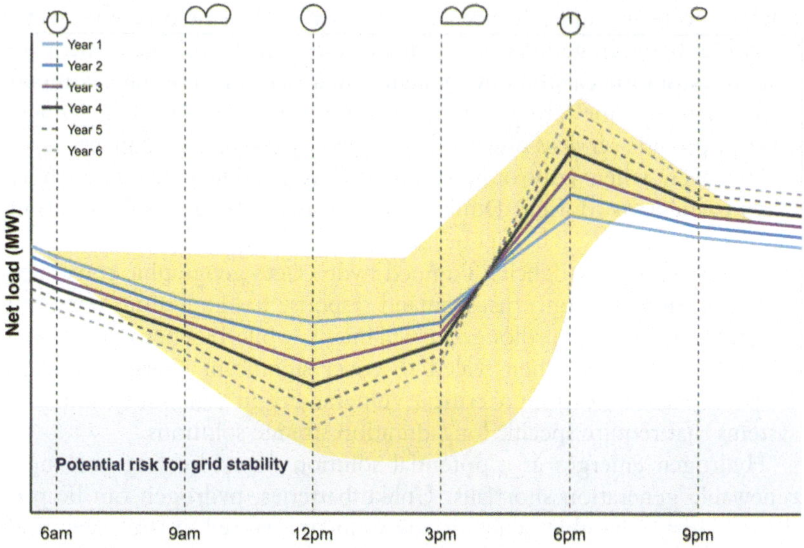


**Fig. 6.2** Duck curve due to overgeneration by solar power during the noon. (Source: Authors)

and spatial disparities, requiring significant ramping capabilities from remaining dispatchable resources.

Seasonal variations pose another challenge for renewable-dominated systems. Winter months typically bring increased demand for heating alongside decreased solar production due to shorter days and lower sun angles, especially in countries located at higher latitudes. More critically, extended periods of low wind and solar generation—such as the 'Dunkelflaute' phenomenon in Europe, where calm, cloudy conditions can persist for days or weeks—create sustained energy shortfalls that cannot be addressed through short-duration balancing mechanisms. These weather patterns test the resilience of renewable-heavy systems, revealing fundamental limitations when weather-dependent generation dominates without adequate long-duration alternatives.

Many low-carbon technologies can address these grid stability challenges. To stabilize frequency, technologies such as grid-forming inverters, synchronous condensers, and virtual inertia systems are employed. Battery storage meets short-term demands, while pumped hydro storage manages energy at larger scales. Transmission expansion, interconnections, and advanced power flow control help resolve spatial disparities between generation and load. Additionally, voltage control and system restoration capabilities are being enhanced through static compensators, dynamic line rating systems, and smart inverters, enabling renewables to provide services previously supplied by conventional plants.

However, when confronting extended renewable generation shortfalls—particularly during Dunkelflaute events—the available solutions narrow considerably. Batteries become prohibitively expensive when scaled to address multi-day deficits. Pumped hydro faces geographic constraints and environmental concerns. Demand response has limitations regarding societal tolerance for prolonged curtailment, while bioenergy raises sustainability questions when scaled to cover significant energy shortfalls. These limitations expose a critical vulnerability in renewable-dominant systems that require specific long-duration storage solutions.

Hydrogen emerges as a potential solution for addressing prolonged renewable generation shortfalls. Unlike batteries, hydrogen can be produced when renewable generation is abundant, stored in large quantities for extended periods, and converted back to electricity through fuel cells or hydrogen-capable turbines when needed. This pathway offers seasonal storage capabilities with energy density far exceeding batteries, making it potentially viable for addressing multi-week generation deficits. While hydrogen-to-power technologies currently face challenges regarding cost and efficiency, their ability to provide dispatchable low-carbon power makes them an option to address the extreme challenge of Dunkelflaute events.

This chapter therefore focuses specifically on the potential role of hydrogen in addressing these extended Dunkelflaute events. Hydrogen is uniquely suited to long-duration and seasonal storage because it can be produced from excess renewable electricity, stored in large quantities for long periods, and later converted back into power when needed. While other low-carbon technologies may be more efficient for short-term balancing or frequency regulation, hydrogen's comparative advantage lies in its ability to provide dispatchable low-carbon electricity over prolonged periods of low renewable output. By narrowing the analytical scope to this distinctive role, the chapter aims to assess where hydrogen-to-power applications can add genuine system value rather than duplicating the functions already served more effectively by other technologies. We also use the United Kingdom as an illustrative case study because it makes the cross-links between power-system adequacy, business model design, and enabling infrastructure particularly visible; the objective is to extract lessons that can inform other markets rather than to treat the United Kingdom as a benchmark. The structure of this chapter is as follows. Section "Dunkelflaute Events and Approaches to Manage Them" outlines the stability and adequacy challenges of renewable-based electricity systems, highlighting why Dunkelflaute events are particularly problematic. Section "Hydrogen-to-Power" evaluates the technological pathways for hydrogen-to-power conversion and their suitability for long-duration storage and reviews how different countries are approaching hydrogen-to-power within their broader energy strategies. Section "Case Study: Hydrogen-to-Power in the UK" provides a case study of hydrogen-to-power in the United Kingdom including discussion on adopted business model. Section "Conclusions" concludes by summarising the findings and identifying where hydrogen can most effectively complement other flexibility options.

## Dunkelflaute Events and Approaches to Manage Them

Dunkelflaute, a German term meaning 'dark doldrums', refers to periods of simultaneously low wind and solar power generation that pose significant challenges for electricity systems with high renewable energy penetration. These events occur when both wind speeds drop and solar radiation decreases, creating a substantial shortfall in renewable electricity supply (Li et al., 2021). While wind and solar generation naturally fluctuate, Dunkelflaute events represent extreme cases where both resources experience prolonged underperformance simultaneously, often lasting from several hours to multiple days or even weeks. Mayer et al. (2023) note that Dunkelflaute events predominantly occur during winter months in Europe, when solar output is already limited by shorter daylight hours, and high-pressure weather systems can cause extended periods of calm winds across entire regions.

Figure 6.3 illustrates Germany's energy dynamics in January 2023, highlighting a prolonged Dunkelflaute period from January 20 to January 28, where renewable energy generation from onshore wind, offshore wind, and solar sources significantly declined, with onshore wind dropping from peaks above 3000 MW to below 1000 MW and solar output remaining negligible during this winter period. Hydro and biomass

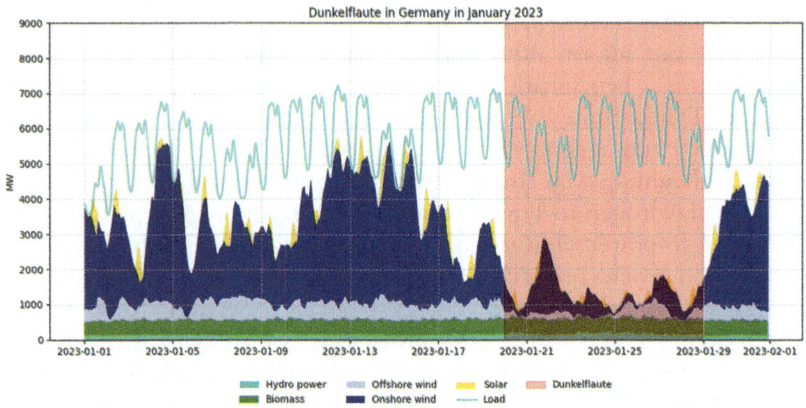


**Fig. 6.3** Dunkelflaute in Germany in January 2023. (Note: The Y-axis is scaled down by the factor of 10 for a better visibility. Source: ENTSO-E (n.d.))

generation remained relatively stable, contributing consistently around 1000 MW and 400 MW, respectively, but were insufficient to offset the shortfall. Meanwhile, the total load (scaled down by the factor of 10 for a better visibility) fluctuated between 4000 and 6000 MW, peaking mid-month, revealing a stark reliance on alternative energy sources or storage to meet demand during this low renewable production phase, underscoring the challenges of maintaining grid stability amidst variable renewable energy availability.

Weather patterns play a crucial role in triggering Dunkelflaute events, with specific meteorological conditions creating these challenging scenarios. Mockert et al. (2023) identify three primary weather regimes responsible for approximately 51% of Dunkelflaute occurrences in Germany: European Blocking (22%), where high-pressure systems directly over Central Europe reduce wind speeds; Scandinavian Blocking (15%), characterized by high pressure over Scandinavia creating weak winds across Northern Europe; and Greenland Blocking (14%), which not only reduces wind generation but also brings cold air outbreaks that increase electricity demand. These blocking high-pressure systems create weak pressure gradients, leading to stagnant air masses and significantly reduced wind generation across wide geographical areas (Li et al., 2020). This issue is particularly severe in winter, when Dunkelflaute conditions peak (Duchêne et al., 2024), as solar generation is already at its lowest, making the system heavily reliant on wind power.

The literature reveals no universally accepted definition of Dunkelflaute, with researchers employing various methodologies to identify and quantify these events. Kittel and Schill (2024) categorise approaches to measuring renewable energy shortages into two main perspectives: supply-based approaches, which identify variable renewable energy (VRE) droughts based purely on low resource availability; and demand-based approaches, which focus on residual load (electricity demand minus renewable supply). Some studies employ fixed thresholds, classifying Dunkelflaute as periods when renewable output falls below specific percentages of installed capacity—for instance, Li et al. (2021) define it as when both wind and solar generation drop below 20% of their nominal capacities during a specific 60 min period. Others use relative thresholds based on statistical measures or adopt more complex methodologies like the Sequent Peak Algorithm to identify extended periods of energy deficit (Kittel & Schill, 2024). This lack of standardisation creates challenges for comparing studies and developing consistent policy responses.

The definition approach significantly impacts how Dunkelflaute events are identified and quantified. Kittel and Schill (2024) emphasise that using a fixed absolute threshold (e.g., 10% of capacity) fails to account for regional differences and seasonal variations, potentially leading to inconsistent identification of events across different contexts. They recommend using relative thresholds—such as a fraction of mean renewable availability—to improve comparability across different systems. Additionally, the time window considered for analysis affects results significantly; short windows might overestimate the frequency while underestimating the duration of Dunkelflaute events, whereas longer windows might miss brief but potentially critical shortfalls. The authors propose more sophisticated methods, such as Variable-Duration Mean-Below-Threshold (VMBT) and Adjusted Sequent Peak Algorithm (SPAadj), to provide more accurate assessments of Dunkelflaute events and better reflect their impact on energy systems.

Dunkelflaute events have profound implications for power system planning and operation. Li et al. (2021) find that events lasting more than 24 h occur between 2 and 10 times per year in European countries, with some lasting up to five days, creating significant challenges for maintaining reliable electricity supply. Particularly concerning is the geographical correlation of these events, with the same study showing that Dunkelflaute events often coincide with each other in neighbouring countries, limiting the effectiveness of cross-border electricity trading as a mitigation strategy. This synchronicity means that energy systems cannot rely solely on imports to address renewable energy shortfalls during severe Dunkelflaute periods. Furthermore, Duchêne et al. (2024) demonstrate that climate change is likely to exacerbate Dunkelflaute risks, with projections indicating wind power production could decline and electricity demand might be affected due to changing temperature patterns.

For the purpose of planning, the characteristics of power systems necessitate appropriate backup solutions and flexibility measures to manage calm periods. Ghanbarzadeh et al. (2024) analyse the context of Australia's South West Interconnected System (SWIS), which is a large but self-contained electricity grid without strong interconnections, and conclude that without flexible backup power, storage alone is not enough to address Dunkelflaute risk in a 100% renewable system.

The optimal energy mix to address Dunkelflaute also depends on event duration; in the context of Belgium, a study shows that sub-daily events benefit from more wind power, mid-term events (1–2 days) require a higher proportion of solar PV, while long-term events (over one week) again favour wind power (Duchêne et al., 2024). Additionally, the timing of Dunkelflaute events matters significantly. For example, in Germany, Greenland Blocking-induced Dunkelflauten are particularly problematic as they coincide with cold temperatures, increasing electricity demand for heating precisely when renewable generation is low (Mockert et al., 2023). These complex interactions between Dunkelflaute characteristics and power system needs underscore the importance of effective planning and operation strategies to ensure system reliability in high-renewable futures.

### *Managing Dunkelflaute Events*

Managing Dunkelflaute events requires a multifaceted approach combining various technological, market, and operational strategies to ensure electricity system reliability. One of the primary solutions is expanding renewable energy capacity beyond what is needed to meet average demand, thus creating an intentional overcapacity buffer. This strategy helps ensure that even during low-generation periods, some renewable output remains available. However, this approach assumes that the outputs of different renewable energy technologies are not perfectly correlated. Moreover, overcapacity alone leads to significant curtailment during normal conditions, necessitating complementary solutions to utilise excess generation efficiently. Research conducted in the context of the South West Interconnected System (SWIS), an isolated system, indicates that an overcapacity ratio of 1.32, when combined with energy storage systems having a 24-hour minimum storage duration, provides the most cost-effective solution, minimising both investment costs and energy curtailment costs (Ghanbarzadeh et al., 2024).

Energy storage systems represent a crucial strategy for bridging renewable generation gaps during Dunkelflaute events. Studies of the European power system demonstrate that the required storage capacity varies significantly based on the level of grid interconnection; in a fully isolated European system, up to 378 TWh of storage might be needed (approximately 7.6% of Europe's annual electricity demand), whilst in a perfectly interconnected European grid (with unlimited energy exchange), this requirement drops to around 159 TWh (3.2% of annual demand) (Kittel et al., 2025). Short-duration storage solutions, such as lithium-ion batteries, efficiently manage fluctuations over hours or days, yet they become prohibitively costly for prolonged low-renewable periods. For multi-day to seasonal shortages in European power systems, long-duration energy storage (LDES) solutions such as hydrogen or compressed-air storage can provide valuable backup, though these complement rather than replace the dominant short-duration storage, interconnection, and demand--response measures. With the ability to retain substantial energy for extended times without major losses, hydrogen is well-suited to address extreme Dunkelflaute events. In the context of the United Kingdom, for instance, hydrogen storage can be deployed through salt caverns and depleted gas fields, providing strategic reserves similar to today's natural gas storage infrastructure (LCP Delta, 2023). Nevertheless, concerns exist regarding the availability of suitable large-scale storage across Europe, as not all countries have sufficient appropriate sites for this purpose.

Cross-border electricity trade and grid interconnections significantly enhance resilience to Dunkelflaute events by enabling regions with surplus renewable generation to support those experiencing shortages. Research demonstrates that pooling renewable resources across 11 countries in the North and Baltic Sea regions can reduce the frequency of Dunkelflaute from 3–9% in individual countries to approximately 3.5% for the entire interconnected system (Li et al., 2021). This approach leverages the geographic diversity of weather patterns, as Dunkelflaute events rarely affect all European regions simultaneously. However, the same study reveals that some neighbouring countries show a particularly high correlation. For example, around 50–60% of Dunkelflaute events in Belgium coincide with similar conditions in the Netherlands (the same applies to Denmark and Sweden), limiting the effectiveness of regional electricity trading during severe events. Furthermore, quantitative analysis of the European power system shows that a fully interconnected European grid reduces aggregated median storage needs by 55% compared to isolated national systems; however, it never drops to zero, and substantial long-duration storage is still required to handle extreme events (Kittel et al., 2025). Additionally, whilst grid interconnections represent a cost-effective solution, they face political, regulatory, and infrastructure challenges, including the need for massive investment in high-voltage transmission lines across national borders.

Diversifying the energy mix beyond variable renewables provides another important strategy for managing Dunkelflaute risks. Conventional approaches include maintaining dispatchable low-carbon generation sources such as nuclear power, hydroelectric facilities, and bioenergy plants. Assessment of the contribution of these technologies in the European context finds that adding 24 GW of nuclear capacity in selected European countries would reduce maximum storage requirements by approximately 6% (Kittel et al., 2025). Whilst this impact seems modest, nuclear power provides stable baseload generation that can be particularly valuable during extended Dunkelflaute periods. In addition, research emphasises the transformative potential of hydrogen-based power generation technologies, contrasting the lower efficiency of hydrogen turbines with the superior efficiency of fuel cells (Dai et al., 2024). Among fuel cell technologies, Solid Oxide Fuel Cells (SOFCs) stand out with expected efficiencies of 60–80%, potentially making them particularly suitable for applications like distributed power generation and co-generation, which could enhance the flexibility and sustainability of power systems as hydrogen infrastructure evolves. Nonetheless, despite constant technological progress and significant research efforts, they have not been fully commercialised yet. Besides, fuel cells have high capital costs per unit of capacity compared to hydrogen-fired gas turbines, making them less suitable for grid-scale dispatch.

Demand-side flexibility represents an increasingly important strategy for mitigating Dunkelflaute impacts without relying solely on supply-side solutions. Demand response programmes that incentivise consumers to reduce consumption during Dunkelflaute periods, particularly during those events that coincide with cold temperatures and increased heating demand, play a crucial role in maintaining system reliability. Smart heating systems that pre-heat buildings before anticipated Dunkelflaute events can significantly reduce electricity demand during critical periods in northern European countries. Furthermore, industrial consumers can shift energy-intensive operations away from Dunkelflaute hours, providing substantial grid relief. However, whilst demand flexibility is highly cost-effective, it faces limitations during extended Dunkelflaute events, as there are practical constraints on how long consumption can be reduced or shifted. Consequently, it is likely that demand flexibility works best when combined with storage and backup generation in a comprehensive approach to Dunkelflaute management.

Advanced forecasting capabilities enable more proactive management of Dunkelflaute events by providing early warning to system operators. Research investigating the predictability of a Dunkelflaute event in the Netherlands—a critical challenge for wind- and solar-dependent grids—using the Weather Research and Forecasting (WRF) model reveals that wind speed reductions, such as those observed during 30 April 2018 event, can be reliably forecast up to three days ahead with Global Forecast System (GFS) operational data (Li et al., 2020). This predictive window offers valuable lead time for grid operators to mitigate supply shortages in a nation increasingly reliant on renewables. However, the study underscores persistent difficulties in accurately forecasting cloud cover, highlighting a key limitation in anticipating solar production deficits during such events.

Overall, better forecasting capability allows grid operators to optimise storage charging before anticipated Dunkelflaute events, schedule demand response programmes, and plan maintenance of critical infrastructure accordingly. Additionally, improved forecasting enables better market coordination, allowing electricity prices to reflect upcoming scarcity and incentivising appropriate responses from market participants. Nevertheless, forecast accuracy diminishes with longer lead times, and unexpected shifts in weather patterns can still create challenges for system operators. Despite these limitations, integrating weather regime forecasting into energy system operations represents a cost-effective supplement to physical infrastructure solutions for Dunkelflaute management.

## Hydrogen-to-Power

Hydrogen can be converted to electricity through several technologies with distinct operational characteristics. Fuel cells directly convert hydrogen to electricity through electrochemical reactions without combustion, achieving high efficiencies. Hydrogen-fired gas turbines represent another option that is suitable for large scale operation and can leverage existing power generation infrastructure. Hydrogen internal combustion engines offer a middle-ground solution for medium-scale applications, adapted from conventional engines with moderate efficiency and cost. Figure 6.4 provides schematic representation of power-to-hydrogen-to-power.

### *Fuel Cells*

Hydrogen fuel cells generate electricity by directly converting the chemical energy of hydrogen combined with an oxidant, most commonly oxygen from the air. This conversion occurs through a pair of redox reactions

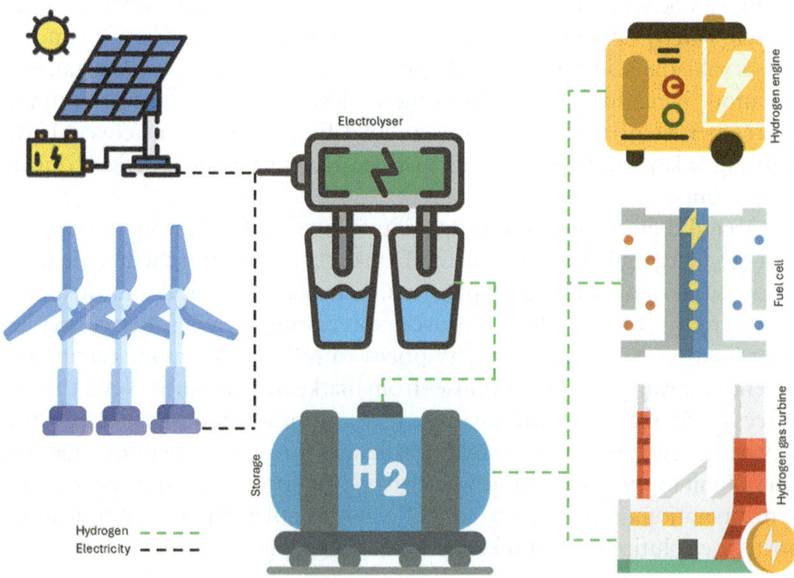


**Fig. 6.4** Schematic representation of power-to-hydrogen-to-power. (Source: Authors)

within the fuel cell, producing water and heat as the primary by-products. This direct conversion of chemical energy to electrical energy inherently bypasses the energy losses associated with the thermal cycles inherent in combustion-based technologies (Bloom Energy, 2025). Several types of fuel cells exist, each with its own electrolyte and operating temperature, influencing their suitability for different applications. These include Polymer Electrolyte Membrane Fuel Cells (PEMFCs), Solid Oxide Fuel Cells (SOFCs), Molten Carbonate Fuel Cells (MCFCs), Phosphoric Acid Fuel Cells (PAFCs), and Alkaline Fuel Cells (AFCs) (US Department of Energy, 2006). For instance, PEMFCs typically operate at lower temperatures (50–100°C) and are well-suited for transportation applications, while SOFCs operate at much higher temperatures (650–1000°C) and are often used for stationary power generation (US Department of Energy, 2006). To obtain the voltage and power necessary for practical use, single fuel cells—each producing relatively low voltage—are arranged in series as fuel cell stacks. The number and size of the cells in a stack can be tailored to meet specific power requirements, making the technology highly modular and scalable.

Hydrogen fuel cells can achieve up to 60% efficiency (and higher with co-generation) in converting hydrogen's energy to electricity (H2FC, 2025). This is roughly 2–3 times more efficient than traditional combustion-based generators (which are ~35% efficient) (US Department of Energy, 2017). High-temperature fuel cells (like solid oxide) reach the upper end of this range, and if the waste heat is captured for cogeneration (CHP), the total energy efficiency can approach 80–90% (Kubert, 2010).

Historically, the capital cost associated with hydrogen fuel cell technology has been a significant barrier to its widespread adoption. In 2010, the price of fuel cells could range from $4000 to $6000 per kilowatt of power output (Horizon Educational, 2023). However, significant advancements in technology and increased manufacturing volumes have led to a substantial decline in prices. By 2023, fuel cells were entering the market at a cost of around USD 1500 per kilowatt (Horizon Educational, ibid.). Looking towards the future, the US Department of Energy (DOE) has set ambitious targets for further cost reductions. For megawatt-scale stationary PEM fuel cell systems, by 2030, the objectives include reducing the cost to around $650 per kilowatt for systems with a 50,000-hour lifetime and around $550 per kilowatt for systems with a 25,000-hour lifetime (Wei, 2022).

Currently, the cost for stationary power fuel cells ranges from $1200 to $2500 per kilowatt of capacity (US Department of Energy, 2024). It is important to recognize that the capital cost of fuel cell systems can vary considerably based on the scale of operation, ranging from small portable devices to residential and vehicle applications, and up to large central power generation facilities.

Fuel cell power output ramps moderately fast, though not as instantaneously as a turbine in some cases. PEM fuel cells, common in smaller and transportation applications, have fast electrical response—studies show they can ramp at 20–30% of rated power per second (Nikiforow et al., 2018). This means a PEM fuel cell could go from 50% to 100% output in only a few seconds. In contrast, other fuel cell types, such as Solid Oxide Fuel Cells (SOFCs), can have significantly longer start-up times as they need to reach their operating temperature. A fast response time is particularly important for applications such as backup power systems, where immediate power is required in the event of a grid failure, and in vehicles, where quick acceleration and power delivery are essential for performance and safety. Overall, fuel cells are good at load following within their operating range (especially PEM fuel cells) but are typically used for steady or slowly varying power outputs. They lack the inertia of large rotating machines, but power electronics can manage output smoothly.

Hydrogen fuel cells have minimal environmental impact at the point of use. Since there is no combustion, they emit no NOx, SOx, CO, or particulate pollution—the exhaust is only water and waste heat (US Department of Energy, 2006). This makes fuel cells a zero-emission technology on-site (assuming the hydrogen is produced cleanly). They operate quietly and feature fewer moving components, which lowers both noise and certain maintenance requirements.

### *Hydrogen Turbines*

Hydrogen turbines represent another promising technology for converting hydrogen into electricity. They leverage proven turbine technology, enabling large-scale power generation (tens to hundreds of MW) with zero $CO_2$ emissions. These systems are essentially gas turbines that have been either adapted or specifically designed to use hydrogen as their primary fuel source. A key advantage of hydrogen turbines is the potential to leverage the extensive existing infrastructure of natural gas power plants. Many conventional natural gas turbines can be modified to co-fire hydrogen with natural gas or, in some cases, to operate on pure hydrogen. Multiple manufacturers have prototypes or early deployments of turbines running on high hydrogen fuels.

The efficiency of a hydrogen gas turbine is comparable to a natural gas turbine of similar design. Modern heavy-duty gas turbines reach about 35–42% efficiency in simple cycle (open cycle) and ~60–62% in combined-cycle configurations (Davison, 2016). While there are technical challenges, using hydrogen instead of methane does not fundamentally change the thermodynamic efficiency of gas turbine. However, in practice many hydrogen turbines will use methods to limit NOx emission, which can slightly reduce efficiency. For instance, injecting nitrogen or steam into the combustor can make a hydrogen turbine 0.4–1.3 points less efficient than a natural gas turbine (Davison, 2016).

The capital cost associated with gas turbine power plants varies depending on the size, technology (simple cycle vs. combined cycle), and fuel type. For purpose-built hydrogen gas turbines, a 2021 study estimated the cost to be around $1320/kW (Hernandez & Gençer, 2021). If an existing natural gas turbine plant is being retrofitted to burn hydrogen, the incremental cost is much lower than a new build. Retrofitting primarily involves modifying or replacing combustors, fuel supply systems, and perhaps turbine materials. According to the US Department of Energy's 'Pathways to Commercial Liftoff: Clean Hydrogen' report (2023), such retrofits can cost approximately $25 million for a 100 MW facility (i.e., around $250/kW), with costs varying based on the targeted hydrogen blending percentage (US Department of Energy, 2023). Notably, retrofitting costs appear particularly favourable for aging plants approaching retirement, potentially offering a pathway for extending their operational life while transitioning to lower-carbon generation.

Gas turbines, in general, are known for their relatively fast start-up times compared to other types of thermal power plants. The relatively quick start-up times and good load-following capabilities of hydrogen turbines make them particularly suitable for complementing intermittent renewable energy sources. They can be rapidly brought online when renewable output is low and quickly adjust their power output to balance supply and demand, playing a crucial role in maintaining the stability and reliability of the electricity grid.

The primary emission from hydrogen combustion is NOx. Because hydrogen contains no carbon, burning it in a turbine emits no $CO_2$, CO, or $SO_2$. This is a huge advantage for climate goals—a hydrogen turbine can generate hundreds of MW with zero carbon emissions (assuming green hydrogen). However, the high flame temperature of hydrogen in air leads to formation of nitrogen oxides (NOx) from the air's $N_2$ and $O_2$ (Altria & Jacobs, 2024). NOx is a regulated pollutant (it contributes to smog and acid rain), so hydrogen turbines must employ mitigation strategies.

### *Hydrogen Internal Combustion Engines (ICEs)*

Hydrogen internal combustion engines are modified reciprocating engines (like modified gasoline or natural gas engines) that burn hydrogen fuel to drive pistons and produce mechanical work, which spins a generator. They are essentially spark-ignition engines running on hydrogen, with adaptations to handle hydrogen's properties. $H_2$ ICEs can be based on existing engine designs (trucks, generators, etc.), offering a potentially lower-cost and familiar pathway to use hydrogen. These engines can range from small (automotive) to large industrial engines. A number of demonstration projects are exploring hydrogen ICEs for stationary power generation, backup generators, and heavy-duty vehicles (like trucks and locomotives), seeing them as a complement or interim step to fuel cells. While they still involve combustion, and thus are not zero-emission in terms of NOx, they eliminate $CO_2$ emissions when running on hydrogen fuel.

Hydrogen ICEs have lower efficiency than fuel cells but can be comparable to or slightly better than conventional hydrocarbon-fuelled engines. A report by McKinsey & Company puts the tank to wheel efficiency at around 30% for ICE engine based on renewable hydrogen. The research on hydrogen ICE is progressing but remains primarily focused on automotive applications rather than utility-scale power generation. As documented by Davison (2016), BMW's prototype hydrogen ICE, featuring a specialised cylinder head and direct hydrogen injection at pressures up to 300 bar, achieved an impressive 42% efficiency—comparable to leading automotive turbo diesel engines. This efficiency benchmark, while encouraging, derives from smaller engines than would be required for utility power generation. In contrast, practical field experience with hydrogen-rich fuels exists in the form of 12 Jenbacher gas engines operating at a Spanish coke factory since 1995, which maintain a consistent 37% efficiency when running on coke oven gas containing 50–60% hydrogen, or when using a 60% coke oven gas mixture with natural gas (Davison, 2016).

One potential advantage of hydrogen internal combustion engines is their potentially lower capital cost compared to hydrogen fuel cell systems (Heid et al., 2021). This cost advantage stems from the fact that hydrogen ICEs largely utilise existing internal combustion engine technology, which is mature and produced at scale. The primary costs associated with hydrogen ICEs involve the necessary engine modifications to ensure compatibility with hydrogen fuel, such as the installation of specialized hydrogen fuel injection systems, adjustments to the intake and exhaust systems, and potentially upgrades to the ignition system. While these modifications do incur costs, the overall capital expenditure for a hydrogen ICE is generally expected to be lower than that for a comparable fuel cell system, which involves more complex and currently less mature technology.

Lastly, although hydrogen internal combustion engines emit no carbon at the tailpipe, NOx emissions remain a concern, requiring ongoing development of emission control technologies to comply with strict environmental standards and support cleaner air.

Among the three types of technology, hydrogen-fired gas turbines are currently the most commercially compatible option for converting hydrogen to electricity, mainly because they can integrate with existing centralised generation assets. These turbines offer a pragmatic pathway for partial decarbonisation of existing dispatchable capacity, allowing utilities to retrofit some natural-gas assets for hydrogen use and reduce barriers to demonstration-scale adoption, though their contribution is likely to complement rather than replace other low-carbon flexibility options. Furthermore, their operational characteristics, including rapid start-up and flexible load-following capabilities, make hydrogen gas turbines particularly suitable for integration into grids increasingly reliant on variable renewable sources. Given the growing need to balance intermittent renewable generation, the adaptability and responsiveness of hydrogen turbines could provide targeted support for maintaining grid stability during rare, extended renewable shortfalls, rather than serving as a routine balancing tool.

In contrast, fuel cells and hydrogen ICE, while promising in certain niche applications, face limitations that reduce their potential for widespread adoption in large-scale electricity generation. Fuel cells provide significant environmental advantages and high energy conversion efficiency, yet their relatively high upfront costs and technical complexity limit large-scale grid deployment. Their applications are likely to remain specialised, such as distributed generation in locations sensitive to emissions or noise.

Similarly, hydrogen ICEs offer the advantage of lower upfront costs and ease of adoption through the conversion of existing engine infrastructure; however, their relatively lower efficiency and operational scale limitations suggest that their role will predominantly be transitional or confined to smaller, decentralised power applications. Consequently, among available hydrogen-based technologies, hydrogen-fired gas turbines are best positioned for early, large-scale demonstrations and limited deployment in the electricity sector because of their compatibility with existing infrastructure and operational flexibility, though their long-term use is expected to remain focused on specific system-balancing needs.

### *Countries with Hydrogen-to-Power Strategy*

Several countries have launched pilot projects and policy measures that explore hydrogen's potential role within their power sectors, notably Japan, South Korea, Germany, the Netherlands, the United States, Australia, and the United Kingdom. In most cases, these initiatives are experimental or complementary rather than core components of national power-sector strategies.

Japan, a pioneer in hydrogen demonstrations for power generation, views hydrogen as one of several tools—alongside renewables, nuclear, and efficiency measures—for enhancing energy security and progressing towards carbon neutrality. Through its Basic Hydrogen Strategy, Japan has invested substantially in demonstration projects involving hydrogen co-firing in gas turbines, aligning hydrogen incentives with broader goals of achieving a hydrogen-based society. A cornerstone of this effort is Mitsubishi Power's establishment of the Takasago Hydrogen Park in February 2022, recognised as the world's first integrated validation centre for hydrogen production and utilization in power generation (Mitsubishi Power, 2023). This facility has achieved a successful demonstration of 30% hydrogen co-firing in a 450 MW class JAC large frame gas turbine connected to the electricity grid at the T-Point 2 combined cycle power plant validation facility (MPS, 2024). Looking forward, Mitsubishi Power has outlined plans for further advancements, including a 100% hydrogen firing demonstration in gas turbine in the next step (Mitsubishi Power, 2023). These developments underscore a strong commitment to advancing hydrogen power generation technologies.

Beyond pilot projects, Japan is witnessing the initial stages of commercial hydrogen utilisation. In November 2024, JERA began the first commercial supply of electricity produced from hydrogen-powered, zero-emission thermal generation to Toho Studios (JERA, 2024). This project employs hydrogen receiving and supply equipment, a 320 kW hydrogen gas engine, and two 35 kW hydrogen fuel cell generators, demonstrating the feasibility of hydrogen for providing clean power to commercial operations. These initiatives, coupled with the strategic establishment of the Takasago Hydrogen Park, signify a momentum in Japan's pursuit of a hydrogen use for power generation.

Similarly, South Korea's Hydrogen Economy Roadmap includes ambitious targets for stationary fuel-cell deployment, mainly to diversify generation and support grid resilience. By 2023, the country had surpassed 1 GW of installed fuel cell capacity for power generation, an achievement that positions South Korea as a leader in the global fuel cell market and home to some of the world's largest fuel cell facilities, such as the 78.96 MW Shinincheon Bitdream Fuel Cell Power Plant (CMS, 2024).

The launch of the world's first auction for clean hydrogen power generation in 2024 represents another crucial step forward for South Korea. The first auction under the Clean Hydrogen Portfolio Standard (CHPS) aimed to award contracts for up to 6500 GWh of electricity per year over a 15-year period, with commercial operation expected to begin by 2028 (Baker McKenzie, 2024). While Korea Southern Power (KOSPO) was selected as the preferred bidder for 750 GWh/year, utilizing ammonia co-firing technology (Atchison, 2024), the auction was reportedly undersubscribed, indicating potential challenges in the current economics of clean hydrogen power generation (S&P Global Commodity Insights, 2024). The government anticipates that future auctions may see greater participation as infrastructure develops and power grid connections improve.

In Europe, Germany and the Netherlands stand out for including hydrogen-to-power pilot and readiness measures within broader national hydrogen strategies and incentive frameworks, while maintaining a primary focus on industrial and system-balancing applications. Germany, driven by aggressive coal phase-out targets, strategically integrates hydrogen through gas turbine hydrogen-fired turbines. Germany's hydrogen power plant strategy initially included three categories: hydrogen sprinters (Purpose-built turbines running on hydrogen from day on), hydrogen hybrids (Co-location of hydrogen capabilities with solar PV or onshore wind for balancing), and hydrogen-ready plants (Gas-fired turbines with a roadmap to switch to hydrogen no later than 2040) (McWilliams & Zachmann, 2024). However, due to a November 2023 constitutional court ruling affecting budget allocations, the plan was revised to focus on hydrogen-ready plants (McWilliams & Zachmann, 2024).

The Netherlands is also making strides in deploying hydrogen for power generation through several pilot projects. A notable initiative is underway at Uniper's Rotterdam Capelle (RoCa) power plant, where Thomassen Energy is retrofitting an existing gas turbine with their HyFlex LEC-III™ combustion system to enable operation with hydrogen-natural gas blends, initially targeting 30% hydrogen with a long-term vision of achieving 0–100% hydrogen flexibility (PSM, 2025). Beyond conventional turbine applications, Dutch startup HyER Power is developing an innovative large-scale plant designed to generate both electricity and heat directly from hydrogen using a combination of heat pump, fuel cell system, and energy storage technology, with operations expected to begin by late 2025 at Innovation Hub KAAP in Vlissingen (PV Magazine, 2025). These diverse pilot projects are expected to collectively contribute to the advancement and understanding of hydrogen production, transportation, and utilisation in the Netherlands.

The United States and Australia similarly combine abundant renewable resources with policy incentives that encourage exploration of hydrogen's role in future low-carbon power generation, primarily through limited demonstration and hydrogen-ready infrastructure. The United States, through the Inflation Reduction Act, provides targeted tax credits to stimulate hydrogen production for the use in various sectors. In the power sector, hydrogen co-firing in existing natural gas turbine plants has emerged as a viable strategy for reducing carbon emissions while leveraging current infrastructure, as demonstrated by several successful projects across the United States. The US Energy Information Administration (EIA) highlights key examples, including the Long Ridge Energy Generation Project in Ohio, a 485-MW combined-cycle facility, which in March 2022 effectively burned a 5% hydrogen blend, confirming initial compatibility with existing systems (EIA, 2024). Similarly, Georgia Power's Jack McDonough plant achieved a 7% reduction in $CO_2$ emissions by co-firing up to 20% hydrogen in June 2022, while the New York Power Authority's Brentwood plant, testing blends up to 44% hydrogen in September 2022, recorded a 14% $CO_2$ reduction at a 35% hydrogen mix. These initiatives underscore the interest in hydrogen gas turbines as a means of facilitating of the United States' transition to clean power generation.

Australia's National Hydrogen Strategy, although oriented towards exports, also aims to incentivise domestic hydrogen utilisation for power generation, focusing on renewable hydrogen projects. Recognizing the long-term potential of hydrogen in the power sector, there is a growing trend towards developing hydrogen-ready infrastructure. The Tallawarra B Power Station in New South Wales is a leading example, using GE's 9F.05 gas turbine that can operate on natural gas and hydrogen blends, starting from 5% with ability to increase to 100% hydrogen (GE, 2024). This 320 MW plant helps stabilize the grid during peak demand and supports NSW's net-zero goal by 2050 (GE, 2024). Similarly, the Brigalow Peaking Power Plant in Queensland is being developed as a 400 MW natural gas power plant with the future capability to operate on hydrogen (Power Technology, 2024). Australia's approach highlights hydrogen as a potential complement for balancing variable renewables and for gradually decarbonising existing gas infrastructure, though its role remains prospective and supplementary within the overall energy transition

*What Does the Review Tell Us?*

The above review shows that Hydrogen's promise as a low-carbon fuel has garnered attention across countries such as Japan, Australia, South Korea, the Netherlands, Germany, the United Kingdom, and the United States, though each country's motivations reflect its particular energy and industrial context. Overall, a key common factor is the drive towards industrial decarbonisation, especially in sectors such as steel, chemicals, and cement, where direct electrification is difficult. Similarly, long-term energy security is another shared rationale: countries with extensive energy import dependencies (e.g., Japan, South Korea) want to diversify their fuel sources, while resource-rich nations (e.g., Australia, the United States) hope to develop robust domestic or export-oriented hydrogen markets.

Despite these broad convergences, differences emerge in how each country positions hydrogen's role alongside other low-carbon technologies. For instance, Japan emphasizes hydrogen not only for industrial or transport applications but also as a cornerstone of its overall energy strategy, seeking to mitigate dependence on imported LNG through an extensive hydrogen supply chain network. By contrast, Australia seeks to leverage its vast solar and wind resources to become a global exporter of green hydrogen, with domestic use often positioned as a secondary but complementary step in building a larger hydrogen economy. In Germany, industrial applications remain pivotal but are heavily underscored by the ambition to integrate hydrogen with a rapidly expanding renewables sector, offering a buffer against the intermittency of wind and solar and supporting the nation's high manufacturing base. Meanwhile, the Netherlands looks to transform its existing gas infrastructure—and its strategic location around the Port of Rotterdam—into a hydrogen hub for broader European markets.

No single country has made power-sector reliability concerns—such as addressing Dunkelflaute—the primary or sole driver for large-scale hydrogen deployment. While countries with high shares of variable renewables (like Germany) do indeed reference hydrogen's potential for storing surplus renewable power and mitigating 'dark doldrums', in practice, that is one reason among several (often secondary to industrial decarbonisation, energy security, or technological leadership). Thus, while power sector needs are a significant factor, they don't take precedence over other goals in any of these nations' strategies.

There are countries that, despite having clean power sector targets and overall net-zero commitments, have chosen alternative decarbonisation pathways rather than incentivising hydrogen in electricity generation. For instance, countries with limited existing gas infrastructure, constrained financial resources, or uncertainty regarding hydrogen's long-term cost-effectiveness have adopted a cautious or observational approach to hydrogen incentives in power generation. These countries typically prefer investing directly in mature renewable technologies, demand-side management, or grid interconnection projects due to quicker returns, lower immediate risks, and clearer economic benefits. Thus, differences in energy resource endowment, infrastructure readiness, economic capacity, and risk tolerance underpin the variation in national strategies regarding hydrogen incentives for electricity generation.

The comparative analysis of international hydrogen strategies also highlights a critical insight: while technical solutions are advancing rapidly across fuel cells, turbines, and internal combustion engines, the economic viability of hydrogen-to-power applications remains heavily dependent on supportive policy frameworks. Countries pursuing hydrogen as part of their power sector decarbonisation strategy face a common challenge-creating mechanism that appropriately value hydrogen's unique contribution to system resilience while managing the substantial investment risks across the nascent value chain. Without carefully designed support policies that recognize both the cross-chain dependencies and the specific value proposition of hydrogen in addressing extended renewable generation shortfalls, market signals alone appear insufficient to drive deployment at the scale needed. The higher capital and operational costs compared to conventional alternatives necessitate targeted interventions that bridge the economic gap during the technology's early commercial phase while establishing a pathway to eventual market competitiveness. In the next section, we analyse the United Kingdom's Hydrogen-to-Power business model as an instructive case study of how one country is addressing these policy challenges and extract key lessons that may guide other nations in designing effective support frameworks for their own hydrogen-to-power initiatives.

## Case Study: Hydrogen-to-Power in the United Kingdom

The UK government has committed to delivering a clean power system by 2030, which will require significant deployment of low carbon flexible generation capacity to complement intermittent renewables (DESNZ, 2024). Within this context hydrogen-to-power (H2P)—the conversion of low carbon hydrogen to produce low carbon electricity—has been identified as a key technology that can perform various functions. This includes functions such as providing dispatchable low carbon electricity generation during extended periods of low renewable output; replacing system services traditionally provided by unabated gas generation; offering a viable decarbonisation pathway for existing gas-fired power plants and finally supporting seasonal energy storage through the conversion of excess renewable electricity to hydrogen.

The National Energy System Operator (NESO) estimates that the UK electricity system could need approximately 40–45 GW of long-duration flexible capacity by 2030, with hydrogen power identified as 'an important requirement for a clean power system' (DESNZ, 2024, p. 4). According to government analysis, hydrogen demand in the power sector could reach 5–30 TWh by 2035, with hydrogen-to-power capacity potentially growing to 5–12 GW in the same timeframe (DESNZ, 2023a).

However, hydrogen-to-power faces several risk and barriers. Therefore, although the UK government acknowledged that certain hydrogen power plants could be implemented via existing market frameworks, further targeted support is required to address major deployment barriers. These include uncertainty and higher investment risks associated with hydrogen power as a First-of-a-Kind (FOAK) technology, as well as reliance on emerging critical infrastructure—production, transport, and storage—leading to 'cross-chain risks' and fuel supply challenges.

To address these barriers, the government commissioned extensive analysis to evaluate potential support mechanisms, starting with a long list of fifteen options that was narrowed down to six contenders for detailed assessment (LCP Delta and Frontier Economics, 2023) as shown in Fig. 6.5.

These options were assessed against criteria including effectiveness, investability, cost efficiency, and strategic fit and deliverability. After further analysis, three models were shortlisted for final consideration: the DPA-style mechanism, Split CM, and Revenue Cap and Floor (DESNZ, 2023a).

The government ultimately decided to discount the Split CM and Revenue Cap and Floor options for the following reasons. First while Split CM model would reduce inframarginal rents compared to the standard CM, it would still expose investors to fuel availability risk through non-delivery penalties. Second, with limited initial H2P plants competing, there were concerns about auction liquidity and competitiveness. The government also noted that implementing CM reforms would take considerable time, potentially delaying H2P deployment (DESNZ, 2024).

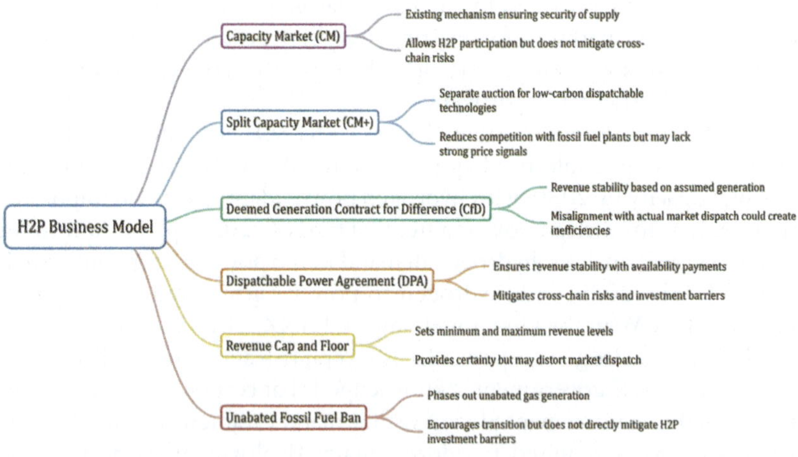


**Fig. 6.5** Options considered for hydrogen-to-power business model in the United Kingdom. (Source: Authors)

Revenue Cap and Floor model was rejected primarily because it could create perverse incentives around dispatch. If operators expected to end a reconciliation period below the floor or above the cap, they would have no economic incentive to dispatch efficiently. The government concluded that this approach is 'more suited to technologies with high CapEx, low and stable operating costs, and where significant barriers to entry exist' rather than dispatchable power technologies with variable operating costs (DESNZ, 2023b, p.14).

Deemed Generation CfD model was found unsuitable for dispatchable technologies as it was designed for intermittent renewables. The concept of providing support based on deemed output introduces additional risks for H2P operators, particularly if metered output diverges from deemed output while electricity prices change (DESNZ, 2023b).

### *The Hydrogen-to-Power Business Model*

Following consultation and stakeholder feedback, the UK government committed in December 2024 to implement a DPA-style mechanism as the Hydrogen-to-Power Business Model (H2P BM). This decision was supported by the majority of consultation respondents, who agreed that a DPA-style approach would be most effective in mitigating key deployment barriers (DESNZ, 2024).

The H2P BM is based on elements of the Dispatchable Power Agreement designed for Power CCUS but adapted to suit the specific needs of hydrogen power. Its primary features include:

1. **Availability Payment**: A fixed capacity-based payment, payable over time irrespective of usage, which generates predictable revenue to cover investment costs and de-risks the project for investors. Crucially, unlike the Capacity Market, this payment would not be strictly tied to security of supply conditions, helping mitigate cross-chain risks by continuing to provide support even if hydrogen fuel becomes unavailable due to infrastructure issues (DESNZ, 2023a).
2. **Optional Variable Payment**: The government is considering whether to include a variable payment component (paid per unit of output) to influence dispatch. Stakeholder views on this were mixed, with some noting it could help H2P dispatch ahead of unabated gas but others warning of potential market distortions (DESNZ, 2024). The government is continuing to analyse whether such a payment is

necessary, particularly given the interaction with the Hydrogen Production Business Model, which already subsidises hydrogen fuel costs.

3. **Allocation Approach**: The government intends to initially allocate H2P BM contracts through bilateral negotiation, transitioning to price-based competitive allocation as the technology matures and enabling infrastructure expands. This addresses concerns about limited initial market liquidity that could undermine a purely competitive approach in the early years (DESNZ, 2023a).
4. **Contract Duration**: While specific details are still being developed, contracts are expected to run for 10–15 years, providing long-term revenue certainty to investors (DESNZ, 2023a).

The H2P BM is designed as a time-limited intervention rather than a permanent subsidy. The government's vision is that as technology costs decline and the hydrogen economy matures, H2P plants will eventually be able to compete through the Capacity Market or other market mechanisms without specific support (DESNZ, 2024).

### *Challenges of UK H2P BM*

Stakeholder feedback through the consultation process highlighted several key challenges that need to be addressed for successful H2P deployment. The most frequently cited concern was the alignment and coordination of policies across the hydrogen value chain (DESNZ, 2024). There are concerns that hydrogen infrastructure (production, transport, storage) may not come forward in the right places, at the right time, or with sufficient capacity to support H2P deployment.

Some market participants expressed significant concerns about hydrogen fuel availability in a nascent market. The Capacity Market's non-delivery penalties were highlighted as a major risk, as plant operators could face penalties during system stress events if hydrogen fuel was unavailable due to cross-chain issues beyond their control (DESNZ, 2024).

Some stakeholders questioned whether the technology is sufficiently mature for widespread deployment, noting challenges related to NOx emissions from hydrogen combustion and the higher capital costs associated with FOAK technology. However, others argued that hydrogen-capable turbines are relatively mature, with several OEMs targeting commercial availability soon (DESNZ, 2024).

### *Lessons for Other Countries*

Several valuable lessons emerge from the United Kingdom's approach to supporting hydrogen-to-power for other countries considering similar initiatives. Recognizing the need for coordinated support across the entire hydrogen value chain—from production to transport, storage, and end use—represents a holistic strategy that acknowledges the 'chicken-and-egg' problem of hydrogen deployment. This challenge, where producers need assured off-take and consumers need reliable supply, suggests that other nations would benefit from similar integrated planning rather than addressing individual segments in isolation.

Specific business models developed for different parts of the hydrogen economy (production, transport, storage, power) demonstrate the necessity for targeted interventions addressing unique challenges and risks in each segment. Implementing a DPA-style mechanism for H2P rather than adapting existing mechanisms like the CM or CfD reflects a clear understanding that nascent technologies may require bespoke support.

A phased transition from government support to market competition offers another important lesson. Beginning with bilateral negotiations for early projects, then moving to competitive allocation within the H2P BM, and eventually transitioning to wider market mechanisms like the Capacity Market provides a clear 'glide path' for the technology. This staged approach could serve as a template for other countries to balance initial deployment targets with long-term market efficiency.

Focusing on developing hydrogen infrastructure within industrial clusters provides a practical model worth emulating. By concentrating initial hydrogen demand and production in these areas, economies of scale can be achieved while reducing infrastructure costs. Locating major H2P projects within these clusters leverages shared infrastructure and reduces cross-chain risks.

Maintaining flexibility in policy approach, with regular consultations and adaptations based on stakeholder feedback and evolving market conditions, represents another crucial strategy. Ongoing analysis regarding whether a variable payment component is necessary in the H2P BM based on mixed stakeholder views exemplifies the adaptability essential in a rapidly evolving technological landscape.

Finally, providing conversion pathways for existing gas-fired power plants rather than solely promoting new-build hydrogen plants maximizes the use of existing assets and grid connections while reducing overall system costs. Nations with substantial gas generation fleets might similarly benefit from focused support for conversion pathways.

## Conclusions

Hydrogen emerges as a potential solution for addressing the fundamental challenge of extended renewable generation shortfalls during Dunkelflaute events—periods of simultaneously low wind and solar output that can persist for days or weeks. Unlike batteries, which become prohibitively expensive when scaled for multi-day energy deficits, hydrogen offers unique capabilities for seasonal storage at the scale required by weather-dependent power systems. It can be produced during periods of renewable abundance, stored in large quantities in geological formations like salt caverns, and converted back to electricity when needed most, providing dispatchable low-carbon power during critical supply shortages.

The United Kingdom's development of a dedicated Hydrogen-to-Power Business Model (H2P BM), featuring availability payments and long-term contracts negotiated bilaterally before transitioning to competitive allocation, demonstrates growing policy recognition of hydrogen's potential contribution to system resilience. This approach specifically addresses the cross-chain risks and investment uncertainties that could otherwise impede deployment, while providing a clear 'glide path' from government support to eventual market competition through mechanisms like the Capacity Market.

Despite these advantages, hydrogen faces significant technical and economic challenges. The hydrogen-to-power pathway suffers from relatively low round-trip efficiency, raising legitimate concerns about energy wastage and overall system costs. Different conversion technologies present distinct trade-offs: fuel cells offer higher efficiency (up to 60–80% for SOFCs) but at higher capital costs per unit capacity, while hydrogen-fired gas turbines enable utility-scale output with established technology but lower efficiency (35–42% in simple cycle, 60–62% in combined cycle) and potential NOx emission challenges. The analysis suggests hydrogen turbines are the most technically compatible option for near-term, large-scale demonstrations, given their alignment with existing infrastructure and ability to use retrofitted gas assets. However, they are expected to complement rather than dominate other low-carbon flexibility sources in future power systems.

Economic challenges further complicate hydrogen's deployment in power systems. The substantial capital requirements across the hydrogen value chain necessitate coordinated policy support for production, transport, storage, and end-use applications. As demonstrated in the UK case study, early hydrogen power projects depend heavily on government intervention to mitigate investment risks associated with first-of-a-kind technology. Without policy frameworks that specifically value multi-day to seasonal flexibility, market signals alone may prove insufficient to drive adequate hydrogen deployment.

The international review reveals that no country deploys hydrogen primarily to address power sector challenges like Dunkelflaute. Instead, hydrogen is consistently positioned as a multi-purpose tool within comprehensive energy transition strategies, addressing industrial decarbonization, energy security, and export opportunities alongside power system needs. Japan and South Korea have made significant progress in hydrogen power demonstrations, including successful co-firing in gas turbines and deployment of fuel cell capacity. Meanwhile, Germany, the Netherlands, the United States, and Australia are advancing various approaches to hydrogen production and power generation, though each with distinct national contexts and priorities.

A balanced path forward recognizes that the bulk of flexibility in renewable power systems will continue to come from batteries, pumped hydro, interconnection, and demand-side response, while hydrogen provides a selective, long-duration complement for rare, multi-day or seasonal supply shortages. This approach depends on three key enablers: significant wind and solar deployment to provide both abundant renewable electricity and the need for long-duration storage; development of essential infrastructure along the hydrogen value chain; and supportive policy and market frameworks that properly value hydrogen's unique capabilities. Under these circumstances, hydrogen-to-power could serve as a flexible, dispatchable, and low-carbon backup option that helps maintain grid stability during prolonged renewable shortfalls, complementing batteries, interconnections, and demand-side flexibility.

In summary, hydrogen's role in the power sector is likely to remain strategic but limited-focused on ensuring reliability during extreme events rather than serving as a routine source of electricity. Its value lies in complementing, not competing with, direct electrification and other flexibility measures.

## References

Altria, G., & Jacobs, H. (2024). *Understanding hydrogen combustion and NOx emissions* [Online]. Retrieved March 19, 2025, from https://www.slrconsulting.com/us/insights/understanding-hydrogen-combustion-and-nox-emissions/

Atchison, J. (2024). *Korea Southern Power selected as final bidder in national clean power auction* [Online]. Retrieved March 20, 2025, from https://ammoniaenergy.org/articles/korea-southern-power-selected-as-final-bidder-in-national-clean-power-auction/.

Baker McKenzie. (2024). *Hydrogen Developments: South Korea* [Online]. Retrieved March 20, 2025, from https://resourcehub.bakermckenzie.com/en/resources/hydrogen-heat-map/asia-pacific/south-korea/topics/hydrogen-developments.

Bloom Energy. (2025). *What are the advantages of hydrogen fuel cells?* [Online]. Retrieved March 19, 2025, from https://www.bloomenergy.com/blog/what-are-the-advantages-of-hydrogen-fuel-cells/.

Calero, I., Cañizares, C. A., Bhattacharya, K., & Baldick, R. (2022). Duck-curve mitigation in power grids with high penetration of PV generation. *IEEE Transactions on Smart Grid, 13*(1), 314–329.

CMS. (2024). *Hydrogen law, regulations & strategy in South Korea* [Online]. Retrieved March 20, 2025, from https://cms.law/en/int/expert-guides/cms-expert-guide-to-hydrogen/south-korea

Dai, X., et al. (2024). Hydrogen energy in electrical power systems: A review and future outlook. *Electronics, 13*(3370), 1–12.

Davison, J. (2016). *A review of gas turbines and their ability to use hydrogen-containing fuel gas.* [Online]. Retrieved March 19, 2025, from https://ukerc.rl.ac.uk/ETI/PUBLICATIONS/AdHoc_CCS_CC1011_12.pdf

DESNZ. (2023a). *Hydrogen to power: Consultation on the need, and design, for a hydrogen to power market intervention.* Department for Energy Security and Net Zero.

DESNZ. (2023b). *The need for government intervention to support hydrogen to power.* Department for Energy Security and Net Zero.

DESNZ. (2024). *Hydrogen to power: Government response to consultation on the need, and design, for a Hydrogen to Power market intervention.* Department for Energy Security and Net Zero.

Duchêne, F., et al. (2024). Current-day and future Dunkelflaute risks for Belgium. *Journal of Applied Meteorology and Climatology, 63*(11), 1–11.

EIA. (2024). *U.S. electric power sector explores hydrogen cofiring at natural gas-fired plants* [Online]. Retrieved March 21, 2025, from https://www.eia.gov/todayinenergy/detail.php?id=63084.

ENTSO-E. (n.d.). *Transparency platform.* European Network of Transmission System Operators for Electricity. Retrieved March 12, 2025, from https://transparency.entsoe.eu/.

GE. (2024). *Opening of Australia's first dual-fuel gas and green hydrogen capable power plant in New South Wales* [Online]. Retrieved March 21, 2025, from https://www.ge.com/news/press-releases/opening-of-australia-first-dual-fuel-gas-and-green-hydrogen-capable-power-plant-in.

Ghanbarzadeh, T., Habibi, D., & Aziz, A. (2024). Generation expansion planning in isolated power systems: A robust approach with Dunkelflaute assessment. *IEEE Access, 12*, 165831–165844.

H2FC. (2025). *H2FC Lab* [Online]. Retrieved November 29, 2025, from https://hydrogenfc.netlify.app/.

Heid, B., Martens, C., & Orthofer, A. (2021). *How hydrogen combustion engines can contribute to zero emissions* [Online]. Retrieved March 19, 2025, from https://www.mckinsey.com/industries/automotive-and-assembly/our-insights/how-hydrogen-combustion-engines-can-contribute-to-zero-emissions

Hernandez, D. D., & Gençer, E. (2021). Techno-economic analysis of balancing California's power system on a seasonal basis: Hydrogen vs. lithium-ion batteries. *Applied Energy, 300*, 11–22.

Horizon Educational. (2023). *Hydrogen guide: Are fuel cell stacks really worth it?* [Online]. Retrieved March 19, 2025, from https://www.horizoneducational.com/hydrogen-guide-are-fuel-cell-stacks-really-worth-it/t1429?currency=usd

JERA. (2024). *Japan's first commercial use of electricity generated with hydrogen-fired zero-emissions thermal – JERA begins supplying hydrogen-generated power to Toho Studios* [Online]. Retrieved March 20, 2025, from https://www.jera.co.jp/en/news/information/20241129_2071.

Kittel, M., Roth, A., & Schill, W.P. (2025). *Coping with the Dunkelflaute: Power system implications of variable renewable energy droughts in Europe* [Online]. Retrieved November 12, 2025, from https://arxiv.org/abs/2411.17683.

Kittel, M., & Schill, W. P. (2024). Measuring the Dunkelflaute: How (not) to analyze variable renewable energy shortage. *Environmental Research: Energy, 1*(035007), 1–11.

Kubert, C. (2010). *Fuel cell technology: A clean, reliable source of stationary power. Clean Energy States Alliance.* [Online]. Retrieved March 19, 2025, from https://www.cesa.org/wp-content/uploads/CESA-fuelcelltechnology-may2010.pdf.

LCP Delta. (2023). *Role of hydrogen in decarbonising UK power generation* [Online]. Retrieved November 12, 2025, from https://www.centrica.com/media/j11h4c5j/h2p-whitepaper.pdf

Li, B., Basu, S., Watson, S. J., & Russchenberg, H. W. J. (2020). Quantifying the predictability of a 'Dunkelflaute' event by utilizing a mesoscale model. *Journal of Physics: Conference Series, 1618*(6), 1–16.

Li, B., Basu, S., Watson, S. J., & Russchenberg, H. W. J. (2021). A brief climatology of Dunkelflaute events over and surrounding the North and Baltic Sea areas. *Energies, 14*(20), 65–68.

Mayer, M. J., Biró, B., Szűcs, B., & Aszódi, A. (2023). Probabilistic modeling of future electricity systems with high renewable energy penetration using machine learning. *Applied Energy, 336*, 120801.

McWilliams, B., & Zachmann, G. (2024). *Four questions for Germany's big hydrogen power plan* [Online]. Retrieved March 20, 2025, from https://www.bruegel.org/analysis/four-questions-germanys-big-hydrogen-power-plan

Mitsubishi Power. (2023). *Takasago hydrogen park, the world's first integrated validation facility for technologies from hydrogen production to power generation, enters full-scale operation - electrolysis hydrogen production begins* [Online]. Retrieved March 19, 2025, from https://power.mhi.com/news/230920.html

Mockert, F., Grams, C. M., Brown, T., & Neumann, F. (2023). Meteorological conditions during Dunkelflauten in Germany: Characteristics, the role of weather regimes, and impacts on demand. *Meteorological Applications*. https://doi.org/10.1002/met.2141.

MPS. (2024). *Mitsubishi power demonstrates 30% $H_2$ in a JAC gas turbine* [Online]. Retrieved March 20, 2025, from https://www.modernpowersystems.com/analysis/mitsubishi-power-demonstrates-30-h2-in-a-jac-gas--turbine-11460855/.

Nikiforow, K., et al. (2018). Power ramp rate capabilities of a 5 kW proton exchange membrane fuel cell system with discrete ejector control. *Journal of Power Sources, 381*, 30–37.

Power Technology. (2024). *Brigalow peaking power plant, Australia* [Online]. Retrieved March 21, 2025, from https://www.power-technology.com/projects/brigalow-peaking-power-plant-australia/.

PSM. (2025). *Thomassen energy provides a hydrogen fuel-flexible retrofit solution to support decarbonization of Uniper gas turbine power plant* [Online]. Retrieved March 20, 2025, from https://www.psm.com/news-press-release-archive/thomassen-energy-provides-a-hydrogen-fuel-flexible-retrofit-solution-to--support-decarbonization-of-uniper-gas-turbine-power-plant.

PV Magazine. (2025). *Dutch startup developing large plant to generate heat, power from hydrogen* [Online]. Retrieved March 20, 2025, from https://www.pv-magazine.com/2025/03/19/dutch-startup-developing-large-plant-to--generate-heat-power-from-hydrogen/

Qvist, S., Al Hammadi, M., & Victor, D. G. (2023). Meeting the challenge of reliability on today's electric grids: The critical role of inertia. *Energy Insight*, 135, Oxford, UK: Oxford Institute for Energy Studies.

S&P Global Commodity Insights. (2024). *Korea's low-carbon hydrogen power tenders may need sweeteners to succeed: Experts* [Online]. Retrieved March 20, 2025, from https://www.spglobal.com/commodity-insights/en/news-research/

latest-news/energy-transition/121624-koreas-low-carbon-hydrogen-power--tenders-may-need-sweeteners-to-succeed-experts.

US Department of Energy. (2006). *Hydrogen fuel cells fact sheet* [Online]. Retrieved March 19, 2025, from https://www.californiahydrogen.org/wp--content/uploads/files/doe_fuelcell_factsheet.pdf.

US Department of Energy. (2017). *Fuel cells for stationary power applications* [Online]. Retrieved March 19, 2025, from https://www.energy.gov/eere/fuelcells/articles/fuel-cells-stationary-power-applications.

US Department of Energy. (2023). *Pathways to commercial liftoff: Clean hydrogen*. Washington, DC: U.S. Department of Energy [Online]. Retrieved March 19, 2025, from https://liftoff.energy.gov/wp-content/uploads/2023/05/LIFTOFF-Clean-Hydrogen_Updated-2.6.25.pdf

US Department of Energy. (2024). *Hydrogen and fuel cell technologies office multi-year program plan* [Online]. Retrieved March 19, 2025, from https://www.energy.gov/sites/default/files/2024-05/hfto-mypp-2024.pdf.

Wei, M. (2022). *Reversible fuel cell cost analysis and megawatt PEM cost analysis for $H_2$ grid storage systems* [Online]. Retrieved March 19, 2025, from https://www.hydrogen.energy.gov/docs/hydrogenprogramlibraries/pdfs/review22/fc332_wei_2022_p-pdf.pdf.

CHAPTER 7

# Hydrogen in Road and Rail Transport

## Introduction

At the moment, the transport sector with all its niches is responsible for at least a quarter of all the industrial carbon emissions (Fig. 7.1). Here, the road and rail transport sectors—currently operating internal combustion engine (ICE) vehicles and diesel-electric locomotives that rely heavily on fossil fuels like petrol, diesel, and, to a lesser extent, compressed natural gas (CNG)—account for approximately 12.5%. For more than a century, these energy sources have driven most global transportation, thanks to their high energy density, broad availability, and established infrastructure. However, the environmental and economic challenges associated with these conventional fuels are becoming increasingly apparent. Road transport alone accounts for approximately 12% of global carbon dioxide ($CO_2$) emissions, while rail transport with around 0.5% $CO_2$ emissions, though more efficient, still contributes significantly to greenhouse gas (GHG) releases, particularly in regions where diesel-powered trains are prevalent (IEA, 2023).

The reliance on fossil fuels in these sectors not only exacerbates climate change but also exposes economies to volatile energy prices and geopolitical risks. For instance, over the past few years, oil prices worldwide have fluctuated sharply due to geopolitical conflicts, disruptions in supply chains, and evolving demand patterns, affecting the cost of fuel. Therefore, these factors have underscored the need for more sustainable and resilient


A. Patonia, R. Poudineh, *Clean Hydrogen for Decarbonisation*,
https://doi.org/10.1007/978-3-032-19442-8_7

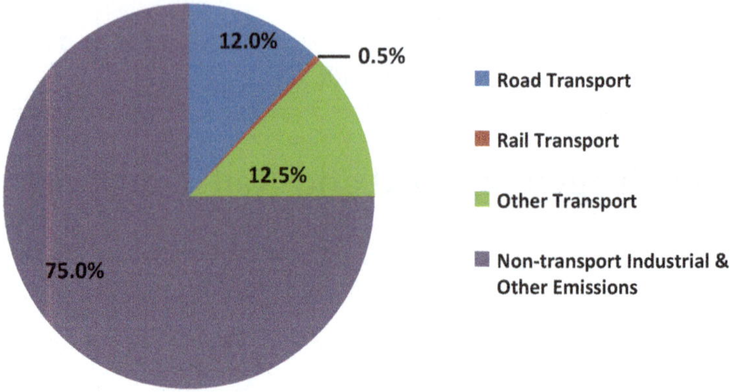


**Fig. 7.1** Approximate share of road and rail transport emissions. (Source: Adapted from IMO (2020), IEA (2021), IPCC (2021), OECD (2023), and World Resources Institute (2023))

energy solutions in the transport sector that will ideally be less vulnerable to such disruptions. Additionally, as with the growing population and economies, rail and road transport emissions will have to rise as well, if no decarbonisation measures are taken, stringent environmental regulations, such as the European Union's Fit for 55 package, are pushing the industry towards net-zero carbon, further highlighting the urgency of transitioning to cleaner energy sources.

Overall, at the moment, around 60% of the road vehicles around the world run on petrol (gasoline), with diesel being the second most popular fuel (Fig. 7.2). Although the sales of electric cars (EVs) are currently on the rise in many countries and regions of the world, including North America and Scandinavia, together with the remaining sustainable fuel alternatives to hydrocarbons-derived conventional propellants of internal combustion engines, currently they only take up to 10%. In the rail transport niche, however, the situation looks different: trains propelled by electricity are more popular and widely used globally compared to other propulsion methods, especially in regions with advanced rail infrastructure. Therefore, electricity's share is over half of the global market with diesel being only the runner-up with around 40% (Fig. 7.3). Here, the remaining sustainable options such as hydrogen, hybrid, and biofuels only constitute around 5%.

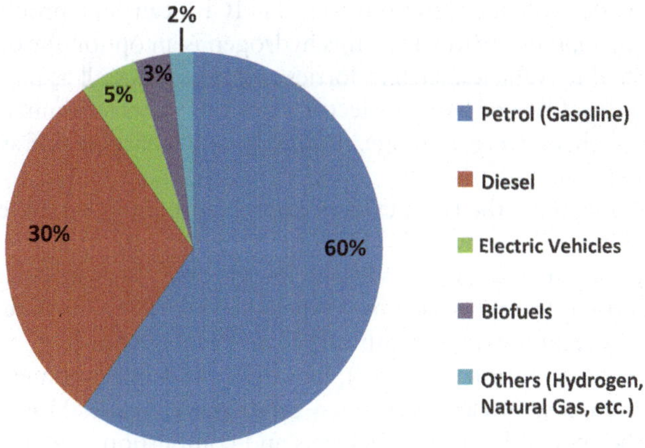


**Fig. 7.2** Approximate shares of key fuels in road transport. (Source: Adapted from EEA (2021), IPCC (2021), EIA (2023), ICCT (2023), IEA (2023a, 2023b, 2024))

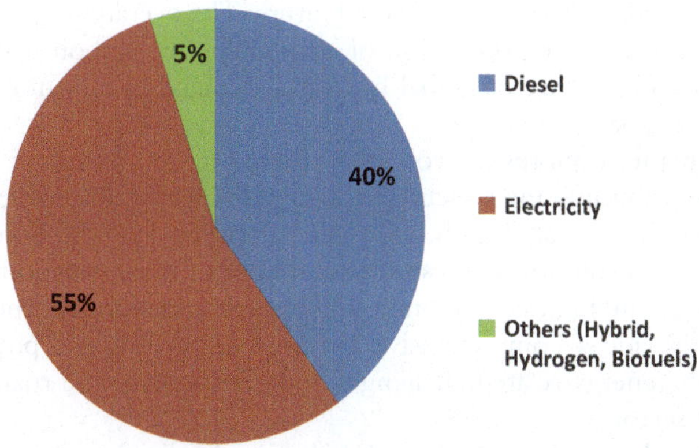


**Fig. 7.3** Approximate shares of key fuels in rail transport. (Source: Adapted from EEA (2021), IPCC (2021), EIA (2023), ICCT (2023), IEA (2023a, 2023b, 2024))

In this context, hydrogen is currently being viewed as an alternative fuel primarily for road and to specific cases of rail transport where other options such as direct electrification may not necessarily represent the most likely solution to the decarbonisation of this sector. Overall clean hydrogen can enable very low tailpipe emissions: fuel cells emit only water vapour, while hydrogen combustion ($H_2$-ICE) can still produce $NO_x$ without appropriate treatment. Thus hydrogen is an option for decarbonising heavy-duty vehicles, such as lorries and buses, as well as rail systems, where overhead line or battery-electric solutions may face limitations due to issues such as weight, range, topology and charging infrastructure constraints.

At the same time, the latest evidence points to a highly selective role for hydrogen: it is not a universal substitute but a niche solution where alternatives are impractical. In fact, despite its potential, hydrogen's adoption in road and rail transport faces several challenges. These include, among others, the need for extensive infrastructure development (e.g., refuelling stations and distribution networks), the current lack of economies of scale, and the high cost of clean hydrogen production overall. Moreover, the energy efficiency of hydrogen fuel cells and combustion engines must be improved to compete with conventional and other sustainable alternatives. Nevertheless, on-going advancements in hydrogen production, storage, and utilisation technologies, coupled with increasing policy support and private sector investment, are often expected to drive the sector towards a partially hydrogen-powered future. The overarching bottleneck, however, remains the production of affordable, low-carbon hydrogen at scale; transport's share of global hydrogen demand is currently less than 1% (IEA, 2023a).

This chapter explores the role of hydrogen in decarbonising road and rail transport, examining the current state of the sector, the challenges and opportunities associated with hydrogen adoption, and the potential for hydrogen to revolutionise these critical modes of transportation. By analysing the technological, economic, and regulatory landscape, this chapter aims to provide a comprehensive overview of hydrogen's potential to address the energy-related challenges and emissions of the road and rail transport sectors.

It proceeds as follows. Section "Hydrogen Applications in the Sector" explores the technological applications of hydrogen in road and rail transport, detailing key solutions like fuel cells and combustion engines, and analysing their advantages, disadvantages, and infrastructure requirements. Section "Economic Aspects" analyses the economic aspects, comparing costs against alternatives like battery-electric vehicles. Section "Policy and Regulatory Landscape" reviews the relevant policy and regulatory landscape governing hydrogen's adoption. Section "Case Studies and Pilot Projects" presents case studies and pilot projects from both road and rail sectors. Finally, Section "Future Outlook and Conclusions" offers a future outlook and conclusions on hydrogen's selective role in the decarbonisation of transport.[1]

## Hydrogen Applications in the Sector

### *Technological Solutions*

The currently suggested hydrogen-based propulsion technologies for road and rail transport primarily include fuel cell systems, hydrogen combustion engines, and hybrid configurations. Each of these solutions offers distinct advantages and challenges, with varying levels of technological maturity. Compared to alternatives such as battery electrification and biofuels, it is expected that hydrogen could present unique benefits, particularly for ***heavy-duty*** and ***long-distance*** applications where energy density and refuelling speed are critical. At the same time, $H_2$ also poses significant challenges, addressing which will need to be done in order for this fuel to successfully compete with other land transport decarbonisation options.

When it comes to fuel cells that transform energy contained in hydrogen into electrical power without generating carbon emissions, at the moment, Proton Exchange Membrane Fuel Cells (PEMFCs) represent the most mature and popular technology considered for transport applications when it comes to both road and rail land niches (Table 7.1). While their efficiencies typically range between 40 and 60% (Jiao & Li, 2021), they are currently viewed particularly suited for road vehicles, including buses and trucks, due to their rapid start-up and dynamic response (Mancino et al., 2023). For rail transport, PEMFCs are being integrated into hydrogen-powered trains, such as Alstom's Coradia iLint, which operates on non-electrified routes (Siwiec, 2021; Alstom, 2023). Here, although Solid Oxide Fuel Cells (SOFCs), which are expected to be able to utilise hydrogen, ammonia, or synthetic fuels, are also under exploration for rail due to their potential higher efficiency (45–65%), they face challenges related to high operating temperatures (700–1000°C), which affect their durability, and therefore currently keep them at a lower

[1] Because Chaps. 4, 5, and 6 already detail hydrogen transport, storage, and system-integration fundamentals, the infrastructure and regulatory discussion in Chaps. 7, 8, 9, 10, 11, 12, and 13 is intentionally limited to sector-specific requirements and bottlenecks; where general points would repeat, we cross-refer back to the earlier infrastructure chapters.

**Table 7.1** Key hydrogen-based transport solutions, their application, and technology readiness levels (TRL)

| *Technology* | *Currently considered key application (Road)* | *TRL (road)* | *Typical efficiency range (%) (Road)* | *Potential cost (Road)* | *Currently considered key application (Rail)* | *TRL (Rail)* | *Typical efficiency range (%) (Rail)* | *Potential cost (Rail)* | *Notes* |
|---|---|---|---|---|---|---|---|---|---|
| *PEMFCs* | Buses, lorries/trucks, cars | 8–9 (commercial) | 40–60 | High | Passenger trains | 7 (early commercial) | 45–55 | Very high | Dominant for road but limited rail deployment (niche applications where batteries are unsuitable) |
| *SOFCs* | Long-haul trucks (prototypes) | 5–6 (demonstration) | 45–65 | Very high | Freight/long-distance trains | 5 (R&D phase) | 50–60 | Very high | Higher efficiency but durability challenges |
| *$H_2$-ICE (Hydrogen Combustion Engines)* | Heavy-duty trucks (retrofits) | 6–7 (pilot deployments) | 35–45 | Moderate | Diesel locomotive conversions | 5–6 (testing phase) | 30–40 | Moderate | $NO_x$ emissions a concern, lower efficiency than fuel cells |
| *Fuel Cell + Battery Hybrid* | Urban buses, delivery vans | 7–8 (early commercial) | 45–55 | High | Regional/commuter trains | 6 (demonstration) | 40–50 | High | Combines fuel cell range with battery boost |

Source: Adapted from Provincie Groningen (2020), Ortega et al. (2021), Alstom (2023), Stępień (2024), Turner (2025)

Technology Readiness Level (TRL 5–6) compared to PEMFCs (TRL 8–9 for road, TRL 7 for rail) (Golkhatmi et al., 2022).

Apart from fuel cells, hydrogen can, in principle, also be used in internal combustion engines ($H_2$-ICEs), in pure form, as a derivative or blended with other fuels. Here, the main advantage is the very fact that these engines operate similarly to conventional diesel engines but emit near-zero $CO_2$ (MAN, 2023). In addition, if $H_2$ blends or derivatives are used, fuel tanks would occupy less space, which will then give more flexibility and space for cargo management. That is why, for road transport, $H_2$-ICEs are currently being tested primarily in heavy-duty trucks and long-distance busses, offering a transitional solution due to estimated lower infrastructure requirements compared to fuel cells (Low et al., 2023). However, they face intense competition from both battery-electric and fuel-cell options.

At the same time, such engines still pose concerns of $NO_x$ emissions, since most of them are unable to secure a 100% effective combustion (Onorati et al., 2022). In addition, their TRL level is lower than that of PEFCs, and many even believe it is a 'dead-end solution for heavy-duty trucks' as fuel cell and EV technologies that normally are more efficient are rapidly developing and advancing (Union of Concerned Scientists, 2023). Similarly, although, in rail transport, hydrogen combustion is being explored as an alternative to diesel locomotives, particularly in freight operations, efficiency (~30–40%) is typically much lower than fuel cells and is similar to that of diesel locomotives, and retrofitting existing engines remains costly (Onorati et al., 2022). Besides, their technical readiness level is currently very low, as they mostly remain at the testing phase (TRL 5–6) (ibid.).

Furthermore, the operational reliability of alternative technologies is a critical factor. Recent data from the German Automobile Club (ADAC) based on 3.6 million service callouts in 2024 indicates that EVs are significantly more dependable than internal combustion engine vehicles of the same age (ADAC, 2025). In particular, for vehicles aged 2–4 years, ICE cars were 2.5 times more likely to require roadside assistance than EVs (ibid.). This inherent reliability of electric powertrains strengthens the case for battery-electric solutions over both conventional and hydrogen options, which face their own unique maintenance challenges.

Apart from fuel cells and $H_2$-ICEs, hybrid configurations, such as fuel cell-battery combinations, are gaining traction, especially in urban buses and regional trains. These systems generally use fuel cells for steady power and batteries for peak demands, improving efficiency and range (Ortega et al., 2021; IEA, 2023b).Therefore, by leveraging the complementary advantages of both technologies, hybrid setups can potentially mitigate some of the limitations of standalone fuel cells, such as transient power shortages, while reducing the infrastructure burden compared to purely battery-electric alternatives (Ortega et al., 2021). However, despite their advantages, such configurations still need further technological improvement (e.g., fully transition to TRL 9 for road and at least to TRL 7 for rail) and face challenges related to cost and system complexity, as integrating multiple energy sources increases maintenance requirements and vehicle weight (ibid.).

### *Advantages/Disadvantages*

While, in principle, hydrogen technologies can offer a promising pathway for decarbonising road and rail transport, they come with significant challenges. For instance, while PEMFCs achieve efficiencies of 40–60% in real-world conditions, which in theory makes them suitable for heavy-duty vehicles and regional trains where energy density is critical and batteries at their current stage of technological development still cannot keep all the needed energy for long periods of time, their efficiency is still significantly lower than that of EVs (70–90%) (Table 7.2). Therefore, their well-to-wheel efficiency is even less significant due to production and compression

**Table 7.2** Efficiency comparison: battery-electric versus fuel cell vehicles

| *Metric* | *battery-Electric Vehicles (BEVs)* | *Hydrogen Fuel Cell Vehicles (FCEVs)* | *Key Findings* |
|---|---|---|---|
| *Well-to-Wheel Efficiency (%)* | 70–90 | 25–35 | BEVs are 2–3 times more efficient due to fewer energy conversions |
| *Energy Losses (%)* | 10–15 (grid-to-battery) | 40–50% ($H_2$ production + compression) | Fuel cell vehicles lose more energy in hydrogen production/storage |
| *Drivetrain Efficiency (%)* | 85–90 (battery to wheels) | 50–60% (fuel cell to wheels) | BEVs optimise energy use more effectively |

Source: Adapted from Sorlei et al. (2021), Pramuanjaroenkij and Kakaç (2023), and Zhang et al. (2023)

losses.[2] This fundamental efficiency gap is reflected starkly in the market: hydrogen fuel cell cars are being commercially outsold by Ferrari sports cars, highlighting their failure to achieve mainstream consumer acceptance compared to the rapidly growing battery-electric vehicle market (Carbon Brief, 2025). This, combined with superior demonstrated reliability of electric powertrains (ADAC, 2025), means that for most light-duty vehicles, battery-electric vehicles (BEVs) are the more economical, energy-efficient, and dependable choice. The evidence points overwhelmingly to BEVs as the main route for cars; FCEVs remain a niche contingent on a future scenario of abundant, cheap renewable hydrogen.

When it comes to rail, although cases like Alstom's Coradia iLint hydrogen trains have demonstrated the technical feasibility of PEMFC technology's application in the sector, their operating costs are still significantly higher if compared to diesel and other equivalents (Table 7.3). Therefore, the decarbonisation of rail networks requires careful selection of

**Table 7.3** Key train propulsion technologies compared

| *Technology* | *Typical efficiency range (%)* | *Approximate infrastructure cost (USD/km)* | *Approximate range* | *Emissions* | *Best use cases* |
|---|---|---|---|---|---|
| *Overhead line (Catenary)* | 85–95 (most efficient) | 1.5–4M (high upfront) | Unlimited (while electrified) | Zero (if renewable-powered) | High-traffic mainlines, urban rail |
| *Battery--electric* | 75–85 | 0.5–1M (charging stations) | 100–300 km per charge | Zero | Regional routes, last-mile gaps |
| *Hydrogen fuel cell* | 30–40 | 2–4M per refuelling station | 600–1000 km per charge | Zero (with green $H_2$) | Non-electrified rural lines |
| *Diesel* | 30–35 | Lowest (existing infrastructure) | 1000+ km | High $CO_2$/ $NO_x$ | Legacy systems, remote areas |

Source: Adapted from Golightly et al. (2019), Ding and Wu (2024), Tabrizi et al. (2024), Marjani et al. (2025)

[2] Obviously, here we also need to consider the source of electricity used by EVs in terms of its carbon content, etc., in order to fully appreciate their decarbonisation potential.

propulsion technologies, each with distinct efficiency, infrastructure, and operational characteristics. Conventional diesel trains, while operationally flexible, are currently facing phase-outs in many regions of the world due to their 30–35% efficiency and high emissions. Transitional solutions like diesel-battery hybrids are being deployed to mitigate emissions on non-electrified lines, but these represent stopgap measures rather than long-term solutions.

Overall, overhead line (catenary) systems remain the gold standard for efficiency, achieving 85–95% well-to-wheel energy conversion when powered by renewable electricity (Golightly et al., 2019). This makes them ideal for high-traffic corridors, such as Japan's Shinkansen or France's TGV networks, where high upfront infrastructure costs (1.5–4 million USD per km) are offset by long-term energy savings (ibid. and Tabrizi et al., 2024). However, the prohibitive expense of electrifying low-density routes has spurred interest in alternatives.

In this context, battery-electric trains have emerged as a potential solution, particularly for regional lines with partial electrification. These systems achieve 75–85% efficiency by combining grid charging with regenerative braking, which recovers around 15–20% of energy during deceleration (Streuling et al., 2021). While projects like the United Kingdom's 'electrified islands' demonstrate their viability for bridging non-electrified gaps, with ranges of 100–300 km per charge and infrastructure costs 60–70% lower than full electrification, battery weight and capacity still remains a constraint for long-haul freight applications[3] (ibid.).

A clear current hierarchy for rail decarbonisation is evident from current planning: electricity where feasible, use batteries to bridge gaps, and reserve hydrogen for the hardest, non-electrified corridors. Following this logic, hydrogen fuel cell trains offer a zero-emission alternative for routes where neither overhead lines nor batteries are practical.[4] While their 30–40% well-to-wheel efficiency lags behind other decarbonisation options due to energy losses in hydrogen production and compression, their 600–1000-kilometer range and rapid refuelling (15–20 min) make them potentially suitable for low-density rural lines (Golightly et al., 2019; Ding & Wu, 2024). Pilot deployments, such as Germany's Coradia iLint

[3] Just like in the case of most EVs.

[4] Hydrogen fuel cell systems (stack + balance of plant) typically operate at 40–60% system-level electrical efficiency; lower numbers quoted elsewhere refer to stack-only or early demonstration systems.

and the United Kingdom's HydroFLEX, highlight this potential, though operating costs remain 2–3 times higher than diesel equivalents (ibid.). Therefore, the future rail energy mix will likely involve tailored combinations of these technologies: overhead lines for high-capacity corridors, batteries for regional routes with partial electrification, and hydrogen for remote lines.

While hydrogen internal combustion engines ($H_2$-ICEs) could potentially provide a transitional solution by leveraging existing engine architectures, they are currently viewed as less attractive option if compared to fuel cells when it comes to land transportation solutions. Overall, these engines deliver power outputs comparable to conventional diesel engines (200–5000 kW) but with efficiencies of 30–45% (Table 7.4) (Verhelst & Wallner, 2009; Onorati et al., 2022). While they reduce $CO_2$ emissions by 85–95%, they still produce notable levels of $NO_x$ emissions, necessitating advanced after-treatment systems (Boretti, 2011; Stępień, 2024). Hybrid systems that combine fuel cells with batteries aim to optimize both efficiency (35–60%) and range, though system integration challenges remain at commercial scales (ibid.).

**Table 7.4** Key decarbonisation technologies for road and rail transport

| *Technology* | *Power output (kW)* | *Approximate efficiency range (%)* | *Performance* | *Emissions reduction* | *Key challenges* |
|---|---|---|---|---|---|
| *Hydrogen Fuel Cells* | 100–500 (road) 200–1000 (rail) | 40–60 | High range, fast fuelling | Zero tailpipe emissions | High CapEx (~900 USD/kW); high fuel cost |
| *H2 combustion engines* | 200–5000 | 30–45 | High power density | Near-zero $CO_2$ | $NO_x$ emissions, 20% higher maintenance; high fuel cost |
| *Battery--electric* | 50–500 (road) 500–2000 (rail) | 70–90 | Limited range | Zero emissions | Battery weight (400+ kg/kWh) |
| *Biofuels* | Engine-dependent | 30–40 | Drop-in solution | 50–80% reduction | 2–4x current fuel costs |

Source: Adapted from Golightly et al. (2019), Stead et al. (2019), Provincie Groningen (2020), Ortega et al. (2021), Popovich et al. (2021), Alstom (2023), Stępień (2024), Ding and Wu (2024), Tabrizi et al. (2024), Marjani et al. (2025), Turner (2025)

Overall, comparative analyses highlight the strengths and limitations of technologies alternative to hydrogen for road and rail transport. For instance, although battery-electric systems achieve superior well-to-wheel efficiencies (70–90%), they are constrained by energy density limitations, particularly for freight transport (Popovich et al., 2021). Biofuels, in turn, offer drop-in compatibility with existing infrastructure and lifecycle emissions reductions of 50–80%, but their scalability is limited by sustainable feedstock availability (Stead et al., 2019). In these circumstances, it is estimated that hydrogen fuel cell trucks could achieve total cost of ownership parity with diesel by 2030, contingent on significant reductions in renewable hydrogen production costs (ICCT, 2020). However, for trucks, BEVs are already the cheapest option across many use cases this decade, and therefore is increasingly viewed by many as the means that will only serve select long-haul niches if fuel and station costs drop dramatically.

At the same time, the infrastructure requirements for hydrogen still remain an extremely significant barrier, with estimated costs of USD 1–2 million per heavy-duty refuelling station (IEA, 2023b). Besides, hydrogen itself poses challenges for vehicle design and operational flexibility, as its compressed storage systems currently require 4–5 times more space than diesel tanks for equivalent energy (ibid. and Xu et al., 2022). Therefore, for rail networks, the International Union of Railways projects that hydrogen solutions will only be economically viable on 30–40% of non-electrified European routes (UIC, 2023). However, current planning and procurements generally prioritise electrification first and battery trains for many gaps, reserving hydrogen for hard-to-electrify lines.

### *Infrastructure Requirements*

The successful integration of hydrogen technologies into road and rail transport systems depends fundamentally on developing appropriate infrastructure tailored to the unique requirements of each sector. Unlike conventional fuels, hydrogen presents distinct challenges and opportunities that necessitate careful consideration of production, distribution, storage, and refuelling systems.

For road transport, the infrastructure requirements vary significantly between light-duty passenger vehicles and heavy-duty freight applications. Fuel cell electric vehicles, such as passenger cars, generally require networks of high-pressure (350–700 bar) refuelling stations capable of delivering hydrogen at purity levels exceeding 99.97% (Samsun et al., 2022).

These stations represent substantial investments, with current costs ranging between USD 1200 and 3000 per kg of hydrogen fuelled per day (US Department of Energy, 2020; Guerra et al., 2021). That is why, at the rapid pace of infrastructure and technological development for EVs, fuel cell passenger cars currently seem to be losing the battle to their battery-electric alternatives. In fact, at the moment, the rollout of BEV charging infrastructure is occurring at a much faster rate, further cementing their dominance in the light-duty segment.

Heavy-duty trucks and buses face even greater infrastructure challenges due to their higher fuel consumption rates, necessitating strategically located refuelling points along major transport corridors (ibid.). Long-haul BEV capability is improving (rising ranges and megawatt charging), and BEV trucks are getting more and more cost-competitive for many regional and some long-haul operations; hydrogen fuel cells may still serve targeted long-range, high-utilisation niches. Therefore, it seems to be up to the speed of this technological and infrastructure development to define the specific niche and size of the share that fuel cells will occupy in the land transport sector.

Rail transport presents a different set of infrastructure considerations. Hydrogen-powered trains, such as those already piloted for operation in countries like Austria, Germany, or Italy, typically rely on centralised refuelling depots rather than extensive networks of stations. These depots often utilise liquid hydrogen ($LH_2$) storage systems to maximise energy density and minimise the frequency of refuelling operations (Xu et al., 2022). However, it is still unclear how much economical and replicable this model can be in comparison to conventional and other sustainable alternatives. Therefore, the application of hydrogen technology to long-haul freight rail within the absence of well-developed $H_2$ infrastructure still remains questionable primarily due to the substantial fuel quantities required and the current limitations of hydrogen storage systems (Marjani et al., 2025).

The scalability of hydrogen infrastructure differs markedly between road and rail applications. In road transport, several European countries have begun establishing hydrogen refuelling networks, with Germany leading the way with over 100 operational stations (World Economic Forum, 2024). However, the pace of expansion remains constrained by high capital costs and relatively low utilisation rates, which deter private investment (Guerra et al., 2021). The situation is further complicated by the competing development of battery-electric vehicle infrastructure, which benefits from lower costs and greater compatibility with existing electrical grids (CleanTechnica, 2024).

For rail applications, hydrogen infrastructure remains highly specialised and geographically limited. Most current implementations involve purpose-built facilities serving specific regional routes, making broader adoption dependent on significant additional investment. Furthermore, retrofitting existing diesel depots for hydrogen use is technically feasible but often not economically viable at current scales (Marjani et al., 2025). Therefore, in these circumstances, electrification still seems to be winning on all fronts despite having its own challenges, followed by biofuels, as they do not require any infrastructure adjustment whatsoever (Table 7.5). When it comes to the widespread deployment of hydrogen infrastructure, it has several critical challenges. In general, the production of clean hydrogen remains constrained by the availability of renewable electricity and electrolyser capacity (for green) as well as slow development of carbon capture and storage solutions (for blue), while distribution logistics add substantial costs—typically increasing final fuel prices at least by 30–50% compared to conventional alternatives (ibid. and CleanTechnica, 2024).

Despite these challenges, in the opinion of many, hydrogen continues to offer compelling advantages for certain transport applications, particularly heavy-duty road freight and regional passenger rail services where battery-electric solutions may be impractical. Nevertheless, realising this potential will require coordinated policy support, targeted infrastructure investments, and continued technological advancements to address current limitations in cost and performance (Marjani et al., 2025; World Economic Forum, 2024). In any case, the development of hydrogen infrastructure for transport must be viewed as part of a broader energy transition strategy, with careful consideration given to the optimal applications where hydrogen can deliver the greatest system benefits relative to alternative decarbonisation pathways. As the technology matures and scale effects begin to reduce costs, hydrogen may yet emerge as a vital component of sustainable transport systems in specific niches where its unique characteristics provide decisive advantages.

**Table 7.5** Hydrogen and alternative fuel technologies for road and rail transport: infrastructure requirements, scalability, and adaptability

| *Technology* | | *Specific infrastructure requirements* | *Current scalability* | *Current adaptability* | *Key challenges* |
|---|---|---|---|---|---|
| *Hydrogen Fuel Cells* | *Road* | • High-pressure refuelling stations (350–700 bar)<br>• Hydrogen purity >99.97% | Low | Low | • High CapEx<br>• Low utilisation rates<br>• Competition from battery-electric infrastructure |
| | *Rail* | • Centralised depots (no roadside stations) | Low-medium | Low-medium | • Storage volume, low energy density<br>• High CapEx |
| *Hydrogen combustion engines* | *Road* | • High-pressure (up to 700 bar) refuelling stations | Low | Low | • 25–30% lower efficiency than fuel cell vehicles<br>• Fuel economy 50% worse than diesel<br>• $NO_x$ emissions |
| | *Rail* | • Centralised refuelling depots<br>• Liquid hydrogen ($LH_2$) storage systems to maximise energy density | Low | Low | • High costs, storage limitations<br>• $NO_x$ emissions<br>• Safety concerns<br>• 35% efficiency (vs. 45% for $H_2$ fuel cells) |

(*continued*)

**Table 7.5** (continued)

| *Technology* | | *Specific infrastructure requirements* | *Current scalability* | *Current adaptability* | *Key challenges* |
|---|---|---|---|---|---|
| *Hybrid ($H_2$ fuel cells + electric)* | *Road* | • Combined hydrogen refuelling stations and battery charging infrastructure | Medium | Medium-high | • Integration challenges between hydrogen storage and battery systems<br>• High upfront costs (CapEx) |
| | *Rail* | • Centralised depots with hydrogen refuelling and battery charging facilities | Medium | Medium-high | • High costs of dual infrastructure<br>• Compatibility with electrified networks |
| *Electricity* | *Road (battery-electric)* | • Fast chargers (50–250 kW)<br>• Megawatt charging | High | High | • Grid upgrades needed |
| | *Rail (electrification)* | • Catenary wires (5M USD/mile) + substantions | High | Medium | • 10-year payback period |
| *Biofuels* | *Road* | • Existing pumps and blending infrastructure | High | Very high | • Limited sustainable feedstock |
| | *Rail* | • Depot storage tanks | High | Very high | • 30% more expensive than diesel |

Source: Adapted from Golightly et al. (2019), Stead et al. (2019), Provincie Groningen (2020), Ortega et al. (2021), Popovich et al. (2021), Alstom (2023), Stępień (2024), Ding and Wu (2024), Tabrizi et al. (2024), Marjani et al. (2025), Turner (2025)

## Economic Aspects

The adoption of hydrogen in road and rail transport could represent a promising pathway to decarbonisation, yet its economic viability hinges on overcoming substantial cost barriers. A comprehensive analysis must consider capital expenditures (CapEx), operational expenditures (OpEx), and fuel costs (as a separate part of OpEx) to evaluate hydrogen's competitiveness against conventional and alternative propulsion technologies. In any case, at the moment, government subsidies, incentives, and carbon pricing mechanisms further play a pivotal role in accelerating hydrogen's market penetration (Roland Berger, 2019; PWC, 2023; Marjani et al., 2025).

Overall, the transition to hydrogen in road and rail transport entails significant CapEx, primarily driven by vehicle manufacturing, refuelling infrastructure, and hydrogen production facilities. For road transport, fuel cell electric vehicles require costly platinum-based catalysts and high-pressure storage tanks, with current fuel cell system costs ranging between EUR 50 and 100 per kW. Therefore, on average, they are significantly more expensive than all other existing alternatives (Fig. 7.4).

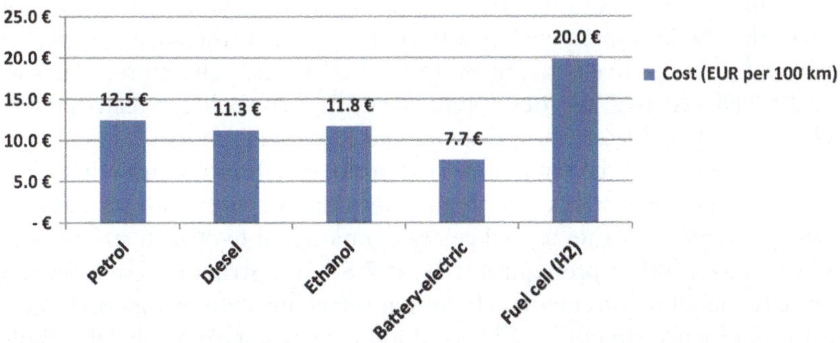


**Fig. 7.4** Comparison of approximate average total cost per 100 km (5-year ownership) (These costs as well as the costs from Fig. 7.5 represent estimated average, as they can vary for different propulsion options depending on factors such as fuel prices, infrastructure costs, operational efficiency, and technological advancements.) (Source: Adapted from Consumer Reports, 2020; ICCT, 2022; PWC, 2023; Bradley, 2024; European Commission, 2025; Marjani et al., 2025)

Here, as seen, battery-electric EVs are increasingly cost-competitive with petrol and diesel cars due to several factors. At the moment, generally, energy costs for EVs range from EUR 0.05 to 0.10 per km, significantly lower than the EUR 0.10–0.15 per km for fossil fuels, reflecting their higher energy efficiency and lower electricity prices compared to gasoline or diesel (Bradley, 2024). In addition, maintenance costs for EVs are expected to be approximately 50% lower than those of internal combustion engine (ICE) vehicles, attributed to simpler powertrains and the absence of oil changes (Consumer Reports, 2020). Battery prices have also decreased substantially and are expected to continue going down, with lithium-ion battery pack prices estimated to drop below USD 100 per kWh by 2026, after declining from over USD 1000 per kWh in 2010 to USD 151 per kWh in 2022 (ICCT, 2022). Furthermore, EVs boast much higher energy efficiency, with electric motors achieving efficiencies of around 80%, compared to the 20–30% efficiency of ICE vehicles (ibid.).

In addition to that, government subsidies further enhance EV affordability. In Europe, incentives vary by country but can reach up to EUR 7000 under programs such as Spain's Moves III initiative (European Commission, 2025). Overall, these advantages contribute to EVs achieving total ownership cost parity with conventional vehicles within 3–5 years in many scenarios (ICCT, 2022). In these circumstances, the future for fuel cell vehicles looks way less attractive, at least in the areas and niches where EVs are actively taking more market shares.[5] Therefore, it is currently believed that the development and use of such cars can only be economically viable for long-distance and heavy-duty modes.

The situation in the rail transport sector generally looks quite similar, as hydrogen-powered trains incur higher upfront costs than diesel or battery-electric alternatives due to fuel cell integration and hydrogen storage systems, among other prerequisites (Fig. 7.5). Infrastructure costs further amplify capital requirements. Hydrogen refuelling stations for road transport require investments of EUR 1–2 million per station, while rail depots need liquefaction or compression systems, adding EUR 5–10 million per site (Roland Berger, 2021). Electrolyser costs for green hydrogen production remain high, averaging EUR 800–1500 per kW, though

[5] The commercial fragility of the hydrogen trucking niche was starkly illustrated by the bankruptcy of Nikola Corporation, which led to the auction of over 100 of its hydrogen fuel cell trucks, highlighting the significant market and financial challenges facing early entrants (Car and Driver, 2025).

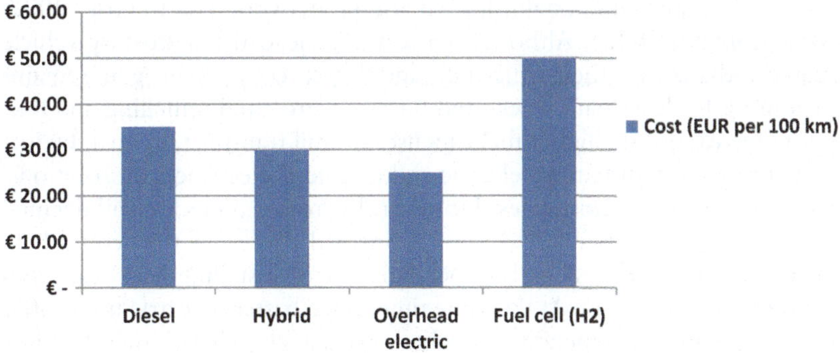


**Fig. 7.5** Comparison of approximate average total cost per 100 km (key train propulsion options). (Source: Adapted from Gnann et al. (2019), Clean Hydrogen Partnership (2021), and Markets and Markets (2022))

economies of scale are expected to reduce this by 2030 (ibid. and PWC, 2023).

Operational expenditures for hydrogen vehicles are influenced by maintenance, fuel, and energy efficiency. Compared with internal combustion engines, hydrogen fuel cells contain fewer moving components, which can reduce maintenance requirements over time. However, rail operators report higher maintenance costs for hydrogen trains due to the complexity of fuel cell systems compared to diesel alternatives. For example, hydrogen trains require additional components such as air handling systems, hydrogen tanks, and fuel cell replacements every three years, which significantly increase maintenance efforts (Argonne National Laboratory, 2019).

At the same time, just like in the case of road transport, fuel costs remain a critical hurdle for hydrogen-powered rail transport. With green hydrogen currently costing more than EUR 5 per kg in Europe, far higher than diesel's EUR 1.20–1.80 per kg on an energy-equivalent basis, dramatic cost reductions need to be achieved before $H_2$ could become a serious competitor to conventional fuels and other sustainable alternatives (Euractiv, 2024). Although advancements in hydrogen production and fuelling infrastructure are expected to reduce costs by 2030, it is still unclear whether it will happen.

Overall, hydrogen's economic competitiveness varies significantly by application. In road transport, fuel cell cars face stiff competition from battery electric vehicles, which benefit from lower electricity costs and a more developed and established charging network (Earth.Org, 2022; MIT Climate, 2023). Although battery EVs lead the light-duty vehicle market, thanks to their efficiency and lower costs, hydrogen remains promising for long-haul trucks and buses, where rapid refuelling and longer range can justify higher fuel expenses. In rail transport, in turn, hydrogen competes with battery-electric and overhead electrification solutions, which win most in most cases. However, hydrogen trains are still deemed to be attractive particularly on non-electrified routes, as they could help avoiding the EUR 1–3 million per km cost of installing overhead lines (Freight Waves, 2021). At the same time, since battery-electric trains offer lower operational expenditures where partial electrification is feasible, recent studies indicate that hydrogen trains could achieve total cost of ownership parity with alternatives such as diesel trains by the end of the decade only if hydrogen prices fall below EUR 3 per kg (Roland Berger, 2019, 2021).

## Policy and Regulatory Landscape

In general, the adoption of hydrogen in road and rail transport should be shaped by policies and regulatory frameworks aimed at decarbonising the transport sector. Globally, the Hydrogen Council and the International Energy Agency (IEA) have advocated for hydrogen as a key enabler of zero-emission mobility, particularly for heavy-duty vehicles (HDVs) and long-haul rail operations (IEA, 2021). However, unlike aviation, which is governed by the International Civil Aviation Organization (ICAO), road and rail transport regulations are more fragmented, with policies varying significantly across regions and nations.

In particular, in the European Union, hydrogen adoption in transport is supported by the Alternative Fuels Infrastructure Regulation (AFIR), which mandates the deployment of hydrogen refuelling stations along major transport corridors by 2030 (European Union, 2023). The AFIR regulation requires Member States to ensure sufficient publicly accessible hydrogen refuelling stations are deployed to enable the circulation of hydrogen-powered vehicles across the EU (ibid.). Additionally, the Fuel Cells and Hydrogen Joint Undertaking (FCH JU), now known as the Clean Hydrogen Partnership, has funded numerous pilot projects for hydrogen-powered buses, trucks, and trains, which aim to demonstrate the viability and benefits of hydrogen technologies in various transport applications (Clean Hydrogen Partnership, 2024).

The EU's Hydrogen Strategy further identifies transport as a priority sector, with a focus on fuel cell electric vehicles and hydrogen-combustion engines (European Commission, 2020). However, similar to aviation, most policies emphasise hydrogen-derived synthetic fuels rather than direct hydrogen use, partly due to infrastructure challenges. This is because synthetic fuels, such as e-kerosene, can be used in existing infrastructure (Korberg et al., 2023).

Nationally, Germany has been a frontrunner, with its National Hydrogen Strategy allocating EUR 9 billion to develop hydrogen infrastructure, including refuelling stations for trucks and trains (Federal Ministry of Economic Affairs and Energy., 2020). Similarly, the United Kingdom's Hydrogen Strategy supports trials for hydrogen-powered trains and freight vehicles, with projects demonstrating the feasibility of hydrogen rail (Department for Transport, 2021). These strategies, however, often emphasise hydrogen-derived synthetic fuels rather than direct hydrogen use, partly due to infrastructure challenges.

Overall, the lack of binding international regulations for hydrogen adoption remains a significant gap. In particular, the absence of harmonised standards for hydrogen storage, refuelling, and safety poses challenges for cross-border operations (IEA, 2021). Furthermore, the lack of binding international standards for hydrogen refuelling, storage, and vehicle safety creates inconsistencies. While the United Nations Economic Commission for Europe (UNECE) has developed regulations for hydrogen vehicles (e.g., Global Technical Regulation No. 13), full harmonisation still remains incomplete (UNECE, 2023).

In general, safety is a critical consideration for hydrogen deployment in transport. Although hydrogen has a high flammability range (4–75% in air), its rapid dispersion reduces explosion risks compared to petrol (US Department of Energy, 2024). Modern hydrogen refuelling stations and vehicles incorporate leak detection sensors, flame arrestors, and pressure-relief systems, enhancing safety (International Association for Hydrogen Safety, 2021). However, public perception remains influenced by historical incidents (e.g., Hindenburg disaster), necessitating awareness campaigns to highlight hydrogen's safety record in modern applications (Scovell, 2022).

At the moment, public acceptance is generally mixed. While hydrogen is viewed as a clean alternative, concerns over safety, refuelling availability, and cost persist (Emodi et al., 2021). Surveys indicate that around 65% of Europeans support hydrogen transport, but only 30% would prefer a fuel cell vehicle over a battery electric car due to refuelling anxiety (Clean Energy Technology Observatory, 2024). Demonstrations like H2Bus Europe and hydrogen train trials in Austria and France aim to build confidence, but broader acceptance requires policy incentives (e.g., subsidies, tax breaks) and consumer education (Clean Hydrogen Partnership, 2023). Supply chain establishment, refuelling infrastructure development, and supportive policies all require substantial investments and international cooperation to enhance public support (IEA, 2021).

Regulatory barriers further complicate the development of hydrogen infrastructure, which is crucial for the large-scale adoption of hydrogen technologies in road and rail transport. Unlike battery-electric vehicles, which benefit from uniform charging standards such as CCS and CHAdeMO, hydrogen refuelling protocols vary significantly by region. For instance, SAE J2601 is widely used in the United States, while ISO 17268 governs refuelling standards in the European Union, creating complexity for manufacturers aiming for global compatibility (Hydrogen Tools, 2023).

Finally, safety certifications for hydrogen vehicles differ across jurisdictions, delaying market entry. In the EU, hydrogen tank safety is regulated under ECE R134, which sets standards for pressure vessels in hydrogen-powered vehicles. However, other regions impose additional local requirements that are not harmonised with international frameworks, further complicating cross-border operations (UNECE, 2023). These regulatory inconsistencies hinder the scalability of hydrogen technologies and contribute to slower adoption rates in transport sectors.

In summary, regulatory inconsistencies across jurisdictions create significant complications for the adoption of hydrogen technologies for road and rail transport. At the same time, more importantly, hydrogen technologies face intense competition from increasingly cost-competitive battery-electric solutions in the road sector and established electrification options in rail. While government policies remain critical to bridging hydrogen's cost gap, it is not clear whether they will unanimously support the promotion of $H_2$ in the transport sector as opposed to other decarbonisation alternatives, which often happen to be cheaper and more scalable.

## Case Studies and Pilot Projects

Hydrogen technologies have evolved significantly over the decades, with fuel cells, combustion engines, and hybrid systems each being potentially capable of contributing to the development of zero-emission solutions in road and rail transport. This progress has been marked by ground-breaking prototypes, real-world deployments, and lessons learned from early projects.

The history of hydrogen fuel cells dates back to 1839 when Sir William Grove developed the first crude fuel cell, which demonstrated the potential of electrochemical reactions between hydrogen and oxygen to generate electricity (Zhu et al., 2024). However, it was not until the mid-twentieth century that Francis Thomas Bacon advanced this technology with the alkaline fuel cell, which later powered NASA's Apollo missions (ibid.). In the automotive sector, General Motors introduced the world's first hydrogen-powered vehicle, the Electrovan, in 1966, which demonstrated a range of 150 miles using a proton exchange membrane (PEM) fuel cell (ibid. and Halder et al., 2024). Nevertheless, as its high costs and safety concerns limited its application to company property, the first commercially viable fuel cell vehicles emerged decades later, with Toyota launching the Mirai in 2014, Hyundai mass-producing the ix35 FCEV in 2013, and Honda introducing the Clarity in 2015 (ibid.). Although these vehicles offered ranges exceeding 300 miles and refuelling times comparable to petrol cars, their adoption was constrained by limited hydrogen infrastructure (ibid. and Li et al., 2022).

At the same time, despite commercial and other challenges, technological development continues. For instance, China has unveiled the 'Track 1000' liquid hydrogen system for trucks, which aims to break the 1000 km range barrier without refuelling (Fuel Cell Works, 2025). If successful, this will represent a significant advancement in storage technology and give further impetus to the development and ramp-up of hydrogen propulsion for land transport. However, most such prototypes must still overcome the overarching economic and infrastructure hurdles to achieve widespread commercial viability.

Fuel cell technology has also made significant strides in rail transport. In particular, Alstom's Coradia iLint, launched in Germany in 2018 and Austria in 2020, became the world's first hydrogen-powered passenger train which uses PEM fuel cells to achieve a range of up to 600 miles while emitting only water vapour (Alstom, 2020). The train has successfully replaced diesel locomotives on regional routes, eliminating over 330 tonnes of $CO_2$ annually per train[6] (ibid. and Durkin et al., 2024). Similarly, California has invested UESD 127 million in Stadler Rail AG's hydrogen-powered trains for Amtrak routes, with operations expected by 2027 (Mass Transit, 2024). At the same time, despite these successes, challenges remain. For instance, Germany's hydrogen trains have faced operational issues such as high maintenance costs and limited refuelling infrastructure (Hydrogen Insight, 2025).

The concept of hydrogen combustion engines ($H_2$-ICEs) dates back to François Isaac de Rivaz's hydrogen-fuelled internal combustion engine in 1806 (Kooij, 2021). At the same time, its modern applications focus on retrofitting diesel engines to burn hydrogen directly, which can potentially offer a transitional decarbonisation pathway. In road transport, Hyundai Doosan Infracore plans to mass-produce $H_2$-ICEs for heavy-duty trucks by mid-2020s, leveraging existing engine designs to achieve near-zero $CO_2$ emissions (Aggregates Business, 2023). Similarly, Toyota has tested $H_2$-ICE prototypes in motorsports, including a hydrogen-burning Corolla in Japan's Super Taikyu endurance series, demonstrating the technology's viability under extreme conditions (Toyota Europe Newsroom, 2024).

In rail transport, however, hydrogen combustion remains mostly experimental and more often focuses on dual-fuel applications. While $H_2$-ICEs can potentially eliminate $CO_2$ emissions, their adoption is constrained primarily by $NO_x$ production, lower efficiency compared to fuel cells, and the same challenge of developing nascent hydrogen infrastructure. Therefore, hydrogen fuel cells currently dominate most zero-emission rail initiatives, and $H_2$-ICEs remain a niche but actively researched alternative, particularly for retrofitting diesel fleets. For instance, Austria's AVL List investigated retrofit kits for legacy diesel trains as part of projects like HY2RAIL, but adoption has been limited due to competition from battery-electric solutions—exemplified by the Zillertalbahn's decision to deploy Stadler FLIRT Akku trains instead (Railway Gazette International, 2024).

[6] Alstom is also planning to launch the first hydrogen-powered train operation in Italy (Alstom Coradia Stream H), which is currently undergoing refuelling trials at Rovato near Brescia in Lombardy (International Railway Journal, 2025).

In these circumstances, hybrid systems that combine hydrogen fuel cells with batteries are increasingly viewed as promising solutions because they can optimise efficiency and extend operational range. One example of these, Siemens' Mireo Plus H hydrogen-powered train integrates fuel cells and lithium-ion batteries to achieve a range of up to 800 km while maintaining compatibility with electrified networks (Siemens Mobility, 2024). Testing began in Bavaria in 2023, and passenger service is scheduled to start in the upcoming years on Bayerische Regiobahn routes so that the train becomes part of Germany's broader strategy to eliminate diesel operations by 2040 and offer a sustainable alternative for non-electrified rail routes (Railway News, 2023). Similarly, in early 2025, Italy's Valcamonica project started to deploy Alstom hybrid trains on mountainous routes where electrification is impractical (FIT Consulting, 2025). These trains integrate hydrogen fuel cells with batteries to reduce emissions significantly while avoiding the high costs associated with overhead catenary systems (ibid.).

In road transport, BMW's iX5 Hydrogen prototype demonstrates promising potential by combining PEM fuel cells with a lithium-ion battery buffer for optimised energy use and enhanced performance (BMW, 2024). With a driving range of around 260–310 miles, the vehicle showcases the adaptability of hybrid systems for heavy-duty applications while leveraging existing hydrogen infrastructure (Car and Driver, 2023). The integration of BMW's fifth-generation eDrive technology with Toyota-sourced core fuel cell components is supposed to ensure efficient energy management and acceleration capabilities (ibid.). However, despite its advanced design, the iX5 Hydrogen also faces scalability challenges due to limited global refuelling infrastructure and high production costs.

Overall, despite their promise, hydrogen technologies face significant hurdles and are currently notably less scalable and adaptable compared to other popular decarbonisation alternatives like direct electrification and biofuels (Table 7.5). Infrastructure costs represent a major barrier and competing technologies such as battery-electric systems often overshadow hydrogen due to their lower operational costs and faster infrastructure rollout. However, as advancements continue and production scales up globally, hydrogen technologies could play a more important role in decarbonising transport systems.

## Future Outlook and Conclusions

Hydrogen's role in surface transport appears selective rather than universal. Across light-duty road transport, recent assessments indicate battery-electric vehicles (BEVs) deliver higher energy efficiency and lower life-cycle emissions, and, crucially, greater demonstrated reliability to date (ADAC, 2025) than alternatives in most contexts. Fuel-cell electric vehicles (FCEVs) for passengers may therefore remain a niche option unless low-carbon hydrogen becomes widely available at competitive cost and refuelling networks expand. This chapter synthesises recent evidence and debates; compares hydrogen with direct electrification across passenger cars, heavy-duty trucks, and regional rail; and clarifies where each technology currently shows advantages. It also reconciles claims in the literature with deployment and cost data and summarises practical implications that emerge for near-term decisions.

In heavy-duty road transport, evidence and early deployments suggest BEV trucks already outperform alternatives in many regional and some long-haul applications, with performance expected to improve as ranges increase and megawatt-class charging is introduced. The staggering growth in the global EV market, led by China but with strong participation from European manufacturers, underscores the massive industrial momentum behind electrification. At the same time, hydrogen fuel-cell trucks continue to be explored for duty cycles that emphasise very long range, high utilisation, challenging climates, or limited depot power—especially where delivered hydrogen prices are favourable and refuelling reliability is high. However, the bankruptcy of pioneers like Nikola serves as a cautionary tale about the commercial risks in this nascent segment. Hydrogen internal-combustion engines ($H_2$-ICE) are also under evaluation for specific use cases, including retrofits and some off-road/non-road mobile machinery, noting that achieving low $NO_x$ requires appropriate combustion strategies and after-treatment.

For rail, a consistent pattern in European planning and procurement points to a hierarchy of options: widespread electrification where feasible; battery trains on partially wired routes or to bridge gaps; and hydrogen trains for corridors that are difficult to electrify, for example, due to low traffic density or challenging topography. This configuration is frequently associated with lower system cost and efficient operations while maintaining a path to full decarbonisation.

Supply-side dynamics are likely to shape the pace and scale of hydrogen use. Although announced pipelines for low-emissions hydrogen are sizeable, conversion to final investment decision (FID) has been slower than anticipated in several regions. In the near term, transport use may therefore compete with other demand centres—such as refining replacement, fertilisers, steel and maritime fuels—and local production costs and logistics arrangements are expected to be decisive.

Policy discussions increasingly reflect these patterns. For road transport, attention often centres on the availability of reliable charging (including megawatt-class charging), alignment of incentives with observed TCO, and interoperability standards. For hydrogen in heavy-duty segments, stakeholders frequently consider corridor-based pilots, co-location with industrial demand, and certification of low-carbon supply, alongside air-quality requirements relevant to $H_2$-ICE. For rail, planning documents commonly examine the balance between electrification programmes, battery multiple units with suitable charging points, and targeted hydrogen deployments on a subset of unelectrified routes.

Market instruments that reward outcomes—such as performance-based procurement, zero-emission sales mandates, and well-to-wheel carbon metrics—are often cited as ways to reveal least-cost pathways while leaving room for hydrogen where it offers distinct operational value.

Areas where further evidence would be useful include thresholds for hydrogen truck competitiveness by duty cycle (as a function of delivered fuel price and station uptime); real-world performance of megawatt-class charging in long-haul operations; comparative corridor appraisals for rail that include partial wiring and battery charging strategies; and regularly updated life-cycle assessments that reflect grid-marginal emissions and verified hydrogen origins.

Overall, the outlook suggested by the evidence is clear. BEVs currently dominate many road applications on efficiency and cost; batteries and electrification feature prominently in rail; and hydrogen's most promising applications lie where it can address specific operational constraints or infrastructure barriers. This framing helps prioritise near-term actions while keeping options open as technologies, fuel prices, and infrastructure evolve.

## References

ADAC. (2025). *ADAC Pannenstatistik 2025: Die Gewinner und Verlierer* [Online]. Retrieved September 25, 2025, from https://www.adac.de/rund-ums-fahrzeug/unfall-schaden-panne/adac-pannenstatistik/.

Aggregates Business. (2023). *Hyundai Doosan Infracore to mass produce hydrogen internal combustion engines in 2025* [Online]. Retrieved April 01, 2025, from https://www.aggbusiness.com/hyundai-doosan-infracore-mass-produce-hydrogen-internal-combustion-engines-2025/

Alstom. (2020). *Alstom's hydrogen train enters regular passenger service in Austria* [Online]. Retrieved April 01, 2025, from https://www.alstom.com/press-releases-news/2020/9/alstoms-hydrogen-train-enters-regular-passenger-service-austria

Alstom. (2023). *Alstom's Coradia iLint, the world's first hydrogen-powered passenger train, will demonstrate green traction in Quebec* [Online]. Retrieved March 29, 2025, from https://www.alstom.com/press-releases-news/2023/2/alstoms-coradia-ilint-worlds-first-hydrogen-powered-passenger-train-will-demonstrate-green-traction-quebec

Argonne National Laboratory. (2019). *Total cost of ownership for line haul, yard switchers and regional passenger locomotives – preliminary results* [Online]. Retrieved April 04, 2025, from https://www.energy.gov/sites/prod/files/2019/04/f62/fcto-h2-at-rail-workshop-2019-ahluwalia.pdf

BMW. (2024). *Think hydrogen: The BMW iX5 hydrogen concept vehicle* [Online]. Retrieved April 02, 2025, from https://www.bmwusa.com/ix5--hydrogen.html

Boretti, A. (2011). Advances in hydrogen compression ignition internal combustion engines. *International Journal of Hydrogen Energy, 36*(1), 12601–12606.

Bradley, S. (2024). *Electric vehicle cost goes beyond the purchase price* [Online]. Retrieved April 03, 2025, from https://www.nerdwallet.com/article/loans/auto-loans/ev-total-ownership-costs.

Car and Driver. (2023). *View photos of the 2023 BMW iX5 hydrogen prototype* [Online]. Retrieved April 02, 2025, from https://www.caranddriver.com/photos/g43023233/2023-bmw-ix5-hydrogen-prototype-drive-gallery/

Car and Driver. (2025). *Nikola, an American electrick-truck startup, has filed for bankruptcy* [Online]. Retrieved September 25, 2025, from https://www.caranddriver.com/news/a63841019/nikola-ev-startup-bankruptcy/

Carbon Brief. (2025). *Guest post: Why hydrogen cars are being outsold by Ferraris* [Online]. Retrieved September 25, 2025, from https://www.carbonbrief.org/guest-post-why-hydrogen-cars-are-being-outsold-by-ferraris/

Clean Energy Technology Observatory. (2024). *Fuel cell technology in the European Union – Status report on technology development, trends, value chains & markets*

[Online]. Retrieved April 04, 2025, from https://www.h2knowledgecentre.com/content/researchpaper6278

Clean Hydrogen Partnership. (2021). *FCH 2JU – MAWP Key Performance Indicators (KPIs)* [Online]. Retrieved April 03, 2025, from https://www.clean-hydrogen.europa.eu/knowledge-management/strategy-map-and-key-performance-indicators/fch-2-ju-mawp-key-performance-indicators-kpis_en

Clean Hydrogen Partnership. (2023). *European partnership for hydrogen technologies* [Online]. Retrieved April 04, 2025, from https://www.clean-hydrogen.europa.eu/index_en

Clean Hydrogen Partnership. (2024). *Projects* [Online]. Retrieved April 04, 2025, from https://www.clean-hydrogen.europa.eu/projects_en

CleanTechnica. (2024). *NREL's cost study on hydrogen for heavy vehicles fuel does not withstand scrutiny* [Online]. Retrieved April 01, 2025, from https://cleantechnica.com/2024/03/06/nrels-cost-study-on-hydrogen-for-heavy-vehicles-fuel-does-not-withstand-scrutiny/

Consumer Reports. (2020). *Electric vehicle owners spending half as much on maintenance compared to gas-powered vehicle owners, finds new CR analysis* [Online]. Retrieved April 03, 2025, from https://advocacy.consumerreports.org/press_release/electric-vehicle-owners-spending-half-as-much-on-maintenance-compared-to-gas-powered-vehicle-owners-finds-new-cr-analysis/

Department for Transport. (2021). *UK Hydrogen Strategy* [Online]. Retrieved April 04, 2025, from https://assets.publishing.service.gov.uk/media/64c7e8bad8b1a70011b05e38/UK-Hydrogen-Strategy_web.pdf

Ding, D., & Wu, X. Y. (2024). Hydrogen fuel cell electric trains: Technologies, current status, and future. *Applications in Energy and Combustion Science, 17*(1), 1–12.

Durkin, K., et al. (2024). Hydrogen-powered vehicles: Comparing the powertrain efficiency and sustainability of fuel cell versus internal combustion engine cars. *Energies, 17*(5), 1–15.

Earth.Org. (2022). *Hydrogen vs. electric cars: Comparing innovative sustainability* [Online]. Retrieved April 04, 2025, from https://earth.org/hydrogen-vs-electric-cars/

EEA. (2021). *Rail and waterborne – best for low-carbon motorised transport* [Online]. Retrieved March 17, 2025, from https://www.eea.europa.eu/publications/rail-and-waterborne-transport.

EIA. (2023). *International energy outlook 2023* [Online]. Retrieved March 17, 2025, from https://www.eia.gov/outlooks/ieo/

Emodi, N., Lovell, H., Levitt, C., & Franklin, E. (2021). A systematic literature review of societal acceptance and stakeholders' perception of hydrogen technologies. *International Journal of Hydrogen Energy, 46*(60), 30669–30697.

Euractiv. (2024). *Making sense of green hydrogen costs and recent market development in Europe* [Online]. Retrieved April 04, 2025, from https://www.euractiv.com/section/energy-environment/opinion/making-sense-of-green-hydrogen-costs-and-recent-market-developments-in-europe/.

European Commission. (2020). *A hydrogen strategy for a climate-neutral Europe* [Online]. Retrieved April 04, 2025, from https://eur-lex.europa.eu/legal-content/EN/TXT/?uri=CELEX:52020DC0301.

European Commission. (2025). *European Alternative Fuels Observatory* [Online]. Retrieved April 03, 2025, from https://alternative-fuels-observatory.ec.europa.eu/transport-mode/road/spain/incentives-legislations.

European Union. (2023). *Regulation (EU) 2023/1804 of the European Parliament and the Council of 13 September 2023 on the deployment of alternative fuels infrastructure, and repealing Directive 2014/94/EU (Text with EEA relevance)* [Online]. Retrieved April 04, 2025, from https://eur-lex.europa.eu/eli/reg/2023/1804/oj.

Federal Ministry of Economic Affairs and Energy. (2020). *The national hydrogen strategy* [Online]. Retrieved April 04, 2025, from https://www.bmwk.de/Redaktion/EN/Hydrogen/Dossiers/national-hydrogen-strategy.html

FIT Consulting. (2025). *Tests underway for the first hydrogen train in Italy: Here's how it works* [Online]. Retrieved April 02, 2025, from https://www.fitconsulting.it/en/tests-underway-for-the-first-hydrogen-train-in-italy-heres-how-it-works/.

Freight Waves. (2021). *Is electrifying the freight rail network cost prohibitive?* [Online]. Retrieved April 04, 2025, from https://www.freightwaves.com/news/is-electrifying-the-freight-rail-network-cost-prohibitive.

Fuel Cell Works. (2025). *China unveils 'Track 1000' liquid hydrogen system for trucks, breaking 1,000 km barrier without refuelling* [Online]. Retrieved September 25, 2025, from https://fuelcellsworks.com/2025/03/21/clean-energy/china-unveils-track-1000-liquid-hydrogen-system-for-trucks-breaking-1-000km-barrier-without-refueling.

Gnann, T., Wietschel, M., Hettsheimer, T., & Kluschke, P. (2019). Market potential of catenary hybrid electric trucks in different world regions. In *3rd Electric Road Systems Conferences 2019*. Frankfurt am Main, Germany, 7–8th of May.

Golightly, D., Gamble, C., Palacin, R., & Pierce, K. (2019). Multi-modelling for decarbonisation in urban rail systems. *Urban Rail Transit, 5*(1), 254–266.

Golkhatmi, S. Z., Asghar, M. I., & Lund, P. D. (2022). A review on solid oxide fuel cell durability: Latest progress, mechanisms, and study tools. *Renewable and Sustainable Energy Reviews, 161*(1), 1–34.

Guerra, C. F., et al. (2021). Sustainability of hydrogen refuelling stations for trains using electrolysers. *International Journal of Hydrogen Energy, 46*(26), 137488–113759.

Halder, P., et al. (2024). Performance, emissions and economic analyses of hydrogen fuel cell vehicles. *Renewable and Sustainable Energy Reviews, 199*(1), 1–19.

Hydrogen Insight. (2025). *Stalled hydrogen-powered trains in Germany back in operation, despite ongoing refuelling problems* [Online]. Retrieved April 01, 2025, from https://www.hydrogeninsight.com/production/stalled-hydrogen-powered-trains-in-germany-back-in-operation-despite-ongoing-refuelling-problems/2-1-1764903.

Hydrogen Tools. (2023). *Hydrogen fuel cell codes & standards* [Online]. Retrieved April 04, 2025, from https://h2tools.org/hydrogen-fuel-cell-codes-standards

ICCT. (2020). *Fuel-cell hydrogen long-haul trucks in Europe: A total cost of ownership analy*sis [Online]. Retrieved March 31, 2025, from https://theicct.org/wp-content/uploads/2022/09/eu-hvs-fuels-evs-fuel-cell-hdvs-europe-sep22.pdf

ICCT. (2022). *Assessment of light-duty electric vehicle costs and consumer benefits in the United States in the 2022–2035 time frame* [Online]. Retrieved April 03, 2025, from https://theicct.org/wp-content/uploads/2022/10/ev-cost-benefits-2035-oct22.pdf.

ICCT. (2023). *Passenger vehicle greenhouse gas emissions and fuel consumption* [Online]. Retrieved March 17, 2025, from https://theicct.org/pv-fuel-economy/.

IEA. (2021). *World Energy Outlook 2021*. International Energy Agency.

IEA. (2023a). *Global EV outlook 2023* [Online]. Retrieved March 17, 2025, from https://iea.blob.core.windows.net/assets/dacf14d2-eabc-498a-8263-9f97fd5dc327/GEVO2023.pdf.

IEA. (2023b). *Rail* [Online]. Retrieved March 17, 2025, from https://www.iea.org/energy-system/transport/rail.

IEA. (2024). *Oil 2023. Analysis and forecast to 2028* [Online]. Retrieved March 17, 2025, from https://iea.blob.core.windows.net/assets/6ff5beb7-a9f9-489f-9d71-fd221b88c66e/Oil2023.pdf.

IMO. (2020). *Fourth IMO Greenhouse Gas Study 2020*. International Maritime Organization.

International Association for Hydrogen Safety. (2021). *Handbook of hydrogen safety* [Online]. Retrieved April 04, 2025, from https://hysafe.info/wp-content/uploads/sites/3/2021/04/D39_2021-01-PRESLHY_ChapterLH2-v3.pdf.

International Railway Journal. (2025). *Italy's first hydrogen train on test* [Online]. Retrieved April 01, 2025, from https://www.railjournal.com/technology/italys-first-hydrogen-train-on-test/.

IPCC. (2021). *Climate Change 2021: The Physical Science Basis. Contribution of Working Group I to the Sixth Assessment Report of the Intergovernmental Panel on Climate Change*. Cambridge University Press.

Kooij, B. J. G. (2021). *How did the general purpose technology 'internal combustion engine' contribute to the third industrial revolution: The power engines* [Online]. Retrieved April 01, 2025, from https://papers.ssrn.com/sol3/papers.cfm?abstract_id=3852628.

Korberg, A. D., et al. (2023). On the feasibility of direct hydrogen utilisation in a fossil-free Europe. *International Journal of Hydrogen Energy, 48*(8), 2877–2891.

Li, J., Gao, C., Lu, X., & Hoseyni, A. (2022). A combined energy system consisting of fuel cell, water electrolyzer and solar technologies to produce hydrogen fuel and electricity. *Energy Sources, 44*(1), 1173–1188.

Low, J. M., Haszeldine, R. S., & Harrison, G. P. (2023). The hidden cost of road maintenance due to the increased weight of battery and hydrogen trucks and buses – a perspective. *Clean Technologies and Environmental Policy, 25*(1), 757–770.

MAN. (2023). *MAN Engines presents groundbreaking hydrogen combustion engine for off-road applications* [Online]. Retrieved March 29, 2025, from https://press.mantruckandbus.com/corporate/man-engines-presents-groundbreaking-hydrogen-combustion-engine-for-off-road-applications/

Mancino, A. N., et al. (2023). (2022) 'PEM fuel cell applications in road transport'. *Energies, 16*(17), 1–27.

Marjani, S. R., et al. (2025). Assessing hydrogen as an alternative fuel for rail transport – a case study. *Scientific Reports, 15*(6449), 1–15.

Markets and Markets. (2022). *Hybrid train market size, share, trends, and forecast report, 2030* [Online]. Retrieved April 03, 2025, from https://www.marketsandmarkets.com/Market-Reports/hybrid-train-market-238438631.html.

Mass Transit. (2024). *Caltrans orders six additional hydrogen-powered trainsets from Stadler* [Online]. Retrieved April 01, 2025, from https://www.masstransitmag.com/rail/vehicles/press-release/53096580/caltrans-california-department-of-transportation-caltrans-orders-six-additional-hydrogen-powered-trainsets-from-stadler.

MIT Climate. (2023). *Why have electric vehicles won out over hydrogen cars (so far)?* [Online]. Retrieved April 04, 2025, from https://climate.mit.edu/ask-mit/why-have-electric-vehicles-won-out-over-hydrogen-cars-so-far.

OECD. (2023). *New estimates provide insights on CO2 emissions from global shipping* [Online]. Retrieved January 06, 2025, from https://oecdstatistics.blog/2023/06/15/new-estimates-provide-insights-on-co2-emissions-from-global-shipping/

Onorati, A., et al. (2022). The role of hydrogen for future internal combustion engines. *International Journal of Engine Research, 23*(4), 529–540.

Ortega, A., Gkoumas, K., Tsakalidis, A., & Pekar, F. (2021). Low-emission alternative energy for transport in the EU: State of play of research and innovation. *Energies, 14*(22), 1–22.

Popovich, N. D., Rajagopal, D., Tasar, E., & Phadke, A. (2021). Economic, environmental and grid-resilience benefits of converting diesel trains to battery-electric. *Nature Energy, 6*(1), 1017–1025.

Pramuanjaroenkij, A., & Kakaç, S. (2023). The fuel cell electric vehicles: The highlight review. *International Journal of Hydrogen Energy, 48*(25), 9401–9425.

Provincie Groningen. (2020). *Main results: Test with hydrogen train in Groningen* [Online]. Retrieved March 29, 2025, from https://www.alstom.com/sites/alstom.com/files/2020/09/30/Rapport%20Waterstoftrein%20Groningen_EN.pdf.

PWC. (2023). *Can hydrogen turn the rail industry green?* [Online]. Retrieved April 02, 2025, from https://www.pwc.com/gx/en/issues/esg/the-energy-transition/sustainable-transportation/can-hydrogen-turn-the-rail-industry-green.html

Railway Gazette International. (2024). *Zillertalbahn hydrogen plan dropped in favour of battery traction* [Online]. Retrieved April 02, 2025, from https://www.railwaygazette.com/traction-and-rolling-stock/zillertalbahn-hydrogen-plan-dropped-in-favour-of-battery-traction/66291.article

Railway News. (2023). *Siemens Mobility tests Mireo Plus H hydrogen train in Bavaria* [Online]. Retrieved April 02, 2025, from https://railway-news.com/siemens-mobility-tests-mireo-plus-h-hydrogen-train-in-bavaria/.

Roland Berger. (2019). *Study on the use of fuel cells & hydrogen in the railway environment* [Online]. Retrieved April 02, 2025, from https://rail-research.europa.eu/wp-content/uploads/2019/04/Report-2.pdf.

Roland Berger. (2021). *Hydrogen transportation* [Online]. Retrieved April 04, 2025, from https://www.rolandberger.com/publications/publication_pdf/roland_berger_hydrogen_transport.pdf.

Samsun, R. C., et al. (2022). Deployment of fuel cell vehicles and hydrogen refuelling station infrastructure: A global overview and perspectives. *Energies, 15*(14), 1–34.

Scovell, M. D. (2022). Explaining hydrogen energy technology acceptance: A critical review. *International Journal of Hydrogen Energy, 47*(19), 10441–10459.

Siemens Mobility. (2024). *Mireo Plus H – The next generation of hydrogen trains* [Online]. Retrieved April 02, 2025, from https://www.mobility.siemens.com/global/en/portfolio/rolling-stock/commuter-and-regional-trains/mireo/mireo-plus-h.html.

Siwiec, J. (2021). Use of hydrogen fuel cells in rail transport. *Railway Reports, 190*(1), 113–117.

Sorlei, I. S., et al. (2021). Fuel cell electric vehicles – A brief review of current topologies and energy management strategies. *Energies, 14*(1), 1–29.

Stead, C., Wadud, Z., Nash, C., & Li, H. (2019). Introduction of biodiesel to rail transport: Lessons from the road sector. *Sustainability, 11*(3), 1–20.

Stępień, Z. (2024). Analysis of the prospects for hydrogen-fuelled internal combustion engines. *Combustion Engines, 197*(2), 32–41.

Streuling, C., Pagenkopf, J., Schenker, M., & Lakeit, K. (2021). Techno-economic assessment of battery electric trains and recharging infrastructure alternatives integrating adjacent renewable energy sources. *Sustainability, 13*(15), 1–30.

Tabrizi, M. K., et al. (2024). Retrofit of diesel engines with H2 for potential decarbonisation of non-electrified railways: Assessment with lifecycle analysis and advanced numerical modeling. *Energies, 17*(5), 1–13.

Toyota Europe Newsroom. (2024). *Evolved liquid hydrogen-powered GR Corolla to participate in Super Taikyu Fuji 24 Hours Race* [Online]. Retrieved April 01, 2025, from https://newsroom.toyota.eu/evolved-liquid-hydrogen-powered-gr-corolla-to-participate-in-super-taikyu-fuji-24-hours-race/.

Turner, J. W. G. (2025). Future technological directions for hydrogen internal combustion engines in transport applications. *Applications in Energy and Combustion Science, 21*(1), 1–14.

UIC. (2023). *Global rail sustainability report* [Online]. Retrieved March 31, 2025, from https://uic.org/IMG/pdf/2023_global_rail_sustainability_report_web_1_1_.pdf

UNECE. (2023). *UN global technical regulation no. 13. Hydrogen and fuel cell vehicles* [Online]. Retrieved April 01, 2025, from https://unece.org/sites/default/files/2023-07/ECE-TRANS-180-Add.13-Amend1e.pdf.

Union of Concerned Scientists. (2023). *Hydrogen combustion is a dead-end technology for heavy-duty trucks* [Online]. Retrieved March 29, 2025, from https://blog.ucs.org/dave-cooke/hydrogen-combustion-is-a-dead-end-technology-for-heavy-duty-trucks/.

US Department of Energy. (2020). *Hydrogen fueling stations cost* [Online]. Retrieved March 31, 2025, from https://www.hydrogen.energy.gov/docs/hydrogenprogramlibraries/pdfs/21002-hydrogen-fueling-station-cost.pdf?Status=Master.

US Department of Energy. (2024). *Hydrogen Program. Safety* [Online]. Retrieved April 04, 2025, from https://www.hydrogen.energy.gov/program-areas/safety.

Verhelst, S., & Wallner, T. (2009). Hydrogen-fueled internal combustion engines. *Progress in Energy and Combustion Science, 35*(6), 490–527.

World Economic Forum. (2024). *This is how hydrogen trains could transform transport* [Online]. Retrieved April 01, 2025, from https://www.weforum.org/stories/2024/09/hydrogen-trains-sustainable-transport/.

World Resources Institute. (2023). *The shipping industry won't meet its decarbonization goals without investing more in low-carbon fuels* [Online]. Retrieved January 06, 2025, from https://www.wri.org/insights/how-to-decarbonize-international-shipping

Xu, Z., et al. (2022). Techno-economic analysis of hydrogen storage technologies for railway engineering: A review. *Energies, 15*(17), 1–22.

Zhang, W., Fang, X., & Sun, C. (2023). The alternative path for fossil oil: Electric vehicles or hydrogen fuel cell vehicles? *Journal of Environmental Management, 341*(1), 1–19.

Zhu, S., Ding, C., Hu, X., & Tian, Y. (2024). Analysis of safety technical standards for hydrogen storage in fuel cell vehicles. *Frontiers in Energy Research, 12*(1), 1–12.

CHAPTER 8

# Hydrogen for Maritime Transport

## Introduction

In the recent past, until 2020, when the International Maritime Organization (IMO) implemented regulations mandating a reduction to no more than 0.5%, the sulphur content of combusted bunker fuel used by large vessels such as cargo ships and tankers was the primary focus of environmental groups, activists, and policymakers seeking to make the maritime sector less polluting (IMO, 2023). At present, however, carbon emissions are at the forefront, as the industry as a whole is responsible for up to 3% of their global release (Fig. 8.1). This is not surprising, as most of these emissions remain insufficiently addressed by the international community because there are currently no internationally recognised binding regulations explicitly limiting their discharge by marine vessels (World Resources Institute, 2023; IMO, 2023).[1]

[1] The International Maritime Organization (IMO) has established a strategy to reduce greenhouse gas (GHG) emissions from ships, aiming for a reduction in the carbon intensity of international shipping by at least 40% by 2030, compared to 2008 levels (IMO, 2023). However, this strategy is not legally binding, and there are currently no internationally binding regulations explicitly limiting carbon emissions from marine vessels. As such, the IMO's approach relies on member states to implement measures at the national level, resulting in a lack of uniform enforcement and regulatory frameworks across the global shipping industry. Many industry leaders, such as Lars Barstad, CEO of Frontline, have therefore criticised it and accused the IMO of inaction in addressing the environmental risks posed by unregulated 'dark fleet' vessels (Financial Times).



A. Patonia, R. Poudineh, *Clean Hydrogen for Decarbonisation*,
https://doi.org/10.1007/978-3-032-19442-8_8

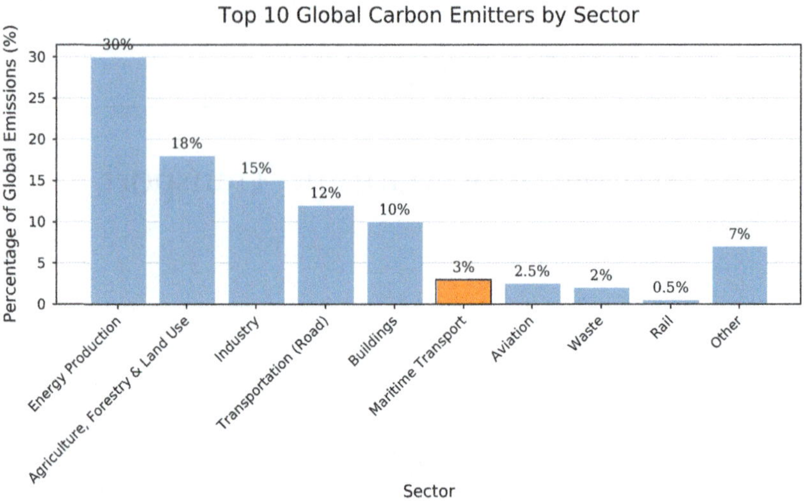


**Fig. 8.1** Top 10 global carbon emitters by sector. (Source: Adapted from IMO (2020), IEA (2021), IPCC (2021), OECD (2023), and World Resources Institute (2023))

In fact, while there are frameworks in place to regulate carbon emissions from maritime activities, the level of enforcement and binding agreements vary. Internationally, the IMO's measures are guiding but not fully binding, whereas the EU has taken more forceful steps by integrating shipping into the EU Emissions Trading System (EU ETS) as of 2024 (European Commission, 2024). Under this system, shipping companies are obliged to monitor and report their emissions and purchase allowances corresponding to their $CO_2$ output (European Commission, 2025). This regulation is legally binding for companies operating within the EU; however, it does not extend to the rest of the world (ibid.).

While the current regulatory environment is not fully equipped to address the challenge of high carbon emissions produced by the maritime sector, the industry itself is increasingly exploring various technical options to tackle this problem. This dynamic was set to change dramatically with the landmark 2025 IMO agreement, which was supposed to establish the world's first global carbon price for an entire industry, scheduled for implementation in 2027–2028. This, however, did not happen, as recent political developments have slowed global consensus. In particular, in

October 2025, the IMO's Marine Environment Protection Committee (MEPC 83) failed to adopt its Net Zero Framework (NZF) after a procedural motion delayed voting for one year (Seas at Risk, 2025; WWF Arctic, 2025). The delay followed political pressure and opposition from several major states, including the United States under Donald Trump, whose administration publicly criticised the IMO's 'green shipping' plans and called them economically damaging (Hydrogen Insight, 2025).

This postponement underscores the fragility of international cooperation on shipping decarbonisation and heightens the need for regional leadership. Nevertheless, industry players are accelerating technological exploration. With the anticipated global carbon-pricing system—now likely deferred to 2028–2029—hydrogen and its derivatives remain central to future fuel strategies.

In this context, alongside initial efforts to electrify ships or replace the combustion of Heavy Fuel Oil (HFO) with that of less polluting Marine Gas Oil (MGO), liquefied natural gas (LNG) or organic (bio) alternatives (Fig. 8.2), hydrogen and its derivatives are being increasingly considered as potential solutions to support the overall decarbonisation of the waterborne transport. At the same time, a critical distinction must be made: while hydrogen is a zero-carbon feedstock, its direct use as a fuel is severely constrained by physics and economics. The most promising applications

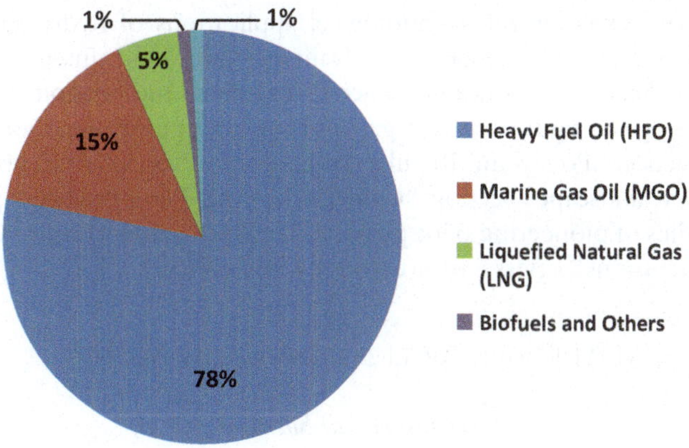


**Fig. 8.2** Key fuels in maritime propulsion and their approximate shares (2022). (Source: Adapted from IMO (2020), IEA (2022), DNV Gl (2022), and Lloyd's Register (2024))

for deep-sea shipping lie in hydrogen-derived energy carriers, such as green ammonia and e-methanol, whose adoption is now directly incentivised by the new global carbon price.

Here, however, just like in many other cases, the environmental challenges associated with the carbon emissions of combusted bunker fuels are only part of the problem. Another issue that hampers replacing it with any other option that has a lower carbon footprint is cost. As the maritime sector needs to consume large volumes of propellants such as HFO, powerful and more fuel-efficient diesel engines (compared to other types of propulsion systems) make this fuel-engine (HFO-diesel) combination cost-effective and very competitive for long-distance travel. The latter is due to the fact that, overall, HFO is normally around 33–66%cheaper than MGO, 20–40% cheaper than LNG, 50–73% cheaper than biofuels, and far cheaper than hybrid/electric systems (IEA, 2020; IMO, 2020; Bureau Veritas, 2021; DNV Gl, 2022). Nevertheless, this cost equation is being radically reshaped by the imminent global carbon price, which will impose a significant financial burden on conventional fossil fuels.

In these conditions, in order to be universally used, hydrogen-based solutions need to offer available, scalable, and cheaper alternative to the already existing and well-spread ones. While this may sound to be extremely challenging to achieve, some important attempts have already been made and first steps have already been taken.

This chapter proceeds as follows. Section "Hydrogen Applications in the Sector" explores the technological applications of hydrogen in the maritime sector and analyses the advantages and disadvantages of these pathways. Section "Economic Aspects" examines the economic aspects, highlighting the significant cost gap and the limitations of carbon pricing alone. Section "Policy and Regulatory Landscape" reviews the policy and regulatory landscape. Section "Case Studies and Pilot Projects" presents case studies of pioneering pilot projects. Finally, Section "Future Outlook and Conclusions" offers a future outlook and conclusions.

## Hydrogen Applications in the Sector

### *Technological Solutions*

At the moment, the key hydrogen-related technologies viewed for the application in the maritime sector could be broadly divided into two groups: *fuel cells* (FCs) and *combustion engines*. Through an electrochemical process, fuel cells transform hydrogen and its carriers, including ammonia and methanol, into electrical energy, with water as the only by-product. Here, Proton Exchange Membrane Fuel Cells (PEMFCs) and alkaline fuel cells (AFC) are particularly notable due to their operational efficiency at lower temperatures, and high technology readiness levels (TRL) making them suitable for the utilisation in marine environments at the moment (Table 8.1). These fuel cells have been in constant

**Table 8.1** Major fuel cell types potentially suitable for maritime transport

| *Fuel cell type* | *Fuel type* | *Typical power output (W)* | *Typical efficiency range (%)* | *Potential cost* | *Technology readiness level (TRL)* | *Notes* |
|---|---|---|---|---|---|---|
| *Proton Exchange Membrane Fuel Cell (PEMFC)* | Hydrogen | 100–200 | 40–60 | High | 7–8 | Limited to small vessels; requires high-purity $H_2$ |
| *Alkaline Fuel Cell (AFC)* | Hydrogen, ammonia | 40–70 | 40–70 | Moderate | 7–8 | Sensitive to $CO_2$ contamination |
| *Solid Oxide Fuel Cell (SOFC)* | Hydrogen, ammonia, methane | 45–65 | 45–65 | Moderate | 6–8 | Operates at high temperatures (500–1000 °C); multi-fuel capability can potentially offer flexibility |
| *Direct Methanol Fuel Cell (DMFC)* | Methanol | 30–40 | 30–40 | High | 5–7 | Suitable for small vessels |
| *Molten Carbonate Fuel Cell (MCFC)* | Hydrogen, methane, biogas | 45–55 | 45–55 | Moderate | 6–7 | Capable of internal reforming |
| *Ammonia Fuel Cell* | Ammonia | 45–60 | 45–60 | Moderate | 4–6 | Requires ammonia reforming; low TRL |

Source: Adapted from Biert et al. (2016), Xing et al. (2021), Khalil and Mughal (2021), ABS (2023), Bosio et al. (2023), Fu et al. (2023), Shi et al. (2023), Vairo et al. (2023), and Bhuiyan and Siddique (2025)

development since the 1960s and have seen growing application in maritime settings since the 1980s, as their scale and efficiency substantially increased (Elkafas et al., 2023; Kołodziejski, 2023).

At the same time, as seen from Table 8.1, different fuel cell technologies vary significantly in terms of not only the ranges of their typical efficiency and power output but also estimated costs and technology readiness. Critically, even the most advanced fuel cells, such as PEMFCs, are constrained by power output limits that make them unsuitable for the multi-megawatt propulsion needs of large ocean-going vessels. Their application is therefore confined to ferries, coastal, and other short-sea shipping where power demands are lower and refuelling is frequent.

In contrast, combustion engines can operate on hydrogen or its derivatives directly or as part of a dual-fuel system, allowing for integration with existing diesel engines. Such flexibility enables a gradual transition to hydrogen for shipping companies, avoiding the need for a complete fleet overhaul. However, the direct use of hydrogen in internal combustion engines ($H_2$-ICEs) faces the same fundamental barrier as fuel cells: its extremely low volumetric energy density (Chiong et al., 2021). Storing sufficient gaseous or cryogenic liquid hydrogen for long voyages would consume an impractical amount of a ship's cargo space. Therefore, combustion engines capable of running on hydrogen derivatives such as ammonia or methanol are currently under active development by the world's leading engine manufacturers, including Wärtsilä, MAN, and Mitsubishi (Al-Aboosi et al., 2021). These derivatives, which are liquids at ambient or mildly refrigerated conditions, offer a far more practical energy storage solution for deep-sea shipping.

Overall, Methanol Internal Combustion Engines are currently at the highest technology readiness levels (TRL) and deliver greater power output than their alternatives (Table 8.2). This should not be surprising, as hydrogen and methanol are much easier to combust than, for example, ammonia, making such engines easier to develop, as hydrogen and methanol ignite more easily and burn more predictably, which simplifies engine design and operation. In fact, due to ammonia's low flammability range, which prevents efficient combustion, the full successful commercialisation of Ammonia Internal Combustion Engines ($NH_3$-ICEs) has not yet been achieved. At the same time, despite being much easier to store and handle—since it is a liquid under ambient (normal) conditions—methanol contains carbon and, therefore, cannot be fully viewed as the ultimate decarbonisation solution, while hydrogen, as mentioned before, due to its low density, requires specific solutions to address its storage challenges

**Table 8.2** Major types of combustion engines potentially suitable for hydrogen and/or its derivatives

| *Engine type* | *Fuel type* | *Typical power output (W)* | *Typical efficiency range (%)* | *Potential cost* | *Technology readiness level (TRL)* | *Notes* |
|---|---|---|---|---|---|---|
| *Hydrogen Internal Combustion Engine ($H_2$-ICE)* | Hydrogen | 200–300 | 30–40 | Moderate | 8–9 | Severe tank space penalty limits to short-range applications; $NO_x$ formation is a concern |
| *Methanol Internal Combustion Engine* | Methanol | 200–300 | 30–40 | Low-moderate | 8–9 | Commercially available; suitable for new builds; carbon emissions unless green methanol |
| *Dual-Fuel Combustion Engine* | Hydrogen or Ammonia + Diesel | 400–600 | 40–45 | Low | ~8 | Lower emission than pure diesel; ammonia dual-fuel is a leading candidate for deep-sea |

(*continued*)

**Table 8.2** (continued)

| *Engine type* | *Fuel type* | *Typical power output (W)* | *Typical efficiency range (%)* | *Potential cost* | *Technology readiness level (TRL)* | *Notes* |
|---|---|---|---|---|---|---|
| *Spark Ignition (SI) Engine* | Hydrogen, methanol, ammonia | 150–200 | 30–40 | Moderate | 7–8 | Hydrogen and methanol work best, ammonia needs additional support for efficient combustion |
| *Compression Ignition (CI) Engine* | Ammonia, methanol, hydrogen | 250–350 | 35–45 | Low-moderate | 6–8 | Operates on a mix of fuels, ammonia requires pilot fuel (e.g., diesel) to ignite |
| *Ammonia Internal Combustion Engine ($NH_3$-ICE)* | Ammonia | 100–200 | 30–38 | Moderate | 6–7 | Requires ammonia decomposition or dual-fuel setups to improve ignition and emits $NO_x$. |

Source: Adapted from Verhelst and Wallner (2009), Tarnatore et al. (2022), Djermouni and Ouahda (2023), Kołodziejski (2023), and Zhang et al. (2024)

effectively. This is why Dual-Fuel Combustion Engines, Spark Ignition (SI) engines, and Compression Ignition (CI) engines that could, in principle, run on a combination of fuels (i.e., hydrogen, methanol, and ammonia) are also approaching commercialisation.

When comparing hydrogen with other alternatives such as electrification and the use of biofuels, several key factors emerge. Battery-electric systems are gaining traction in short-distance shipping; however, they face limitations due to weight and energy density, making them less suitable for larger vessels or long-haul routes. Hydrogen fuel cells offer a promising solution for smaller ships where battery weight could be prohibitive (EMSA, 2023). Although biofuels offer a lower-carbon alternative to conventional fossil fuels, they frequently compete with agricultural land and food production. In contrast, hydrogen—especially green hydrogen produced from renewable sources—presents a more sustainable long-term solution without these trade-offs, primarily when used as a feedstock for ammonia and e-methanol (Kołodziejski, 2023).

The maturity of these technologies varies significantly. Hydrogen fuel cells are at a demonstration phase for maritime applications, with only niche commercial operations. Numerous demonstration projects are underway globally to test hydrogen as a marine fuel, serving as platforms for evaluating different technological solutions in real-world conditions (Kołodziejski, 2023). Many hydrogen combustion engine systems are still in the pilot phase, with ongoing research aimed at optimising performance and reducing costs. The transition from pilot projects to commercial viability will depend on advancements in production infrastructure and regulatory support (EMSA, 2023). In conclusion, the technological pathway is bifurcating: direct hydrogen for small, short-range vessels, and hydrogen-derived fuels for the large vessel, deep-sea segment that constitutes the bulk of the sector's emissions.

### *Advantages and Disadvantages*

Since fuel cells and combustion engines currently represent two primary technologies for the use of hydrogen and its derivatives, which, in turn, are viewed as potential alternative to traditional fossil fuels, highlighting the advantages and drawbacks of either seems important. Overall, fuel cells demonstrate higher operational efficiency (typically between 40 and 60 or even 70%) than combustion engines (normally between 30 and 45%), while also having lower environmental impact (Minnehan & Pratt,

2017; Vairo et al., 2023). In addition, they operate quieter and have fewer moving parts, which can ultimately lead to lower maintenance costs over time (Bosio et al., 2023; Kołodziejski, 2023).

On the other hand, the adoption of fuel cells in maritime applications still faces significant challenges that go beyond their full commercialisation that is yet to be achieved. In general, being less powerful than combustion engines, at the moment, they cannot be utilised by most of the heavy-load, largest, and therefore most polluting marine vessels and can instead be used only by relatively small ships and boats (Table 8.1). This is a fundamental constraint unlikely to be overcome, cementing their role as a niche solution. In most cases, they also require high purity hydrogen, which significantly complicates supply chains and results in high costs associated with the infrastructure adjustment (Kołodziejski, 2023). This factor also limits their use by large vessels as the tank-cargo issue mentioned before stemming from $H_2$'s low volumetric density has still not been properly addressed (ibid. and Fu et al., 2023). Finally, the initial investment for fuel cell technology is relatively high, which provides further arguments in favour of combustion engines.

In contrast, while combustion engines can utilize hydrogen directly, they can also use dual-fuel systems with diesel or other derivatives like ammonia and methanol. This flexibility potentially allows for easier integration with existing diesel fleets, making it a more attractive option for shipping companies looking to transition without significant overhauls (Volvo Group, 2024). Methanol Internal Combustion Engines are currently at highest technology readiness levels (TRLs) and can deliver substantial power outputs (200–300 kW), making them suitable for newbuild vessels. However, combustion engines are not without drawbacks. While they can operate on hydrogen derivatives, they still produce nitrogen oxides ($NO_x$) and other emissions, which cause environmental concerns though less significant than those associated with conventional diesel engines (Verhelst & Wallner, 2009; Svanberg et al., 2018). The use of such hydrogen derivatives as methanol, in turn, introduces carbon emissions into the equation, further complicating the pursuit of complete decarbonisation. Finally, ammonia combustion poses significant technical challenges due to its low flammability range, which hinders efficient operation (ibid.).

### *Infrastructure Requirements*

The transition to alternative fuels and technologies in the maritime transport sector greatly depends on the development of sector-specific infrastructure. Here, each fuel—such as hydrogen, ammonia, methanol, LNG, or hybrid/electric solutions—requires tailored storage, transportation, and refuelling systems to ensure functionality and scalability. As shown in Table 8.3, it is therefore unsurprising that combustion engines designed to run on more sustainable alternatives to HFO are generally more scalable and adaptable than fuel cells or electric/hybrid options partially because much of the infrastructure that would be required for their application often happens to already be in place. Specifically, methanol bunkering can leverage existing liquid fuel infrastructure with minimal adjustments, while ammonia requires new but manageable systems similar to LPG. Hydrogen infrastructure, in contrast, is the most capital-intensive and complex to deploy.

In general, for fuel cells, particularly PEMFCs and AFCs, dedicated refuelling stations are essential to supply high-purity hydrogen (Table 8.3). While these stations must be strategically located in major ports to facilitate the refuelling of vessels, their design should consider safety protocols due to hydrogen's flammability and the need for specialized equipment to handle pressurized gas or liquefied $H_2$, which should be kept under cryogenic temperatures[2] (Xing et al., 2021). In fact, hydrogen's specific features place additional pressure on the development of $H_2$ infrastructure, as both the compression and liquefaction of this fuel not only require precautionary measures to ensure safe handling but are also associated with additional energy losses and costs[3] (Veldhuizen et al., 2023; Vairo et al., 2023). Therefore, at the moment, the scalability of fuel cell infrastructure is low for PEMFCs due to the high costs associated with developing high-purity hydrogen refuelling stations (Bosio et al., 2023). Although AFCs have a slightly better scalability potential, they are still limited by $CO_2$ contamination issues, and SOFCs present moderate scalability but require

[2] Safety protocols for hydrogen refuelling (or bunkering) of maritime vessels are still in development, and while progress has been made, there are no universally recognised international standards fully adopted across the maritime industry as of now. However, there are efforts underway to establish such standards.

[3] Using today's technology, liquefaction typically consumes more than 30% of the energy content of the hydrogen (US Department of Energy, 2024).

**Table 8.3** Key technological alternatives to HFO, their infrastructure requirements, current scalability and adaptability

| *Technology* | | *Specific infrastructure requirements* | *Current scalability* | *Current adaptability* | *Current key challenges* |
|---|---|---|---|---|---|
| *Hybrid/electric* | | • Charging infrastructure<br>• Grid integration | Low | Moderate (battery limits) | • Charging speed<br>• Grid readiness<br>• Heavy-duty compatibility |
| *Fuel cells* | PEMFC | • High-purity hydrogen refuelling stations<br>• Cryogenic or high-pressure storage | Very low | Limited (hydrogen only) | • High hydrogen purity requirements<br>• Extremely costly and complex bunkering infrastructure |
| | AFC | Hydrogen/ammonia refuelling infrastructure | Low | Limited ($CO_2$-sensitive) | • $CO_2$ contamination issues<br>• Hydrogen handling |
| | SOFC | Multi-fuel pipelines and storage systems | Moderate | High | • High operating temperatures<br>• Infrastructure upgrades required |
| | DMFC | Methanol refuelling systems | Low | Low (small-scale only) | • Limited to small vessels<br>• High cost |
| | MCFC | Hydrogen/methane storage and reforming | Moderate | Moderate | • Internal reforming complexity |
| | Ammonia | Ammonia-specific storage and bunkering | Low | Limited (early-stage tech) | • Ammonia reforming and safety challenges |

| | | | | | |
|---|---|---|---|---|---|
| *Combustion engines* | $H_2$-ICE | High-pressure or cryogenic hydrogen storage, modified refuelling systems | Moderate | Moderate | • Prohibitive tank space requirements<br>• $NO_x$ emissions |
| | Methanol ICE | Minor adjustments to liquid fuel infrastructure | High | High | • Carbon content limits its potential for full decarbonisation |
| | $NH_3$-ICE | Ammonia-specific storage and enhanced safety systems | Low | Limited | • Safety concerns (toxicity)<br>• Inefficient ammonia combustion requiring pilot fuel |
| | Dual-fuel engine | Infrastructure for traditional and alternative fuels | Moderate | High | • Maintaining efficiency with mixed fuel use |
| | Spark ignition | Fuel-specific storage Methanol requires minimal changes | Moderate | Moderate | • Ammonia's low flammability<br>• Hydrogen storage complexity |
| | Compression ignition | Adjustments for ammonia and hydrogen storage Minor changes for methanol | Moderate | Moderate | • Ammonia requires pilot fuel<br>• Hydrogen ignition challenges |
| | CI MGO | Mature bunkering and distribution networks | Very high | Very high | • Moderate emissions compared to HFO but still significant |
| | CI LNG | Cryogenic storage, bunkering | High | Moderate | • Methane leakage<br>• Limited carbon neutrality |
| | CI Biofuels | Minor system upgrades, storage | High | High | • Feedstock availability<br>• Land use concerns |

*Source:* Adapted from Verhelst and Wallner (2009), Biert et al. (2016), Xing et al. (2021), Tarnatore et al. (2022), ABS (2023), Bosio et al. (2023), Djermouni and Ouahda (2023), Fu et al. (2023), Kołodziejski (2023), Shi et al. (2023), Vairo et al. (2023), Zhang et al. (2024), and Bhuiyan and Siddique (2025)

significant infrastructure upgrades to support their operation effectively (ibid.).

The overall adaptability of fuel cells is also limited. PEMFCs are primarily designed for hydrogen use only. This creates a 'chicken-and-egg' problem: investment in widespread hydrogen bunkering is stalled by limited demand from a small fleet of compatible vessels, and the fleet growth is constrained by the lack of bunkering infrastructure.

Combustion engines running on hydrogen and its derivatives also have specific infrastructure needs. For instance, Hydrogen Internal Combustion Engines ($H_2$-ICEs) require high-pressure or cryogenic hydrogen storage with modified refuelling systems (Svanberg et al., 2018). At the same time, Methanol Internal Combustion Engines can often leverage existing liquid fuel infrastructure with minor adjustments, enhancing their adaptability (Kołodziejski, 2023). In contrast, ammonia-based engines necessitate ammonia-specific storage and enhanced safety systems due to toxicity concerns (ibid.).

Overall, combustion engines using methanol and ammonia demonstrate higher adaptability compared to fuel cells. Methanol ICEs represent the lowest-barrier entry for alternative fuels, while dual-fuel systems allow vessels to utilize a mix of fuels efficiently, enhancing operational flexibility. However, significant challenges are still in place regarding maintaining efficiency with mixed fuel use in dual-fuel engines and addressing $NO_x$ emissions from $H_2$-ICEs.

When it comes to the scalability of combustion engine infrastructure, it varies significantly. $H_2$-ICEs have moderate scalability due to the need for specialized storage solutions for hydrogen. In contrast, Methanol ICEs exhibit high scalability because they can integrate with existing fuel systems without extensive modifications (Svanberg et al., 2018). Dual-fuel engines also present moderate scalability as they can operate on traditional diesel fuels alongside alternative fuels.

In general, both technologies face unique challenges related to infrastructure development. Fuel cells are normally hindered by the high costs of establishing dedicated refuelling stations and the need for high-purity hydrogen. Combustion engines, in their turn, must often contend with safety concerns associated with ammonia storage and the environmental impact of $NO_x$ emissions from the combustion process itself. While both fuel cells and combustion engines have their respective strengths and weaknesses regarding infrastructure scalability and adaptability in maritime transport, combustion engines currently offer greater flexibility in utilizing existing infrastructure. Nevertheless, ongoing technological improvements and evolving regulatory frameworks could greatly enhance the scalability and versatility of fuel cells.

## Economic Aspects

Adopting hydrogen in the maritime sector necessitates substantial investments across the value chain, encompassing capital expenditures (CapEx), operational expenditures (OpEx), and fuel costs (as a significant separate part of OpEx). Here, CapEx primarily includes the cost of acquiring new hydrogen-powered vessels or retrofitting existing ones with fuel cells or hydrogen combustion engines. Retrofitting existing vessels to run on direct hydrogen is considered economically unfeasible at scale due to the profound space and weight penalties of hydrogen storage systems, among others. For newbuilds, the CapEx for a vessel powered by hydrogen-derived fuels (e.g., ammonia engines) is estimated to be 20–50% higher than a conventional vessel, while a hydrogen fuel cell vessel can be up to twice as expensive (DNV, 2023).

OpEx, in turn, comprises, among others, fuel costs, maintenance, and crew training. When it comes to fuel costs, which is absolutely critical to OpEx, although hydrogen fuel is expected to become cost-competitive in the future, current production methods of clean $H_2$ and its derivatives are much more expensive than those associated with conventional maritime fuels, which makes this cost component very significant. Green ammonia and e-methanol are currently 2–4 times more expensive than VLSFO (Very Low Sulphur Fuel Oil), and this gap is not projected to close significantly without massive policy intervention (BloombergNEF, 2023) (Fig. 8.3).

Retrofitting ships with hydrogen fuel cells present a substantial financial undertaking, impacting both CapEx and OpEx. The cost of fuel cell systems varies considerably, typically ranging from USD 1000 to 3000 per kW (DNV, 2023). For vessels requiring megawatts of power, installation costs can easily reach millions of dollars. Hydrogen storage and distribution infrastructure contribute further substantial expenses; cryogenic tanks for liquid hydrogen or high-pressure gas storage can cost between USD 500,000 and 5 million, depending on capacity (EMSA, 2023). Integrating fuel cells into a ship's power system involves additional costs for components like DC/AC power conversion and battery buffers (ibid.). It is therefore estimated that the CapEx for a hydrogen combustion

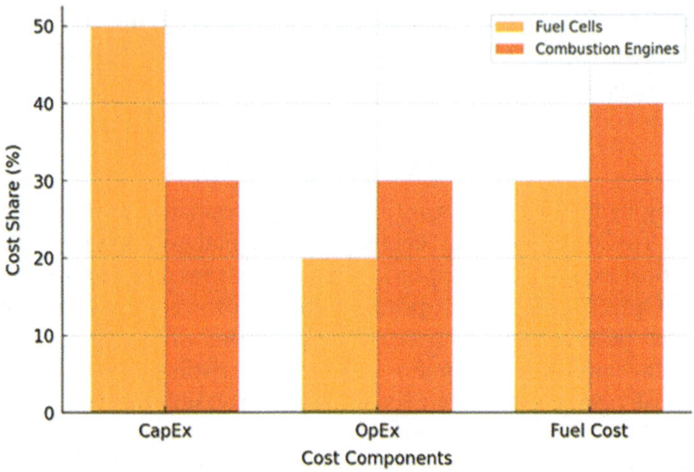


**Fig. 8.3** Approximate cost breakdown for hydrogen fuel cells and combustion engines. (Source: Adapted from Bureau Veritas (2021), DNV (2023), EMSA (2023), World Resources Institute (2023))

engine-powered vessel could be two to three times higher than that of a comparable conventional vessel (ibid.). Similar analyses indicate that fuel cell-powered vessels might require a cost premium in the same range—approximately two to three times the CapEx of conventional vessels, and in some cases, depending on vessel design and integration complexity, the premium for fuel cell systems could approach 3 to 3.5 times higher (ibid.). At the same time, as technology matures and economies of scale are realised, these cost differentials are projected to decline.

Overall, comparing hydrogen with current technologies requires a holistic assessment, considering direct costs and externalities like environmental impact and regulatory compliance. As noted, the operation of hydrogen-fuelled vessels currently incurs higher costs compared with traditional HFO-powered ships, reflecting greater CapEx and OpEx. However, while hydrogen costs will presumably decrease and conventional fuel costs, coupled with carbon pricing, will increase, clean $H_2$ and its derivatives will become more competitive. The primary benefit of using these new fuels is, therefore, different—i.e., that of the near-elimination of greenhouse gas emissions and air pollutants, contributing to maritime decarbonisation, which aligns with increasingly stringent environmental regulations and enhances environmental credentials. That is why, although hydrogen has higher upfront costs, long-term benefits of reduced emissions and potential carbon pricing advantages could make it more attractive with time.

In this context, carbon pricing, such as emissions trading systems or carbon taxes, is a core mechanism to incentivise emission reductions. The landmark IMO agreement in 2025 establishes a global carbon price for shipping, starting at USD 100 per tonne of $CO_2$ from 2028. This is a pivotal development, but evidence suggests that this price alone is insufficient to bridge the entire cost gap; it must be complemented by direct subsidies, mandates, and fuel standards to make green fuels competitive (IRENA, 2022). The IMO mechanism is also complex, applying a higher fee (USD 380/t) to the most intensive portion of emissions and USD 100/t to remaining emissions above a threshold. While it is projected to generate USD 11–13 billion annually to support clean fuel deployment, some analysts warn its complexity may blunt its effectiveness, potentially creating a cost burden without fully catalysing the hydrogen fuel transition (Hydrogen Insight, 2025). Therefore, consistent, long-term policy support is essential to build investor confidence and drive innovation. A level playing field, where all fuels are assessed on a full lifecycle emissions basis, is crucial for fair competition and optimal decarbonisation.

Effective government policies are therefore critical mechanisms. More specifically, direct subsidies for hydrogen vessel construction or retrofitting reduce initial CapEx, tax incentives, loan guarantees, and R&D grants could further encourage investment in the field. Policies like the EU FuelEU Maritime, mandating stepwise cuts in the GHG intensity of maritime energy, are key because they establish demand for low-carbon fuels irrespective of pure cost considerations. The EU's own targets—a 6% reduction in shipping GHG intensity by 2030 and 80% by 2050—run in parallel to the global IMO measures, creating a layered regulatory push (European Commission, 2023).

## Policy and Regulatory Landscape

Globally, maritime policy is heavily influenced by the International Maritime Organization (IMO), which sets the standards for shipping emissions through instruments such as the International Convention for the Prevention of Pollution from Ships (MARPOL) and its Annex VI regulations. In 2018, the IMO approved its initial strategy to cut greenhouse gas emissions from ships, aiming for a 50% reduction by 2050 relative to 2008 levels (IMO, 2018). In 2023, this was revised to a net-zero GHG emissions target 'by or around' 2050, a much stronger signal that necessitates a shift towards zero-carbon fuels (IMO, 2023).

Crucially, in April 2025, IMO Member States reached political agreement on a Net Zero Framework combining a well-to-wake GHG-intensity standard and a global carbon-pricing mechanism (IMO, 2025). Yet, in October 2025, its formal adoption was postponed after a procedural motion was introduced just before the vote, deferring implementation for at least a year (Seas at Risk, 2025). The postponement—which observers described as a 'lost year' for maritime decarbonisation—came amid strong lobbying and political resistance, including outright criticism from Donald Trump, who accused the IMO of threatening US trade interests (Hydrogen Insight, 2025). Environmental groups and some Member States called the delay 'deeply disappointing', noting that it risks pushing the sector further off track for its 2030 targets (WWF Arctic, 2025).

As a result, the timeline for the global carbon-pricing mechanism—initially expected to begin in 2027—is now likely to shift to 2028 or later. This adds uncertainty for shipowners and fuel producers investing in hydrogen and its derivatives, though the EU and other regions continue to advance their own schemes (European Commission, 2025). In general, however, analysts suggest that, even if reached in 2026, the agreement may deliver only around an 8–10% absolute emissions reduction by 2030, falling short of the IMO's own target of 20–30%, highlighting an ambition gap that may require further policy strengthening (Reuters, 2025).

At the same time, regionally, for instance at the European level, the situation looks more promising, as the European Green Deal and the subsequent Fit for 55 package have intensified focus on shipping emissions, including maritime transport in the EU Emissions Trading System (ETS) and introducing the FuelEU Maritime regulation (European Commission, 2021). The EU's Alternative Fuels Infrastructure Regulation (AFIR) supports the deployment of alternative fuel refuelling points in major ports, which will include ammonia and methanol bunkering facilities, thus laying foundational infrastructure for hydrogen-derived fuel adoption (European Commission, 2022). The European Commission has welcomed the IMO deal as a 'meaningful step' and a 'strong foundation', while noting that it will assess the interaction between the new global rules and existing EU legislation to maintain environmental integrity and avoid double burdens (European Commission, 2025).

Nevertheless, although global alignment under the IMO has temporarily stalled, the EU remains the most ambitious regional actor, enforcing its FuelEU Maritime regulation and extending the ETS to shipping, and other nations such as Japan, South Korea, and Norway maintain active hydrogen-based maritime strategies. In these circumstances, hydrogen-derived fuels such as ammonia and methanol are currently viewed as key candidates for driving decarbonisation in the maritime sector.

Nationally, although many countries have adopted their hydrogen strategies in expectations to ramp-up the development of their local clean $H_2$ sector, countries like Japan and South Korea have specifically articulated maritime applications for the use of hydrogen and its derivatives in their national hydrogen documents. In particular, Japan's Basic Hydrogen Strategy identifies hydrogen-fuelled vessels and ammonia bunkering as strategic priorities, supported by subsidies and research initiatives, while South Korea's 'Hydrogen Economy Roadmap' aims to make the country a leader in hydrogen-powered ship technology, including infrastructure development and pilot projects (METI, 2017; Baker McKenzie, 2024).

Outside of Asia, the Norwegian government has been particularly proactive in advancing cleaner vessels through targeted regulation and strategic planning. One example is the zero-emission requirement for cruise ships, ferries, and tourist boats operating in Norway's World Heritage fjords: as of 1 January 2026, passenger ships under 10,000 gross tonnage must comply, and from 1 January 2032 the same rule will apply to larger passenger ships (Norwegian Maritime Authority, 2025). Ships will be allowed to use biogas alternatives where conditions are met, and shore power must be used where available. These policies are helping to stimulate development of low- or zero-emission vessel technology, including hydrogen fuel cell ferries, although no universally binding global framework yet mandates these, and financing still presents a major barrier.

Overall, while some national and even regional policies have started promoting hydrogen and its derivatives, the lack of a universally binding and comprehensive regulatory framework remains a significant barrier. The high cost disparity, coupled with the capital intensity of new infrastructure, creates a persistent 'chicken-and-egg' problem that regional policies alone cannot fully resolve. Here, even the use of hydrogen derivatives still does not eliminate all the problems because the existing combustion engines need to be significantly adjusted, which has not been fully successful (ABS, 2021). The durability and efficiency of fuel cells in maritime environments, in turn, is characterized by saltwater corrosion, and variable loads, among other challenged, also require further R&D (ibid.). While some of these barriers can potentially be mitigated in the future with technical progress, they are not the only ones that have to be addressed.

For instance, economically, the cost competitiveness of clean hydrogen and its derivatives still remains a very significant (if not the most important) hurdle. Despite all the efforts made by countries where the cost of renewable power generation is low, green hydrogen is currently a lot more expensive than blue or conventionally produced grey $H_2$ and obviously much more expensive than fossil fuels and even other low-carbon alternatives like LNG (Fig. 8.4). This cost disparity is exacerbated by the capital-intensive nature of hydrogen infrastructure—such as refuelling stations and onboard storage retrofits, which require substantial upfront investments and create a 'chicken-and-egg' dilemma in demand and supply development (DNV, 2023).

Supply chain issues also present a significant challenge. The production of green hydrogen and its derivatives is geographically constrained to regions with abundant renewable resources, requiring robust international

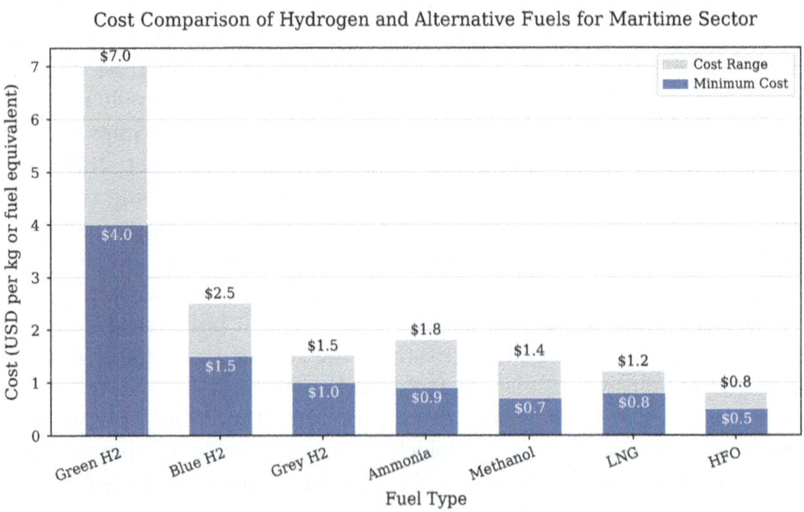


**Fig. 8.4** Average cost ranges of hydrogen and alternative fuels for maritime sector. (Source: Adapted from IEA (2020), IMO (2020), World Bank (2021), Sphera (2022), BloombergNEF (2023))

supply chains to transport $H_2$ or its carriers to major maritime hubs (IRENA, 2022). That is why the scalability of hydrogen production and the development of global supply networks are pivotal for the widespread maritime adoption of hydrogen.

When it comes to regulatory barriers, apart from the mentioned absence of universally binding regulations on carbon emissions, some of the most important ones include the lack of harmonised international standards for hydrogen bunkering and safety protocols. While the IMO has made strides with guidelines for using hydrogen as fuel under the IGF Code (International Code of Safety for Ships Using Gases or Other Low-flashpoint Fuels), detailed standards specific to hydrogen are still under development (IMO, 2024). Moreover, national regulations often vary, creating fragmented market conditions that complicate the operation of hydrogen-fuelled vessels across different jurisdictions.

Overall, safety is a paramount concern in the deployment of hydrogen in maritime settings. Hydrogen's flammability and wide ignition range necessitate rigorous safety measures, particularly in the confined and potentially isolated environment of a ship. Similar (if not stricter) measures should be applied to hydrogen derivatives such as ammonia, which is toxic and can cause severe respiratory irritation, chemical burns, and environmental hazards in case of leaks. Therefore, developing effective leak detection systems, ventilation strategies, and emergency response protocols are critical for operational safety (DNV, 2023).

The issue of safety is very closely related to the one of public acceptance, which, in turn, is often overlooked. At the same time, for hydrogen and its derivatives to become viable alternatives to conventional marine fuels, all the maritime industry stakeholders—ranging from shipowners and operators to port authorities and regulators—must be convinced of hydrogen's viability as a safe and sustainable alternative to incumbent fuels. Since this, however, is unlikely to be the case at the moment, education and awareness campaigns, coupled with transparent demonstration projects, will have to be conducted to help build confidence and foster a favourable public and industry perception (European Maritime Safety Agency, 2023).

## Case Studies and Pilot Projects

As the maritime industry is increasingly adopting hydrogen as a potentially viable fuel source, several significant milestones marking its progress have been achieved. In this respect, one of the most notable examples is Sea Change, the 'world's first entirely hydrogen-powered ferry', which was officially launched in 2024 (Renewable Energy Magazine, 2024). Developed by All American Marine, this 70-foot (~22-metre) ferry utilizes a hydrogen fuel cell system from Zero Emission Industries (Zero Emission Industries, 2021). With a capacity for 75 passengers and the ability to operate on renewable hydrogen, Sea Change is supposed to exemplify the potential of $H_2$ in reducing maritime emissions while maintaining operational efficiency (ibid.). It is a quintessential example of the niche where direct hydrogen fuel cells are viable: a small, short-route ferry.

While Sea Change definitely represents an interesting case and may seem an impressive milestone on the way to decarbonise the marine sector, previous historic examples actually demonstrate that physically replacing conventional diesel engines with fuel cells may not necessarily be the greatest challenge to overcome on the way to successfully introduce hydrogen into the industry. In fact, the FCS Alsterwasser, launched in 2008 in Hamburg, Germany, was one of the world's first hydrogen fuel cell-powered passenger ferries, which used a hybrid propulsion system, combining hydrogen fuel cells (50 kW) with batteries (Barett, 2008). Built by Alster Touristik GmbH (ATG) as part of the EU-funded Zemships (Zero Emission Ships) project, it was designed to carry up to 100 passengers while operating on the city's Alster River (ibid.). Although FCS Alsterwasser successfully demonstrated the feasibility of fuel cell technology in commercial ferry services, the project faced challenges due to hydrogen refuelling infrastructure limitations, leading to its eventual discontinuation (European Commission, 2011). This underscores the criticality of simultaneous infrastructure development.

As most current $H_2$ fuel cell projects in the maritime sector are relatively small-scale, compressed hydrogen is currently preferred over liquefied hydrogen for storage tanks. At the same time, as longer distances and larger scales are likely to make the use of liquefied hydrogen more relevant, its application in maritime conditions and in fuel cells needs to be tested. In this respect, the MF Hydra is noteworthy as one of the world's first vessels powered by liquid hydrogen and hydrogen fuel cells (Ballard, 2023). Since entering operation in 2023, MF Hydra, which features two

200 kW fuel cell modules, has successfully completed over 20,000 crossings, demonstrating the viability of liquid hydrogen in fuel cell-powered maritime transport (ibid.). Nevertheless, we have yet to see similar success stories replicated in other parts of the world, and it remains unclear whether this pilot will be scaled up and transformed into a universally adopted mainstream solution.

At the moment, the two ferries that are being developed for Torghatten in Norway and that are going to be equipped with 6.4 MW PowerCell fuel cells are likely to become the largest marine hydrogen fuel cells ever produced (Seatrade Maritime News, 2023). Designed to operate on Norway's longest ferry route, they are set to commence service in October 2025 and are expected to have the capacity to carry up to 599 passengers and 120 cars each (ibid.). This project represents the upper limit of scalability for pure hydrogen fuel cells and remains an exception rather than a norm.

While hydrogen is a promising zero-carbon fuel, its low energy density by volume, storage challenges, and infrastructure requirements make it less practical for widespread use in the maritime sector at present. Therefore, the industry's main focus has shifted to hydrogen-derived fuels. For instance, Wärtsilä, a global leader in marine technology, has been developing engines for ammonia and methanol. Wärtsilä has achieved a ground-breaking milestone with the development of the four-stroke Wärtsilä 25 ammonia engine, the world's first ammonia dual-fuel marine engine (Wärtsilä, 2022). During testing, the engine demonstrated its ability to efficiently combust ammonia while maintaining performance and reliability, achieving significant reductions in $CO_2$ emissions (Wärtsilä, 2023). This represents a strategic bet on ammonia as a future deep-sea fuel.

Wärtsilä is also exploring the use of ammonia as a fuel, with plans to introduce a wide spectrum of ammonia-ready engines within this decade. By now, the company has already achieved a ground-breaking milestone in maritime decarbonisation with the development of the four-stroke Wärtsilä 25 ammonia engine, the world's first ammonia dual-fuel marine engine, which is designed to operate on ammonia as well as traditional marine fuels like diesel or LNG (Wärtsilä, 2022). During testing, the engine demonstrated its ability to efficiently combust ammonia while maintaining performance and reliability, achieving significant reductions in $CO_2$ emissions (Wärtsilä, 2023). For Wärtsilä 25, the company's innovative approach includes advanced fuel injection and combustion technologies to address challenges such as ammonia's lower flammability and higher nitrogen oxide ($NO_x$) emissions (Melideo & Desideri, 2024). While the company plans to fully commercialise this product in 2025, offering shipowners a practical pathway to decarbonise their fleets, it appears to be a relatively small-scale (1.7–3.4 MW) application for medium-speed vessels (Wärtsilä, 2023); therefore, this technology will need to be significantly scaled up if it is to play a decisive role in the decarbonisation of the maritime sector (Melideo & Desideri, 2024).

MAN Energy Solutions has also been actively developing ammonia-powered engines for maritime applications, with the full-scale testing of a two-stroke ammonia dual-fuel engine currently taking place at their Research Centre in Copenhagen (MAN Energy Solutions, 2023). This ME-LGIA engine is designed for vessels with significant power demands. Even though, just like the Wärtsilä 25, this engine would require a small pilot flame of conventional fuel (like diesel) to initiate combustion, the goal is to reduce this to as low as 5%, representing a 95% well-to-wake emissions reduction (Melideo & Desideri, 2024).

Although not representing the ultimate solution due to its carbon content, methanol is also gaining significant attention among manufacturers of marine engines, primarily due to its liquid form at ambient temperatures, which significantly simplifies its storage and handling. A prominent example is MAN Energy Solutions' dual-fuel methanol engines, which are available in both two-stroke and four-stroke configurations and offer operational flexibility (MAN Energy Solutions, 2023). Methanol-fuelled newbuilds are already being ordered in significant numbers, indicating its role as a leading transitional fuel.

In summary, at present, hydrogen fuel cells for marine applications remain viable primarily for smaller-scale solutions like ferries. They are not yet widely adaptable to existing marine infrastructure and face scalability challenges. In contrast, combustion engines running on ammonia and methanol are more adaptable and scalable, especially for larger vessels and newbuilds. The pilot projects and commercial developments from major engine manufacturers clearly signal that the industry's trajectory is centred on hydrogen-derived fuels, not direct hydrogen, for the bulk of maritime decarbonisation.

## Future Outlook and Conclusions

Hydrogen and its derivatives remain core to the sector's decarbonisation vision. However, the 2025 IMO stalemate and one-year delay of the Net Zero Framework have introduced new uncertainty into the timeline for global action. Analysts warn that this could slow investment in green fuel infrastructure and divert resources to short-term transitional fuels. At the same time, the controversy has galvanised calls from the EU and Pacific states for more ambitious regional measures if global consensus falters.

In the meantime, industry momentum has not stopped—pilot projects for hydrogen, ammonia, and e-methanol continue, but financiers are seeking regulatory clarity before committing to large-scale infrastructure. Therefore, while hydrogen and its derivatives will remain central to the maritime decarbonisation portfolio, the political fractures exposed in 2025 demonstrate that technological progress must be matched by stable international governance. Without binding and timely rules, the sector risks missing its 2030 and 2040 milestones. Ultimately, achieving net-zero shipping will require a combination of global carbon pricing, regional regulation, and accelerated deployment of hydrogen-derived fuels. The postponed IMO framework is a reminder that even as technology advances, political will remains the decisive variable.

Therefore, in the short term, the adoption of hydrogen in maritime transport is likely to remain largely experimental and limited to pilot projects, short-haul routes, and smaller vessels. Current regulatory frameworks, including the EU ETS, FuelEU Maritime, and Norway's zero-emission fjord mandates, create important incentives for early adoption, particularly along emerging green corridors that connect prepared ports. The imminent IMO carbon price, starting at USD 100/tonne, will begin to internalise the cost of pollution for shipowners, making fossil fuels less attractive. Hydrogen fuel cells will remain focused on ferries and coastal vessels where refuelling is frequent, while hydrogen-derived fuels such as ammonia and e-methanol are expected to dominate early commercial uptake in larger ships due to their higher energy density and easier handling.

However, the high cost of clean hydrogen and its derivatives, combined with limited supply and underdeveloped bunkering infrastructure, remains a significant barrier. Analyses suggest the IMO measures alone may not be sufficient to overcome this barrier entirely, potentially creating a cost burden without fully unlocking investment in green hydrogen fuels, due to complexity and perceived insufficient stringency. In addition, fuel cells, while promising for small-scale operations, are not yet scalable for large ocean-going vessels requiring megawatt-class propulsion. Combustion engines operating on ammonia or e-methanol, often in dual-fuel configurations, are therefore expected to provide more immediate decarbonisation potential, leveraging existing engine platforms and ship designs.

As hydrogen's volumetric energy density constraint is unlikely to be fully overcome, hybrid and dual-fuel approaches using hydrogen derivatives (ammonia, e-methanol) are expected to gain traction as near-term pragmatic solutions. Engine manufacturers such as Wärtsilä and MAN will continue refining these systems, aiming to reduce pilot fuel use and control emissions such as $NO_x$ and $N_2O$.

To accelerate this transition, governments and industry stakeholders must deploy a diverse set of policy tools—including direct subsidies, loan guarantees, carbon pricing, and binding lifecycle-based fuel-intensity standards—to foster investment confidence. The USD 11–13 billion in annual revenue expected from the IMO carbon price, which is ring-fenced for maritime decarbonisation, represents a monumental source of funding that must be deployed strategically to bridge the cost gap and finance first-mover projects. Coordinated international standards and safety guidelines under the IMO will also be essential to harmonise bunkering, crew training, and operational practices.

In the medium term, hydrogen-derived fuels such as ammonia and e-methanol are expected to scale across the sector, driven by technological learning, cost reductions, and coordinated infrastructure build-out through green corridors and international public-private partnerships. As electrolyser capacity grows and renewable power expands, green fuel costs should decline, though they are likely to remain above fossil fuels without robust policy support. The success of this phase hinges on the effective implementation and potential strengthening of the IMO's global fuel standard and carbon price mechanism to close the ambition gap and meet the 2030 targets.

At this stage, standardisation of bunkering procedures and comprehensive safety frameworks for ammonia, e-methanol, and hydrogen will be essential to enable safe, scalable deployment. Dedicated hydrogen-fuelled vessels will remain concentrated in short-sea routes and auxiliary systems, while deep-sea ships will rely mainly on hydrogen-derived fuels optimised for long-range operation. Gradual adoption will depend on overcoming the 'chicken-and-egg' challenge between demand and infrastructure investment, requiring government-backed off-take mechanisms and the creation of green shipping corridors.

In the long term, hydrogen-derived fuels—primarily green ammonia and e-methanol—are projected to become the dominant zero-carbon energy carriers for deep-sea shipping, while direct hydrogen will likely remain confined to short-sea, ferry, or auxiliary uses. By this stage, global renewable deployment and electrolyser innovation should enable large-scale, competitively traded green fuels, supporting widespread decarbonisation of international shipping.

The regulatory landscape will need to be consolidated, with binding international agreements mandating lifecycle-based carbon neutrality across the sector and stringent emission controls progressively phasing out fossil-based fuels. The IMO's 2023 strategy, with its net-zero by 2050 goal and interim targets for 2030 and 2040, provides the long-term direction, but the 2025 agreement must be viewed as a starting point that requires increased ambition over time to ensure the sector fully contributes to the Paris Agreement goals.

Overall, hydrogen will be an essential enabler of maritime decarbonisation, primarily as a feedstock for zero-carbon fuels rather than as a direct propulsion energy source. The success of this transition will depend on rapid expansion of renewable energy, harmonisation of global safety and environmental standards, and coordinated investment in green corridors that connect early adopters and accelerate the shift towards a sustainable, zero-carbon shipping system. While the new global carbon price could be a game-changer, its ultimate impact hinges on the effective use of revenues to de-risk and drive growth in the hydrogen market and on raising its ambition to meet the challenge's magnitude.

## References

ABS. (2021). *Hydrogen as marine fuel.* Global Sustainability Center.

ABS. (2023). *Fuel cell power systems for marine and offshore applications.* Global Sustainability Center.

Al-Aboosi, F., El-Halwagi, M., Moore, M., & Nielsen, R. (2021). Renewable ammonia as an alternative fuel for the shipping industry. *Current Opinion in Chemical Engineering, 31*(1), 1–10.

Baker McKenzie. (2024). *Hydrogen developments* [Online]. Retrieved February 03, 2025, from https://resourcehub.bakermckenzie.com/en/resources/hydrogen-heat-map/asia-pacific/south-korea/topics/hydrogen-developments.

Ballard. (2023). *World's first liquid-powered hydrogen ship, MF Hydra, is powered by Ballard's fuel cells* [Online]. Retrieved January 30, 2025, from https://blog.ballard.com/marine/worlds-first-liquid-powered-hydrogen-ship-mf-hydra-is-powered-by-ballards-fuel-cells.

Barett, S. (2008). Proton for world's first fuel cell passenger ship. *Fuel Cells Bulletin, 2*(1), 2.

Bhuiyan, M. H., & Siddique, Z. (2025). Hydrogen as an alternative fuel: A comprehensive review of challenges and opportunities in production, storage, and transportation. *International Journal of Hydrogen Energy, 102*(1), 1026–1044.

Biert, L., Godjevac, M., Visser, K., & Aravind, P. V. (2016). A review of fuel cell systems for maritime applications. *Journal of Power Sources, 327*(1), 345–364.

BloombergNEF. (2023) *2H 2023 hydrogen market outlook: The demand question* [Online]. Retrieved February 04, 2025, from https://about.bnef.com/blog/2h-2023-hydrogen-market-outlook-the-demand-question/

Bosio, B., Archetti, M., Audasso, E., & Bove, D. (2023). Process analysis of a molten carbonate fuel cell on-board application to reduce vessel CO2 emissions. *Chemical Engineering and Processing – Process Intensification, 190*(1), 1–29.

Bureau Veritas. (2021). *Alternative fuels for shipping: The options ahead.* Bureau Veritas.

Chiong, M. C., et al. (2021). Advancements of combustion technologies in the ammonia-fuelled engines. *Energy Conversion and Management, 244*(1), 1–17.

Djermouni, M., & Ouahda, A. (2023). Thermodynamic analysis of methanol, ammonia, and hydrogen as alternative fuels in HCCI engines. *International Journal of Thermofluids, 19*(1), 1–7.

DNV. (2023). *Hydrogen forecast to 2050* [Online]. Retrieved February 05, 2025, from https://www.dnv.com/focus-areas/hydrogen/forecast-to-2050/.

DNV GL. (2022). *Maritime forecast to 2050* [Online]. Retrieved January 24, 2025, from https://www.dnv.com/maritime/publications/maritime-forecast/

Elkafas, A., et al. (2023). Fuel cell systems for maritime: A review of research development, commercial products, applications, and perspectives. *Processes, 11*(97), 1–33.

EMSA. (2023). *Potential of hydrogen as fuel for shipping.* European Maritime Safety Agency.

European Commission. (2011). *Zero emission ships* [Online]. Retrieved January 30, 2025, from https://webgate.ec.europa.eu/life/publicWebsite/project/LIFE06-ENV-D-000465/zeroemissionships.

European Commission. (2021). *'Fit for 55': Delivering the EU's 2030 climate target on the way to climate neutrality* [Online]. Retrieved February 03, 2025, from https://eur-lex.europa.eu/legal-content/EN/TXT/HTML/?uri=CELEX:52021DC0550

European Commission. (2023). *FuelEU Maritime Initiative: Proposal for a Regulation on the use of renewable and low-carbon fuels in maritime transport.* Brussels, Belgium: European Commission.

European Maritime Safety Agency (2023) *Potential of hydrogen as fuel for shipping*. Lisbon, Portugal: EMSA..

European Commission. (2022). *Alternative fuels infrastructure regulation* [Online]. Retrieved February 03, 2025, from https://transport.ec.europa.eu/transport-themes/clean-transport/alternative-fuels-sustainable-mobility-europe/alternative-fuels-infrastructure_en.

European Commission. (2024). *Reducing emissions from the shipping sector* [Online]. Retrieved January 09, 2025, from https://climate.ec.europa.eu/eu-action/transport/reducing-emissions-shipping-sector_en

European Commission. (2025). *FAQ – Maritime transport in EU Emissions Trading System (ETS)* [Online]. Retrieved January 09, 2025, from https://climate.ec.europa.eu/eu-action/transport/reducing-emissions-shipping-sector/faq-maritime-transport-eu-emissions-trading-system-ets_en.

Financial Times. (2025). *Oil tanker boss says UN maritime body 'sleeping' over dark fleet threat* [Online]. Retrieved January 07, 2025, from https://www.ft.com/content/4cd90c84-9fd2-47e8-a035-9b7bf1a21445

Fu, Z., et al. (2023). Fuel cell and hydrogen in maritime application: A review on aspects of technology, cost and regulations. *Sustainable Energy Technologies and Assessments, 57*(1), 1026–1044.

Hydrogen Insight. (2025). *'Outraged' Trump slams IMO green shipping plans before knife-edge vote* [Online]. Retrieved November 11, 2025, from https://www.hydrogeninsight.com/transport/outraged-trump-slams-imo-green-shipping-plans-before-knife-edge-vote/2-1-1887876?utm.

IEA. (2020). *The future of hydrogen: Seizing today's opportunities*. International Energy Agency.

IEA. (2021). *World energy outlook 2021*. International Energy Agency.

IEA. (2022). *The role of alternative fuels in reducing shipping emissions*. International Energy Agency.

IMO. (2018). *2018 initial IMO strategy* [Online]. Retrieved February 03, 2025, from https://www.imo.org/en/OurWork/Environment/Pages/Vision-and-level-of-ambition-of-the-Initial-IMO-Strategy.aspx.

IMO. (2020). *Fourth IMO greenhouse gas study 2020*. International Maritime Organization.

IMO. (2023). *2023 IMO strategy on reduction of GHG emissions from Ships* [Online]. Retrieved January 06, 2025, from https://www.IMO.org/en/OurWork/Environment/Pages/2023-IMO-Strategy-on-Reduction-of-GHG-Emissions-from-Ships.aspx

IMO. (2024). *International code of safety for ships using gases or other low-flashpoint fuels (IGF code)*. International Maritime Organization.

IMO. (2025). *IMO approves net-zero regulations for global climate* [Online]. Retrieved October 03, 2025, from https://www.imo.org/en/mediacentre/pressbriefings/pages/imo-approves-netzero-regulations.aspx?utm

IPCC. (2021). *Climate Change 2021: The Physical Science Basis. Contribution of Working Group I to the Sixth Assessment Report of the Intergovernmental Panel on Climate Change*. Cambridge University Press.

IRENA. (2022). *Global Hydrogen Trade to Meet the 1.5°C Climate Goal: Part I – Trade Outlook for 2050 and Way Forward*. Abu Dhabi, UAE: International Renewable Energy Agency.

Khalil, M., & Mughal, M. (2021). Molten Carbonate Fuel Cells (MCFCs) in maritime applications. *Renewable Energy and Marine Science, 4*(2), 89–102.

Kołodziejski, M. (2023). Review of hydrogen-based propulsion systems in the maritime sector. *Archives of Thermodynamics, 44*(4), 335–380.

Lloyd's Register. (2024). *Ship readiness for zero carbon fuels*. Maritime Decarbonisation Hub.

MAN Energy Solutions. (2023). *MAN B&W ME-LGI engines*. MAN Energy Solutions.

Melideo, D., & Desideri, U. (2024). The use of hydrogen as alternative fuel for ship propulsion: A case study of full and partial retrofitting of roll-on/roll-off vessels for short distance routes. *International Journal of Hydrogen Energy, 50*(B), 1045–1055.

METI. (2017). *Basic hydrogen strategy* [Online]. Retrieved February 03, 2025, from chrome-extension://efaidnbmnnnibpcajpcglclefindmkaj/ https://www.meti.go.jp/shingikai/enecho/shoene_shinene/suiso_seisaku/pdf/20230606_5.pdf

Minnehan, J. J., & Pratt, J. W. (2017). *Practical application limits of fuel cells and batteries for zero emission vessels*. Sandia National Laboratories.

Norwegian Maritime Authority. (2025). *Adoption of zero-emission requirements for cruise ships, tourist boats and ferries in the World Heritage fjords* [Online]. Retrieved October 03, 2025, from https://www.sdir.no/contentassets/ac4f83e167b749c3b3ffccbed0e730ff/eng-rsr-om-miljosikkerhetsforskriften-vaf.pdf.

OECD. (2023). *New estimates provide insights on CO2 emissions from global shipping* [Online]. Retrieved January 06, 2025, from https://oecdstatistics.blog/2023/06/15/new-estimates-provide-insights-on-co2-emissions-from-global-shipping/.

Renewable Energy Magazine. (2024). *World's first entirely hydrogen-powered ferry welcomes passengers in San Francisco Bay* [Online]. Retrieved January 30, 2025, from https://www.renewableenergymagazine.com/hydrogen/world-s-first-entirely-hydrogenpowered-ferry-welcomes-20240808.

Reuters. (2025). *Policy Watch: Unambitious global shipping deal a 'lost opportunity' for climate* [Online]. Retrieved October 03, 2025, from https://www.reuters.com/sustainability/boards-policy-regulation/policy-watch-unambitious-global-shipping-deal-lost-opportunity-climate-2025-04-17/?utm.

Seas at Risk. (2025). *A year's delay for shipping's decarbonisation: What happened at the IMO* [Online]. Retrieved November 11, 2025, from https://seas-at-risk.org/general-news/a-years-delay-for-shippings-decarbonisation-what-happened-at-the-imo/.

Seatrade Maritime News. (2023). *Largest marine hydrogen fuel cells ordered for Norwegian ferry pair* [Online]. Retrieved January 30, 2025, from https://www.seatrade-maritime.com/alternative-fuels/largest-marine-hydrogen-fuel-cells-ordered-for-norwegian-ferry-pair.

Shi, J., et al. (2023). A prompt decarbonisation pathway for shipping: Green hydrogen, ammonia, and methanol production and utilization in marine engines. *Atmosphere, 14*(3), 1–29.

Sphera. (2022). *1st life cycle GHG emission study on the use of alternative marine fuels*. Sphera.

Svanberg, M., Ellis, J., Lundgren, J., & Landälv, I. (2018). Renewable methanol as a fuel for the shipping industry. *Renewable and Sustainable Energy Reviews, 94*(1), 1217–1228.

Tarnatore, C., Marchitto, L., Sabia, P., & Joannon, M. (2022). Ammonia as green fuel in internal combustion engines: State-of-the-art and future perspectives. *Frontiers in Mechanical Engineering, 8*(1), 1–16.

US Department of Energy. (2024). *Liquid hydrogen delivery* [Online]. Retrieved January 28, 2025, from https://www.energy.gov/eere/fuelcells/liquid-hydrogen-delivery.

Vairo, T., et al. (2023). Solid oxide fuel cells for shipping: A machine learning model for early detection of hazardous system deviations. *Process Safety and Environmental Protection, 172*(1), 184–194.

Veldhuizen, B., Biert, L., Aravind, P., & VIsser, K. (2023). Solid oxide fuel cells for marine applications. *International Journal of Energy Research, 1*(1), 1–35.

Verhelst, S., & Wallner, T. (2009). Hydrogen-fueled internal combustion engines, *Progress in Energy and Combustion Science, 35* (6), 490–527.

Volvo Group. (2024). *Hydrogen combustion engines: Development and applications for heavy-duty transport*. Gothenburg, Sweden: Volvo Group.

Wärtsilä. (2022). *Launch of Wärtsilä 25 engine paves the way towards maritime decarbonisation* [Online]. Retrieved February 02, 2025, from https://www.wartsila.com/media/news/07-09-2022-launch-of-wartsila-25-engine-paves-the-way-towards-maritime-decarbonisation-3152432.

Wärtsilä. (2023). *Commercially operated Wärtsilä engine runs on 25 vol% hydrogen blend, a world first* [Online]. Retrieved February 02, 2025, from https://www.wartsila.com/media/news/23-03-2023-commercially-operated-wartsila-engine-runs-on-25-vol-hydrogen-blend-a-world-first-3245232.

World Bank. (2021). *The role of LNG in the transition to a low-carbon shipping sector*. The World Bank.

World Resources Institute. (2023). *The shipping industry won't meet its decarbonization goals without investing more in low-carbon fuels* [Online]. Retrieved January 06, 2025, from https://www.wri.org/insights/how-to-decarbonize-international-shipping

WWF. (2025). *Even as the IMO net zero framework is postponed, the work for cleaner shipping must continue* [Online]. Retrieved November 11, 2025, from https://www.arcticwwf.org/newsroom/features/the-imo-net-zero-framework-postponed/.

Xing, H., Stuart, C., Spence, S., & Chen, H. (2021). Fuel cell power systems for maritime applications: Progress and perspectives. *Sustainability, 13*(3), 1–34.

Zero Emission Industries. (2021). *Sea change* [Online]. Retrieved January 30, 2025, from https://www.zeroei.com/sea-change.

Zhang, R., et al. (2024). A comparative study on $NH_3/H_2$ and $NH_3/CH_3OH$ combustion and emission in an optical SI engine. *Fuel, 369*(1), 1–9.

CHAPTER 9

# Hydrogen in Aviation

## Introduction

The aviation sector is currently dominated by conventional jet fuels, primarily derived from petroleum, which power the vast majority of commercial aircraft. These fuels, while energy-dense and well suited for long-haul flights, are a significant source of greenhouse gas (GHG) emissions, particularly carbon dioxide ($CO_2$) and nitrogen oxides ($NO_x$). At the moment, the aviation industry in general is responsible for around 2.5–3% of global carbon emissions, which places it right behind the maritime sector in the list of top 10 carbon emitters among the main economic sectors (ATAG, 2024). This figure, however, is projected to rise significantly further as air travel demand is constantly growing (Fig. 9.1). Since unfortunately these emissions have been largely unregulated until most recently, they pose a significant challenge to international climate goals, as there are no internationally recognised binding regulations explicitly limiting their discharge by aircraft.

While, in principle, there are frameworks in place to regulate carbon emissions from aviation activities, the level of enforcement and binding agreements vary. Overall, the International Civil Aviation Organization (ICAO)'s measures are not fully binding but can lead to legally enforceable regulations through treaties. In contrast, the EU Emissions Trading System (ETS) has been extended to cover $CO_2$ emissions from flights within Europe, as, under this system, aviation companies are obliged to



A. Patonia, R. Poudineh, *Clean Hydrogen for Decarbonisation*,
https://doi.org/10.1007/978-3-032-19442-8_9

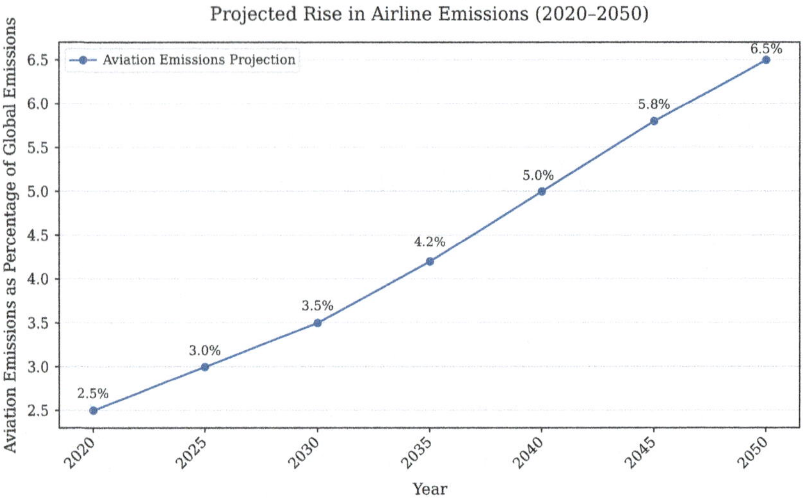


**Fig. 9.1** Projected rise in airline emissions (2020–2050). (Source: Adapted from IPCC (2018), UNEP (2019), Lee et al. (2021), World Resources Institute (2021), ICAO (2022))

monitor and report their emissions and purchase allowances corresponding to their $CO_2$ output (European Commission, 2023). Nevertheless, even though this regulation is legally binding for companies operating within the European Union, it does not extend to the rest of the world.

This is one of the key reasons why currently the global aviation sector still relies heavily on kerosene-based jet fuel,[1] a well-established and energy-dense source of propulsion, which also appears to be the main source of carbon emissions (Fig. 9.2). In fact, an average jet engine running on this type of fuel releases approximately 71.5 kg of $CO_2$ per gigajoule of energy produced (ICAO, 2020). This means that burning one tonne of jet fuel would release roughly 3.15 tonnes of carbon dioxide

[1] Conventional kerosene-based jet fuels include Jet A, primarily used in the United States with a freezing point of -40 °C, and Jet A-1, the global standard with a lower freezing point of -47 °C and added static dissipater additives (ExxonMobil, 2022; Shell, 2023). Jet B, a blend of kerosene and gasoline, offers better cold-weather performance but is more volatile, while TS-1 is optimised for low temperatures and used mainly in Russia and CIS countries (IATA, 2024). JP-8, a military variant of Jet A-1, includes corrosion inhibitors and anti-icing agents for enhanced operational flexibility (Repsol, 2024).

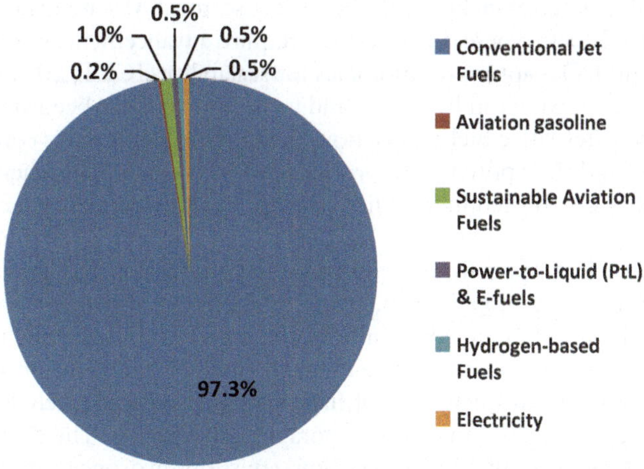


**Fig. 9.2** Approximate global aviation fuel share (2025) (aviation gasoline (or 'avgas') is distinct from kerosene-based jet fuels and represents the main propellant for piston-engine aircraft due to its high octane and specialised additives (Shell, 2023)). (Sources: Adapted from European Commission (2022), ATAG (2023), European Parliament (2023), OECD (2023), WEF (2024))

(Aviation Benefits Beyond Borders, 2024; ATAG, 2021). This is why alternatives like electric propulsion, the so-called Sustainable Aviation Fuels (SAFs), 'e-fuels', and hydrogen-based fuels have been actively explored and promoted as more environmentally friendly substitutes for kerosene-based conventional jet propellants.

Here, SAFs are biofuels made from renewable feedstock like plant oils or waste, produced primarily through processes such as Hydroprocessed Esters and Fatty Acids (HEFA), while Power-to-Liquid (PtL) or e-fuels are synthetic fuels created using renewable electricity, water, and captured $CO_2$ via Fischer-Tropsch synthesis (IATA, 2024). It is crucial to distinguish between the direct use of hydrogen (e.g., as liquid hydrogen in fuel cells or combustion engines) and its indirect use as a feedstock for producing synthetic kerosene (PtL/e-fuels). While SAFs are already used in blends with conventional jet fuel, PtL/e-fuels are still in pilot phases due to high costs and energy demands (ibid. and European Commission, 2022). Although both are considered carbon-neutral, SAFs offset emissions through feedstock $CO_2$ absorption, and PtL/e-fuels use captured $CO_2$ during production, each technology has significant limitations. In particular, just like biofuels for other branches of the transport sector, SAFs are generally limited by feedstock, whereas PtL/e-fuels require advancements in renewable energy and $CO_2$ capture technologies for scalability (ICCT, 2021).

In this context, clean hydrogen and its derivatives have been viewed as a promising alternative fuel for aviation due to their high energy content per unit mass and their potential to produce zero $CO_2$ emissions when used in fuel cells or combusted in modified jet engines. However, they have yet to secure a significant market share greater than the current approximate 0.5% (Fig. 9.2). Here, apart from the high cost of production and the establishment of a robust supply chain, some of the most significant challenges associated with $H_2$'s introduction into the sector and large-scale universal adoption lie in the adaptation of aircraft themselves and their infrastructure to accommodate this new type of fuel, which has an extremely low volumetric energy density and complex storage requirements. The climate benefit of hydrogen aviation hinges on a low-emissions hydrogen supply (green hydrogen), and its use in combustion engines introduces non-$CO_2$ effects, such as $NO_x$ emissions and contrail formation, which must be managed. At the same time, it is quite clear that if these challenges are successfully addressed, the aviation sector has a strong chance of being dramatically transformed, though this impact is expected to be gradual and segment-specific through 2050, with hydrogen complementing rather than replacing SAF/PtL fuels for fleet-wide decarbonisation.

This chapter provides a comprehensive analysis of hydrogen's role in aviation. It begins by examining the technological solutions, including fuel cells and combustion engines (Section "Hydrogen Applications in the Sector"). Section "Economic Aspects" analyses economic aspects, while Section "Policy and Regulatory Landscape" reviews the policy and regulatory landscape . Section "Case Studies and Pilot Projects", in turn, focuses on key initiatives around the world, and Section "Future Outlook and Conclusions" conclused the chapter with an assessment of hydrogen's realistic pathway in the sector.

## Hydrogen Applications in the Sector

### *Technological Solutions*

The propulsion technologies running on hydrogen and its derivatives that are currently being considered for use in aviation can be broadly categorised into *fuel cell systems*, *combustion engines*, and *hybrid systems*. Here, just like in the maritime industry, hydrogen is not the only option viewed as the main fuel because its derivatives, such as ammonia and methanol, are being explored as alternative fuels due to their easier storage and transport characteristics. Overall, each of these approaches has unique advantages and challenges, and their development is progressing at varying levels of maturity.

In essence, fuel cells convert hydrogen and oxygen into electricity via an electrochemical process, generating only water as a by-product. This electricity can then power electric motors, offering a zero-emission propulsion solution. At the moment, several types of fuel cells are being explored for aviation applications, each with unique characteristics and levels of maturity (Table 9.1). In particular, Proton Exchange Membrane Fuel Cells (PEMFCs), which are the most technologically mature option at the moment, have a typical efficiency range between 40 and 60% and operate at relatively low temperatures, which makes them particularly suitable for aviation (Schröder et al., 2021; Schmelcher & Häβy, 2022; Kösters et al., 2023). They rely on pure hydrogen as fuel and, since their typical power output ranges from 100 to 200 kW, they are currently mostly suitable for rather small aircraft and regional applications (ibid.).

Although, in theory, potentially suitable for use by larger aircraft in the future, Solid Oxide Fuel Cells (SOFCs) that are expected to have higher power output (200–500 kW) and efficiency (45–65%) and be able to utilise hydrogen, ammonia, methane, and methanol, they are currently not viewed as the most suitable type of technology for aviation (ibid.). This is so because SOFCs normally operate at high temperatures (500–1000 °C) and therefore they face challenges related to thermal management and durability and hence are currently at a lower technology readiness level (6–7) (Zhang et al., 2024). Similarly, Direct Methanol Fuel Cells (DMFCs) and Ammonia Fuel Cells, in turn, can directly use methanol and ammonia, respectively, which, in theory, makes them easier to handle than hydrogen-based systems. However, their lower efficiency and power output currently limit their application to small aircraft, and they still need to be improved before they can reach full commercialisation (ibid.).

Combustion systems generally adapt conventional jet engines to burn hydrogen or its derivatives instead of traditional jet fuel (Soleymani et al., 2024). This approach normally leverages existing gas turbine technology while replacing carbon-emitting fuels with hydrogen; when hydrogen is

**Table 9.1** Major fuel cell types currently considered for use in aviation

| *Fuel cell type* | *Fuel type* | *Typical power output (kW)* | *Typical efficiency range (%)* | *Potential cost* | *Technology readiness level (TRL)* | *Notes* |
|---|---|---|---|---|---|---|
| *Proton Exchange Membrane Fuel Cell (PEMFC)* | Hydrogen | 100–200 | 40–60 | High | 7–8 | Relies on pure hydrogen, suitable for small and regional aircraft |
| *Solid Oxide Fuel Cell (SOFC)* | Hydrogen, ammonia, methane, methanol | 200–500 | 45–65 | High | 6–7 | Operates at high temperatures (500–1000 °C), potentially suitable for larger aircraft |
| *Direct Methanol Fuel Cell (DMFC)* | Methanol | 100–200 | 30–40 | Moderate | 5–6 | Suitable for small aircraft, lower efficiency |
| *Ammonia Fuel Cell* | Ammonia | 100–500 | 45–60 | Moderate | 4–6 | Requires ammonia reforming, early development stage |

Source: Adapted from Schröder et al. (2021), Schmelcher and Häßy (2022), Kösters et al. (2023), Zhang et al. (2024)

burned it avoids $CO_2$ but can still generate $NO_x$ and contrails that contribute to climate impact. These non-$CO_2$ effects, particularly persistent contrail formation, are a significant climate impact that must be addressed. At present, combustion engines in aviation are also being adapted to run on ammonia and methanol, offering a potential route to reduce emissions while making use of existing engine designs (ibid.). These engines are expected to be able to operate on pure fuels or in dual-fuel configurations, providing flexibility for different aircraft types and mission profiles. Nevertheless, although ammonia and methanol are generally easier to handle than hydrogen, due to ammonia's low flammability range and methanol's low energy density and flashpoint, they are not the primary candidates for broad use in aviation and are currently in the early stages of development (Table 9.2).

In these circumstances, hydrogen gas turbines as well as hydrogen internal combustion engines ($H_2$-ICEs) that burn hydrogen directly are currently considered the most promising combustion technologies in this context (Maciorowski et al., 2024; Soleymani et al., 2024). Here, hydrogen gas turbines primarily viewed for larger and more powerful aircraft that would normally use conventional jet engines are currently demonstrating output of 1000–5000 kW with a typical efficiency range of 35–45% (Boretti, 2024). In contrast, $H_2$-ICE is expected to work like traditional piston engines that burn hydrogen instead of aviation gasoline (avgas)

**Table 9.2** Major types of combustion engines potentially suitable for hydrogen and/or its derivatives

| *Engine type* | *Fuel type* | *Typical power output (kW)* | *Typical efficiency range (%)* | *Potential cost* | *Technology readiness level (TRL)* | *Notes* |
|---|---|---|---|---|---|---|
| *Hydrogen gas turbine* | Hydrogen | 1000–5000 | 35–45 | High | 6–7 | Modified jet engines; ground tests completed; produces $NO_x$ and can form contrails |
| *Hydrogen internal combustion engine ($H_2$-ICE)* | Hydrogen | 200–300 | 30–40 | moderate | 6–7 | Retrofits possible; $NO_x$ emissions a concern |
| *Ammonia combustion engine* | Ammonia | 100–300 | 30–38 | moderate | 5–6 | Requires dual-fuel setup; emits $NO_x$ |
| *Methanol combustion engine* | Methanol | 200–400 | 30–40 | Low-moderate | 5–6 | Can be used for dual-fuel mode; carbon emissions |

Source: Adapted from Boretti (2024), IATA (2023), Maciorowski et al. (2024), and Soleymani et al. (2024)

(IATA, 2024). Therefore, they would demonstrate lower power output of 200–300 kW with average efficiency of 30–40% (ibid.).

Hybrid systems that are currently being developed for the aviation sector typically either combine hydrogen fuel cells with batteries or integrate hydrogen combustion with electric motors to optimise performance and efficiency. Essentially, these systems combine hydrogen fuel cells to provide baseline power with batteries handling peak demand. At the moment, they are being developed for regional aircraft, with first commercial niches more plausibly in the later-2030s/2040s and a small fleet share before 2050. Just like hybrid cars, hybrid applications that combine hydrogen combustion and electric systems in aviation integrate hydrogen combustion engines with electric motors to ensure high power output and flexibility. At the same time, they are currently less technologically developed and efficient than the previously mentioned ones (Table 9.3). Finally, as mentioned before, due to the complexities associated with the use of ammonia and methanol, hybrid systems that combine ammonia/methanol fuel cells and battery systems are currently facing a number of challenges related to system integration, etc. and therefore are also in the early stages of development.

### *Advantages/Disadvantages*

Overall, hydrogen, whether used in fuel cells or combustion engines, offers the potential for zero or near-zero carbon emissions, depending on the source of hydrogen production. However, the well-to-wake climate benefit is only significant if the hydrogen is produced from low-carbon sources (green hydrogen). Unlike SAF and PtL fuels, which can be used as drop-in replacements in existing jet engines and infrastructure, hydrogen requires entirely new storage, refuelling, and propulsion systems, making its adoption more complex and capital-intensive. Here, one of the most important barriers for its wider implementation is its low volumetric energy density, which necessitates larger storage tanks and impacts aircraft design and operational efficiency. Its gravimetric energy density is superior to batteries, but liquid hydrogen's low volumetric density and tank integration penalties mean early feasibility is strongest for regional to some narrow-body missions; long haul remains most challenging.

On the other hand, SAF and PtL fuels, derived from biomass or renewable electricity, can seamlessly integrate into current aviation infrastructure and aircraft engines. Accordingly, their main strength lies in leveraging

**Table 9.3** Main hybrid-electric systems currently considered for use in aviation

| *Hybrid system type* | *Fuel type* | *Typical power output (kW)* | *Typical efficiency range (%)* | *Potential cost* | *Technology readiness level (TRL)* | *Notes* |
|---|---|---|---|---|---|---|
| *Hydrogen fuel cell + battery* | Hydrogen | 100–200 | 40–60 | High | 6–7 | Suitable for regional aircraft; batteries for peak power |
| *Hydrogen combustion + electric* | Hydrogen | 200–500 | 35–45 | Moderate | 5–6 | Hydrogen power output; flexibility in operation; managing $NO_x$ and contrails is a key challenge |
| *Ammonia fuel cell + battery* | Ammonia | 50–100 | 40–50 | Moderate | 4–5 | Early development stage; requires ammonia reforming |
| *Methanol fuel cell + battery* | Methanol | 50–100 | 30–40 | Moderate | 4–5 | Suitable for small aircraft; lower efficiency |

Source: Adapted from Zeroavia (2023), Zhang et al. (2024), and H2FLY (2024)

current supply chains while delivering substantial carbon savings under sustainable sourcing. Nevertheless, at the moment, their production costs remain significantly higher than conventional jet fuel, and current manufacturing capacity is insufficient to meet global aviation demand. Moreover, some types of feedstock used for synthesising SAF raise concerns over land use and sustainability.

In contrast, although battery-electric aircraft offer true zero-emission propulsion, they are severely limited by battery weight and energy density. At the moment, the limitations of battery technologies restrict their use to short-haul flights and regional aviation, making them unsuitable for long-haul applications. Although, in theory, advances in solid-state batteries and other high-energy-density storage solutions may extend their range in the future, at present, electrification does not appear to be a scalable solution for large commercial aircraft.

Overall, while hydrogen presents an attractive long-term pathway for decarbonising aviation, its infrastructure and storage challenges are substantial (Table 9.4). Its impact will be gradual and segment-specific, complementing rather than replacing SAF and PtL fuels for fleet-wide decarbonisation this side of 2050. SAF and PtL fuels offer a more immediate but partial solution, while battery-electric propulsion remains viable only for niche markets. A combination of these technologies, tailored to specific aviation needs, will likely shape the industry's path towards sustainability.

### *Infrastructure Requirements*

Like in other niches of the transport industry, the transition to hydrogen-based propulsion in aviation is heavily dependent on the development of sector-specific infrastructure, including storage, refuelling, and transportation systems. Each type of hydrogen-based technology—fuel cells, combustion engines, and hybrid systems—requires tailored infrastructure to ensure functionality and scalability. As shown in Table 9.5, not surprisingly, combustion engines and hybrid systems may scale in some respects, but $LH_2$ handling imposes substantial new infrastructure and certification demands: scalability is constrained compared to fuel cells, recognising that existing kerosene infrastructure is not directly usable for $LH_2$ without building parallel cryogenic capabilities. However, fuel cells, while quieter and more environmentally friendly, face significant challenges in

**Table 9.4** Hydrogen technologies with alternatives

| *Technology* | *Typical power output (kW)* | *Typical efficiency range (%)* | *Performance* | *Emissions reduction* | *Key challenges* |
|---|---|---|---|---|---|
| *Hydrogen fuel cells* | 100–500 | 40–60 | High | Zero $CO_2$ emissions at point of use | High cost, storage issues |
| *Hydrogen combustion engines* | 200–5000 | 30–45 | High | Near-zero $CO_2$ emissions | Produces $NO_x$ and contrails $NO_x$ emissions, infrastructure, non-$CO_2$ effects |
| *Hybrid systems* | 50–500 | 35–60 | Medium | Zero/ near-zero emissions | System integration, technological maturity |
| *SAF/PtL fuels* | N/A (varies by engine) | 30–40 | High | Up to 80% reduction on a lifecycle basis | High production costs, land use concerns |
| *Battery-- electric systems* | 50–500 | 70–90 | Low | Zero emissions | Limited range, weight issues |

Source: Adapted from Schmelcher and Häβy (2022), Schröder et al. (2021), Boretti (2024), IATA (2024), Maciorowski et al. (2024), Soleymani et al. (2024), and Zhang et al. (2024)

infrastructure development, particularly due to the need for high-purity hydrogen and specialised handling systems.

Fuel cells, particularly Proton Exchange Membrane Fuel Cells (PEMFCs), require dedicated refuelling stations to supply high-purity hydrogen. In fact, this high-purity $H_2$ requirement puts additional pressure on the design of the aircraft themselves, as readjusting larger tanks (due to hydrogen's lower volumetric density compared to jet fuel) within the fuselage will have a direct negative impact on the volume of cargo and/or the number of passengers that the aircraft will be able to carry. In addition, the refuelling stations themselves must be strategically located at airports and adhere to stringent safety protocols due to hydrogen's flammability and the need for pressurised or cryogenic storage (Schröder et al., 2021). This will require the readjustment of the entire airport infrastructure, adapting infrastructure to support additional $LH_2$ systems while

**Table 9.5** Key technological alternatives to kerosene-based jet fuels, their infrastructure requirements, current scalability, and adaptability

| *Technology* | | *Specific infrastructure requirements* | *Current scalability* | *Current adaptability* | *Current key challenges* |
|---|---|---|---|---|---|
| *Fuel cells (hydrogen-electric)* | PEMFC | High-purity hydrogen refuelling stations | Low | Limited (hydrogen only) | • High hydrogen purity requirements<br>• Costly infrastructure |
| | SOFC | Multi-fuel pipelines and storage systems | Moderate | High | • High operating temperatures<br>• Infrastructure upgrades required |
| *Combustion engines* | Hydrogen gas turbine<br>$H_2$- ICE | High-pressure or cryogenic hydrogen storage | Moderate | Moderate | • $NO_x$ emissions<br>• Hydrogen's low volumetric energy density<br>• Hydrogen storage complexity |
| *Hybrid systems* | Hydrogen fuel cell + battery<br>Hydrogen combustion + electric | Hydrogen refuelling and charging systems | Moderate | Moderate | • System integration<br>• Technological maturity |
| *SAF* | | Existing fuel infrastructure (minor modifications required) | High | High | • High production costs<br>• Limited feedstock availability<br>• Certification and scaling |

| | | | | |
|---|---|---|---|---|
| *PtL and e-fuels* | Renewable electricity, $CO_2$ capture, and synthesis facilities | Low-Moderate | Moderate | • High energy requirements<br>• High capital costs<br>• Limited production capacity and scalability |
| *Battery-electric* | Charging infrastructure, high-capacity battery storage, and grid upgrades | Low | Low-moderate | • Battery energy density limitations<br>• Charging time<br>• Infrastructure investment |

Source: Adapted from Verhelst and Wallner (2009), Biert et al (2016), Xing et al (2021), Tarnatore et al (2022), ABS (2023), Bosio et al (2023), Djermouni and Ouahda (2023), Fu et al (2023), Kołodziejski (2023), Shi et al (2023), Vairo et al (2023), Zhang et al. (2024), and Bhuiyan and Siddique (2025)

maintaining kerosene/SAF/PtL capacity during the multi-decade transition. In these circumstances, the scalability of infrastructure that should accommodate the use of pure $H_2$ currently remains low due to high costs and technical challenges, which are further complicated by the fact that the compression and liquefaction of hydrogen also introduce energy losses (Zhang et al., 2024).

Similarly, hydrogen combustion engines, including hydrogen gas turbines and hydrogen internal combustion engines, require high-pressure or cryogenic hydrogen storage systems and modified refuelling infrastructure. While combustion engines are generally described as more adaptable than fuel cells in airplane design, they still face challenges such as $NO_x$ emissions. More importantly, hydrogen's low volumetric energy density also has a significant negative impact on the tank-cargo/passenger considerations and operational efficiency, though, in principle, hydrogen gas turbines' ability to integrate with existing gas turbine technology enhances their scalability compared to fuel cells (Boretti, 2024; IATA, 2024).

In turn, hybrid systems, which combine hydrogen fuel cells or combustion engines with batteries or electric motors, require a mix of hydrogen refuelling infrastructure and charging stations. These systems are particularly promising for regional aircraft but currently face challenges related to system integration and technological maturity (Zeroavia, 2023; H2FLY, 2024). While they potentially offer flexibility in operation, their infrastructure requirements are also complex and currently limit their scalability, as they face challenges similar to those of fuel cell and combustion engine technologies. At the same time, combustion engines and hybrid systems generally demonstrate higher scalability and adaptability compared to fuel cells, as they are expected to leverage existing infrastructure with relatively minor modifications. In contrast, fuel cells require entirely new infrastructure, making their adoption more complex and capital-intensive. However, as technology advances and regulatory frameworks evolve, the potential for fuel cells to become more scalable and adaptable may increase significantly.

Nevertheless, in principle, the development of hydrogen infrastructure in aviation is critical for the adoption of all three key types of hydrogen technologies: fuel cells, combustion engines, and hybrid systems. New aircraft designs and major airport $LH_2$ infrastructure are prerequisites, not simple retrofits. In this respect, SAFs and e-fuels that do not require significant infrastructure adjustments are currently viewed more favourably in light of being the 'low-hanging fruits' of sustainable aviation. Therefore, it is likely that the foreseeable future of hydrogen use in the aviation industry will be greatly influenced by advancements in infrastructure development and regulatory frameworks.

## Economic Aspects

Although the adoption of hydrogen as a fuel in the aviation sector presents a transformative opportunity to decarbonise one of the most challenging industries in terms of emissions reduction, this transition is accompanied by significant economic considerations, including capital expenditures (CapEx), operational expenditures (OpEx), and fuel costs, which could, in principle, be related to OpEx but are normally viewed separately, as they constitute a very significant share of overall expenses. Therefore, conducting a comprehensive cost-benefit analysis comparing hydrogen solutions to current technologies, alongside the role of subsidies, incentives, and carbon pricing, is essential to understanding the economic viability of hydrogen in aviation (CSIRO, 2020).

Overall, the integration of hydrogen into aviation requires substantial investments across the value chain, encompassing aircraft design, infrastructure development, and fuel production. These costs can be broadly categorised into CapEx, OpEx, and fuel costs (ibid., Yusaf et al., 2022, 2024). Here, the most significant CapEx in hydrogen aviation relates to the development of hydrogen-powered aircraft and the associated infrastructure (ibid.). Hydrogen propulsion systems, whether based on fuel cells or hydrogen combustion engines, require entirely new aircraft designs or extensive retrofitting of existing models.

For instance, hydrogen fuel cells necessitate modifications to accommodate fuel storage, power distribution, and thermal management systems (Alsulaiman, 2024). Hydrogen combustion engines, in turn, while potentially easier to integrate into existing aircraft architectures, still require significant redesigns to handle hydrogen's unique properties, such as its low energy density and cryogenic storage requirements (ibid.). This is perhaps why not so much progress has been achieved with respect to their flight testing, and only ground tests of such engines have been conducted so far in many cases, which underscores that widespread commercial entry is unlikely before the late 2030s/2040s.

Overall, the cost of developing hydrogen-powered aircraft is estimated to be significantly higher than that of conventional aircraft. For instance, the cost of hydrogen fuel cells themselves can range from approximately

250 to 1000 USD per kilowatt (kW), depending on the technology and scale of production (Argonne National Laboratory, 2020). However, when considering the entire system, including power conditioning, storage, and other necessary components, the total cost for large commercial aircraft could potentially reach hundreds of millions of dollars (ibid.). For example, if a large commercial aircraft requires a 10 MW power system, and assuming an average cost of $500/kW for the fuel cells alone, the fuel cell component would cost around $5 million.

Similarly, although projected to be less significant than that of fuel cells, the cost of developing hydrogen combustion systems for aviation is expected to be quite substantial as well (Fig. 9.3). In principle, hydrogen combustion engines will need new $LH_2$ ground infrastructure—such as cryogenic storage, transfer systems, safety zones, and personnel training—separate from existing kerosene facilities, yet overall costs remain dominated by investments in hydrogen production, storage, and distribution. For instance, the cost of liquid hydrogen is estimated to range from 3.45 to 4.00 EUR per kilogram by 2050 in Europe, with hydrogen production

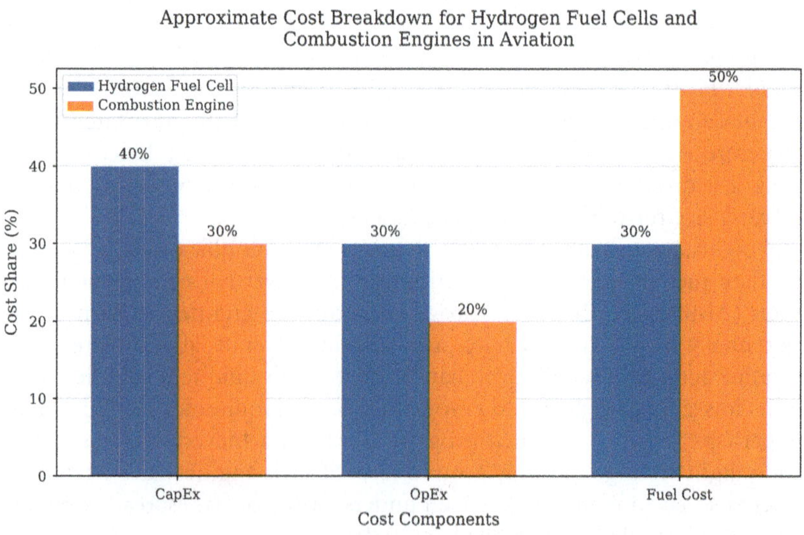


**Fig. 9.3** Approximate cost breakdown for hydrogen fuel cells and combustion engines. (Source: Adapted from Roland Berger (2020), IEA (2022), Steer and DLR (2023)), and European Climate Foundation (2023))

alone accounting for 54% of total costs in hydrogen aviation systems (Steer & DLR, 2023; European Climate Foundation, 2023). It is important to note that green hydrogen (from renewables) is significantly more expensive than grey hydrogen (from fossil fuels without CCUS); consistent cost estimates are crucial for comparison. In 2021, the costs of green hydrogen were typically in the range of 3–8 USD/kg, while grey hydrogen was around 0.5–1.5 USD/kg (IEA, 2021).

Aircraft redesign is another major expense for hydrogen combustion systems. In general, these engines require modified conventional thrust systems and additional fuselage space for hydrogen storage due to its lower volumetric energy density compared to jet fuel. This redesign could lead to increased drag or necessitate innovative aircraft structures such as blended wing bodies (Roland Berger, 2020). Adding other system components and infrastructure could significantly increase costs to tens or even hundreds of millions of dollars.

Moreover, establishing hydrogen production, storage, and distribution infrastructure at airports entails significant capital expenditure (CapEx). This includes liquefaction plants, cryogenic storage tanks, and refueling systems. According to McKinsey & Company, the global investment needed for hydrogen infrastructure in aviation could range between USD 700 billion and 1.7 trillion by 2050, with up to 90% allocated off-airport for facilities such as hydrogen production, pipelines, and liquefaction systems (McKinsey & Company, 2023). Despite the high upfront costs, many governments and transport-sector companies view hydrogen-powered aviation as a central element of decarbonisation strategies. While long-term operational savings and environmental benefits may justify the initial investment, deep $CO_2$ reductions from hydrogen propulsion are most feasible for long-haul routes, with near- and mid-term decarbonisation relying primarily on SAF or PtL fuels.

When considering operational expenditures (OpEx) for hydrogen aviation, they encompass fuel costs, maintenance, and training. Not surprisingly, hydrogen fuel costs are currently higher than those of conventional jet fuel due to the energy-intensive processes required for clean hydrogen production, such as electrolysis powered by renewable energy. While $H_2$ has higher energy content per unit of mass than jet fuel, its low volumetric energy density necessitates larger storage systems, which increase aircraft weight and operational complexity (European Climate Foundation, 2023; Steer & DLR, 2023).

At the moment, maintenance costs for hydrogen systems remain uncertain due to the limited experience with large-scale commercial applications. However, hydrogen's unique properties, e.g., its potential to embrittle metals and its flammability, are likely to require specialised maintenance procedures and materials, potentially increasing OpEx (Arup, 2023). Additionally, crew training for handling hydrogen, a much more flammable substance than jet fuel, will add to operational costs. This includes training for safe refuelling procedures and emergency response protocols at airports (European Commission, 2020).

Most importantly, fuel costs are a critical factor in the adoption of hydrogen aviation. Currently, green hydrogen (produced via electrolysis using renewable energy) is significantly more expensive than conventional jet fuel. In particular, while green hydrogen costs start climbing up from around 3.45 USD per kilogram in Europe, jet fuel prices generally vary from approximately 0.70 to 1.50 USD per kilogram (European Climate Foundation, 2023; Steer & DLR, 2023). Although improvements in technology, scaling effects, and decreasing renewable energy prices could eventually bring clean hydrogen costs down to 1–2 USD per kilogram worldwide, the achievement of such competitiveness with conventional fuels is not expected in the foreseeable future (Hydrogen Insight, 2024).

When comparing hydrogen solutions for the aviation sector with currently available technologies and alternatives, one must consider both direct costs and externalities, such as environmental impact and regulatory compliance (ATAG, 2022). Speaking about the direct costs, we should make it straightforwardly clear that hydrogen-powered aircraft are currently more expensive to develop and operate than conventional aircraft, which is not surprising. Specifically, while the CapEx for hydrogen aircraft is estimated to be two to three times higher than that of traditional jet fuel-powered aircraft, primarily due to the need for new propulsion systems and infrastructure, their OpEx is also higher, as it is driven by elevated fuel and maintenance costs.

However, while considering the use of hydrogen in aviation, we should not omit its potential benefits, as the primary advantage and benefit of hydrogen for the sector would be its potential to eliminate greenhouse gas emissions and air pollutants. Here, since hydrogen combustion produces only water vapour and hydrogen fuel cells emit no pollutants, the use of $H_2$ technologies in aviation will bring external benefits associated with improved air quality and lower greenhouse gas content of the atmosphere. At the same time, the well-to-wake emissions, including hydrogen production, are critical for assessing the true climate benefit. This aligns with increasingly stringent environmental regulations, such as ICAO's Carbon Offsetting and Reduction Scheme for International Aviation (CORSIA). Therefore, by adopting hydrogen, airlines can enhance their environmental credentials and avoid potential carbon taxes or penalties (ICAO, 2025).

Nevertheless, this will definitely not be enough to convince the key players in the aviation sector to transition to a more expensive but also more environmentally friendly fuel, if the cost of carbon they will have to pay for is too low. As carbon pricing mechanisms become more widespread, the cost of conventional jet fuel is expected to rise, narrowing the gap between hydrogen and traditional fuels. Until that happens, the economic viability of hydrogen in aviation will be doomed to be heavily influenced by government policies such as subsidies, incentives, and carbon pricing mechanisms. Therefore, at the moment, government support is crucial to bridging the cost gap between hydrogen and conventional aviation technologies. For instance, while direct subsidies for the development of hydrogen-powered aircraft and infrastructure can reduce initial CapEx, making hydrogen more accessible to airlines, tax incentives, such as credits for clean energy investments, can further encourage adoption.

To drive innovation and reduce cost of research and development over time, R&D grants are also essential. For example, at the moment, the European Union's Clean Aviation initiative and the US Department of Energy's Hydrogen Program provide funding for hydrogen-related R&D and demonstration projects. These initiatives aim to accelerate the commercialisation of hydrogen technologies in aviation (European Commission, 2020).

At the same time, in the long term, carbon pricing mechanisms such as emissions trading systems (ETS) and carbon taxes are critical for incentivising the adoption of hydrogen in aviation. By internalising the external costs of carbon emissions, these policies make hydrogen more competitive with conventional fuels. For instance, under the EU ETS, airlines are required to purchase carbon allowances for their emissions, increasing the cost of using fossil fuels. A robust carbon price signal can drive investment in clean technologies and accelerate the transition to hydrogen (ICAO, 2020).

Moreover, clear and consistent regulatory frameworks are essential for building investor confidence and ensuring the global adoption of hydrogen in aviation. International cooperation—such as through ICAO—is necessary to harmonise safety standards, carbon pricing mechanisms, and incentive programmes. A level playing field, where all fuels are assessed based on full lifecycle emissions, is crucial for fair competition and effective decarbonisation (ATAG, 2021).

## Policy and Regulatory Landscape

Although technological and economic challenges hamper the implementation of $H_2$ in the aviation sector, the success of the adoption of hydrogen-powered propulsion by the industry will also be significantly influenced by existing and future policy and regulatory frameworks. At the moment, globally, the aviation sector is regulated by the International Civil Aviation Organization (ICAO), which sets international standards and recommended practices for aviation safety, security, efficiency, and environmental protection. In 2016, ICAO introduced the Carbon Offsetting and Reduction Scheme for International Aviation (CORSIA), designed to maintain net $CO_2$ emissions at 2020 levels by mandating airlines to offset any growth through carbon credits (ICAO, 2016). While CORSIA represents a significant step towards addressing aviation emissions, it does not mandate the use of zero-emission fuels like hydrogen, focusing instead on market-based measures. This leaves the adoption of hydrogen to voluntary initiatives and national policies, limiting its effectiveness in driving widespread hydrogen adoption (Schäfer et al., 2018; Yusaf et al., 2022).

At the regional level, the European Union has emerged as a leader in promoting hydrogen adoption in aviation, since the European Union's Hydrogen Strategy, published in 2020, identifies aviation as a key sector for hydrogen deployment, particularly for short- and medium-haul flights (European Commission, 2020). In addition, the European Green Deal and the Fit for 55 package have set ambitious targets for reducing greenhouse gas emissions across all sectors, including aviation (European Commission, 2021). In particular, The ReFuelEU Aviation Initiative, part of the Fit for 55 package, proposes blending mandates for Sustainable Aviation Fuels (SAFs), including hydrogen-derived fuels like synthetic kerosene, starting from 2025 (ibid.). However, none of the EU-wide initiatives has explicitly supported hydrogen as a primary propellant to replace kerosene-based jet fuels, instead focusing on hydrogen-derived synthetic fuels and SAFs. While part of the reason for this is undoubtedly the high cost of clean hydrogen production and its relatively small scale, another—if not more significant—prerequisite is the high complexity and cost of infrastructure adjustments required if hydrogen is to be used as a dominant fuel.

Nationally, several countries have incorporated hydrogen aviation into their hydrogen strategies. For instance, Japan's Basic Hydrogen Strategy identifies hydrogen as a key component of its aviation decarbonisation efforts, with a focus on developing hydrogen fuel cells for regional aircraft (Ministry of Economy, Trade and Industry, 2017). Similarly, the United Kingdom's Hydrogen Strategy, published in 2021, highlights the potential of hydrogen for decarbonising aviation and commits to supporting research and development (R&D) in hydrogen propulsion technologies (Department of Energy Security & Net Zero, 2021). In the United States, the FAA has initiated the Continuous Lower Energy, Emissions, and Noise (CLEEN) programme to support the advancement of hydrogen fuel cell and hydrogen combustion technologies for aviation (FAA, 2020).

Despite these initiatives, the lack of binding international regulations for hydrogen adoption in aviation remains a significant gap. While ICAO provides a platform for international cooperation, its non-binding nature limits its effectiveness in driving the widespread adoption of hydrogen technologies (Schäfer et al., 2018; Yusaf et al., 2024). Furthermore, the absence of harmonised standards for hydrogen storage, refuelling, and safety in aviation poses challenges for cross-border operations (IEA, 2021). This could be attributed to the overall challenges of hydrogen adoption associated with $H_2$'s low energy density by volume, which presents significant challenges for aircraft design and operation and overall hampers rapid technological progress, deployment, and ramp-up of hydrogen solutions.

Since, economically, the high cost of clean $H_2$ production remains a major hurdle, clean hydrogen-based fuels appear to be significantly more expensive than its conventional version and most other sustainable alternatives (Fig. 9.4). This cost disparity is exacerbated by the need for significant investments in hydrogen production, storage, and distribution infrastructure, including airport refuelling facilities and transportation networks (Schäfer et al., 2020). Since most of the relevant policies and regulations in this domain are currently missing, the slow pace of the hydrogen value chain's progress is further hampering the adoption of $H_2$ in aviation.

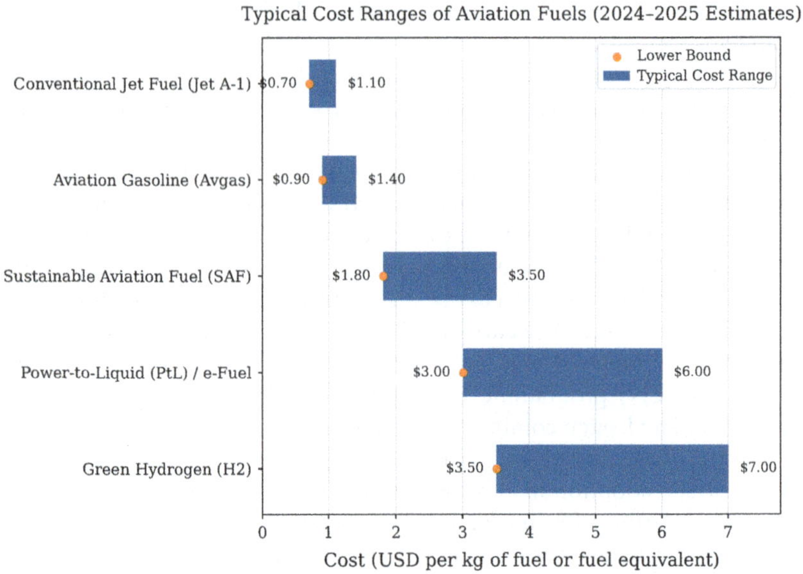


**Fig. 9.4** Average cost ranges of hydrogen and alternative fuels for aviation. (Source: Adapted from ICCT (2019), IEA (2021), WEF (2020), ATAG (2021), and IATA (2022))

Apart from costs, regulatory barriers further complicate the adoption of hydrogen in aviation. More specifically, the lack of harmonised international standards for hydrogen storage, refuelling, and safety creates uncertainty for manufacturers, airlines, and infrastructure developers. While ICAO has established guidelines for the safe handling of hydrogen, detailed standards specific to aviation applications are still under development. Additionally, national regulations often vary, creating fragmented market conditions that hinder the scalability of hydrogen technologies.

Overall, because of relative technological novelty, the certification process for hydrogen-powered aircraft is more stringent than for conventional aircraft, requiring extensive testing and validation to ensure safety and reliability (Spencer, 2022). In general, safety is a paramount concern in the deployment of hydrogen in aviation, since hydrogen's high flammability and wide ignition range necessitate rigorous safety measures, particularly in the confined and pressurised environment of an aircraft. While $H_2$ has been used safely in industrial applications for decades, its use in aviation requires specialised handling procedures, leak detection systems, and emergency response protocols (Maciorowski et al., 2024). Therefore the development of robust safety standards and training programmes for ground crew and flight personnel is critical to mitigating these risks. This, however, has not been properly done yet, as the sector is in its nascence.

Supply chain issues also present significant challenges. The production of clean hydrogen is geographically constrained to regions with abundant renewable energy resources and geological formations suitable for $CO_2$ storage. Therefore, just like other fuels used in aviation, clean $H_2$ will have to be transported to airports and stored there for further use. However, transporting hydrogen to airports, particularly in remote or landlocked locations, requires the development of efficient and cost-effective supply chains, which is complicated by the same notorious properties of hydrogen itself—low volumetric density and small molecular size. Although liquid hydrogen has long been used in the space industry by entities like NASA to make storing larger volumes of $H_2$ economically and technically more attractive, dealing with sub-zero temperatures that are close to absolute zero[2] will require specialised cryogenic transport and storage infrastructure that will have to minimise boil-off gas losses, further complicating the supply chain (Brewer, 1976; Choi & Lee, 2022).

Public acceptance is a critical factor for the successful adoption of hydrogen in aviation. While hydrogen is often perceived as a clean and sustainable fuel, concerns about its safety and the environmental impact of its production (e.g., water usage for electrolysis) can influence public opinion (Scovell, 2022). Overall, the negative perception of hydrogen use in aviation can be traced back to historical events, particularly the Hindenburg disaster of 1937, which left a lasting stigma on hydrogen's safety in the public's mind.[3] This perception has influenced more recent hydrogen aviation projects, where initial concerns about the fuel's flammability and storage caused hesitation among airlines and passengers. That is why education and awareness campaigns, coupled with transparent demonstration projects, are essential to building confidence among stakeholders.

[2] At atmospheric pressure, gaseous hydrogen is liquefied at a temperature of -252.87 °C.

[3] The Hindenburg disaster occurred on 6 May 1937, when the hydrogen-filled German airship LZ 129 attempted to land in Lakehurst, New Jersey. A fire erupted, destroying the vessel and killing 36 individuals, illustrating the risks of using hydrogen for lift (Lancaster, 2023).

## Case Studies and Pilot Projects

At the moment, hydrogen is gaining traction as a zero-emission solution for aviation, particularly for regional and short-haul flights. Airbus is a key player in this space, with its ZEROe initiative exploring two main hydrogen-powered aircraft propulsion concepts: hybrid (hydrogen fuel cell + battery electric) and direct hydrogen combustion (Airbus, 2025). One of the key projects under development is a regional turboprop aircraft that would be propelled by electric motors powered by hydrogen fuel cells with batteries performing supporting role for transient power needs—the design that is expected to be particularly suited for shorter flights, where the energy density and efficiency of fuel cells are advantageous (ibid.). In addition to the hybrid fuel cell concept, Airbus is also developing two other ZEROe designs: a turbofan aircraft, which will use an A380 as a testbed, and a blended-wing body aircraft, both of which would use hydrogen combustion in modified gas turbines to allow for longer-range flights (ibid.).

At the same time, despite being a lot more active in their attempts to decarbonise the aviation sector than many competitors like, e.g., Boeing, Airbus has recently acknowledged significant challenges. In particular, despite originally planning flight testing of a new hydrogen aircraft for 2026, in early 2025, the company officially announced that it should only be expected to happen 'later than 2035' (Aerospace Global News, 2025). Here, while the complete redesign of the aircraft itself appeared to be part of the problem, the real and most important challenge was admitted to be lack of a sufficiently developed sustainable hydrogen ecosystem, including infrastructure, production, distribution, and regulatory frameworks (Financial Times, 2025). This delay underscores the segment-specific and gradual nature of hydrogen's impact, with regional/short-haul applications being the first viable niche.

In terms of companies and projects focusing primarily on fuel cells, H2FLY should be mentioned as a key player in the pure fuel cell-electric aviation sector. In fact, the company has made notable progress with its HY4 aircraft, a four-seater powered entirely by hydrogen fuel cells, which has successfully completed multiple test flights demonstrating the feasibility of hydrogen-electric propulsion (H2FLY, 2024). While H2FLY is currently working on scaling the technology for regional aircraft to address challenges such as energy density and system integration, it has not yet been able to extend fuel cells to larger aircraft, primarily due to limitations in power output and durability.

In fact, similar progress was demonstrated by ZeroAvia, who successfully flight-tested their fuel cell and electric motor technology in 2023 that was powered by compressed $H_2$ stored in tanks (ZeroAvia, 2023). The company retrofitted their prototype ZA600 engine to run the left-side propeller of a Dornier 228, with fuel cells used for power generation and an electric motor for propulsion (ibid.). At the same time, similar to the previous case of H2FLY, this product has neither been fully commercialised nor scaled up for larger aircraft and is only planned to be so by 2030 (ibid.). Here, as with other fuel cell-powered aviation systems, the main roadblocks appear to relate to fuel cell durability. In addition, the infrastructure and hydrogen ecosystem challenges that were faced by Airbus are also applicable here and, therefore, should be addressed to enable the sustainable ramp-up of such applications (International Airport Review, 2024).

At the moment, for larger aircraft, combustion engines seem to be attracting greater attention than fuel cells, which is not surprising, given the scalability and adaptability limitations of the latter. However, none of the existing projects has so far been able to reach the stage of full commercialisation. For instance, Rolls-Royce and easyJet achieved a milestone in 2022 by successfully conducting a ground test of the world's first aero engine powered by hydrogen derived from wind and tidal power (Rolls-Royce, 2022). At the same time, while being inspired by this success, which demonstrated the feasibility of hydrogen combustion for aviation, the companies plan to conduct the first flight tests and expand the technology to larger aircraft only in the coming years. The next milestone for the foreseeable future is set to be the ground testing of a Rolls-Royce Pearl 15 jet engine, which is normally used to power the Bombardier Global 5500 and 6500 private jet series (Rolls-Royce, 2024). A key challenge for such combustion concepts is managing non-$CO_2$ effects like $NO_x$ and contrails.

Similarly, GE Aerospace and CFM International are collaborating with Airbus on a hydrogen-powered open-fan engine, with flight tests expected by the mid-2030s (GE, 2022). This project aims to leverage the high efficiency of open-fan designs while integrating hydrogen combustion technology (ibid.). Just like in the previous case, apart from $NO_x$ emissions, key challenges include managing the high temperatures and pressures associated with hydrogen combustion and ensuring compatibility with existing airport infrastructure (ibid).

To help mitigate this challenge, Universal Hydrogen proposed using modular aluminium tanks containing liquid $H_2$, which could be delivered to airports and loaded directly onto aircraft, eliminating the need for permanent hydrogen infrastructure (Hydrogen Wire, 2024). However, despite the initial success of the ground test run with its megawatt-class fuel cell powertrain using its proprietary liquid hydrogen module to supply the fuel and the first flight of their partially hydrogen-powered De Havilland Canada Dash 8–300 in 2023, the company was forced to shut down a year later due to insufficient funding (Green Air, 2024). Therefore, currently, it seems unlikely that this approach will be widely adopted by companies working on hydrogen propulsion systems in aviation in the coming years. This case highlights the significant financial and infrastructure challenges facing the sector.

Finally, hybrid systems, which combine hydrogen fuel cells with batteries, are being developed to address the limitations of standalone hydrogen technologies. However, just like most other projects, their technological maturity remains at a very low level and the complexity of infrastructure adjustment has not even been considered in most cases. For instance, just like Airbus with one of its ZEROe concept prototypes, GKN Aerospace is working on the H2GEAR system, which uses hydrogen fuel cells to drive electric motors, supported by batteries for peak power demands (Airbus, 2025). The system is aimed at regional aircraft, with a goal once discussed for ~2035, though the later-2030s/2040s are now more realistic for service entry. Nevertheless, challenges such as system integration and technological maturity remain significant barriers and it is therefore unclear whether full commercialisation will be achieved within the upcoming decade (GKN Aerospace, 2023).

H2FLY and Deutsche Aircraft, in turn, are collaborating on a hydrogen-electric hybrid version of the Dornier 328 regional aircraft. This project combines fuel cells and batteries to create a propulsion system that balances energy density and power output. The collaboration also aims to achieve commercial flights by 2035, but challenges include managing the weight and complexity of hybrid systems and ensuring the reliability of hydrogen fuel cells in commercial operations (H2FLY, 2024).

Overall, the progress made by companies like Airbus, H2Fly, Rolls-Royce, and ZeroAvia demonstrates some potential of hydrogen-based technologies to transform the aviation industry. However, for such initiatives to ramp up and become universally used solutions, challenges such as technological maturity and lack of financial backing will have to be addressed in parallel with those of hydrogen storage complexity and generally high costs of airport infrastructure adjustment. The collective evidence from these projects points to a gradual, segment-specific impact for hydrogen, complementing SAF/PtL fuels rather than replacing them at scale before 2050.

## Future Outlook and Conclusions

The aviation sector is at a pivotal moment in its quest to decarbonise, with hydrogen emerging as a promising yet complex solution. This chapter has explored the multifaceted challenges and opportunities associated with hydrogen's adoption, analysing its technological feasibility, infrastructure requirements, economic viability, and the surrounding policy landscape. The evidence points to a future where hydrogen plays a critical but specific role, shaped by a clear consensus on its complementary nature.

The overarching conclusion is that hydrogen's impact is most likely to be gradual and segment-specific. The transition will not be a rapid, wholesale replacement of conventional fuels but an evolution marked by distinct phases. In the short term (to 2035), hydrogen's application will be confined to niche markets, primarily small regional aircraft powered by fuel cells, as demonstrated by projects from H2FLY and ZeroAvia. These will serve as vital proof-of-concept demonstrations.

The medium term (2035–2050) will likely see hydrogen gaining a foothold in the short- to medium-haul segment, with hydrogen combustion engines enabling larger aircraft, as envisioned by Airbus' ZEROe programme (if successfully materialised). However, it is crucial to recognise that during this period, hydrogen will most likely complement, rather than replace, Sustainable Aviation Fuels and Power-to-Liquid fuels for fleet-wide decarbonisation. SAF/PtL will remain the primary solution for long-haul flights and the existing fleet, while hydrogen carves out a role in new, specific aircraft segments. In these circumstances, the long-term prospect (post-2050) of hydrogen powering zero-emission long-haul flights remains a possibility but is contingent on overcoming immense technological hurdles related to storage and aircraft design.

This entire pathway is predicated on two non-negotiable prerequisites: the development of new aircraft architectures and major hydrogen infrastructure at airports. The industry cannot retrofit its way into this future; it requires purpose-built aircraft, such as blended-wing-body designs, to efficiently integrate large cryogenic fuel tanks. Simultaneously, airports must undergo a fundamental transformation, investing in parallel cryogenic storage, refuelling, and safety systems. This represents a colossal coordination and investment challenge that demands unprecedented public–private partnerships.

Economically, the business case for hydrogen remains challenging. High capital and operational expenditures currently make hydrogen-powered aircraft significantly more expensive than conventional alternatives. The climate benefit of hydrogen aviation is entirely contingent on a low-emissions hydrogen supply, making the well-to-wake perspective paramount. The scaling up of affordable green hydrogen production is an absolute prerequisite; without it, the $CO_2$ reduction benefits are negated. While subsidies, incentives, and robust carbon pricing can help bridge the cost gap, widespread adoption hinges on dramatic reductions in green hydrogen production costs.

Finally, the environmental focus must extend beyond $CO_2$. Non-$CO_2$ climate effects, particularly nitrogen oxide ($NO_x$) emissions and contrail formation from hydrogen combustion, remain material concerns that require active research and mitigation. This underscores that fuel cells and combustion engines present different environmental trade-offs that must be carefully managed.

In conclusion, hydrogen represents an important strategic option for a sustainable aviation industry, but its journey will be one of incremental progress. Its successful integration depends on a synchronised advancement of technology, the creation of a new global infrastructure, the availability of cost-competitive clean hydrogen, and a nuanced understanding of its full climate impact. The path forward requires coordinated efforts from governments, industry, and international organisations to harmonise regulations, fund innovation, and build public acceptance. The coming decades will see hydrogen working in tandem with SAFs, PtL fuels, and efficiency improvements—not in competition with them—to chart a credible and multifaceted path towards the aviation sector's net-zero ambitions.

## References

ABS (2023) *Fuel cell power systems for marine and offshore applications*. Spring, TX: American Bureau of Shipping Global Sustainability Center.

Aerospace Global News. (2025). *Airbus ZEROe project could be delayed by up to a decade* [Online]. Retrieved March 08, 2025, from https://aerospaceglobalnews.com/news/airbus-zeroe-project-could-be-delayed-by-up-to-a-decade/.

Airbus. (2025). *ZEROe* [Online]. Retrieved March 08, 2025, from https://www.airbus.com/en/innovation/energy-transition/hydrogen/zeroe.

Alsulaiman, A. (2024). *Navigating turbulence: Hydrogen's role in the decarbonisation of the aviation sector.* Oxford Institute for Energy Studies.

Argonne National Laboratory. (2020). *Total Cost of Ownership (TCO) analysis of hydrogen fuel cells in aviation – preliminary results* [Online]. Retrieved March 13, 2025, from https://www.energy.gov/sites/prod/files/2020/12/f81/hfto-h2-airports-workshop-2020-ahluwalia.pdf.

Arup. (2023). *Hydrogen in aviation* [Online]. Retrieved March 13, 2025, from https://www.arup.com/globalassets/downloads/insights/hydrogen-in-aviation.pdf.

ATAG. (2021). *Waypoint 2050 2nd edition: September 2021 (full report and summary)* [Online]. Retrieved March 11, 2025, from https://atag.org/resources/waypoint-2050-2nd-edition-september-2021.

ATAG. (2023). *Sustainable aviation fuel* [Online]. Retrieved February 21, 2025, from https://atag.org/industry-topics/sustainable-aviation-fuel.

ATAG. (2024). *Facts & figures* [Online]. Retrieved February 17, 2025, from https://atag.org/facts-figures.

Aviation Benefits Beyond Borders. (2024). *Aviation: Benefits beyond borders 2024* [Online]. Retrieved February 19, 2025, from https://aviationbenefits.org/downloads/aviation-benefits-beyond-borders-2024/.

Biert, L., Godjevac, M., Visser, K., and Aravind, P.V. (2016) 'A review of fuel cell systems for maritime applications', *Journal of Power Sources*, 327 (1), pp. 345–364.

Bhuiyan, M.H. and Siddique, Z. (2025) 'Hydrogen as an alternative fuel: A comprehensive review of challenges and opportunities in production, storage, and transportation', *International Journal of Hydrogen Energy*, 102 (1), pp. 1026–1044.

Boretti, A. (2024). Towards hydrogen gas turbine engines aviation: A review of production, infrastructure, storage, aircraft design and combustion technologies. *International Journal of Hydrogen Energy, 88*(1), 279–288.

Bosio, B., Archetti, M., Audasso, E., and Bove, D. (2023) 'Process analysis of a molten carbonate fuel cell onboard application to reduce vessel $CO_2$ emissions', *Chemical Engineering and Processing – Process Intensification*, 190, pp. 1–29.

Brewer, G. D. (1976). Aviation usage of liquid hydrogen fuel – prospects and problems. *International Journal of Hydrogen Energy, 1*(1), 65–88.

Choi, Y., & Lee, J. (2022). Estimation of liquid hydrogen fuels in aviation. *Aerospace, 9*(10), 1–18.

CSIRO. (2020). *Opportunities for hydrogen in commercial aviation* [Online]. Retrieved March 13, 2025, from https://www.csiro.au/-/media/Do-Business/Files/Futures/Boeing-Opportunities-for-hydrogen-in-commercial-aviation.pdf.

Department of Energy Security & Net Zero. (2021). *UK hydrogen strategy* [Online]. Retrieved March 11, 2025, from https://www.gov.uk/government/publications/uk-hydrogen-strategy/uk-hydrogen-strategy-accessible-html-version.

Djermouni, M. and Ouahda, A. (2023) 'Thermodynamic analysis of methanol, ammonia, and hydrogen as alternative fuels in HCCI engines', *International Journal of Thermofluids*, 19, pp. 1–7.

European Climate Foundation. (2023). *The cost of hydrogen aviation – Final briefing* [Online]. Retrieved March 13, 2025, from https://te-cdn.ams3.cdn.digitaloceanspaces.com/files/The-cost-of-hydrogen-aviation-Final-Briefing-2.pdf.

European Commission. (2020). *A hydrogen strategy for a climate-neutral Europe* [Online]. Retrieved March 11, 2025, from https://energy.ec.europa.eu/system/files/2020-07/hydrogen_strategy_0.pdf.

European Commission. (2021). *'Fit for 55': Delivering the EU's 2030 Climate Target on the way to climate neutrality* [Online]. Retrieved March 11, 2025, from https://eur-lex.europa.eu/legal-content/EN/TXT/HTML/?uri=CELEX:52021DC0550.

European Commission. (2022). *Sustainable aviation fuels (SAF) and other alternative fuels used for aviation* [Online]. Retrieved February 21, 2025, from https://alternative-fuels-observatory.ec.europa.eu/transport-mode/aviation/general-information-and-context.

European Commission. (2023). *EU Emissions Trading System* (EU ETS) [Online]. Retrieved February 18, 2025, from https://ec.europa.eu/clima/eu-action/eu-emissions-trading-system-eu-ets_en.

European Parliament. (2023). *Assessment of the potential of sustainable fuels in transport* [Online]. Retrieved February 21, 2025, from chrome-extension://efaidnbmnnnibpcajpcglclefindmkaj/ https://www.europarl.europa.eu/RegData/etudes/STUD/2023/733103/IPOL_STU(2023)733103_EN.pdf

ExxonMobil. (2022). *Aviation fuels* [Online]. Retrieved February 21, 2025, from https://www.exxonmobil.com/en/aviation/products-and-services/products/categories/fuels.

FAA. (2020). *Continuous Lower Energy, Emissions, and Noise (CLEEN) program* [Online]. Retrieved March 11, 2025, from https://www.faa.gov/sites/faa.gov/files/2022-07/eeSC-Mar2020-CLEENBenefitsSummary.pdf.

Fu, Z., et al. (2023) 'Fuel cell and hydrogen in maritime application: A review on aspects of technology, cost and regulations', *Sustainable Energy Technologies and Assessments*, 57, pp. 1026–1044.

Financial Times. (2025). *Airbus pushes back plants to fly hydrogen plane by 2035* [Online]. Retrieved March 08, 2025, from https://www.ft.com/content/12490140-dd6d-4191-9495-a0dadb68874c.

GE. (2022). *Hydrogen takes flight: Airbus and CFM International to partner on hydrogen-fueled demonstration* [Online]. Retrieved March 09, 2025, from https://www.ge.com/news/reports/hydrogen-takes-flight-airbus-and-cfm-international-to-partner-on-hydrogen-fueled-0.

Green Air. (2024). *Hydrogen aviation pioneer Universal Hydrogen fails, citing lack of funding* [Online]. Retrieved March 09, 2025, from https://www.greenairnews.com/?p=5860.

H2FLY. (2024). *Why hydrogen is the best solution to decarbonize aviation* [Online]. Retrieved February 25, 2025, from https://www.h2fly.de/.

Hydrogen Insight. (2024). *Green hydrogen is not going to cost €2/kg in Europe any time soon – so do we need to rethink our policies?* [Online]. Retrieved March 14, 2025, from https://www.hydrogeninsight.com/policy/green-hydrogen-is-not-going-to-cost-2-kg-in-europe-any-time-soon-so-do-we-need-to-rethink-our-policies-/2-1-1738481.

Hydrogen Wire. (2024). *Universal Hydrogen reveals first fully functional liquid hydrogen module made of aluminium* [Online]. Retrieved March 09, 2025, from https://hydrogenwire.com/2024/04/11/universal-hydrogen-reveals-first-fully-functional-liquid-hydrogen-module-made-of-aluminium/.

IATA. (2022). *Developing Sustainable Aviation Fuel (SAF)* [Online]. Retrieved March 11, 2025, from https://www.iata.org/en/programs/sustainability/sustainable-aviation-fuels/.

IATA. (2023). *Hydrogen power – boldly going to the heart of climate-neutral aviation* [Online]. Retrieved February 25, 2025, from https://www.icao.int/environmental-protection/Documents/EnvironmentalReports/2022/ENVReport2022_Art32.pdf.

IATA. (2024). *ReFuelEU aviation handbook* [Online]. Retrieved February 21, 2025, from https://www.iata.org/contentassets/d13875e9ed784f75bac90f000760e998/refuel-eu-aviation-handbook.pdf.

ICAO. (2020). *ICAO carbon emissions calculator methodology* [Online]. Retrieved February 19, 2025, from https://applications.icao.int/icec/Methodology%20ICAO%20Carbon%20Emissions%20Calculator_v13_Final.pdf.

ICAO. (2022). *ICAO environmental report 2022* [Online]. Retrieved February 19, 2025, from https://www.icao.int/environmental-protection/Pages/envrep2022.aspx.

ICAO. (2025). *Carbon Offsetting and Reduction Scheme for International Aviation (CORSIA)* [Online]. Retrieved March 11, 2025, from https://www.icao.int/environmental-protection/CORSIA/Pages/default.aspx

ICCT. (2019). *The cost of supporting alternative jet fuels in the European Union* [Online]. Retrieved March 11, 2025, from https://theicct.org/sites/default/files/publications/Alternative_jet_fuels_cost_EU_20190320.pdf.

ICCT. (2021). *Assessing the sustainability implications of alternative aviation fuels* [Online]. Retrieved February 22, 2025, from https://theicct.org/wp-content/uploads/2021/06/Alt-aviation-fuel-sustainability-mar2021.pdf.

IEA (2021) *World Energy Outlook* 2021. Paris, France: International Energy Agency.

IEA (2022) *World Energy Outlook* 2022. Paris, France: International Energy Agency.

ATAG (2022) Waypoint 2050 – *Aviation sector decarbonisation roadmap update*. Geneva: Air Transport Action Group.

ICAO (2016) *Carbon Offsetting and Reduction Scheme for International Aviation (CORSIA)*. Montreal: International Civil Aviation Organization.

International Airport Review. (2024). *How can airports ensure they have the correct infrastructure in place in time for commercial hydrogen aircraft?* [Online]. Retrieved March 08, 2025, from https://www.internationalairportreview.com/article/232817/how-can-airports-ensure-they-have-the-correct-infrastructure-in-place-in-time-for-commercial-hydrogen-aircraft/.

IPCC. (2018). *Global warming of 1.5°C: An IPCC special report on the impacts of global warming of 1.5°C above pre-industrial levels and related global greenhouse gas emission pathways* [Online]. Retrieved February 17, 2025, from https://www.ipcc.ch/sr15/.

Kösters, T. L., et al. (2023). Experimental study and simulations of hydrogen cooling for aviation PEM fuel cells. *Scientific Reports, 13*(1), 1–11.

Kołodziejski, M. (2023) 'Review of hydrogen-based propulsion systems in the maritime sector', *Archives of Thermodynamics*, 44 (4), pp. 335–380.

Lancaster, O. (2023). *Inferno in the sky: The Hindenburg disaster*. BookBaby.

Lee, D. S., et al. (2021). The contribution of global aviation to anthropogenic climate forcing for 2000 to 2018. *Atmospheric Environment, 244*(117834), 1–29.

Maciorowski, D., Ludwiczak, A., & Kozakiewicz, A. (2024). Hydrogen, the future of aviation. *Combustion Engines, 197*(2), 126–131.

McKinsey & Company. (2023). *Target true zero: Infrastructure for alternative propulsion flight* [Online]. Retrieved March 13, 2025, from https://www.mckinsey.com/industries/aerospace-and-defense/our-insights/target-true-zero-infrastructure-for-alternative-propulsion-flight.

Ministry of Economy, Trade and Industry. (2017). *Basic Hydrogen Strategy* [Online]. Retrieved March 11, 2025, from https://www.meti.go.jp/shingikai/enecho/shoene_shinene/suiso_seisaku/pdf/20230606_5.pdf.

OECD. (2023). *The potential of e-fuels to decarbonise ships and aircraft* [Online]. Retrieved February 21, 2025, from https://www.oecd.org/content/dam/oecd/en/publications/reports/2023/01/the-potential-of-e-fuels-to-decarbonise-ships-and-aircraft_bb1e7c98/3d96e0d9-en.pdf.

Repsol. (2024). *The best product for military use* [Online]. Retrieved February 22, 2025, from https://www.repsol.com/en/products-and-services/aviation/jp-8/index.cshtml.

Roland Berger. (2020). *Hydrogen: A future fuel for aviation?* [Online]. Retrieved March 13, 2025, from https://www.rolandberger.com/publications/publication_pdf/roland_berger_hydrogen_the_future_fuel_for_aviation.pdf.

Rolls-Royce. (2022). *Rolls-Royce and easyJet set new world first* [Online]. Retrieved March 09, 2025, from https://www.rolls-royce.com/media/press-releases/2022/28-11-2022-rr-and-easyjet-set-new-aviation-world-first-with-successful-hydrogen-engine-run.

Rolls-Royce. (2024). *Rolls-Royce and easyJet to perform hydrogen testing at NASA's Stennis Space Center* [Online]. Retrieved March 09, 2025, from https://www.rolls-royce.com/media/press-releases/2024/22-07-2024-rr-and-easyjet-to-perform-hydrogen-testing-at-nasas-stennis-space-center.aspx.

Schäfer, A.W., et al. (2018). *Technological, economic, and environmental prospects of all-electric aircraft* [Online]. Retrieved March 11, 2025, from https://dspace.mit.edu/bitstream/handle/1721.1/126682/Schafer_Technological%2C%20Economic%20and%20Environmental%20Prospects%20of%20All-Electric%20Aircraft_AAM.pdf?sequence=2&isAllowed=y.

Schmelcher, M., & Häβy, J. (2022). *Hydrogen fuel cells for aviation? A potential analysis comparing difference thrust categories.* German Aerospace Center.

Schröder, M., Becker, F., Kallo, J., & Genter, C. (2021). Optimal operating conditions of PEM fuel cells in commercial aircraft. *International Journal of Hydrogen Energy, 46*(66), 33218–33240.

Scovell, M. D. (2022). Explaining hydrogen energy technology acceptance: A critical review. *International Journal of Hydrogen Energy, 47*(19), 10441–10459.

Shell. (2023). *Aviation fuel grades* [Online]. Retrieved February 21, 2025, from https://www.shell.com/business-customers/aviation/aviation-fuel/guide-to-grades-specifications-additives.html.

Shi, J., et al. (2023) 'A prompt decarbonisation pathway for shipping: Green hydrogen, ammonia, and methanol production and utilization in marine engines', *Atmosphere*, 14 (3), pp. 1–29.

Soleymani, M., et al. (2024). Hydrogen propulsion systems for aircraft, a review on recent advances and ongoing challenges. *International Journal of Hydrogen Energy, 91*(1), 137–171.

Spencer, R. (2022). Certification considerations for the configuration of a hydrogen-fuelled aeroplane. *The Aeronautical Journal, 127*(1308), 213–231.

Steer & DLR. (2023). *Analysing the costs of hydrogen aircra*ft [Online]. Retrieved March 13, 2025, from https://te-cdn.ams3.cdn.digitaloceanspaces.com/files/Study-Analysing-the-costs-of-hydrogen-aircraft.pdf.

Tarnatore, C., Marchitto, L., Sabia, P., and Joannon, M. (2022). 'Ammonia as green fuel in internal combustion engines: State-of-the-art and future perspectives', *Frontiers in Mechanical Engineering 8*(1), 1–16.

UNEP. (2019). *Emissions gap report 2019* [Online]. Retrieved February 17, 2025, from https://www.unep.org/resources/emissions-gap-report-2019.

Vairo, T., et al. (2023). 'Solid oxide fuel cells for shipping: A machine learning model for early detection of hazardous system deviations'. *Process Safety and Environmental Protection*, 172, 184–194.

Verhelst, S. and Wallner, T. (2009). 'Hydrogen-fueled internal combustion engines', *Progress in Energy and Combustion Science*, 35 (6), pp. 490–527.

WEF. (2020). *Clean skies for tomorrow: Sustainable aviation fuels as a pathway to net-zero aviation* [Online]. Retrieved March 11, 2025, from https://www3.weforum.org/docs/WEF_Clean_Skies_Tomorrow_SAF_Analytics_2020.pdf.

WEF. (2024). *Aviation industry net-zero tracker* [Online]. Retrieved February 21, 2025, from chrome-extension://efaidnbmnnnibpcajpcglclefindmkaj/https://reports.weforum.org/docs/WEF_Net_Zero_Industry_Tracker_2024_Aviation.pdf.

World Resources Institute. (2021). *Climate watch: Historical GHG emissions* [Online]. Retrieved February 17, 2025, from https://www.climatewatchdata.org/ghg-emissions.

Xing, H., Stuart, C., Spence, S., & Chen, H. (2021). 'Fuel cell power systems for maritime applications: Progress and perspectives'. *Sustainability 13*(3), 1–34.

Yusaf, T., et al. (2022). Sustainable aviation – Hydrogen is the future. *Sustainability, 14*(548), 1–17.

Yusaf, T., et al. (2024). Sustainable hydrogen energy in aviation – A narrative review. *International Journal of Hydrogen Energy, 52*(2), 1026–1045.

Zeroavia. (2023). *The future of zero-emission, hydrogen-electric flight* [Online]. Retrieved February 25, 2025, from https://zeroavia.com/wp-content/uploads/2023/07/ZeroAvia_Brochure_DIGITAL-2023-06-2.pdf.

Zhang, Y., et al. (2024). Fuel cell system for aviation applications: Modeling, parameter sensitivity, and control. *Energy Conversion and Management, 312*(1), 1–19.

CHAPTER 10

# Hydrogen for Steel Production

## Introduction

Until quite recently, the environmental footprint of steelmaking had received less public scrutiny than that of sectors such as power generation or transport. Yet the steel industry is among the largest emitters of carbon dioxide globally, responsible for approximately 7–9% of global anthropogenic $CO_2$ emissions (UNECE, 2022). This is so largely due to its reliance on coal as both a fuel and a chemical reductant in primary production processes (Jeswani et al., 2025). Here, primary steelmaking, which is by far the most $CO_2$-intensive part of the steel value chain, entails the conversion of iron, typically in the form of pig iron or direct reduced iron, into crude steel through processes involving oxidation and controlled melting (Weigel et al., 2016). Secondary steelmaking (or ladle metallurgy), in turn, involves refining the molten steel by adjusting its chemical composition via the addition or removal of alloying elements and dissolved gases, optimising properties for specific applications (Cavaliere, 2016; Shamsuddin, 2021). Finally, tertiary steelmaking, or casting, solidifies the refined molten steel into semi-finished products such as slabs, billets, or blooms, which can subsequently be rolled or forged (ibid.).

At the moment, despite a variety of primary and secondary steel production techniques that were used in the past like Bessemer-Thomas or Siemens-Martin processes (Fig. 10.1), global steelmaking is currently generally split between blast furnace-basic oxygen furnace (BF-BOF) and



A. Patonia, R. Poudineh, *Clean Hydrogen for Decarbonisation*,
https://doi.org/10.1007/978-3-032-19442-8_10

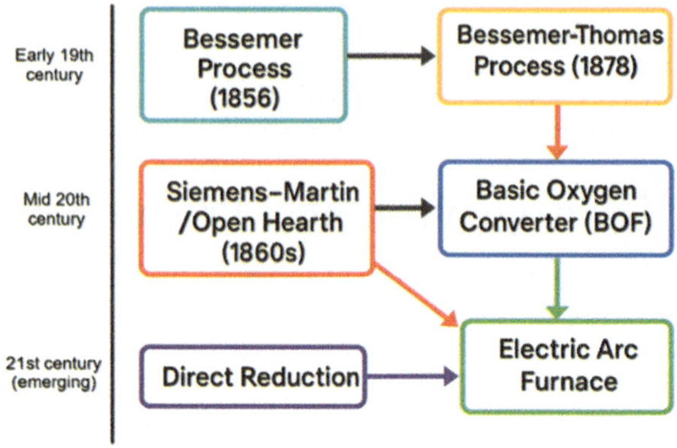


**Fig. 10.1** Evolution of steel production by methods. (Source: Adapted from Birat (1996), Nill (2008), and Fischedick et al. (2014))

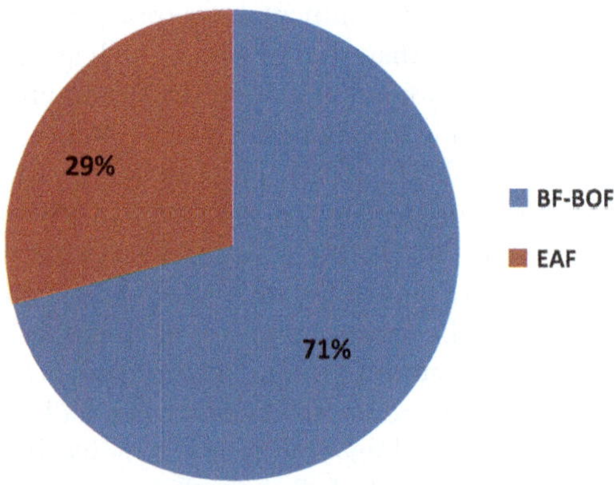


**Fig. 10.2** Current steel production methods by approximate share. (Source: Adapted from Global Energy Monitor (2024))

direct reduction combined with electric arc furnace (EAF) methods (Fig. 10.2). In this connection, since BF-BOF occupies over 70% of the world's steelmaking, it should not be surprising that the sector is considered to be one of the key carbon emitters, as the global average $CO_2$ emissions from conventional BF-BOF steel production are typically between 1.8 and 2.2 tonnes of $CO_2$ per tonne of crude steel (Shahabuddin et al., 2023). This is so because the BF-BOF route depends heavily on metallurgical coal (coke) to reduce iron ore to iron in a high-temperature, carbon-intensive environment (ibid.). That is why the steel industry is increasingly shifting from this backbone of the sector towards EAF as the most progressive method allowing for the most significant reduction of carbon emissions. This would be particularly important in rising economies like China and India, where demand for new steel is constantly growing.

Since the less carbon-intensive alternative pathway—the electric arc furnace (EAF)—uses electricity to melt scrap steel or direct reduced iron (DRI), it depends on the availability of clean electricity and high-quality scrap, both of which vary regionally (Taylor, 2022; Makkiabadi et al., 2024). Therefore, in many regions, especially in emerging economies, steel production remains structurally linked to fossil fuels, with relatively few binding regulatory constraints on carbon emissions compared to other heavy industries. However, this dynamic is beginning to shift as national and regional climate targets become more ambitious and pressure mounts on steel producers to decarbonise their operations.

In addition to the environmental dimension, the economic side of steel production presents its own set of challenges. The sector is energy-intensive and highly sensitive to input costs, which is so particularly for coal, natural gas, and electricity. At the same time, volatile commodity prices and growing investor interest in low-carbon technologies are pushing steelmakers to explore new production pathways that align with future market and policy conditions. In addition, carbon pricing mechanisms, whether in the form of emissions trading systems or border adjustment measures, are increasingly shifting the cost equation against traditional carbon-heavy processes. It is within this context that clean hydrogen produced with minimum or no emissions is emerging as a potential game-changer for the steel industry.

One of the main reasons for this is the fact that hydrogen can be used as a reducing agent to produce DRI, replacing the role traditionally played by carbon in removing oxygen from iron ore. The resulting product—hydrogen-based DRI—can then be fed into electric arc furnaces, allowing for a near-zero carbon steelmaking process when powered by renewable electricity. While several demonstration projects, such as HYBRIT in Sweden and HyIron in Namibia, are already showcasing the feasibility of this approach, major hurdles still remain in terms of cost, scalability, infrastructure, and technological maturity. This chapter explores these challenges in detail, outlines the potential pathways for hydrogen deployment in steelmaking, and assesses the prospects for industrial transformation in the upcoming decades.

This chapter proceeds as follows. Section "Technological Solutions" explores the technological applications of hydrogen in steel production, detailing the hydrogen-based DRI-EAF route and contrasting it with other decarbonisation options. Section "Advantages/Disadvantages" analyses the advantages and disadvantages of these technological pathways and examines the extensive infrastructure requirements for a hydrogen-based steel industry. Section "Economic Aspects" delves into the economic aspects, including production costs and the impact of carbon pricing and subsidies. Section "Policy and Regulatory Landscape" reviews the policy, regulatory, and certification landscape. Section "Case Studies and Pilot Projects" presents case studies of pioneering pilot projects. Finally, Section "Future Outlook and Conclusions" offers a revised future outlook and conclusions on hydrogen's role in the sector's decarbonisation.

## Hydrogen Applications in the Sector

### *Technological Solutions*

In steelmaking, hydrogen is mainly considered for use in the direct reduction of iron (DRI) process, in combination with electric arc furnace (EAF) production. Although hydrogen is not the only decarbonisation option in this context, it can potentially offer significant reduction of emissions and process flexibility. At the heart of hydrogen-based steelmaking is the DRI-EAF route, where hydrogen acts as the reducing agent to remove oxygen from iron ore, producing direct reduced iron (sponge iron). This process replaces fossil carbon (traditionally coke) with pure hydrogen gas:

$$Fe_2\mathrm{O}_3 + 3\mathrm{H}_2 \rightarrow 2Fe + 3\mathrm{H}_2\mathrm{O}$$

As seen, unlike conventional BF-BOF production, this reaction emits only water vapour as a by-product, eliminating $CO_2$ emissions from the reduction stage. The resulting direct reduced iron can then be fed into an EAF, which melts the metallic input using electricity, preferably sourced from low-carbon or renewable grids (Fig. 10.1). The combination of hydrogen-based DRI and renewable-powered EAF represents one of the most promising near-zero emission steelmaking routes currently under consideration.

At the same time, applying hydrogen for steelmaking is not the only pathway that is currently being considered for the decarbonisation of steel. In fact, several other technological pathways are actively being developed in parallel (IEA, 2023; Witecka et al., 2024). For instance, carbon capture and storage (CCS) technologies for retrofitting existing BF-BOF plants aim to capture a substantial proportion of emissions from conventional steelmaking facilities. While this approach could allow for the continued use of established infrastructure and raw material supply chains, at the moment, it faces several challenges primarily related to capture efficiency, long-term $CO_2$ storage capacity, and economic viability (IEEFA, 2024).

Alternative reducing agents such as natural gas (in the DRI process), biogas, or biochar are also being explored. Natural gas-based DRI plants are already commercially operational today. In fact, one of them—the Al Reyadah project in the United Arab Emirates (UEA)—is actively using CCS technology and still remains the world's only operational commercial-scale CCUS plant for steelmaking (ibid.). However, in 2023 it captured only 26.6% of emissions from the gas-based steel plant, which were subsequently used for enhanced oil recovery (ibid.). This highlights a critical point often overlooked in lifecycle assessments: the overall emissions reduction of blue hydrogen (from natural gas with CCS) or NG-DRI with CCS is highly dependent on the $CO_2$ capture rate and the mitigation of methane leakage along the entire natural gas supply chain.

At the same time, although such facilities still emit $CO_2$, they produce less carbon than traditional BF-BOF production. Overall, they are often viewed as transition-ready assets. This is so because it is expected that DRI plants can potentially be converted to hydrogen operation once hydrogen supply and infrastructure become available (Zhang et al., 2023).

The maturity of these technologies varies significantly. As shown in Table 10.1, hydrogen-based DRI and EAF systems are moving from demonstration to early commercialisation, with operational pilot plants already online (HYBRIT) and under construction (Stegra, 2024) in Sweden and planned projects in Germany, Austria, and Canada, among other countries (European Commission, 2022; OMV, 2025). CCS retrofits for BF-BOF plants, in turn, are at a pilot to demonstration stage, with full-scale applications remaining limited due to high costs and infrastructure requirements (IEEFA, 2024; Transition Asia, 2024). Scrap-based EAFs, in contrast, are a fully commercial and widely deployed technology, although their further expansion is constrained by scrap availability and quality considerations, especially in emerging economies (ACCR, 2024).

**Table 10.1** Average maturity level of key low-carbon steelmaking technologies[a]

| *Technology* | *Process type* | *Main energy/reducing agent* | *Typical emissions reduction potential (%)*[b] | *Overall energy efficiency (%)* | *Technology readiness level (TRL)* | *Notes* |
|---|---|---|---|---|---|---|
| *Hydrogen-based DRI + EAF* | Primary | Hydrogen gas | 85–95 | 50–55 | 7–8 | Demonstration plants operational; commercialisation expected by 2030 |
| *Natural gas-based DRI + EAF* | Primary | Natural gas ($CH_4$) | 50–60[c] | 55–65 | 9 | Commercially available; expected to be convertible to hydrogen |
| *CCS on BF-BOF* | Primary | Coke + CCS | 60–80[d] | 40–50 | 6–7 | High capture costs; infrastructure dependent |
| *Scrap-based EAF* | Secondary | Electricity | 80–90 | 70–85 | 9 | Commercially mature; limited by scrap availability |
| *Hydrogen plasma smelting* | Primary | Hydrogen plasma | 95–100 | 30–40 | 4–5 | Laboratory/pilot stage; high technical barriers |

Source: Adapted from Filho et al. (2021), Reclaim Finance (2024), Witecka et al. (2024), and Rumsa et al. (2025)

[a]This highlights a critical point often overlooked in lifecycle assessments: the overall emissions reduction of blue hydrogen (from natural gas with CCS) or NG-DRI with CCS is highly dependent on the $CO_2$ capture rate and the mitigation of methane leakage along the entire natural gas supply chain

[b]Capture rate is highly variable; 90% is often theorised but not yet consistently achieved at scale in steelmaking

[c]Emissions reduction is highly dependent on the carbon intensity of the hydrogen production and electricity source. A full lifecycle assessment (LCA) is necessary for accurate comparison

[d]***Reduction potential decreases significantly if methane leakage from the natural gas supply chain is accounted for***

In addition to hydrogen-based DRI, emerging technologies like hydrogen plasma smelting reduction are being tested at laboratory and pilot scale. This method uses a high-temperature hydrogen plasma to directly reduce iron ore without the need for pellets or sinter, offering near-complete decarbonisation potential (Filho et al., 2021). However, despite its promising nature, it remains at a low TRL (4–5) due to many factors, with challenges in plasma generation, reactor design, and energy consumption being among the core ones (ibid.). Other electrolysis-based routes for direct iron electrowinning are at an even lower TRL (<5), with commercial maturity not expected until well after 2040.

As seen, while the decarbonisation of steel represents a significant challenge, hydrogen can potentially play an important role in maximising its emission reduction. Therefore, hydrogen holds transformative potential in the sector, particularly for primary steel production, which is responsible for the bulk of the industry's carbon emissions. This is so primarily because alternative decarbonisation strategies such as CCS are at a lower TRL while others such as expanded scrap-based EAF production are limited primarily to secondary steelmaking and therefore do not cover the most polluting primary stage of the process. Nevertheless, it is likely that the pace of deployment of steelmaking based on clean hydrogen will depend on many factors, with the availability of low-cost green hydrogen, supportive policy frameworks, and the establishment of infrastructure for hydrogen transport, storage, and use at industrial scale among some of the core ones.

### *Advantages/Disadvantages*

The decarbonisation of steel production through hydrogen-based processes offers both significant advantages and notable limitations when compared to alternative low-carbon steelmaking routes. From an emissions perspective, as seen from Table 10.1, hydrogen-based direct reduced iron combined with electric arc furnace operations is expected to achieve the highest reduction potential among mature and near-mature technologies, typically abating between 85 and 95% of $CO_2$ emissions relative to conventional blast furnace-basic oxygen furnace systems (Yadav et al., 2021; Eurometal, 2025). Therefore, when coupled with renewable-powered EAFs, hydrogen-based DRI can offer a near-zero emission pathway, with only water vapour generated during the reduction process (SEI, 2018).

Performance-wise, hydrogen-based steelmaking has the inherent potential for operational flexibility. However, this flexibility is primarily confined to the hydrogen production stage, as the DRI shaft furnace itself requires a continuous and stable supply of hydrogen and the EAF needs firm power, though limited buffering is possible via hydrogen or hot briquetted iron storage. This means the overall steelmaking process has limited ability to act as a demand-side flexibility resource for the grid compared to more interruptible processes (Reclaim Finance, 2024). In addition, the process's overall energy efficiency is lower than that of natural gas-based DRI, with additional conversion losses in hydrogen production, storage, and delivery (Table 10.1) (Yadav et al., 2021). While natural gas-based DRI systems currently achieve a roughly 50–70% reduction in emissions depending on system boundaries, they offer higher process efficiencies and established commercial viability, with the added advantage of potential conversion to hydrogen once infrastructure matures (Materials Processing Institute, 2021).

When it comes to further promotion and ramp-up of key steel decarbonisation options, hydrogen-based DRI expansion remains constrained primarily by the availability of low-cost clean hydrogen and the capital intensity of new reduction plants and hydrogen supply chains (Table 10.2) (ibid. and Eurometal, 2025). Furthermore, contrary to some claims, $H_2$-DRI is often more sensitive to iron ore quality than blast furnaces; low-grade ores can lead to increased slag formation, clogging, and higher energy use in the EAF, necessitating high-grade DR-grade pellets. By contrast, the deployment of carbon capture and storage (CCS) in BF-BOF plants, which offers another emissions reduction pathway of up to 80%, is hindered by high capture costs, limited transport and storage infrastructure, and public acceptance issues (IEEFA, 2024). Similarly, while scrap-based EAFs are widely commercialised and capable of achieving up to 90% emissions reductions, they are dependent on scrap availability, which is inherently limited in emerging economies with growing demand for primary steel (ACCR, 2024). Finally, although, as mentioned, emerging technologies such as hydrogen plasma smelting present theoretical decarbonisation rates approaching 100%, they remain at low technology readiness levels, facing substantial barriers primarily in terms of reactor design, energy consumption, and technical scalability, and therefore are not ready for full commercialisation and broader use at the moment (Table 10.2) (Filho et al., 2021).

**Table 10.2** Overall energy efficiency, deployment potential, and challenges of emerging low-carbon steelmaking technologies

| *Technology* | *Deployment status* | *Key deployment barriers* | *Expected commercialisation timeline* |
|---|---|---|---|
| *Hydrogen-based DRI + EAF* | Demonstration plants running | Hydrogen infrastructure, scale-up risks | By 2030 |
| *Natural gas-based DRI + EAF* | Widely commercialised | Long-term dependency on fossil fuels, retrofitting for $H_2$ | N/a-already operational |
| *CCS on BF-BOF* | Pilot and demonstration projects | High capture costs, $CO_2$ transport/storage infrastructure | Post-2030 depending on CCS rollout |
| *Scrap-based EAF* | Fully commercialised | Scrap availability, grid decarbonisation pace | N/a-already operational |
| *Hydrogen plasma smelting* | Laboratory/early pilot | Very high energy intensity, technical immaturity | Expected after 2040 |

Source: Adapted from Filho et al. (2021), Reclaim Finance (2024), Witecka et al. (2024), and Rumsa et al. (2025)

In this connection, while it looks like hydrogen-based steelmaking holds the greatest long-term potential for decarbonising primary steel production, its future will be shaped by economic competitiveness, technology maturation, infrastructure development, and supportive policy environments. Therefore, in the interim, hybrid strategies combining scrap-EAFs, natural gas-based DRI, and selective CCS deployment are likely to form the transitional landscape of low-carbon steel.

### *Infrastructure Requirements*

As in numerous other industries, the decarbonisation of primary steel production via low-carbon technologies relies heavily on the development of new, industry-specific infrastructure. Traditional steelmaking via the blast furnace-basic oxygen furnace route relies on mature logistical systems for handling, storing, and transporting raw materials such as coal, coke, and iron ore. Given the long history of conventional steelmaking, most of these systems and networks have long been existing and functioning. In contrast, emerging technologies like hydrogen-based direct reduced iron, hydrogen plasma smelting, and CCS-equipped processes require either completely new or heavily modified infrastructure systems, many of which are currently represented only at demonstration or pilot scale (OECD, 2025).

In particular, for hydrogen-based DRI and hydrogen plasma smelting, infrastructure requirements include hydrogen storage facilities (most likely high-pressure or cryogenic tanks and/or underground geological formations), dedicated pipeline networks, and distribution systems tailored to hydrogen's physical properties (Table 10.3). Here, hydrogen's high diffusivity, low volumetric energy density, and potential to cause metal embrittlement will pose operational risks that existing natural gas networks are not designed to manage (Jia et al., 2023). While repurposing natural gas pipelines for hydrogen transport is possible, this option is limited by material compatibility, pressure constraints, and safety regulations (ibid. and Télessy et al., 2024). In this respect, most steelmaking sites would require new tailor-made hydrogen pipelines and storage systems, which will, in turn, increase capital costs and construction timelines (Rechberger et al., 2020).

By contrast, natural gas-based DRI facilities, already operational, offer higher adaptability (Table 10.3). Existing natural gas infrastructure can in many cases be partially or fully converted to accommodate hydrogen with safety upgrades and material adjustments (Lipiäinen et al., 2023). That is why this adaptability positions natural gas-based DRI as a transitional option, enabling a phased shift to hydrogen as supply and infrastructure expand (Rechberger et al., 2020; OECD, 2025).

Scrap-based electric arc furnaces, the most commercially mature low-carbon steelmaking technology, require minimal dedicated infrastructure modifications compared to hydrogen-based processes. In their case, the primary need is a reliable low-carbon electricity supply, necessitating grid reinforcements, renewable energy integration, and expanded local distribution networks, particularly in regions with multiple EAF installations (Graupner et al., 2023). Therefore, their scalability is constrained not by infrastructure but by limited high-quality scrap availability, especially in areas where steel demand outpaces scrap generation (OECD, 2025). However, since they are designed for secondary steelmaking, in order to contribute to the decarbonisation of the entire steelmaking process, they should be supplemented with a sustainable primary steelmaking component either in the form of scrap or sustainably manufactured DRI.

CCS-equipped BF-BOF systems, in turn, need $CO_2$ capture units, pipeline networks, and access to storage sites like depleted hydrocarbon fields

**Table 10.3** Infrastructure requirements, scalability, and adaptability of low-carbon steelmaking technologies

| *Technology* | *Specific infrastructure requirements* | *Current scalability* | *Current adaptability* | *Key challenges* |
|---|---|---|---|---|
| *Hydrogen-based DRI + EAF* | • High-pressure or cryogenic hydrogen storage<br>• Dedicated pipelines<br>• Gigawatt-scale renewable electricity & grid connections | Low | Limited | • Expensive hydrogen infrastructure<br>• Embrittlement issues<br>• Low hydrogen availability |
| *Natural gas-based DRI + EAF* | • Existing natural gas pipelines and storage<br>• Convertible to hydrogen | High | High | • Hydrogen retrofit costs<br>• Long-term methane dependency if not converted |
| *CCS on BF-BOF* | • $CO_2$ capture units<br>• Transport pipelines<br>• Access to $CO_2$ storage facilities | Moderate | Low | • High capture costs<br>• Infrastructure highly location-dependent |
| *Scrap-based EAF* | • Reinforced electricity grid<br>• Renewable integration | High | High | • Scrap availability<br>• Grid capacity and renewable sourcing |
| *Hydrogen plasma smelting* | • High-purity hydrogen supply<br>• Plasma generators<br>• Advanced storage systems | Very low | Very low | • Technical immaturity<br>• High capital costs<br>• Significant energy losses |

Source: Adapted from Rechberger et al. (2020), Graupner et al. (2023), Jia et al. (2023), Lipiäinen et al. (2023), Perpiñán et al. (2023), and Télessy et al. (2024)

or saline aquifers where carbon dioxide could be stored (Perpiñán et al., 2023). In this respect, the overall feasibility of such projects depends on proximity to storage infrastructure and the economic viability of high-volume $CO_2$ transport, making scalability highly location-dependent (ibid. and IEEFA, 2024). Given that the geological distribution of suitable carbon dioxide storage formations is uneven, it is likely that both their adaptability and scalability will be limited.

Overall, as seen, infrastructure scalability and adaptability vary by technology. Natural gas-based DRI and scrap-EAF routes benefit from higher immediate adaptability, while hydrogen-based technologies and CCS solutions necessitate extensive new infrastructure networks.

## Economic Aspects

The integration of hydrogen as a primary energy and reductant source in the steel sector involves substantial economic considerations, including capital expenditures (CapEx), operational expenditures (OpEx), and external cost factors like carbon pricing and subsidies. Overall, in the steelmaking sector, CapEx generally includes the expenditures required to build or retrofit production facilities capable of operating with hydrogen, while OpEx encompasses the recurring costs of fuel, maintenance, and operational management. Providing a thorough analysis, this section evaluates hydrogen adoption costs in steelmaking, compares them with conventional technologies, and considers the impact of economic incentives and regulations on the sector's financial outlook.

It is not surprising that the transition to hydrogen-based steelmaking requires significant capital investments. In this context, one of the most capital-intensive processes is the construction of DRI plants using hydrogen as a reductant. The CapEx for a hydrogen-based DRI plant is estimated to be around USD 300–600 per tonne of annual production capacity, which is roughly 30–50% higher than that of traditional coal-based blast furnaces, although some studies suggest that actual capital requirements may be even higher depending on project specifics and regional factors (Hüttel & Lehner, 2024). This increased cost stems primarily from the need to develop entirely new infrastructure, including hydrogen storage and distribution systems, as well as safety systems to manage hydrogen's unique properties, such as high flammability and embrittlement risks (ibid.).

Operational expenditures for hydrogen-based steel production are, in turn, heavily influenced by hydrogen fuel costs, which currently remain significantly higher than those of conventional fuels like coal and natural gas. As of 2024, green hydrogen prices typically range from approximately USD 4.8 per kilogram in the United States to over USD 7.2 per kilogram in the Netherlands, compared to about USD 0.12 per kilogram for coal

(IMARC Group, 2024). Since hydrogen accounts for over 70% of OpEx in hydrogen-based steel production, fuel costs are the primary economic barrier to adoption (Kim & Heo, 2024). Maintenance costs are also expected to rise initially, given the need for specialised equipment and handling protocols for hydrogen, although these are projected to decrease with technological maturation and industry learning effects (Hüttel & Lehner, 2024).

At the same time, when comparing hydrogen-based steelmaking to current production methods, it is essential to consider both direct economic costs and environmental externalities. At the moment, conventional steel production through blast furnaces remains economically advantageous primarily due to lower fuel costs and established infrastructure. In particular, the levelised cost of steel (LCoS) for traditional BF-BOF routes is estimated at USD 450–600 per tonne, while hydrogen-based DRI-EAF routes currently range between USD 600 and 1200 per tonne, depending on hydrogen prices and regional factors (Kim & Heo, 2024).

On the other hand, hydrogen steelmaking provides significant environmental benefits by eliminating $CO_2$ emissions from the reduction process. Specifically, BF-BOF production emits approximately 1.8–2.2 tonnes of $CO_2$ per tonne of steel, while hydrogen-based DRI can achieve near-zero direct emissions if powered by renewable electricity (Hüttel & Lehner, 2024). Therefore, factoring in carbon pricing or emissions trading schemes alters the cost competitiveness between these technologies. With the global rise of carbon prices, the relative cost advantage of conventional steelmaking will diminish (Hasanbeigi, 2024). Therefore, although, as illustrated by Fig. 10.3, BF-BOF remains the least costly option today, the gap is expected to narrow as hydrogen production scales up and carbon pricing intensifies.

At the same time, since this gap is yet to be bridged, the economic feasibility of hydrogen-based steelmaking is currently intrinsically linked to policy support mechanisms such as subsidies, tax incentives, and carbon pricing frameworks. Therefore, in the absence of government interventions, the current cost disparity between hydrogen-based and conventional steel production would likely prevent large-scale adoption (Hüttel & Lehner, 2024). Subsidies and financial incentives can significantly lower both CapEx and OpEx. For instance, the European Union's Important Projects of Common European Interest (IPCEI) on hydrogen provides direct financial support to large-scale industrial projects (ibid.). Germany's national hydrogen strategy earmarks EUR 9 billion for hydrogen

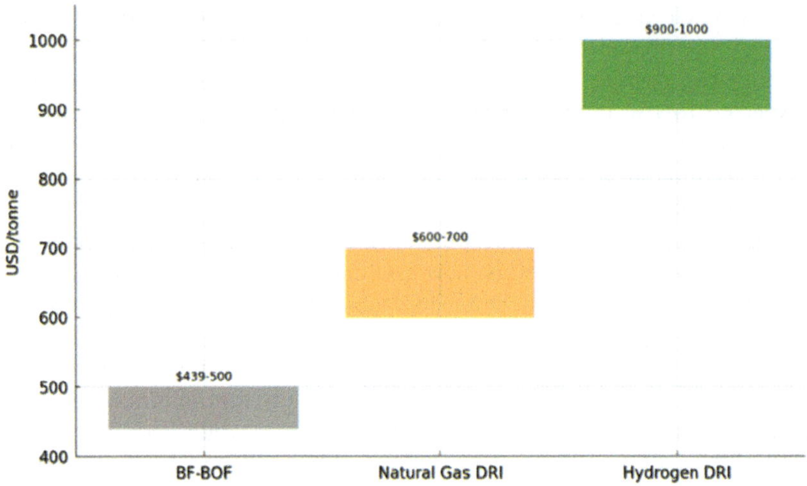


**Fig. 10.3** Estimated levelised cost of steel production (USD/Tonne). (Source: Adapted from Vogl, Åhman, & Nilsson (2018), IEA (2020), Argonne National Laboratory (2021), Li et al. (2021), Cavaliere et al. (2024), and Reznicek et al. (2025))

development, with substantial allocations for industrial decarbonisation projects, including steelmaking (German Government, 2020; BMWK, 2023).

Carbon pricing mechanisms also play a pivotal role in influencing the economic attractiveness of hydrogen solutions. Under the EU Emissions Trading System (ETS), the carbon price reached over EUR 90 per tonne in 2023, substantially increasing the operational costs of carbon-intensive BF-BOF routes (IEEFA, 2024). At such price levels, the additional costs of hydrogen-based steel production begin to be offset by the avoided expenses associated with carbon allowances. Moreover, carbon border adjustment mechanisms (CBAM), like those proposed by the European Union, aim to prevent carbon leakage by imposing levies on imported steel from regions with lower carbon costs, further enhancing the competitive position of hydrogen steelmaking in regulated markets (European Parliament, 2022 cited in Hüttel & Lehner, 2024). Beyond subsidies and carbon pricing, governments are introducing market incentives, such as green steel certification schemes, which can enable producers to command premium prices for low-emission steel. At the moment, a growing number of customers in sectors like automotive and construction are willing to pay a green premium of 10–20% for certified green steel, potentially improving revenue streams for hydrogen-based producers (Hasanbeigi, 2024).

Therefore, although the upfront costs of hydrogen adoption in steelmaking currently remain high, a combination of financial incentives, rising carbon prices, and market-driven demand for green steel is expected to enhance its economic viability (Material Economics, 2019; Hüttel and Lehner, 2024). That is why, in order to ensure hydrogen's competitiveness, policymakers must maintain robust support frameworks, which will enable and stimulate the sector's long-term decarbonisation.

## Policy and Regulatory Landscape

In recent years, policymakers and regulators across Europe, Asia, and North America have increasingly recognised the strategic importance of decarbonising the steel sector, given its contribution to roughly 7–9% of global $CO_2$ emissions (UNECE, 2022). As a result, several countries have introduced policies and frameworks aimed at incentivising low-carbon steel production pathways, with hydrogen-based technologies playing a central role in long-term decarbonisation strategies. Most notably, within the European Union, the European Green Deal and its accompanying Fit for 55 package have established ambitious climate neutrality targets by 2050 and the EU Hydrogen Strategy, adopted in 2020, has explicitly identified hard-to-abate sectors, including steel, as key priority areas for renewable hydrogen deployment (European Commission, 2023). In addition, funding mechanisms such as the Innovation Fund and the Important Projects of Common European Interest (IPCEI) on hydrogen aim to support demonstration projects and infrastructure build-out, including hydrogen-based DRI plants and associated supply chains (ibid.).

When it comes to specific countries, Germany, one of Europe's largest steel producers, has advanced this agenda further through its National Hydrogen Strategy, offering financial support for hydrogen clusters and infrastructure. In particular, the German government has committed over EUR 9 billion for hydrogen development, with EUR 1.5 billion specifically allocated to industrial decarbonisation, which includes steelmaking as one of the most important sectors (Eversheds Sutherland, 2020; BMWK, 2023). Similarly, Sweden's HYBRIT initiative, backed by both public funds and private capital, exemplifies an integrated policy approach combining R&D grants, tax incentives, and regulatory adjustments for infrastructure planning (Vogl, Åhman, & Nilsson, 2018; HYBRIT, 2024). In Asia, Japan's Green Growth Strategy and South Korea's Hydrogen Economy Roadmap include specific provisions for hydrogen-based steelmaking pilot projects (CSIRO, 2020; Government of Japan, 2024). Meanwhile, in the United States, the Inflation Reduction Act (IRA) of 2022 introduced generous tax credits for clean hydrogen production and investments in industrial decarbonisation hubs, including the steel sector (US Department of Energy, 2022).

These policy frameworks are increasingly supported by emerging standards and certification schemes specifically relevant to hydrogen use in steelmaking. In particular, CertifHy in Europe provides a robust framework for certifying renewable and low-carbon hydrogen, which is critical for its use in steelmaking to ensure hydrogen's sustainability credentials. CertifHy operates under the EU Renewable Energy Directive (RED II) and issues Guarantees of Origin (GOs) and Supply Certificates, facilitating traceability and compliance with regulatory targets for renewable hydrogen consumption in industrial sectors, including steel (CertifHy, 2023; IEA, 2023). The scheme's governance involves certification bodies accredited to ISO standards, ensuring rigorous auditing of hydrogen production pathways and greenhouse gas emissions (Hydrogen Council, 2023).

However, a critical and evolving debate in certification revolves around the granularity of electricity sourcing for green hydrogen. To ensure true additionality and avoid indirect emissions, there is a growing consensus that hydrogen production must be matched with new, time-correlated renewable generation. Schemes are now moving beyond annual matching of electricity consumption with renewable GOs towards more stringent hourly or monthly temporal matching requirements. This ensures electrolysers do not draw from carbon-intensive grid power during periods of low renewable availability, which would undermine the carbon savings of the resulting 'green' steel. Furthermore, robust certification must define clear lifecycle boundaries, accounting for all emissions from electricity generation, water treatment, electrolyser construction, and any hydrogen storage and transport. For blue hydrogen (from natural gas with CCS), certification must rigorously account for methane leakage rates across the gas supply chain and the actual $CO_2$ capture rate at the production facility, as these factors drastically impact the overall lifecycle emissions.

At the global level, the International Partnership for Hydrogen and Fuel Cells in the Economy (IPHE) coordinates efforts to harmonise hydrogen certification standards, promoting mutual recognition and facilitating international trade of certified hydrogen. These initiatives support the steel sector's transition by providing credible assurance mechanisms that hydrogen used in steelmaking meets low-carbon or renewable criteria, thus enabling the development of green steel markets (ibid. and IPHE, 2024). Together, these certification frameworks and pilot projects illustrate how policy, technology, and standards converge to enable hydrogen's role in decarbonising steel production, supporting the emergence of green steel with defined emission intensity thresholds and ratings to quantify greenness.

At the same time, despite policy momentum, significant barriers impede the widespread adoption of hydrogen-based steelmaking technologies. On the technical side, apart from hydrogen's low volumetric energy density and storage complexities, key challenges include the nascent maturity of hydrogen plasma smelting and high-purity hydrogen DRI processes. As mentioned, while conventional electric arc furnaces (EAFs) operating on scrap are well-established, primary steelmaking using hydrogen DRI combined with EAFs remains at demonstration or early commercialisation stages. As seen from Fig. 10.3, this early commercialisation results in significantly higher costs of alternative sustainable steelmaking, which still wards off most of the common consumers.

From a regulatory perspective, uncertainties regarding future carbon pricing trajectories and the scope of subsidies or tax credits hinder investment decisions. While the EU Emissions Trading System (ETS) provides a price signal for carbon-intensive processes, fluctuating allowance prices and the phased introduction of the Carbon Border Adjustment Mechanism (CBAM) create an unpredictable regulatory environment for steelmakers contemplating large-scale hydrogen investments (European Commission, 2023). Infrastructure permitting processes for hydrogen production, pipelines, and storage facilities also present regulatory bottlenecks. Lengthy approval procedures, coupled with overlapping jurisdictional competences, often delay project implementation. In some cases, the lack of clear definitions for hydrogen infrastructure within existing energy and industrial regulations further complicates matters (Witecka et al., 2024).

Hydrogen use in many applications including industrial processes such as steelmaking introduces safety concerns that must be carefully managed. Hydrogen's high flammability poses requirements for pressurised or cryogenic storage since it creates significant risks of leaks or explosions if it is not handled properly. Although, in principle, industrial users are accustomed to working with gases like oxygen and natural gas, hydrogen's specific physical and chemical properties necessitate stringent safety protocols and workforce retraining (Calabrese et al., 2024). In this respect, regulatory frameworks for industrial hydrogen safety are still under development in many countries, despite the fact that ISO standards and national guidelines are beginning to converge (IEA, 2023).

Another key obstacle for the steel sector is supply chain limitations. In particular, scaling hydrogen steelmaking to meet global demand would necessitate enormous volumes of clean hydrogen, far exceeding current production levels. The IEA (2023) projects that full decarbonisation using hydrogen would require over 50 Mt of green hydrogen annually by 2050. This is roughly equivalent to the world's entire clean hydrogen production target for all sectors combined by 2030 (ibid.).

Additionally, specifically for green hydrogen, the availability of critical raw materials, such as electrolyser metals (nickel, platinum, iridium) and zero-carbon electricity, presents important supply chain vulnerability. Without coordinated infrastructure development, which includes dedicated hydrogen pipelines, storage terminals, and port facilities, steel producers are likely to face localised hydrogen shortages or logistical bottlenecks (Witecka et al., 2024).

Finally, just like in other sectors where hydrogen is supposed to be applied, public acceptance is also likely to play a pivotal role, especially when it comes to the creation of $H_2$ infrastructure that would be necessary. While decarbonising steel production enjoys broad public support in principle, local opposition to hydrogen infrastructure projects (including pipelines and storage facilities) is likely to emerge driven by safety concerns and land use conflicts, among others (ibid.). Therefore, transparent risk communication, participatory planning processes, and early stakeholder engagement will be crucial to securing social licence for large-scale hydrogen steel projects. At the same time, public awareness regarding the environmental footprint of steel and the benefits of hydrogen-based alternatives remains limited. That is why consumer-facing labelling initiatives and public procurement standards for low-carbon steel products could help address this gap and create market demand for hydrogen-based steel (IPHE, 2024).

## Case Studies and Pilot Projects

Hydrogen adoption in the steel industry is no longer an entirely theoretical exercise solely confined to academic modelling and laboratory trials. In fact, in recent years, several pilot and commercial-scale projects have been launched across Europe to test hydrogen-based technologies under real operational conditions. Although these initiatives are not extremely numerous, they are critical for understanding the economic, technical, and logistical challenges of integrating hydrogen into an industry traditionally dominated by coal and natural gas.

Among the most high-profile examples is the Swedish venture Stegra (previously known as H2 Green Steel and rebranded in 2024), which plans to build one of the world's first large-scale, hydrogen-based direct reduction iron plants integrated with electric arc furnaces (Stegra, 2025). Announced in 2020, the project aims to produce up to 5 million tonnes of green steel annually by 2030 at their plant in Boden using renewable hydrogen generated through electrolysis powered by local hydropower and wind energy (ibid. and OECD, 2023). Although the production process has not been launched yet, the construction of the facility has begun, with the first deliveries expected by 2026. To date, the initiative has attracted significant investor interest, raising over EUR 6.5 billion in combined equity, debt, and state-backed guarantees (ESG News, 2024).

The primary advantage of Stegra's model lies in its fully integrated green hydrogen supply chain. By securing renewable electricity generation assets alongside electrolyser capacity and steel production infrastructure, the company seeks to mitigate the supply risks and high costs associated with green hydrogen procurement on the open market (OECD, 2023). Moreover, by locating its plant in northern Sweden, the company benefits from one of Europe's lowest-cost renewable electricity markets, further improving its cost-competitiveness relative to regions with higher power prices (ibid.).

However, despite these advantages, challenges remain. The capital expenditure for the project is exceptionally high, reportedly around EUR 6 billion, much of which is tied to the construction of new electrolysers, DRI modules, and EAF units (ESG News, 2024). Even with relatively cheap electricity, green hydrogen production costs are projected to remain at least twice those of natural gas-based alternatives until the early 2030s (IEA, 2020; OECD, 2023). Additionally, while Boden is situated near high-quality iron ore deposits, infrastructure and supply limitations have prevented the use of locally sourced ore, forcing the project to rely on imported pellets from international suppliers such as Rio Tinto and Vale (GMK Center, 2023). This further raises concerns over the scalability and replicability of similar projects in less favourable locations.

Another noteworthy initiative, which is located outside Europe, is the HyIron project in Namibia, that aims to combine Africa's rich renewable energy resources with green hydrogen-based steelmaking. Spearheaded by a German-Namibian consortium, the project plans to produce direct reduced iron using hydrogen generated from on-site solar and wind power installations (HyIron, 2024a; Global Hydrogen Review, 2025). The facility is being developed in phases, with the first stage targeting an annual production of 15,000 tonnes of DRI by early 2025–2026, primarily for export to European steelmakers seeking low-carbon feedstock (HyIron, 2024b; Mining & Energy, 2025). At the moment, future expansion envisions scaling up production capacity to several hundred thousand tonnes annually, contingent on market demand and infrastructure development (The Brief, 2024).

HyIron's strategic advantage lies in Namibia's excellent solar and wind potential, which allows for some of the world's lowest projected renewable electricity costs—a critical factor in reducing the price gap between green hydrogen and fossil-based alternatives (HyIron, 2024b). Moreover, the project highlights the potential for cross-border industrial partnerships in the decarbonisation of hard-to-abate sectors, while simultaneously offering economic development opportunities for resource-rich emerging economies (Climate Fund Managers, 2024). Nonetheless, the initiative faces challenges related to water availability for electrolysis, infrastructure development for DRI export, and the financial viability of long-distance hydrogen or DRI transport, particularly in a still-nascent global green steel market (IDOS, 2024).

These early experiences illustrate both the opportunities and limitations of hydrogen steelmaking. The primary advantage of hydrogen-based DRI lies in its potential to virtually eliminate most direct $CO_2$ emissions from the iron reduction process when coupled with renewable electricity. Unlike carbon capture, utilisation, and storage retrofits, which typically reduce emissions by 60–80% depending on capture rates and system integration, hydrogen DRI paired with EAFs offers a pathway to near-zero emissions (OECD, 2023). Nevertheless, as mentioned, hydrogen DRI processes are more sensitive to iron ore quality than conventional blast furnaces; the use of lower-grade ores can lead to higher slag formation, increased energy consumption, and operational challenges unless suitable pretreatment or beneficiation steps are applied (ibid.).

Several disadvantages temper these benefits. It should be of no surprise that chief among them is the high cost of green hydrogen, which remains several times more expensive than natural gas on an energy-equivalent basis (IEA, 2020; OECD, 2023). Furthermore, the requirement for vast quantities of renewable electricity to produce green hydrogen presents a logistical and infrastructural challenge (ibid.). For instance, producing 1 tonne of DRI using hydrogen is estimated to require around 50–60 kg of hydrogen, which in turn necessitates approximately 2.5–3 MWh of renewable electricity per tonne of steel manufactured (Vogl, Åhman, & Nilsson, 2018). At the scale of a typical commercial plant, this would entail gigawatt-scale renewable generation and electrolyser capacity, which may not be feasible or cost-competitive in all regions (OECD, 2023).

Comparatively, CCUS-equipped blast furnaces or natural gas-based DRI processes are expected to offer more immediate and lower-cost pathways for reducing emissions in the steel sector. As mentioned, gas-based DRI paired with electric arc furnaces (EAF) is already commercially proven in countries like the United States and the Middle East, where natural gas is abundant and relatively inexpensive (IEA, 2020; IEEFA, 2024). These processes are estimated to be able to reduce emissions by up to 50–60% relative to conventional blast furnace routes without requiring a complete overhaul of existing infrastructure (ibid.). Similarly, CCUS retrofits are expected to achieve significant emission reductions at lower upfront costs compared to building entirely new hydrogen-based DRI plants (IEA, 2023; Global CCS Institute, 2024). As of early 2025, six commercial-scale CCUS projects for iron and steelmaking are in development globally, doubling the number reported in 2023, although limited public disclosure casts doubt on their precise timelines and operational viability (IEEFA, 2024).

In any case, lessons from early hydrogen pilot projects suggest that while hydrogen-based steelmaking holds promise as a long-term decarbonisation strategy, its immediate deployment is constrained by cost, infrastructure, and regional energy availability. Projects like those of Stegra have demonstrated the technical feasibility of hydrogen-based steelmaking, and their success in attracting financing highlights growing investor confidence in the sector's green transformation (ESG News, 2024). Nonetheless, the high CapEx and OpEx, coupled with uncertainties over future hydrogen prices and carbon pricing policies, continue to act as significant barriers to replication elsewhere.

Moreover, these experiences underscore the importance of policy and market support in enabling hydrogen projects to compete with incumbent technologies. Without adequate subsidies, carbon pricing, or green premiums paid by consumers, hydrogen steel projects are unlikely to achieve financial viability in the short term. While CCUS and gas-based DRI seem to offer more cost-effective decarbonisation pathways for the current decade, their limited potential for achieving near-zero emissions means they are best viewed as transitional technologies rather than end-state solutions.

Ultimately, the case studies mentioned above reveal a complex landscape where no single decarbonisation strategy is universally optimal. Hydrogen steelmaking presents unmatched emissions reduction potential but is hindered by high costs and infrastructure demands. In contrast, CCUS and gas-based DRI potentially provide more affordable and technically mature alternatives but fall short of delivering full decarbonisation. Future progress will therefore likely depend on a diversified strategy that leverages regional resource advantages, targeted public policy interventions, and continued technological innovation.

## Future Outlook and Conclusions

The steel sector finds itself at a decisive stage in its journey towards reducing carbon emissions. As one of the largest industrial emitters of $CO_2$, the sector must undergo a fundamental transformation to align with global climate goals. This chapter examines the evolving role of hydrogen in steel decarbonisation, reviewing current technological developments, cost and infrastructure challenges, and policy mechanisms that enable deployment. It synthesises recent industrial and scientific evidence to assess when and under what conditions hydrogen-based routes could become competitive and highlights the complementary roles of transitional options such as natural gas-based DRI and CCUS. In doing so, the chapter situates hydrogen within a broader portfolio of decarbonisation strategies for the global steel sector.

Hydrogen remains a key enabler for deep decarbonisation, particularly in primary steelmaking where conventional blast furnace-basic oxygen furnace routes depend heavily on coal (SteelWatch, 2025). While alternative pathways such as carbon capture and storage (CCS) and natural gas-based direct reduced iron (DRI) offer lower-cost, near-term mitigation, hydrogen-based steelmaking holds the greatest long-term potential for achieving near-zero emissions.

Nevertheless, in the short term, hydrogen's contribution to global steel production will remain limited to pilot and early demonstration projects. Initiatives such as HYBRIT in Sweden and HyIron in Namibia demonstrate the technical feasibility of hydrogen-based DRI paired with electric arc furnaces (EAFs). However, high costs—with green hydrogen still priced several times above natural gas—combined with limited renewable electricity, electrolyser capacity, and hydrogen storage infrastructure, restrict deployment. These projects remain viable only under strong policy support, including instruments such as the EU Innovation Fund, the US Inflation Reduction Act (IRA), and national carbon pricing mechanisms.

In these circumstances, during the 2020s and early 2030s, hybrid approaches are expected to dominate. Natural gas-based DRI, when combined with CCS, offers a transitional pathway by leveraging existing gas infrastructure and partially reducing emissions. Scrap-based EAFs will therefore continue expanding, particularly in developed regions with abundant scrap, though limitations in scrap availability in emerging economies will prevent this route from meeting total demand. Combined, these interim solutions offer substantial short-term emissions reductions and help establish the foundation for later integration of hydrogen.

Looking ahead, hydrogen-based steelmaking is projected to scale progressively from the late 2030s onward, contingent upon major declines in hydrogen and renewable electricity costs. Widespread commercialisation is only likely to be feasible after 2040, once (and if) hydrogen production costs approach parity with natural gas under robust carbon pricing. Even then, deployment will likely concentrate in regions with abundant, low-cost renewable energy such as Scandinavia, Australia, and parts of the Middle East and North Africa. In other regions, incremental retrofits of existing gas-based DRI facilities for hydrogen use are expected.

Technological innovations such as hydrogen plasma smelting reduction could further reduce process emissions, but remain at low technology readiness levels (TRL 4–5) and are unlikely to contribute meaningfully before mid-century. Similarly, assumptions that hydrogen steelmaking can easily and flexibly respond to electricity market fluctuations are overstated; the process requires stable, continuous electricity supply, reinforcing the need for firm renewable power rather than variable surplus generation. Indeed, hydrogen-based steelmaking has the potential for operational flexibility, but this flexibility is concentrated in the hydrogen production stage rather than the entire steelmaking process.

In this context, achieving global decarbonisation through hydrogen-based steelmaking will demand an unprecedented scale-up of renewable capacity as well as expansion of hydrogen transport and storage infrastructure. Supply chain constraints for electrolyser materials (e.g., nickel, iridium) and the need for DR-grade iron ore will remain critical challenges. International coordination, technology transfer, and green finance will be essential to avoid widening disparities between industrialised and developing economies.

In conclusion, hydrogen is not a silver bullet, but it is a cornerstone of the steel sector's long-term decarbonisation. The transition will be gradual and regionally differentiated: BF-BOF production will steadily decline, natural gas-based DRI with CCS will serve as a bridge technology, and hydrogen-based routes are expected to gain significant traction after 2040. Realising this vision will require sustained policy support—through carbon pricing, R&D investment, and infrastructure funding—alongside robust certification schemes (e.g., CertifHy) that enforce strict lifecycle boundaries and temporal matching of renewable electricity and market mechanisms that reward low-emission steel. Ultimately, a pragmatic, diversified strategy combining hydrogen, CCS, and circular scrap-based approaches offers the most credible path towards near-zero emission steelmaking by mid-century.

## References

ACCR. (2024). *Forging pathways: Insights for the green steel transformation* [Online]. Retrieved May 10, 2025, from https://www.accr.org.au/downloads/ACCR_ForgingPathways_GreenSteel_March2024_1.pdf.

Argonne National Laboratory. (2021). *Technoeconomic and life cycle analysis of synthetic fuels and steelmaking* [Online]. Retrieved May 14, 2025, from https://www.hydrogen.energy.gov/docs/hydrogenprogramlibraries/pdfs/review21/sa174_elgowainy_2021_o-pdf.pdf?Status=Master.

Birat, J. P. (1996). Evolution of steel. *Steel Times, 224*(4), 136–138.

BMWK. (2023). *National hydrogen strategy update*. The Federal Government.

Calabrese, M., et al. (2024). Hydrogen safety challenges: A comprehensive review on production, storage, transport, utilization, and CFD-based consequence and risk assessment. *Energies, 17*(6), 1–26.

Cavaliere, P. (2016). *Ironmaking and steelmaking processes*. Springer.

Cavaliere, P., Dijon, L., Laska, A., & Koszelow, D. (2024). Hydrogen direct reduction and reoxidation behaviour of high-grade pellets. *International Journal of Hydrogen Energy, 49*(1), 1235–1254.

CertifHy. (2023). *EU RFNBO Scheme documents* [Online]. Retrieved May 15, 2025, from https://www.certifhy.eu/eu-rfnbo-scheme-documents/.

Climate Fund Managers. (2024). *Nam-H2 fund managers and HyIron sign development funding agreement for Africa's first-ever green iron plant in Namibia* [Online]. Retrieved May 18, 2025, from https://climatefundmanagers.com/2024/10/25/nam-h2-fund-managers-and-hyiron-sign-development-funding-agreement-for-africas-first-ever-green-iron-plant-in-namibia/.

CSIRO. (2020). *Republic of Korea (South Korea)* [Online]. Retrieved May 15, 2025, from https://research.csiro.au/hyresource/policy/international/republic-of-korea-south-korea/.

ESG News. (2024). *H2 Green Steel raises EUR 4 billion in debt financing for the world's first large-scale green steel plant* [Online]. Retrieved May 17, 2025, from https://esgnews.com/ru/h2-green-steel-raises-e4-billion-in-debt-financing-for-the-worlds-first-large-scale-green-steel-plant/.

Eurometal. (2025). *Hydrogen should be prioritised for steel production: OECD* [Online]. Retrieved May 10, 2025, from https://eurometal.net/hydrogen-should-be-prioritised-for-steel-production-oecd/.

European Commission. (2022). *HYBRIT Demonstration: Swedish large-scale steel value chain demonstration of Hydrogen Breakthrough Iron-making Technology* [Online]. Retrieved May 07, 2025, from https://climate.ec.europa.eu/system/files/2022-07/if_pf_2022_hybrit_en.pdf.

European Commission. (2023). *Hydrogen* [Online]. Retrieved May 15, 2025, from https://energy.ec.europa.eu/topics/eus-energy-system/hydrogen_en.

Eversheds Sutherland. (2020). *German Government's action plan sets the path towards green steel through the use of hydrogen* [Online]. Retrieved May 15, 2025, from https://www.eversheds-sutherland.com/en/germany/insights/german-governments-action-plan-sets-the-path-towards-green-steel-through-the-use-of-hydrogen.

Filho, I. R. S., et al. (2021). Sustainable steel through hydrogen plasma reduction of iron ore: Process, kinetics, microstructure, chemistry. *Acta Materialia, 213*(1), 1–16.

Fischedick, M., Marzinkowski, J., Winzer, P., & Weigel, M. (2014). Techno-economic evaluation of innovative steel production technologies. *Journal of Cleaner Production, 84*(1), 563–580.

German Government. (2020). *German government adopts hydrogen strategy* [Online]. Retrieved May 14, 2025, from https://www.bundesregierung.de/breg-en/service/archive/wasserstoffstrategie-kabinett-1758982.

Global CCS Institute. (2024). *Global status of CCS 2024* [Online]. Retrieved May 18, 2025, from https://www.globalccsinstitute.com/resources/global-status-report/.

Global Energy Monitor. (2024). *Global iron and steel tracker* [Online]. Retrieved April 20, 2025, from https://globalenergymonitor.org/projects/global-iron-and-steel-tracker/#:~:text=Iron%20and%20steel%20are%20typically%20produced%20through,map%20and%20underlying%20data%20are%20updated%20annually.

Global Hydrogen Review. (2025). *HyIron produces first green hydrogen in Namibia* [Online]. Retrieved May 18, 2025, from https://www.globalhydrogenreview.com/hydrogen/24032025/hyiron-produces-first-green-hydrogen-in-namibia/.

GMK Center. (2023). *H2 Green Steel has entered into agreements with Rio Tinto and Vale for the supply of DRI pellets* [Online]. Retrieved May 17, 2025, from https://gmk.center/en/news/h2-green-steel-has-entered-into-agreements-with-rio-tinto-and-vale-for-the-supply-of-dri-pellets/.

Government of Japan. (2024). *The road to net-zero with green steel* [Online]. Retrieved May 15, 2025, from https://www.japan.go.jp/kizuna/2024/03/net_zero_with_green_steel.html.

Graupner, Y., Weckenborg, C., & Spengler, T. S. (2023). Low-carbon primary steelmaking using direct reduction and electric arc furnaces: Prospective environmental impact assessment. *Procedia CIRP, 116*(1), 696–701.

Hasanbeigi, A. (2024). *Green steel economics. Comparing economics of green H2-DRI and traditional steelmaking around the world.* SFOC.

Hüttel, A., & Lehner, J. (2024). *Revisiting investment costs for green steel: Capital expenditures, firm level impacts, and policy implications.* DIW Berlin.

HYBRIT. (2024). *Pilot scale direct reduction with hydrogen* [Online]. Retrieved May 9, 2025, from https://www.hybritdevelopment.se/en/a-fossil-free-development/direct-reduction-hydrogen-pilotscale/.

Hydrogen Council. (2023). *Hydrogen certification 101* [Online]. Retrieved May 16, 2025, from https://hydrogencouncil.com/wp-content/uploads/2023/08/Hydrogen-Certification-101.pdf.

HyIron. (2024a). *Project Oshivela* [Online]. Retrieved May 18, 2025, from https://hyiron.com/oshivela/.

HyIron. (2024b). *Green iron – Zero emissions and a new perspective* [Online]. Retrieved May 18, 2025, from https://hyiron.com/.

IDOS. (2024). *Green hydrogen in Namibia: Opportunities and risks* [Online]. Retrieved May 18, 2025, from https://www.idos-research.de/fileadmin/user_upload/pdfs/publikationen/discussion_paper/2024/DP__6.2024.pdf.

IEA. (2020). *Iron and steel technology roadmap. Towards more sustainable steelmaking* [Online]. Retrieved May 14, 2025, from https://iea.blob.core.windows.

net/assets/eb0c8ec1-3665-4959-97d0-187ceca189a8/Iron_and_Steel_Technology_Roadmap.pdf.

IEA. (2023). *Global hydrogen review 2023* [Online]. Retrieved May 07, 2025, from https://iea.blob.core.windows.net/assets/ecdfc3bb-d212-4a4c-9ff7-6ce5b1e19cef/GlobalHydrogenReview2023.pdf.

IEEFA. (2024). *Carbon capture for steel? CCUS will not play a major role in steel decarbonisation* [Online]. Retrieved May 09, 2025, from https://ieefa.org/sites/default/files/2024-04/Carbon%20capture%20for%20steel-April24.pdf.

IMARC Group. (2024). *Green hydrogen price trend, chart, index, monitor, historical data, news 2024 and forecast* [Online]. Retrieved May 13, 2025, from https://www.openpr.com/news/3550820/green-hydrogen-price-trend-chart-index-monitor-historical

IPHE. (2024). *Comparison of hydrogen certification schemes – Methodology and results* [Online]. Retrieved May 16, 2025, from https://www.iphe.net/_files/ugd/45185a_e097bcac08984a3a87201790b30b145c.pdf.

Jeswani, H. K., Zapata-Boada, S., Spallina, V., & Azapagic, A. (2025). Towards net-zero in steel production: Process simulation and environmental impacts of carbon capture, storage and utilisation of blast furnace gas. *Carbon Capture Science & Technology, 15*(1), 1–16.

Jia, G., et al. (2023). Hydrogen embrittlement in hydrogen-blended natural gas transportation systems: A review. *International Journal of Hydrogen Energy, 48*(82), 32137–32157.

Kim, D., & Heo, E. H. (2024). *Green steel economics – Comparing economics of green H2-DRI and traditional steelmaking around the world* [Online]. Retrieved May 13, 2025, from https://forourclimate.org/research/520.

Li, S., et al. (2021). The direct reduction of iron ore with hydrogen. *Sustainability, 13*(16), 1–15.

Lipiäinen, S., Lipiäinen, K., Ahola, A., & Vakkilainen, E. (2023). Use of existing gas infrastructure in European hydrogen economy. *International Journal of Hydrogen Energy, 48*(80), 31317–31329.

Makkiabadi, M., Tang, H., & Rashidi, M. M. (2024). A comprehensive review of simulation of electric arc furnace (EAF) and its processes. *Heliyon, 1*(1), 1–42.

Material Economics. (2019). *Industrial transformation. Pathways to net-zero emissions from EU heavy industry* [Online]. Retrieved May 16, 2025, from https://materialeconomics.com/node/13.

Materials Processing Institute. (2021). *Decarbonising the DRI feed for EAF using H2.* 12th European Electric Steelmaking Conference, Sheffield, 13–15 September.

Mining & Energy. (2025). *HyIron completes iron production plant, operations to begin in late February* [Online]. Retrieved May 18, 2025, from https://miningandenergy.com.na/hyiron-completes-iron-production-plant-operations-to-begin-in-late-february/.

Nill, J. (2008). Diffusion as time-dependent result of technological evolution, competition, and policies: The case of cleaner iron and steel technologies. *Journal of Cleaner Production, 16*(1), S58–S66.
OECD. (2023). *H2 Green Steel* [Online]. Retrieved May 17, 2025, from https://www.oecd.org/content/dam/oecd/en/about/programmes/cefim/green-hydrogen/H2-green-steel-case-study.pdf.
OECD. (2025). *Hydrogen in steel* [Online]. Retrieved May 07, 2025, from https://www.oecd.org/en/publications/hydrogen-in-steel_7e2edc69-en.html.
OMV. (2025). *A blueprint for the future: Austria's largest green hydrogen plant is here* [Online]. Retrieved May 10, 2025, from https://www.omv.com/en/media/insights/2025/a-blueprint-for-the-future-austria-s-largest-green-hydrogen-plant-is-here.
Perpiñán, J., et al. (2023). Integration of carbon capture technologies in blast furnace based steel making: A comprehensive and systemic review. *Fuel, 336*(1), 1–30.
Rechberger, K., et al. (2020). Green hydrogen-based direct reduction for low-carbon steelmaking. *Steel Research, 91*(1), 1–10.
Reclaim Finance. (2024). *Steeling our future. The banks propping up coal-based steel* [Online]. Retrieved May 10, 2025, from https://reclaimfinance.org/site/wp-content/uploads/2024/03/Steeling-_our_future_March_2024.pdf.
Reznicek, E. P., et al. (2025). Techno-economic analysis of low-carbon hydrogen production pathways for decarbonizing steel and ammonia production. *Cell Reports Sustainability, 2*(4), 1–22.
Rumsa, M., John, M., & Biswas, W. (2025). Global steel decarbonisation roadmaps: Near-zero by 2050. *Environmental Impact Assessment Review, 112*(1), 1–12.
SEI. (2018). *Hydrogen steelmaking for a low-carbon economy. EESS report no 109* [Online]. Retrieved May 10, 2025, from https://www.sei.org/wp-content/uploads/2018/09/hydrogen-steelmaking-for-a-low-carbon-economy.pdf.
Shahabuddin, M., Brooks, G., & Rhamdhani, M. A. (2023). Decarbonisation and hydrogen integration of steel industries: Recent development, challenges and technoeconomic analysis. *Journal of Cleaner Production, 395*(1), 1–21.
Shamsuddin, M. (2021). *Physical chemistry of metallurgical processes*. Springer.
SteelWatch. (2025). *SteelWatch Explainer: Why smart use of green hydrogen is critical for steel decarbonisation* [Online]. Retrieved May 07, 2025, from https://steelwatch.org/steelwatch-explainers/hydrogen/.
Stegra. (2024). *Stegra granted state aid from the Industrial Leap and The Swedish Energy Agency* [Online]. Retrieved May 10, 2025, from https://stegra.com/news-and-stories/stegra-granted-state-aid-from-the-industrial-leap-and-the-swedish-energy-agency.
Stegra. (2025). *We are Stegra* [Online]. Retrieved May 17, 2025, from https://stegra.com/about-us.

Taylor, P. (2022). Unlocking the potential of electric arc furnaces in modern steelmaking. *Journal of Steel Structures & Construction, 8*(11), 1–2.

Télessy, K., Barner, L., & Holz, F. (2024). Repurposing natural gas pipelines for hydrogen: Limits and options from a case study in Germany. *International Journal of Hydrogen Energy, 80*(1), 821–831.

The Brief. (2024). *HyIron secures off-taker, eyes N$3.8bn phase 2 investment* [Online]. Retrieved May 18, 2025, from https://thebrief.com.na/2024/11/hyiron-secures-off-taker-eyes-n3-8bn-investment-for-phase-2/.

Transition Asia. (2024). *Explainer – Carbon capture in the steel sector; BF-BOF abatement* [Online]. Retrieved May 10, 2025, from https://transitionasia.org/explainer-carbon-capture-in-the-steel-sector/.

UNECE. (2022). *COP27: UN report shows pathways to carbon-neutrality in 'energy intensive' steel, chemicals and cement industries* [Online]. Retrieved April 20, 2025, from https://unece.org/media/press/372890.

US Department of Energy. (2022). *Inflation reduction act of 2022* [Online]. Retrieved May 15, 2025, from https://www.energy.gov/lpo/inflation-reduction-act-2022.

Vogl, V., Åhman, M., & Nilsson, L. J. (2018). Assessment of hydrogen direct reduction for fossil-free steelmaking. *Journal of Cleaner Production, 203*(1), 736–745.

Weigel, M., Fischedick, M., Marzinkowski, J., & Winzer, P. (2016). Multicriteria analysis of primary steelmaking technologies. *Journal of Cleaner Production, 112*(1), 1064–1076.

Witecka, W. et al. (2024). *Low-carbon technologies for the global steel transformation* [Online]. Retrieved May 07, 2025, from https://portal.research.lu.se/files/193592305/Agora_WUppertal_Lund_Steel_report.pdf.

Yadav, D., Guhan, A., & Biswas, T. (2021). *Greening steel. Moving to clean steelmaking using hydrogen and renewable energy.* Council on Energy, Environment and Water.

Zhang, G., et al. (2023). Cost and life cycle analysis for deep CO2 emissions reduction for steelmaking: Direct reduced iron technologies. *Steel Research International, 94*(6), 1–17.

CHAPTER 11

# Hydrogen for Cement Production

## Introduction

Historically, cement production has attracted less focus in public discussions on industrial decarbonisation than sectors like power generation or automotive transport. Nevertheless, it remains a major industrial source of greenhouse gas emissions, accounting for roughly 7–8% of global anthropogenic $CO_2$ (IEA, 2023). This is largely due to the dual-emission nature of the cement-making process: both from the combustion of fossil fuels to heat kilns and from the chemical reactions inherent to the transformation of limestone (calcium carbonate) into clinker, the key ingredient in cement (Scrivener et al., 2018).

The cement manufacturing process is typically split into four main stages: raw material preparation, clinker production, cement grinding, and dispatch (Fig. 11.1) (Benhelal et al., 2013). Among these, clinker production is by far the most carbon-intensive, accounting for roughly 90% of the sector's emissions (ibid.). This stems from two principal sources: direct process emissions released during the calcination of limestone, and fuel-related emissions associated with maintaining kiln temperatures exceeding 1450 °C (IEA, 2023). Historically, these kilns have been powered by coal, petcoke, and natural gas, although in some regions alternative fuels such as waste-derived biomass have been introduced in recent years (Okeke et al., 2024).



A. Patonia, R. Poudineh, *Clean Hydrogen for Decarbonisation*,
https://doi.org/10.1007/978-3-032-19442-8_11

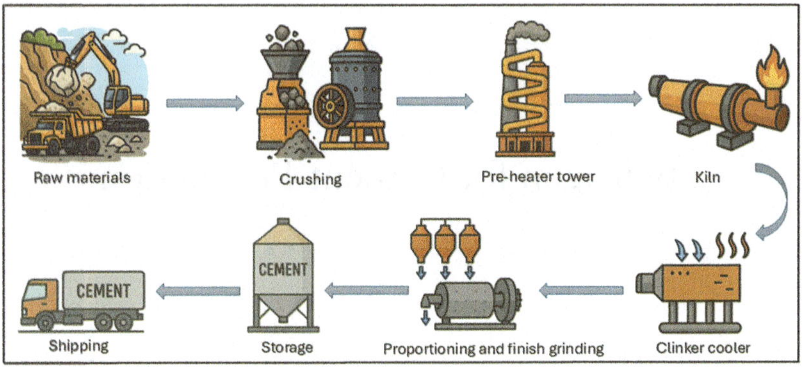


**Fig. 11.1** Main stages in the cement manufacturing process. (Source: Authors)

At present, cement production routes are broadly standardised worldwide, with rotary kilns remaining the dominant technology since their widespread adoption in the early twentieth century. These kilns operate under different process configurations—wet, semi-wet/semi-dry (including Lepol), and predominantly modern dry processes with preheaters and precalciners (Fig. 11.2). While incremental efficiency improvements and partial fuel switching have somewhat reduced emissions intensity over time, the fundamental chemistry of cement production poses a unique challenge to full decarbonisation. Unlike in steelmaking, where a transition from blast furnaces to electric arc furnaces is technically feasible, cement has no equivalent alternative to clinker-based production at commercial scale.

Although the technological decarbonisation 'menu' is broadly similar worldwide, cement demand and production are highly concentrated outside Europe. This matters because regions with the largest clinker output face different constraint sets (fuel availability, grid carbon intensity, CCUS access, and policy enforcement), and many decarbonisation strategies in major markets emphasise clinker substitution, alternative fuels, and—where feasible—CCUS, with hydrogen typically treated as a niche high-heat option rather than a central lever. We therefore use European pilots for detail, but interpret them against the reality that large-scale uptake will ultimately be driven by decisions in major producing and consuming economies.

Within this context, clean hydrogen is nevertheless being currently viewed by some as a potential option to decarbonise the combustion-related component of cement production. Hydrogen could, in principle,

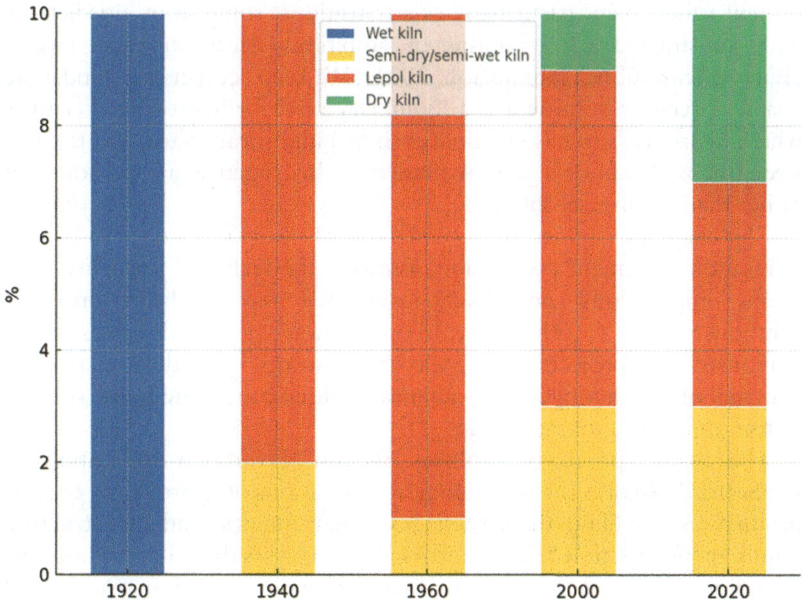


**Fig. 11.2** Evolution of key cement production methods. (Source: Adapted from Schneider et al. (2011) and Mohamad et al. (2022))

be used as a high-temperature, low-carbon fuel for kiln heating, displacing coal and other fossil-based alternatives. However, this pathway presents significant technical and economic hurdles. In particular, cement kilns require a consistent and controllable flame profile, with specific radiative and convective heat properties, which hydrogen combustion may struggle to replicate without extensive modifications to kiln design and operation (Kätelhön et al., 2019; Williams et al., 2024).

Moreover, just like in most other applications, the availability and cost of clean hydrogen—whether produced via electrolysis or steam methane reforming with carbon capture and storage (CCS)—still remain prohibitive for large-scale deployment in the sector in the near to medium term (ibid.). In parallel, other decarbonisation strategies such as carbon capture and storage (CCS), clinker substitution, and alternative binders are progressing and, in many cases, are seen as more immediately viable for deep emission reductions. Therefore, clean hydrogen is more increasingly viewed as a technological path for specific niche applications within the cement value chain, particularly as a transitional solution in jurisdictions with constrained CCS options or ambitious decarbonisation targets (Energy Transitions Commission, 2021). We keep cement as a standalone chapter precisely because it is a 'boundary case' for hydrogen: it clarifies where hydrogen's role is marginal even in a high-heat sector, and thereby strengthens the book's central thesis that hydrogen is a precision tool rather than a universal solution.

This chapter examines the potential role of clean hydrogen in the decarbonisation of cement production, assessing the technical feasibility, economic implications, and likely competitiveness of hydrogen-based solutions relative to other low-carbon pathways. It also discusses recent demonstration projects and policy frameworks, providing a realistic appraisal of whether hydrogen can meaningfully contribute to the sector's transition in the coming decades.

This chapter proceeds as follows. Section "Hydrogen Applications in the Sector" explores the technological applications of hydrogen in cement production, detailing the advantages, disadvantages, and infrastructure requirements. Section "Economic Aspects" analyses the economic aspects, including costs and the impact of carbon pricing. Section "Policy and Regulatory Landscape" reviews the relevant policy and regulatory landscape. Section "Case Studies and Pilot Projects" presents case studies of pilot projects. Finally, Section "Future Outlook and Conclusions" offers a future outlook and conclusions on hydrogen's role in the sector's decarbonisation.

## Hydrogen Applications in the Sector

### *Technological Solutions*

In cement production, the potential applications of clean hydrogen are primarily focused on fuel substitution within high-temperature kiln processes. This process is responsible for the overwhelming majority of the sector's $CO_2$ emissions not because of fuel burn but because of a chemical process that leads to release of carbon dioxide. Unlike in steelmaking, where hydrogen can act as a chemical reductant in iron ore reduction, the decarbonisation challenge in cement lies largely in the calcination of limestone ($CaCO_3$), which releases $CO_2$ as a process emission independent of fuel choice:

$$CaCO_3 \rightarrow CaO + CO_2$$

Approximately 60% of cement plant emissions arise from this unavoidable chemical reaction, while the remaining 40% are linked to the combustion of fossil fuels to heat kilns to temperatures exceeding 1400 °C (IEA, 2023).

The use of hydrogen in cement manufacturing is thus limited to displacing fossil fuels in the thermal energy supply for clinker production, the intermediate product in cement manufacturing. This is so because, as a combustion fuel, hydrogen produces only water vapour when burnt, eliminating $CO_2$ emissions from the fuel side of the process. It is technically feasible to adapt cement kilns to hydrogen combustion, with several pilot projects underway in Europe and the United Kingdom, such as Hanson Cement's trials in the United Kingdom under the HyNet industrial decarbonisation cluster (MPA, 2021). However, this approach does not address process emissions from calcination, which would require parallel deployment of carbon capture and storage (CCS) technologies to achieve near-zero emission cement production (Lehne & Preston, 2018).

Several technological pathways for decarbonising cement are being explored, often in combination rather than competition. These strategies involve raising the share of supplementary cementitious materials (SCMs) such as fly ash, slag, and calcined clays to lower clinker content, using alternative fuels like biogas and refuse-derived fuel, and retrofitting existing plants with carbon capture, utilisation, and storage (CCUS) technologies (IEA, 2023).

As seen in Table 11.1, while technologies such as supplementary cementitious materials (SCMs) and biomass fuels offer modest emissions savings, more substantial reductions can be achieved through CCUS retrofits and hydrogen combustion when combined with other measures. The variation in technology readiness levels (TRLs) underscores the importance of a multi-pathway strategy, with mature options supporting near-term decarbonisation and newer technologies requiring continued research, pilot projects, and supportive policy frameworks to reach commercial viability.

Overall, however, while hydrogen-fuelled kilns can decarbonise the combustion-related portion of emissions, it is important to acknowledge that their economic and technical viability remains uncertain. Hydrogen's low volumetric energy density and high flame temperature pose challenges for retrofitting

**Table 11.1** Average maturity level of key low-carbon cement production technologies

| *Technology* | *Process type* | *Main energy/ decarbonisation agent* | *Typical emissions reduction potential (%)* | *Technology readiness level (TRL)* | *Notes* |
|---|---|---|---|---|---|
| *Hydrogen fuel substitution* | Thermal energy | Hydrogen gas | 20–40 (combustion only) | 6–7 | Pilot trials ongoing; requires integration with CCS for full decarbonisation |
| *Biomass/ alternative fuels* | Thermal energy | Biomass, refuse-derived fuels | 10–30 | 9 | Commercially deployed; constrained by fuel availability and emissions regulation |
| *CCUS retrofits* | Process emissions | Post/oxy-combustion capture | 60–90 (process + combustion) | 5–7 | High capital cost; demonstration plants operating (e.g., Brevik CCS project) |
| *Clinker substation (SCMs)* | Material efficiency | Fly ash, slag, calcined clays | 20–40 | 9 | Mature technology; constrained by SCM availability |
| *Carbon mineralisation* | Process emissions | Carbonation of industrial waste | 5–10 | 3–5 | Emerging; limited to niche applications |
| *Novel low-clinker cements* | Material substitution | Belite cements, $LC^3$ | 30–50 | 4–6 | Pilot scale; performance and durability trials ongoing |

Source: Adapted from Lehne and Preston (2018), Energy Transitions Commission (2021), MPA (2021), IEA (2023)

existing cement kilns, which are typically designed for fossil fuel combustion. In addition, just like in most other cases, the current high cost of clean hydrogen particularly green hydrogen produced via electrolysis using renewable electricity—limits its competitiveness against lower-cost alternatives like biomass and waste-derived fuels in many markets (IRENA, 2022).

Recent pilot projects have demonstrated partial hydrogen fuel substitution of up to 100% in laboratory kilns and up to 20% in industrial-scale trials (Nhuchhen et al., 2022). However, full-scale deployment will depend on the development of hydrogen infrastructure, reductions in hydrogen production costs, and alignment with industrial decarbonisation policy frameworks such as the UK Industrial Decarbonisation Strategy (HM Government, 2021). In any case, unlike the DRI-EAF route in steel, which offers a transformative primary production pathway, hydrogen's role in cement is essentially auxiliary—a means to decarbonise thermal energy supply in combination with carbon capture for process emissions. As a result, while hydrogen can play a role in decarbonising cement production, it is unlikely to become the sector's primary decarbonisation solution on its own.

In summary, the use of hydrogen in cement production represents a promising, albeit partial, decarbonisation lever. Therefore, its deployment will most likely be complementary to other strategies such as clinker substitution, alternative fuels, and CCUS retrofits. That is why the long-term pace of hydrogen adoption in the sector will be determined by regional hydrogen availability, industrial cluster development, and the evolution of carbon pricing and emissions trading schemes, particularly in jurisdictions such as the United Kingdom and European Union.

### *Advantages/Disadvantages*

The decarbonisation of cement production through hydrogen-based fuel substitution offers both important benefits and discernible limitations when assessed against alternative low-carbon pathways for the sector. From an emissions perspective, as shown in Table 11.1, substituting fossil fuels with clean hydrogen in cement kilns could abate approximately 20–40% of total plant $CO_2$ emissions—specifically those linked to fuel combustion—with the remaining emissions from calcination requiring parallel carbon capture solutions (Energy Transitions Commission, 2021; IEA, 2023). Therefore, even under optimal conditions, hydrogen combustion alone cannot achieve full decarbonisation of cement production, but can play a significant role in reducing emissions when deployed as part of an integrated decarbonisation strategy.

Performance-wise, hydrogen combustion offers advantages in terms of zero-carbon heat generation and compatibility with high-temperature processes. Additionally, hydrogen combustion eliminates emissions of sulphur oxides ($SO_x$) and particulate matter typically associated with coal and petcoke combustion, thereby improving local air quality around cement plants (Lehne & Preston, 2018). However, the use of hydrogen as a fuel in cement kilns also presents notable technical and economic challenges. Hydrogen's high flame temperature (around 2000 °C in air) can lead to non-uniform heating in rotary kilns and increased formation of nitrogen oxides ($NO_x$) unless advanced burner designs and combustion controls are deployed (Energy Transitions Commission, 2022). Furthermore, hydrogen's low volumetric energy density complicates its storage and delivery at industrial scale, necessitating significant upgrades to on-site infrastructure (IRENA, 2022).

From an economic perspective, unsurprisingly, the primary limitation again lies in the current high cost of clean hydrogen—particularly green hydrogen produced via renewable-powered electrolysis—which remains several times more expensive than conventional fossil fuels per unit of thermal energy delivered (IEA, 2023). Until hydrogen prices fall below a competitive threshold, estimated at around USD 2/kg for industrial heat applications (IRENA, 2022), its adoption will likely depend on supportive policy frameworks, carbon pricing mechanisms, and industrial decarbonisation subsidies.

When it comes to scaling up hydrogen-based cement decarbonisation options, the primary constraints are linked to hydrogen's economic competitiveness, the need for extensive retrofitting of kiln systems, and the availability of low-carbon hydrogen at industrial cluster scale (Table 11.2) (IRENA, 2022). By contrast, alternative decarbonisation levers such as clinker substitution through supplementary cementitious materials (SCMs) and biomass fuel substitution are already widely deployed in many markets, though their long-term emissions reduction potential is constrained by resource availability and material performance limitations (IEA, 2023). Meanwhile, CCUS retrofits—the only currently available option capable of abating both combustion and process emissions—face substantial barriers in terms of capital costs, public acceptance, and $CO_2$ transport and storage infrastructure development (Energy Transitions Commission, 2022). Novel cement formulations such as belite-rich and Limestone Calcinated Clay ($LC^3$) cements, in turn, offer considerable abatement potential but remain at pilot scale, facing commercialisation delays due to technical validation and standards certification requirements (Lehne & Preston, 2018).

**Table 11.2** Emissions reduction potential, deployment barriers and commercialisation outlook for low-carbon cement production technologies

| *Technology* | *Deployment status* | *Key deployment barriers* | *Expected commercialisation timeline* |
|---|---|---|---|
| *Hydrogen fuel substitution* | Pilot and demonstration trials | Hydrogen supply infrastructure, high fuel costs, burner retrofitting | Early 2030s |
| *Biomass/ alternative fuels* | Commercially deployed | Limited sustainable feedstock | Already operational |
| *CCUS retrofits* | Demonstration and early pilots | High capture costs, CO2 transport/storage infrastructure, public acceptance | Mid-late 2020s |
| *Clinker substation (SCMs)* | Widely commercialised | SCM availability constraints, regulatory cement standards | Already operational |
| *Carbon mineralisation* | Laboratory/early pilot | Limited market scale, high material handling costs | Post-2035 |
| *Novel low-clinker cements* | Pilot scale | Performance validation, industry acceptance, durability data gaps | 2030–2040 |

Source: Adapted from Lehne and Preston (2018), Energy Transitions Commission (2021), MPA (2021), IEA (2023)

In this regard, while hydrogen holds potential as a partial decarbonisation solution for cement kilns, its future role will be contingent upon rapid cost reductions in hydrogen supply, burner technology adaptation, and the co-development of CCUS and SCM deployment. In the short to medium term, hybrid strategies combining biomass fuels, CCUS, and clinker substitution are likely to dominate the decarbonisation landscape of the cement sector (IEA, 2023).

### *Infrastructure Requirements*

As in other energy-intensive industrial sectors, the decarbonisation of cement production through hydrogen-based solutions will critically depend on the development and adaptation of appropriate infrastructure systems. At the moment, conventional cement production processes rely on well-established logistics networks for the supply of fuels such as coal, petcoke, and natural gas, as well as the transport and handling of raw materials like limestone and clinker. These systems are deeply embedded within industrial clusters and are designed around the physical and operational properties of traditional fossil fuels (Leeson et al., 2017; Bacatelo et al., 2024). Therefore, in contrast, integrating hydrogen as a primary fuel in cement kilns—whether for partial substitution or complete replacement of fossil fuels—will require new infrastructure components, many of which are currently absent or available only at demonstration scale[1] (Energy Transitions Commission, 2022).

In particular, the shift towards hydrogen-based cement production would necessitate the deployment of dedicated hydrogen storage facilities, high-capacity pipelines for hydrogen distribution within and between industrial sites, and modified burner systems capable of managing hydrogen's unique combustion characteristics (ibid.). Just like in other industrial applications like steelmaking, due to hydrogen's low volumetric energy density and high diffusivity, existing natural gas networks and onsite storage systems would not be inherently compatible with its use at scale (IEA, 2023). In addition, while repurposing current gas infrastructure could be technically feasible in some contexts, limitations related to material integrity, pressure thresholds, and embrittlement risks would restrict its applicability for high-temperature cement production processes (Jayachandran et al., 2024; Sánchez et al., 2025).

Overall, compared to sectors such as steel, cement production presents additional infrastructural challenges due to its decentralised plant locations and the typically smaller scale of individual cement kilns relative to blast furnaces or steel plants (Bacatelo et al., 2024). As a result, hydrogen supply and distribution networks would need to be developed or expanded across a more dispersed industrial geography, increasing capital investment and operational coordination requirements (ibid. IEA, 2023). Moreover, the combustion of hydrogen in cement kilns requires significant modifications to existing burner systems, given hydrogen's higher flame speed and combustion temperature compared to natural gas (CSTEP, 2024). These factors raise concerns over kiln refractory durability, $NO_x$ emissions, and clinker quality consistency, necessitating additional technological adjustments and operational trials (ibid. and Energy Transitions Commission,

[1] The general properties and constraints of hydrogen transport and storage infrastructure are discussed in Chaps. 4 and 5; here we focus on the cement-specific implications of dispersed plant geography, burner retrofits, and operational constraints in kilns.

2022). Consequently, the scalability and adaptability of hydrogen-based cement decarbonisation is currently low, with only a handful of pilot projects operating in Europe and Japan (Table 11.3).

By contrast, CCS-equipped kilns are estimated to moderate infrastructure scalability, primarily because many capture technologies can be retrofitted to existing plants. However, as in the steel sector, the viability of these projects is highly dependent on proximity to $CO_2$ transport pipelines and suitable geological storage formations (Leeson et al., 2017; Royal White Cement, 2024). In regions lacking such infrastructure, the costs and logistical complexities of developing new carbon storage and transport systems may impede large-scale CCS deployment (ibid.). In this context, while hydrogen holds long-term potential for decarbonisation of cement production, its deployment will rely on the parallel development of hydrogen supply networks, storage facilities, and burner modification solutions, as well as regulatory frameworks to manage operational safety and environmental performance. In the interim, hybrid approaches combining partial fuel switching, CCS, and increased use of supplementary cementitious materials are likely to dominate the decarbonisation landscape of the cement sector.

## Economic Aspects

The integration of hydrogen as a fuel in the cement industry entails significant economic implications, encompassing capital expenditures (CapEx), operational expenditures (OpEx), and external factors such as carbon pricing and subsidies. In the context of cement production, CapEx refers to the costs associated with modifying existing kilns or constructing new facilities capable of operating on hydrogen, as well as installing associated infrastructure such as hydrogen storage, burners, and safety systems. OpEx, in turn, includes recurring costs for fuel, maintenance, operational management, and the expenses of supplementary systems such as oxygen production in oxyfuel applications.

As in the steel sector, the transition to hydrogen-fired cement kilns is highly capital-intensive. Retrofitting existing cement kilns for hydrogen combustion typically incurs substantial capital expenditure, largely due to the need for specialised hydrogen burners, onsite hydrogen storage systems, and safety upgrades (IEA, 2023; RMI, 2022). According to sector estimates, these retrofits can increase capital costs by 30–60% compared to conventional kiln upgrades (IEA, 2023). For greenfield installations,

**Table 11.3** Infrastructure requirements, scalability, adaptability, and challenges of hydrogen-based low-carbon cement technologies

| *Technology* | *Specific infrastructure requirements* | *Current scalability* | *Current adaptability* | *Key challenges* |
|---|---|---|---|---|
| *Hydrogen combustion in kilns* | • Onsite hydrogen storage (high-pressure or cryogenic)<br>• Modified kiln burners<br>• Dedicated or repurposed hydrogen pipelines | Low | Limited | • High hydrogen costs<br>• Infrastructure build-out costs<br>• Burner retrofit complexity |
| *Oxyfuel combustion + hydrogen* | • $O_2$ production and distribution systems<br>• Hydrogen storage and supply networks<br>• $CO_2$ capture and compression units | Very low | Very low | • High capital intensity<br>• Limited demonstration experience |
| *CCS-equipped conventional kilns* | • $CO_2$ capture units<br>• Pipeline transport to storage<br>• Access to $CO_2$ storage sites | Moderate | Moderate | • High capture costs<br>• Limited proximity to storage infrastructure |
| *Electrification of cement process* | • Large-scale renewable electricity supply<br>• High-capacity electrical connections and backup systems | Very low | Very low | • High electricity demand<br>• Limited kiln electrification readiness |

Source: Adapted from Energy Transitions Commission (2022), IEA (2023), Bacatelo et al. (2024), and CSTEP (2024)

particularly those integrating hydrogen-oxyfuel combustion or combined hydrogen-carbon capture systems, total CapEx can rise even further—in some cases exceeding EUR 200–300 per tonne of annual production capacity, depending on project scale and infrastructure availability (Bolt et al., 2023; RMI, 2022). Moreover, many cement plants are located in areas without established hydrogen pipeline networks, necessitating either onsite electrolysis or hydrogen deliveries by road, both of which add to capital and logistical expenses (ibid. and IEA, 2023).

Operational expenditures for hydrogen-fuelled cement kilns are predominantly driven by hydrogen fuel costs, which remain significantly higher than those of coal or natural gas. As of mid-2024, green hydrogen prices in Europe typically ranged from EUR 4.5 to EUR 7 per kilogram, compared to EUR 0.10–0.15 per kilogram for thermal coal (Hydrogen Council, 2024). Given that fuel accounts for 40–60% of operational expenditure in cement manufacturing, these high hydrogen prices present a major economic barrier to widespread adoption (Energy Transitions Commission, 2022). Additionally, operational costs are increased by greater maintenance requirements for hydrogen infrastructure, specialised safety systems, and, where applicable, oxygen production for oxyfuel systems. While these maintenance costs are expected to decrease over time due to learning-by-doing and economies of scale, they currently contribute to the overall cost premium of hydrogen-based cement production (IEA, 2023).

Comparing hydrogen-fuelled cement production to conventional methods highlights the economic disparity. The levelised cost of cement (LCoC) for conventional fossil-fuelled production ranges between EUR 65 and EUR 90 per tonne in Europe, while hydrogen-based processes are estimated at EUR 120–160 per tonne, depending on hydrogen and electricity prices, carbon pricing, and proximity to hydrogen infrastructure (CSTEP, 2024; Jibran & Mahat, 2023).

The environmental benefits of hydrogen-fuelled cement production are substantial. Conventional cement kilns emit approximately 0.6–0.9 tonnes of $CO_2$ per tonne of cement, with fuel combustion responsible for around 35–40% of these emissions (IEA, 2023). Hydrogen combustion can virtually eliminate fuel-related $CO_2$ emissions, although process emissions from limestone calcination persist. In addition, it is estimated that, when combined with carbon capture and storage, total emissions can be reduced by over 90% (CSTEP, 2024).

Consequently, carbon pricing mechanisms and emissions trading systems (ETS) play a pivotal role in shaping the economic feasibility of hydrogen solutions. Under the EU ETS, carbon prices in 2023 generally ranged between EUR 60 and EUR 80 per tonne of $CO_2$, with occasional short-term spikes approaching EUR 90 (IEEFA, 2024). However, the operating costs of conventional cement plants have been partially mitigated by substantial free carbon allowances, which covered a significant share of their emissions in 2023. As these free allowances are gradually phased out and carbon prices potentially rise further, the additional costs of hydrogen-based cement production are expected to be increasingly offset by avoided carbon allowance expenses, improving the economic case for hydrogen adoption. It is nevertheless uncertain when it will really happen.

In these circumstances, financial incentives and subsidies are critical for closing the current economic gap in hydrogen-based cement production. European policy frameworks such as the EU Innovation Fund and national hydrogen strategies provide direct financial support for industrial decarbonisation projects, including cement (European Commission, 2023). For example, Germany's National Hydrogen Strategy allocates approximately EUR 9 billion for hydrogen infrastructure and industrial applications, explicitly including cement and lime production (BMWK, 2023). Additionally, emerging market-based mechanisms such as green cement certification schemes and low-carbon public procurement policies may enable producers to command premium prices for low-carbon cement in infrastructure and construction projects, as evidenced by early initiatives from major public procurement bodies in the Netherlands and Sweden (Energy Transitions Commission, 2022).

Thus, while the current costs of hydrogen use in cement production remain high relative to conventional fuels, a combination of rising carbon prices, direct financial support, and growing market demand for low-carbon materials is expected to improve the economic viability of hydrogen-based solutions over the coming decade. To secure this pathway, consistent and robust policy interventions will be necessary to accelerate infrastructure development, stimulate demand for green cement, and enhance the competitiveness of hydrogen as a decarbonisation option for the cement industry.

## Policy and Regulatory Landscape

Hydrogen-based solutions have gained increasing recognition within national and regional climate frameworks as part of comprehensive long-term strategies to reduce emissions in the cement sector (Cembureau, 2023). At the EU level, the European Green Deal and the Fit for 55 legislative package set ambitious targets for carbon neutrality by 2050, explicitly prioritising hard-to-decarbonise sectors such as cement and steel (European Commission, 2023). The EU Hydrogen Strategy of 2020 identifies renewable hydrogen deployment in these sectors as a key enabler of decarbonisation (European Commission, 2020).

Complementing these efforts, the European Commission's Innovation Fund—one of the world's largest funding programmes for low-carbon technologies—has begun allocating resources to cement decarbonisation projects incorporating hydrogen and alternative fuels. In its 2023 call, the Innovation Fund awarded grants to 14 cement projects across nine European countries, supporting initiatives expected to avoid significant $CO_2$ emissions, primarily through carbon capture and storage but also including hydrogen technologies (European Commission, 2025).

Furthermore, the Important Projects of Common European Interest (IPCEI) framework on hydrogen extends eligibility for funding to hydrogen infrastructure projects supporting industrial users, including cement producers. Germany's IPCEI programme, jointly funded by federal ministries, has allocated over EUR 10 billion to integrated hydrogen projects, encompassing green hydrogen production, pipeline construction, and industrial applications, with the steel and cement sectors among the primary beneficiaries (BMWK, 2023). Among individual member states, Germany's National Hydrogen Strategy initially committed approximately EUR 9 billion to hydrogen development, with industrial decarbonisation—including cement production—as a central focus. The strategy was updated in 2023 to increase targets, notably raising the domestic electrolysis capacity goal to at least 10 GW by 2030, reinforcing hydrogen's role in decarbonising energy-intensive industries such as cement and steel (ibid.).

France's National Low-Carbon Strategy and updated Hydrogen Deployment Plan similarly include support for pilot projects deploying hydrogen in high-temperature industrial processes, encompassing cement kilns. The country aims to reach 4.5 GW of electrolysis capacity by 2030, with hydrogen positioned as a key lever for industrial decarbonisation (France Hydrogène, 2025). In Northern Europe, in turn, the Nordic Hydrogen Route initiative seeks to establish cross-border hydrogen infrastructure by the early 2030s to serve industrial clusters in Finland and Sweden, including cement and lime production sites, facilitating a regional hydrogen economy (Nordic Hydrogen Route, 2025).

In North America, the United States' Inflation Reduction Act (IRA) of 2022 introduced significant tax credits for clean hydrogen production, notably the 45 V credits, and funding for regional clean hydrogen hubs. Some of these hubs are expected to support cement plants as part of broader industrial decarbonisation zones (US Department of Energy, 2022). By contrast, Canada's Hydrogen Strategy, published in 2020, identifies hydrogen as a critical tool for heavy industry decarbonisation, with particular emphasis on provinces such as Alberta and Quebec, where cement production represents a substantial emissions source (Government of Canada, 2020).

Finally, in Asia, Japan's Green Growth Strategy and South Korea's Hydrogen Economy Roadmap outline plans for industrial hydrogen applications, although cement-sector projects remain in early conceptual or pilot stages (CSIRO, 2019; Green Hydrogen Organisation, 2025).

At the regulatory level, hydrogen use in cement production raises unique challenges distinct from other sectors. The EU Emissions Trading System (ETS) covers cement production, subjecting it to carbon pricing and the gradual reduction of free emission allowances. The ETS is increasingly influencing investment decisions in decarbonisation technologies, including hydrogen-based solutions (Carbon Market Watch, 2022). As of 2023, carbon prices surpassed EUR 90 per tonne, narrowing the economic gap between conventional and low-carbon cement production pathways (ibid. and ERCST, 2025). Furthermore, the Carbon Border Adjustment Mechanism (CBAM), which applies to cement imports from 2026, is expected to incentivise domestic producers to adopt hydrogen and other emissions-reduction technologies to maintain competitiveness in EU markets (European Commission, 2023).

Despite these overarching policy incentives, regulatory uncertainties and infrastructure constraints persist. Hydrogen pipeline and storage permitting frequently entails long lead times and overlapping authorities, complicating project implementation (Agora Energiewende, 2021). Furthermore, hydrogen infrastructure is not yet fully integrated into many EU member states' energy and industrial regulations, creating additional barriers for cement producers seeking to incorporate hydrogen supply (ibid.).

Safety regulations also present significant challenges. While industrial operators possess experience handling combustible gases, hydrogen's unique properties—such as high flammability, diffusivity, and potential for material embrittlement—necessitate stricter safety protocols, specialised equipment, and workforce retraining (Calabrese et al., 2024). Although ISO and European standards are converging on hydrogen safety for industrial applications, national regulations and enforcement practices remain uneven across jurisdictions (IEA, 2023).

Low-carbon hydrogen certification programmes, such as Europe's CertifHy, are essential for validating the sustainability of hydrogen employed in cement production. CertifHy issues Guarantees of Origin and Supply Certificates, enabling cement producers to demonstrate compliance with emissions reduction targets under the EU Renewable Energy Directive (RED II) and the ETS (CertifHy, 2025). At the international level, initiatives like the International Partnership for Hydrogen and Fuel Cells in the Economy (IPHE) continue to coordinate the harmonisation of certification standards, facilitating trade in certified low-carbon hydrogen for industrial use (IPHE, 2024).

Social acceptance is another key factor influencing the deployment of hydrogen infrastructure near cement plants. Local communities may raise concerns regarding hydrogen storage safety, pipeline routing, and land use conflicts, especially in urban or peri-urban areas where many cement plants operate (ibid. and Agora Energiewende, 2021). Transparent stakeholder engagement and effective risk communication strategies will be essential to securing public support for hydrogen infrastructure projects linked to the cement sector. Demand-side policies, including public procurement rules favouring low-carbon building materials and consumer-facing eco-labelling schemes, are emerging to stimulate market demand for low-emission cement. Drawing lessons from the steel sector, such initiatives can help close the business case for hydrogen adoption by enabling producers to command green price premiums and secure market access (IPHE, 2024).

In summary, while European and national policy frameworks increasingly recognise hydrogen's role in cement decarbonisation, regulatory bottlenecks, infrastructure constraints, safety requirements, and public acceptance issues continue to impede large-scale implementation. Addressing these challenges through coordinated policy, infrastructure planning, and demand-side incentives will be critical to accelerating the adoption of hydrogen solutions in the cement industry over the coming decade.

## Case Studies and Pilot Projects

Unlike in the steel sector, where hydrogen-based direct reduction processes have reached commercial pilot scale and are progressing rapidly, the use of clean hydrogen in cement production remains largely experimental, with only a limited number of real-world projects undertaken to date. This is mainly attributable to technical constraints—as noted, hydrogen alone cannot fully decarbonise cement production since a substantial portion of emissions stems from limestone calcination—and economic hurdles associated with the high cost of hydrogen production and its integration into existing clinker kilns. Nonetheless, several projects across Europe and beyond have tested partial substitution of fossil fuels with hydrogen in cement kilns, often alongside other decarbonisation measures such as carbon capture and alternative binders.

Among the most notable initiatives is the LEILAC 2 (Low Emissions Intensity Lime and Cement) project, led by Australian technology firm Calix in partnership with Heidelberg Materials, CEMEX, and other European cement producers (Calix, 2023). LEILAC primarily focuses on developing a modular carbon capture system for cement and lime kilns but also includes trials using hydrogen as a supplemental fuel in the preheater and calciner (ibid.). The LEILAC 2 demonstration plant, under construction at Heidelberg Materials' Hanover facility in Germany, is designed to capture a portion of the plant's process emissions without fundamental changes to the rotary kiln design (ibid.). While hydrogen is not a core component of the LEILAC concept, its consideration alongside such projects reflects broader industry interest in combining carbon capture with low-carbon fuel switching.

Another significant effort is Cemex's hydrogen project at its Rugby cement plant in the United Kingdom. Cemex Ventures, in partnership with HiiROC, is deploying hydrogen produced via thermal plasma electrolysis—a process that produces hydrogen and solid carbon black with minimal $CO_2$ emissions—to partially substitute fossil fuels in clinker production (Cemex, 2024). This project marks a strategic step towards integrating clean hydrogen at industrial scale and aligns with Cemex's 2050 net-zero ambitions. Earlier, in 2021, Cemex conducted hydrogen co-firing trials at Rugby, injecting small amounts of hydrogen alongside fossil fuels to evaluate impacts on flame stability and clinker quality. Results indicated potential for marginal fuel-related $CO_2$ reductions but also highlighted operational challenges at higher hydrogen shares, consistent with other industry trials (Global Cement, 2024).

Similarly, Hanson Cement, a Heidelberg Materials subsidiary, conducted hydrogen fuel trials at its Port Talbot plant in Wales as part of the HyNet Industrial Fuel Switching programme. These trials demonstrated that hydrogen could be integrated into existing fuel systems without major hardware changes, but the high flame speed and low radiative heat transfer of hydrogen flames caused instability at higher substitution rates, underscoring the need for burner redesign to enable full fuel switching (HyNet,

2020). Hanson concluded that hydrogen's role would likely remain supplementary unless paired with carbon capture technologies (ibid.).

Outside the United Kingdom, Lafarge Zementwerke partnered with OMV and other Austrian firms under the Carbon2ProductAustria (C2PAT) initiative to test hydrogen co-firing at the Mannersdorf plant (OMV, 2020). Early trials showed up to 10% fuel substitution with hydrogen without compromising clinker quality, but high hydrogen costs and infrastructure limitations constrained scale-up potential (Holcim, 2020). Lafarge positions hydrogen as a niche complement to biomass, waste-derived fuels, and carbon capture (ibid.).

These case studies demonstrate a clear trend: although partial hydrogen substitution in cement kilns is technically achievable, fully decarbonising through hydrogen fuel alone is unlikely in the near to medium term. As mentioned, approximately 60–65% of cement emissions stem from calcination, which hydrogen combustion cannot address by any means (IEA, 2023). Thus, hydrogen's role is limited to reducing fuel-related emissions, which constitute roughly 35–40% of total emissions.

In addition, most of these mentioned pilot projects identified several operational challenges such as high flame temperatures and speeds causing kiln instability and refractory wear (HyNet, 2020; Cemex, 2024), lower radiative heat transfer of hydrogen flames affecting clinker formation efficiency (Calix, 2023), and substantial capital costs for burner redesign and hydrogen supply infrastructure, especially beyond 30% fuel substitution (IEA, 2023). That is mostly why cement producers and policymakers increasingly regard hydrogen as one component of a broader decarbonisation portfolio alongside carbon capture and storage (CCS), alternative clinker formulations, and low-carbon cementitious materials. This strategy is reflected in Heidelberg Materials' and Cemex's recent commitments prioritising full-scale CCS projects in Germany, Norway, and the United States over expanded hydrogen fuel trials (Heidelberg Materials, 2024; Cemex, 2024).

As seen, real-world experience of the most promising pilot projects indicates that hydrogen can, in principle, contribute to reducing fuel-related emissions in cement production but faces technical, economic, and infrastructure barriers that limit its standalone impact. Unlike steelmaking—where hydrogen-based direct reduction can virtually eliminate $CO_2$ emissions from ironmaking—cement decarbonisation requires integrated approaches combining hydrogen with CCS and material innovations. This underscores the need for site-specific assessments and continued investment in complementary technologies to realise deep decarbonisation.

## Future Outlook and Conclusions

The cement industry faces an equally important decarbonisation imperative, being responsible for nearly 7% of global $CO_2$ emissions. However, unlike steelmaking, the pathways for achieving deep emissions reductions are more constrained. This chapter has critically examined the potential and limitations of hydrogen in decarbonising cement production. It has reviewed the latest scientific and industry evidence, assessed pilot projects, and situated hydrogen's role within the wider set of technological pathways available to the sector. The chapter clarifies both where hydrogen can make a meaningful contribution and where its role is likely to remain constrained.

Hydrogen has been explored as a potential enabler of low-carbon cement production, particularly as a substitute for fossil fuels in high-temperature kilns. Yet, its role in this sector is expected to remain considerably narrower than in steelmaking and other sectors, limited by both technical constraints and economic considerations.

In the short to medium term, hydrogen is therefore likely to see limited application within cement manufacturing. Demonstration projects such as those initiated by Heidelberg Materials in Germany and Cemex in the United Kingdom have proven the technical feasibility of hydrogen co-firing in cement kilns. Nonetheless, the fundamental challenge persists and is unlikely to be addressed by hydrogen: the majority of cement process emissions—accounting for around 60%—are released from the calcination of limestone, a process that hydrogen fuel-switching alone cannot address. As a result, even full hydrogen substitution in kiln operations would leave substantial process emissions intact.

Moreover, the economic viability of hydrogen use in cement is highly uncertain. With clean hydrogen prices projected to be several times higher than those of conventional hydrogen beyond 2030, the cost premium over existing fuel options remains prohibitive, particularly in a sector characterised by low profit margins and limited capacity for product price differentiation. Unlike the steel industry, where early adopters of low-carbon products can potentially command green premiums or benefit from green steel certification schemes, equivalent mechanisms in the cement market are far less developed. Following this logic, over the coming decade, hydrogen use in cement production is expected to remain confined to pilot initiatives, niche applications, or facilities with privileged access to low-cost renewable hydrogen. That is why alternative decarbonisation levers—including process innovations such as novel clinker substitutes, carbon capture and storage (CCS), and alternative binders like calcined clays or alkali-activated materials—are likely to play a much more significant role in the sector's transition pathway.

Looking further ahead, to the 2030s and beyond, a marginal expansion of hydrogen utilisation may occur as electrolyser and renewable electricity costs decline, and as hydrogen production hubs proliferate in industrial regions. However, hydrogen's use will likely remain limited to partial fuel substitution in kilns or as a complementary technology within integrated decarbonisation strategies involving CCS or alternative cements. Unlike in other industries like steelmaking or chemical sector, there is little prospect for hydrogen to fundamentally transform core process chemistry or deliver near-zero emissions independently.

By mid-century, the cement sector's decarbonisation will likely rely on a complex portfolio of measures tailored to regional conditions. These will include a combination of carbon capture, alternative binders, energy efficiency improvements, and selective hydrogen use. Regions with abundant, low-cost renewable energy may incorporate hydrogen more readily, but global deployment at scale appears improbable given the sector's decentralised nature and the cost sensitivities of construction markets, particularly in emerging economies.

In conclusion, while hydrogen can contribute to reducing cement production emissions, particularly from kiln fuel combustion, it simply cannot address the majority of the sector's process-related emissions and is therefore unlikely to become a cornerstone decarbonisation option. In these circumstances, its role will remain limited and complementary within a broader decarbonisation framework dominated by CCS and material innovations. As such, policy priorities should focus on accelerating the development of these alternative pathways, while supporting targeted hydrogen demonstration projects to identify niche applications where its deployment may prove both technically and economically feasible. Overall, hydrogen's transformative potential in cement production is, at best, partial—offering one piece of a complex, multi-technology strategy required for the sector's sustainable future.

## References

Agora Energiewende. (2021). *Breakthrough strategies for climate-neutral industry in Europe* [Online]. Retrieved July 07, 2025, from https://epub.wupperinst.org/frontdoor/deliver/index/docId/7751/file/7751_Climate-Neutral_Industry.pdf.

Bacatelo, M., et al. (2024). Carbon-neutral cement: The role of green hydrogen. *International Journal of Hydrogen Energy, 63*(1), 382–395.

Benhelal, E., Zahedi, G., Shamsaei, E., & Bahadori, A. (2013). Global strategies and potentials to curb CO2 emissions in cement industry. *Journal of Cleaner Production, 511*(1), 142–161.

BMWK. (2023). *National hydrogen strategy update* [Online]. Retrieved July 06, 2025, from https://www.bundeswirtschaftsministerium.de/Redaktion/EN/Publikationen/Energie/national-hydrogen-strategy-update.pdf?__blob=publicationFile&v=2.

Bolt, A., Dincer, I., & Agelin-Chaab, M. (2023). Design of a multigenerational energy system with hydrogen production for clean cement plants. *Journal of Cleaner Production, 405*(1), 1–11.

Calabrese, M., et al. (2024). Hydrogen safety challenges: A comprehensive review on production, storage, transport, utilization, and CFD-based consequence and risk assessment. *Energies, 17*(6), 1–26.

Calix. (2023). *Leilac-2 demonstration plant FEED study published* [Online]. Retrieved July 07, 2025, from https://calix.global/reports-and-white-papers/leilac-2-demonstration-plant-feed-study-published/.

Carbon Market Watch. (2022). *Concrete solutions for decarbonising the EU's cement sector* [Online]. Retrieved July 07, 2025, from https://carbonmarketwatch.org/publications/decarbonising-cement-options-for-reforming-the-eus-emissions-trading-system/#pdf_embed.

Cembureau. (2023). *Activity report 2023* [Online]. Retrieved July 06, 2025, from https://cembureau.eu/media/dnbf4xzc/activity-report-2023-for-web.pdf.

Cemex. (2024). *Cemex kickstarts first-of-a-kind low-carbon hydrogen project using thermal plasma electrolysis in cement production* [Online]. Retrieved July 07, 2025, from https://www.cemex.com/w/cemex-kickstarts-first-of-a-kind-low-carbon-hydrogen-project-using-thermal-plasma-electrolysis-in-cement-production.

CertifHy. (2025). *About us* [Online]. Retrieved July 07, 2025, from https://www.certifhy.eu/.

CSIRO. (2019). *Hydrogen economy roadmap of Korea* [Online]. Retrieved July 07, 2025, from https://docs.wixstatic.com/ugd/45185a_551e67dca75340569e68e37eea18f28e.pdf.

CSTEP. (2024). *Advanced process simulation modelling for hydrogen application in steel and cement* [Online]. Retrieved July 04, 2025, from https://cstep.in/drupal/sites/default/files/2024-12/Advanced%20process%20simulation%20modelling%20for%20hydrogen%20application%20in%20steel%20and%20cement%20–%20A%20technical%20and%20economic%20assessment.pdf.

Energy Transitions Commission. (2021). *Making the hydrogen economy possible: Accelerating clean hydrogen in an electrified economy* [Online]. Retrieved June 30, 2025, from https://www.energy-transitions.org/publications/making-clean-hydrogen-possible/.

Energy Transitions Commission. (2022). *Toward net zero: Decarbonization roadmap for China's cement industry* [Online]. Retrieved July 04, 2025, from https://www.energy-transitions.org/publications/decarbonization-roadmap-for-chinas-cement-industry-2/.

ERCST. (2025). *2025 State of the EU ETS Report* [Online]. Retrieved July 07, 2025, from https://ercst.org/wp-content/uploads/2025/05/20250520-2025-State-of-the-EU-ETS-Report-Final.pdf.

European Commission (2020) A hydrogen strategy for a climate-neutral Europe [Online]. Available from: https://energy.ec.europa.eu/system/files/2020-07/hydrogen_strategy_0.pdf (Accessed: 17 July 2025).

European Commission. (2023). *Commission welcomes completion of key 'Fit for 55' legislation, putting EU on track to exceed 2030 targets* [Online]. Retrieved July 06, 2025, from https://ec.europa.eu/commission/presscorner/detail/en/ip_23_4754.

European Commission. (2025). *Innovation Fund* [Online]. Retrieved July 06, 2025, from https://climate.ec.europa.eu/eu-action/eu-funding-climate-action/innovation-fund_en.

France Hydrogène. (2025). *National hydrogen strategy: Harnessing the hydrogen's full potential in pursuit of France's decarbonisation and reindustrialization* [Online]. Retrieved July 07, 2025, from https://www.france-hydrogene.org/publication/national-hydrogen-strategy-harnessing-the-hydrogen-sectors-full-potential-in-pursuit-of-frances-decarbonization-and-reindustrialization/.

Global Cement. (2024). *Cemex to use hydrogen at Rugby* [Online]. Retrieved July 07, 2025, from https://www.globalcement.com/news/item/18128-cemex-to-use-hydrogen-at-rugby.

Government of Canada. (2020). *Hydrogen strategy for Canada. Seizing the opportunities for hydrogen* [Online]. Retrieved July 07, 2025, from https://natural-resources.canada.ca/sites/nrcan/files/environment/hydrogen/NRCan_Hydrogen-Strategy-Canada-na-en-v3.pdf.

Green Hydrogen Organisation. (2025). *Accelerating the truly low-carbon hydrogen transition in Japan* [Online]. Retrieved July 07, 2025, from https://gh2.org/sites/default/files/2025-04/Copy%20of%20Japanese%20Publication%20%28English%20Version%29.pdf.

Heidelberg Materials. (2024). *Compass and roadmap* [Online]. Retrieved July 07, 2025, from https://www.heidelbergmaterials.com/en/sustainability.

HM Government. (2021). *Industrial decarbonisation strategy* [Online]. Retrieved July 03, 2025, from https://assets.publishing.service.gov.uk/media/6051cd04e90e07527f645f1e/Industrial_Decarbonisation_Strategy_March_2021.pdf.

Holcim. (2020). *Holcim's net-zero journey* [Online]. Retrieved July 07, 2025, from https://www.holcim.com/sites/holcim/files/2024-02/08042022-holcim-climate-report-2021.pdf.

Hydrogen Council. (2024). *Hydrogen Insights 2024* [Online]. Retrieved July 06, 2025, from https://hydrogencouncil.com/wp-content/uploads/2024/09/Hydrogen-Insights-2024.pdf.

HyNet. (2020). *HyNet industrial fuel switching* [Online]. Retrieved July 07, 2025, from https://hynet.co.uk/wp-content/uploads/2020/02/hynet-ifs-report-for-publication.pdf.

IEA. (2023). *Cement* [Online]. Retrieved June 28, 2026, from https://www.iea.org/energy-system/industry/cement.

IEEFA. (2024). *Carbon pricing: Governments increasingly make polluters pay for climate change* [Online]. Retrieved July 06, 2025, from https://ieefa.org/sites/default/files/2024-05/Carbon%20Pricing%20Govts%20Make%20Polluters%20Pay%20for%20Climate%20Change_May%202024.pdf.

IPHE. (2024). *Hydrogen certification 101* [Online]. Retrieved July 07, 2025, from https://www.iphe.net/hydrogen-certification-101-oct-24.

IRENA. (2022). *Green hydrogen for industry: A guide to policymaking* [Online]. Retrieved July 07, 2025, from https://h2.pe/uploads/IRENA_Green_Hydrogen_Industry_2022_-1.pdf.

Jayachandran, M., et al. (2024). Challenges and opportunities in green hydrogen adoption for decarbonizing hard-to-abate industries: A comprehensive review. *IEEE Access, 12*(1), 23363–23388.

Jibran, J. A., & Mahat, C. (2023). Application of green hydrogen for decarbonizaiton of cement manufacturing process: A technical review. *Journal of Physics: Conference Series, 2629*(2023), 1–8.

Kätelhön, A., Meys, R., Deutz, S., & Bardow, A. (2019). Climate change mitigation potential of carbon capture and utilization in the chemical industry. *PNAS, 116*(23), 11187–11194.

Leeson, D., et al. (2017). A techno-economic analysis and systematic review of carbon capture and storage (CCS) applied to the iron and steel, cement, oil refining and pulp and paper industries, as well as other high purity sources. *International Journal of Greenhouse Gas Control, 61*(1), 71–84.

Lehne, J., & Preston, F. (2018). *Making concrete change: Innovation in low-carbon cement and concrete* [Online]. Retrieved July 03, 2025, from https://www.chathamhouse.org/sites/default/files/publications/2018-06-13-making-concrete-change-cement-lehne-preston-final.pdf.

Mohamad, N., et al. (2022). Environmental impact of cement production and solutions: A review. *Materials Today: Proceedings, 48*(4), 741–746.

MPA. (2021). *World first UK hydrogen trials demonstrate pathway to net zero cement* [Online]. Retrieved July 03, 2025, from https://mineralproducts.org/News-CEO-Blog/2021/release31.aspx.

Nhuchhen, D. R., Sit, S. P., & Layzell, D. B. (2022). Decarbonization of cement production in a hydrogen economy. *Applied Energy, 317*(1), 1–19.
Nordic Hydrogen Route. (2025). *About the project* [Online]. Retrieved July 07, 2025, from https://nordichydrogenroute.com/project/.
Okeke, I. J., Thirumaran, K., Nimbalkar, S. U., & Cresko, J. (2024). Role of hydrogen as fuel in decarbonizing US clinker manufacturing for cement production: Costs and CO2 emissions reduction potentials. *Foundations of Computer-Aided Process Design, 1*(1), 1–8.
OMV. (2020). *Lafarge, OMV, VERBUND and Borealis join hands to capture and utilize CO2 on an industrial scale* [Online]. Retrieved July 07, 2025, from https://www.omv.com/en/media/press-releases/2020/200624-lafarge-omv-verbund-and-borealis-join-hands-to-capture-and-utilize-co2-on-an-industrial-scale.
RMI. (2022). *Toward net zero: Decarbonization roadmap for China's cement industry* [Online]. Retrieved July 06, 2025, from https://rmi.org.cn/wp-content/uploads/2022/08/final-RMI-Cement-Report-EN-02012023.pdf.
Royal White Cement. (2024). *Update on hydrogen use at cement plants* [Online]. Retrieved July 04, 2025, from https://www.royalwhitecement.com/07/update-on-hydrogen-use-at-cement-plants-july-2024/.
Sánchez, M., Marinova, N., Silveira, E., & Larrosa, N. (2025). Standards and codes for hydrogen in pipeline infrastructure: Testing, qualification, and integrity assessment. *Journal of Pipelines Science and Engineering, 1*(1), 1–30.
Schneider, M., Romer, M., Tschudin, M., & Bolio, H. (2011). Sustainable cement production—present and future. *Cement and Concrete Research, 41*(7), 642–650.
Scrivener, K. L., John, V. M., & Gartner, E. M. (2018). Eco-friendly cements: Potential economically viable solutions for a low-CO2 cement-based materials industry. *Cement and Concrete Research, 114*(1), 2–26.
US Department of Energy. (2022). *Inflation Reduction Act of 2022* [Online]. Retrieved July 07, 2025, from https://www.energy.gov/lpo/inflation-reduction-act-2022#:~:text=The%20President's%20Inflation%20Reduction%20Act,energy%20manufacturing%2C%20and%20putting%20the.
Williams, F., Yang, A., & Nhuchhen, D. R. (2024). Decarbonisation pathways of the cement production process via hydrogen and oxy-combustion. *Energy Conversion and Management, 300*(1), 1–11.

CHAPTER 12

# Hydrogen for Chemical Industry

## Introduction

Chemical production has traditionally occupied a relatively peripheral position in mainstream policy and public debates on industrial decarbonisation. Yet the chemical industry remains one of the largest industrial sources of greenhouse gas (GHG) emissions globally, responsible for an estimated 5–7% of total anthropogenic $CO_2$ emissions (IEA, 2023). The sector's emissions stem both from the combustion of fossil fuels for process heat and from the inherent chemical reactions involved in the synthesis of key industrial chemicals, many of which are carbon-intensive by design.Overall, the chemical industry encompasses a wide and diverse range of production processes and products—from fertilisers and plastics to solvents, pharmaceuticals, and synthetic fuels. However, a small number of high-volume commodity chemicals account for the majority of its emissions. In particular, ammonia, methanol, ethylene, and other olefins are particularly significant in this regard, both in terms of production volume and carbon footprint. This is so because these chemicals are typically produced using fossil fuel-derived feedstocks and energy, with natural gas and coal dominating in regions such as North America, Europe, China, and parts of the Middle East (ibid. and Material Economics, 2019).

In fact, ammonia production alone accounts for approximately 1.8% of global $CO_2$ emissions (IEA, 2023), making it one of the largest single-emitting processes in the industrial sector. This is primarily due to its



A. Patonia, R. Poudineh, *Clean Hydrogen for Decarbonisation*,
https://doi.org/10.1007/978-3-032-19442-8_12

reliance on hydrogen produced via steam methane reforming (SMR) or coal gasification, processes which release significant quantities of carbon dioxide (Fig. 12.1) (Patonia & Poudineh, 2020). Similarly, methanol and olefins (such as ethylene and propylene) also depend heavily on carbon-intensive feedstocks, with production routes such as coal-to-chemicals in China posing particularly acute challenges for decarbonisation (Saygin & Gielen, 2021; US Department of Energy, 2022).

Within this context, clean hydrogen—produced either via water electrolysis using renewable electricity or via natural gas reforming with carbon capture and storage (CCS)—has emerged as a leading candidate for deep decarbonisation in selected areas of chemical production. Unlike sectors such as cement, where hydrogen's role is largely limited to substituting combustion fuels, in chemicals it has the potential to act as both a

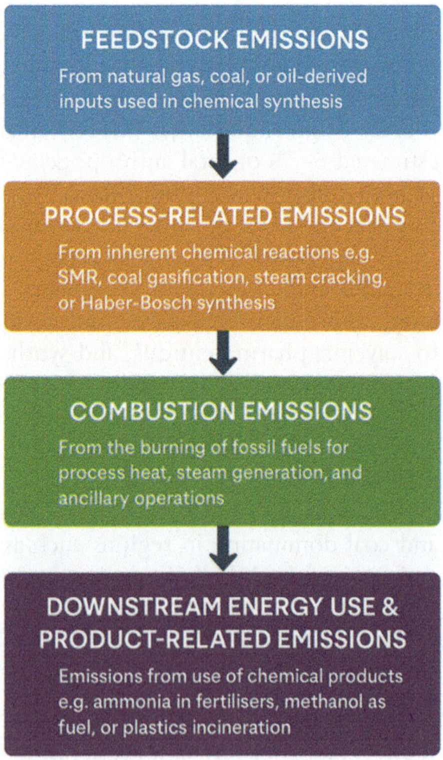


**Fig. 12.1** Principal sources of emissions in chemical production. (Source: Adapted from Material Economics (2019), Saygin and Gielen (2021), and IEA (2023))

zero-carbon energy carrier and a low-carbon feedstock, replacing fossil-derived hydrogen or syngas in key synthesis processes.

In particular, ammonia production presents the most immediate and technically mature opportunity for clean hydrogen deployment. The Haber-Bosch process, which converts hydrogen and nitrogen into ammonia, already consumes around up to 60% of the world's hydrogen supply, the majority of which is currently produced from unabated SMR (Patonia & Poudineh, 2020; Irfan et al., 2024). Substituting this with green or blue hydrogen could, in principle, decarbonise a substantial portion of the industry's emissions footprint without requiring fundamental changes to process chemistry (ibid.). However, a key technical challenge for green ammonia is the need for flexible Haber-Bosch operation to handle intermittent hydrogen supply from variable renewables, which may require significant hydrogen and nitrogen buffer storage or a redesign of the synthesis loop to maintain economic utilisation rates. More importantly, several large-scale projects, including Neom's green ammonia plant in Saudi Arabia and Yara's decarbonisation initiatives in Norway and Australia, are already demonstrating the commercial and technical feasibility of this transition.

Similarly, methanol production, which accounts for over 10% of global hydrogen demand, offers a promising decarbonisation pathway through clean hydrogen substitution (IRENA, 2021). Methanol's versatility as a feedstock for chemicals, plastics, and fuels—and its potential role in emerging markets such as maritime fuel—further strengthens the case for prioritising hydrogen-based production routes in this subsector (Saygin & Gielen, 2021; US Department of Energy, 2022). It is critical to be explicit that for e-methanol to achieve net-zero emissions, the $CO_2$ used in its synthesis must be sourced from biogenic processes or direct air capture (DAC); using carbon dioxide captured from fossil point sources only displaces emissions rather than eliminating them, a distinction often misunderstood in policy and industry circles.

By contrast, decarbonising olefins and other high-volume chemicals remains more technically and economically challenging. While emerging processes such as electrified steam crackers and methanol-to-olefins pathways using green methanol offer some long-term potential, it is important to underline that for olefins, primary decarbonisation levers centre on process electrification and energy efficiency; hydrogen's role is largely supplementary, for example, as a clean fuel in crackers or a feedstock only if a green methanol-to-olefins route is used. These technologies remain at early stages of development, with high capital costs and uncertain operational reliability at commercial scale (Material Economics, 2019; Saygin & Gielen, 2021).

In general, as with other sectors, clean hydrogen faces significant barriers in chemical production, including high production costs, infrastructure limitations, and the availability of low-cost renewable electricity for electrolysis. Nonetheless, unlike cement or even steel, the chemical sector's reliance on hydrogen as an essential feedstock gives it a unique position in the hydrogen economy, where clean hydrogen can directly displace its fossil-based equivalent without necessarily requiring profound changes to existing industrial processes. In this connection, this chapter explores the potential role of clean hydrogen in the decarbonisation of chemical production, with a particular focus on ammonia, methanol, and selected derivatives. It assesses the technical feasibility of hydrogen-based production routes, the economic implications of scaling up green and blue hydrogen supplies for chemical applications, and the likely competitiveness of these pathways relative to other decarbonisation options such as carbon capture and utilisation (CCU) or process electrification.

This chapter proceeds as follows. Section "Hydrogen Applications in the Sector" explores the technological applications of hydrogen as a feedstock and fuel in chemical production, detailing the advantages, disadvantages, and specific infrastructure requirements. Section "Economic Aspects" analyses the economic aspects, including production costs and the pivotal impact of carbon pricing and certification. Section "Policy and Regulatory Landscape" reviews the policy and regulatory landscape shaping hydrogen's adoption in the chemical sector. Section "Case Studies and Pilot Projects" presents case studies of pioneering pilot projects in ammonia and methanol production. Finally, Section "Future Outlook and Conclusions" offers a future outlook and conclusions on hydrogen's transformative potential for the sector's decarbonisation.

## Hydrogen Applications in the Sector

### *Technological Solutions*

In the chemical industry, the decarbonisation potential of clean hydrogen is concentrated in a select number of high-emission production processes that either already use hydrogen as a feedstock or could substitute fossil-based hydrogen with low-carbon alternatives. Globally, the chemical sector is the third-largest industrial emitter after steel and cement (IEA, 2023). Within this sector, ammonia, methanol, and certain refining and petrochemical processes represent the most immediate and technically viable applications for clean hydrogen substitution. In particular, unlike in cement production, where hydrogen's role is largely restricted to fuel switching for thermal processes, the chemical sector already relies on hydrogen as an essential feedstock for key reactions. This makes the transition from fossil-derived, so-called grey hydrogen to 'green' (produced via electrolysis using renewable electricity) or 'blue' hydrogen (from natural gas reforming with CCS) a more direct and scalable decarbonisation pathway for several high-volume chemicals (Hydrogen Council, 2021).

Ammonia production stands out as the single largest industrial consumer of hydrogen globally, which originates from ammonia synthesis via the Haber-Bosch process (IEA, 2023). In this reaction, hydrogen combines with nitrogen under high temperature and pressure to produce ammonia ($NH_3$):

$$\mathrm{N}_2 + 3\mathrm{H}_2 \rightarrow 2NH_3$$

Traditionally, hydrogen for ammonia production is produced from natural gas or coal through steam methane reforming (SMR) or coal gasification, both of which are highly carbon-intensive processes (Patonia & Poudineh, 2020). Clean hydrogen could therefore directly replace fossil-derived hydrogen in existing Haber-Bosch plants, either by retrofitting current facilities or integrating new electrolysis-based hydrogen production units (Bazzanella & Ausfelder, 2017). As noted earlier, successful integration, particularly with variable renewable power, necessitates solutions for flexible ammonia synthesis. Following this logic, several demonstration projects, including the Yara and Ørsted green ammonia project in Norway and ENGIE and Fertiberia's initiative in Spain, are piloting this substitution at industrial scale (Hydrogen Europe, 2024).

Methanol production represents the second key opportunity for clean hydrogen in the chemical sector, since it is conventionally produced via the catalytic hydrogenation of carbon monoxide and carbon dioxide, processes that again rely on hydrogen sourced primarily from fossil fuels:

$$CO_2 + 2\mathrm{H}_2 \rightarrow CH_3OH$$

Here, clean hydrogen could replace grey hydrogen in this synthesis, either within existing methanol plants fitted with carbon capture or via the development of green methanol projects using renewable hydrogen and captured $CO_2$. Notably, green methanol is gaining strategic attention as a zero-carbon shipping fuel, further enhancing the case for clean hydrogen adoption in this segment (IRENA, 2023). Again, the climate benefit of e-methanol is contingent on the $CO_2$ source, with biogenic or DAC $CO_2$ being essential for a net-zero pathway.

In addition, beyond ammonia and methanol, clean hydrogen offers potential for decarbonising refining and petrochemical processes, including hydrocracking, desulphurisation, and the production of synthetic fuels. While these applications are technically feasible, their economic viability is highly sensitive to hydrogen availability, infrastructure integration, and carbon pricing frameworks (IEA, 2023).

Overall, as shown in Table 12.1, the highest emissions reduction potential exists in ammonia and synthetic fuel production, where clean hydrogen could directly replace grey hydrogen with minimal process disruption. Methanol production similarly offers substantial decarbonisation potential, particularly when integrated with $CO_2$ capture technologies or biogenic $CO_2$ sources (IRENA, 2023).

While clean hydrogen applications in refining and petrochemicals are technically proven, their economic competitiveness is currently constrained by high hydrogen production costs and limited infrastructure. Regional industrial cluster developments, for instance in Europe's North Sea hydrogen valleys and the US Gulf Coast, are expected to play a pivotal role in enabling these transitions over the coming decade (IEA, 2024).

In summary, clean hydrogen presents a technically mature and emission-intensive decarbonisation lever for the chemical industry, particularly in ammonia and methanol production. However, scaling these applications will depend on significant cost reductions in green and blue hydrogen production, regulatory incentives, and the coordinated development of industrial hydrogen hubs.

### *Advantages/Disadvantages*

The use of clean hydrogen in the chemical sector offers a combination of strategic opportunities and recognised limitations when compared with other decarbonisation options. Just like in most other cases, from an environmental standpoint, hydrogen offers a critical advantage as a

**Table 12.1** Maturity and emissions reduction potential of clean hydrogen applications in chemical production

| *Technology* | *Process type* | *Main decarbonisation agent* | *Typical emissions reduction potential (%)* | *Technology readiness level (TRL)* | *Notes* |
|---|---|---|---|---|---|
| *Ammonia production* | Feedstock substitution | Green/blue hydrogen | 85–100 | 7–8 | Mature technology; industrial pilots underway in Europe and Asia; flexible Haber-Bosch operation for intermittent $H_2$ is a key R&D area |
| *Methanol production* | Feedstock substitution | Green/blue hydrogen | 60–95 | 6–7 | Emerging projects; strong interest in shipping fuel applications; net-zero carbon requires biogenic/DAC $CO_2$ |
| *Refining (hydrotreating)* | Process hydrogen substitution | Green/blue hydrogen | 20–50 | 6–7 | Feasible; subject to hydrogen infrastructure and carbon pricing |
| *Synthetic fuels* | Power-to-liquid synthesis | Green hydrogen + captured $CO_2$ | 80–100 | 5–6 | High costs; niche aviation and maritime fuel markets developing |

(*continued*)

**Table 12.1** (continued)

| *Technology* | *Process type* | *Main decarbonisation agent* | *Typical emissions reduction potential (%)* | *Technology readiness level (TRL)* | *Notes* |
|---|---|---|---|---|---|
| *Petrochemical processes* | Process hydrogen substitution | Green/blue hydrogen | 10–30 | 5–7 | Dependent on cluster development and integrated hydrogen supply |

Source: Adapted from Bazzanella and Ausfelder (2017), Energy Transitions Commission (2021), IEA (2023), and Hydrogen Europe (2024)

zero-carbon energy vector at the point of use, producing only water vapour upon combustion or via electrochemical conversion in fuel cells (IEA, 2023). This quality makes it particularly suitable for replacing fossil fuels in high-temperature processes or off-grid applications where direct electrification is technically or economically impractical.

A key benefit of hydrogen utilisation lies in its compatibility with existing high-temperature industrial operations, enabling decarbonisation of combustion-related emissions without fundamentally altering core production processes (Energy Transitions Commission, 2021). Moreover, efficient hydrogen combustion eliminates local air pollutants such as sulphur oxides ($SO_x$), particulates, and, when appropriately controlled, can reduce nitrogen oxides ($NO_x$), thereby contributing to improved local air quality and occupational health conditions in industrial sites (ibid. and Bazzanella & Ausfelder, 2017).

However, as in other energy-intensive sectors, the deployment of hydrogen technologies is accompanied by notable technical and economic limitations. In particular, hydrogen's high flame temperature—exceeding 2000°C in air—poses a risk of localised overheating, material degradation, and elevated $NO_x$ emissions unless sophisticated burner systems and advanced combustion controls are employed (DNV, 2023). Furthermore, the relatively low volumetric energy density of hydrogen complicates its storage, compression, and on-site distribution, necessitating capital-intensive retrofitting of storage tanks, pipelines, and burners (Hydrogen Europe, 2025).

As seen from Table 12.2, it should be of no surprise that, economically, the principal barrier remains the current cost differential between clean hydrogen and conventional fossil fuels. Despite significant cost reductions in electrolyser technology and renewable electricity, green hydrogen produced via water electrolysis remains considerably more expensive than incumbent fuels on a delivered energy basis (IEA, 2023). Similarly, blue hydrogen, though cheaper than green, is also quite far from becoming cost competitive in the near future. Therefore, it is estimated that until hydrogen prices fall towards a competitive threshold of approximately USD 2/kg for industrial heat applications (IRENA, 2023), its large-scale adoption will be reliant on carbon pricing frameworks, financial incentives, and industrial decarbonisation grants.

Deployment-wise, scaling up hydrogen applications within the sector faces structural limitations linked to the availability of low-carbon hydrogen, particularly in regions lacking industrial cluster infrastructure or pipeline connectivity (Energy Transitions Commission, 2021). Additionally, the need for extensive retrofitting of existing industrial assets to safely accommodate hydrogen combustion, etc. further complicates near-term

**Table 12.2** Emissions reduction potential, deployment barriers, and commercialisation outlook for low-carbon technologies in the sector

| *Technology* | *Deployment status* | *Key deployment barriers* | *Expected commercialisation timeline* |
|---|---|---|---|
| *Hydrogen fuel substitution* | Pilot and early demonstration | Hydrogen supply costs, infrastructure upgrades, $NO_x$ control | Early 2030s |
| *Biomass/alternative fuels* | Commercially operational | Sustainable feedstock availability, emissions compliance | Already operational |
| *Electrification (where possible)* | Early pilots and feasibility studies | Technology sustainability, electricity infrastructure, grid capacity | Post-2030 |
| *CCUS retrofits* | Demonstration projects | High capture costs, $CO_2$ transport and storage, public acceptance | Mid-late 2020s |

Source: Adapted from Energy Transitions Commission (2021), IRENA (2021), IEA (2023)

uptake. By contrast, as seen in Table 12.2, alternative decarbonisation options—such as electrification where feasible, or switching to sustainable biomass and waste-derived fuels—are in many cases commercially available and operational, albeit constrained by feedstock availability, emissions regulations, and technical performance considerations (IEA, 2023).

In this context, while hydrogen represents a credible medium- to long-term decarbonisation lever, its deployment is unlikely to emerge as a standalone solution in the near term. Instead, hybrid strategies combining incremental fuel switching, process optimisation, CCUS retrofits, and in some cases electrification, will shape the sector's decarbonisation trajectory over the next two decades. Therefore, the future competitiveness of hydrogen will be closely tied to regional hydrogen production costs, the pace of infrastructure roll-out, and policy mechanisms such as carbon pricing and industrial decarbonisation subsidies designed to level the playing field with incumbent fossil fuels.

### *Infrastructure Requirements*

The decarbonisation of the chemical sector—one of the most energy- and emission-intensive branches of heavy industry—will critically depend on the availability and suitability of enabling infrastructure. Traditionally, the chemical industry relies on extensive and highly integrated infrastructure networks for fossil-based feedstocks and fuels, such as natural gas pipelines, ammonia and methanol distribution systems, and high-temperature steam generation units. These systems, optimised over decades, are deeply embedded within industrial clusters and chemical parks designed around the physical, operational, and economic properties of hydrocarbons (Leeson et al., 2017; IEA, 2023).

Introducing clean hydrogen as a low-carbon alternative would require substantial modifications and additions to this infrastructure base. Central to this transformation is the requirement for a dependable, large-scale hydrogen supply, delivered through dedicated pipelines, high-pressure trailers, liquid hydrogen tankers, or onsite electrolysers, depending on regional supply strategies and end-use needs (Energy Transitions Commission, 2021). Additionally, hydrogen's distinct physical properties, notably its low volumetric energy density and high diffusivity, render much of the existing natural gas infrastructure unsuitable without significant retrofitting or repurposing (Jayachandran et al., 2024; Morales-España et al., 2024).

In the chemical sector, infrastructure requirements diverge depending on the intended application of clean hydrogen. For fuel switching in high-temperature processes (e.g., steam crackers, furnaces), infrastructure upgrades would include hydrogen-compatible burners and safety systems to manage its higher flame speed and combustion temperature, alongside dedicated hydrogen storage and distribution systems (IRENA, 2023). Where hydrogen is used as a feedstock—for ammonia, methanol, or olefin production—significant investments in large-scale, uninterrupted hydrogen delivery and storage infrastructure would be necessary to maintain continuous, high-purity supply (IEA, 2023).

Alternative low-carbon technologies for the chemical sector—such as direct electrification, carbon capture and storage (CCS), bio-based feedstocks, and novel chemical processes (like methane pyrolysis or plasma cracking)—each entail different infrastructure demands, with varying degrees of compatibility with existing assets. For instance, CCS-equipped chemical plants require $CO_2$ capture units, pipeline transport networks, and access to storage sites, which in many regions remain underdeveloped (Leeson et al., 2017). Electrification of certain low- and medium-temperature processes would, in turn, necessitate substantial grid reinforcement and the expansion of high-capacity renewable electricity supply, which can be challenging in heavily industrialised areas with limited grid flexibility (Energy Transitions Commission, 2021).

Comparatively, as seen from Table 12.3, bio-based feedstocks can often be integrated into existing process infrastructure with moderate adjustments, though their scalability is constrained by sustainable biomass availability and supply chain limitations (IEA, 2023). Novel processes like methane pyrolysis (producing hydrogen and solid carbon) offer the advantage of generating clean hydrogen without $CO_2$ emissions, but require entirely new reactor designs and carbon handling logistics, with very limited commercial demonstration to date (IRENA, 2023).

In this context, clean hydrogen's infrastructure requirements are particularly capital-intensive and technically demanding, notably due to the need for dedicated hydrogen supply networks, high-capacity onsite storage, and extensive process modifications. Moreover, the scalability of hydrogen-based solutions is heavily dependent on the development of industrial hydrogen hubs, enabling economies of scale in production, storage, and distribution (Energy Transitions Commission, 2021). By contrast, alternatives like CCS retrofits or limited bio-feedstock substitution

**Table 12.3** Infrastructure requirements, scalability, adaptability, and challenges of hydrogen-based low-carbon chemical production technologies

| *Technology* | *Specific infrastructure requirements* | *Current scalability* | *Current adaptability* | *Key challenges* |
|---|---|---|---|---|
| *Hydrogen fuel switching (heat)* | • Dedicated hydrogen supply and storage<br>• Hydrogen-compatible burners<br>• Process safety upgrades | Low | Limited | • High hydrogen costs<br>• Extensive burner and kiln retrofitting |
| *Hydrogen as feedstock* | • High-purity hydrogen supply<br>• Dedicated pipelines or electrolysers<br>• Storage and distribution systems | Low | Low | • Supply intermittency<br>• High production and storage costs |
| *CCS retrofits* | • $CO_2$ capture units<br>• $CO_2$ transport pipelines<br>• Access to geological storage | moderate | moderate | • High capital intensity<br>• Limited proximity to storage sites |
| *Direct electrification* | • Large-scale renewable electricity supply<br>• High-capacity grid connections | Very low | Very low | • Limited readiness for high-temperature processes<br>• Grid constraints |
| *Bio-based feedstocks* | • Sustainable biomass supply chains<br>• Pre-treatment and blending facilities | Low-moderate | moderate | • Feedstock availability<br>• Sustainability and land-use constraints |

(*continued*)

**Table 12.3** (continued)

| *Technology* | *Specific infrastructure requirements* | *Current scalability* | *Current adaptability* | *Key challenges* |
|---|---|---|---|---|
| *Methane pyrolysis* | • New reactor designs<br>• Solid carbon handling and logistics infrastructure | Very low | Very low | • Limited demonstration experience<br>• High operational costs |
| *Plasma/electrification cracking* | • Specialised high-voltage plasma units<br>• High-capacity renewable grid supply | Very low | Very low | • Immature technology<br>• High electricity demand |

Source: Adapted from Bazzanella and Ausfelder (2017), Energy Transitions Commission (2021), IEA (2023), and Hydrogen Europe (2024)

can often leverage portions of existing infrastructure but face other constraints, including $CO_2$ storage proximity and feedstock resource limitations (ibid.).

In summary, while clean hydrogen holds considerable long-term decarbonisation potential for the chemical sector—both as a fuel and feedstock—its infrastructure requirements are extensive and currently represent a major barrier to rapid deployment. At this stage, alternative options such as CCS and bio-based feedstocks seem to offer more immediate, albeit partial, abatement potential with lower infrastructure transformation demands. However, they face their own limitations in terms of scalability, public acceptance, and sustainable resource availability, among other factors. Therefore, as such, the decarbonisation of the chemical industry will likely require a multi-vector strategy, combining gradual hydrogen adoption in industrial clusters with incremental CCS deployment, limited bio-feedstock integration, and targeted electrification of suitable processes, depending on regional infrastructure readiness and resource constraints.

## Economic Aspects

Although the transition to clean hydrogen is increasingly viewed as central to the decarbonisation of the chemical sector, its economic competitiveness will ultimately be defined by several interlinked factors: capital investment requirements, operational expenditures, and the evolving landscape of regulatory incentives.

Overall, investing in green hydrogen infrastructure entails significant upfront costs. Electrolyser capacity development typically ranges from USD 900 to 1500 per kilowatt (kW), translating to approximately USD 200–400 per tonne of annual hydrogen production capacity (IEA, 2023; Hydrogen Council, 2024). In comparison, modifying existing steam methane reforming plants to incorporate carbon capture (blue hydrogen) accumulates costs from USD 100–200 per tonne for SMR upgrades and an additional USD 300–400 per tonne for the carbon capture and storage (CCS) infrastructure required (Belmehdi et al., 2024). In addition, the adaptation of ammonia and methanol plants to accommodate clean hydrogen introduces supplementary investment—often an estimated 15–30%—to cover new compression, purification systems, and upgraded process controls (Material Economics, 2019).

Operational expenditure, in turn, is predominantly shaped by the cost of hydrogen itself. With mid-2024 broad estimates of green hydrogen production at around USD 3.5–6.5 per kilogram and blue hydrogen production at approximately USD 1.5–2.5 per kilogram, grey hydrogen production costs of USD 1–1.5 per kilogram are still hard to match (IEA, 2023; IRENA, 2023). Therefore, since hydrogen feedstock expenses often constitute 50–70% of the operating costs for hydrogen-intensive chemical processes, the importance of cost-competitive supply chains for the chemical sector cannot be underestimated. That is why, when assessed through the levelised cost of production, blue and green chemical routes remain substantially more expensive than conventional pathways.

As seen in Fig. 12.2, the cost of conventional ammonia generally sits between USD 250–400 per tonne, blue ammonia at USD 350–550 per tonne, and green ammonia currently at USD 500–800 per tonne. Methanol production exhibits a similar cost pattern, reflecting the persistent economic challenge clean hydrogen faces (IEA, 2023; Evans et al., 2024). Therefore, the integration of carbon pricing is pivotal for enhancing the competitiveness of cleaner hydrogen. In this context, blue hydrogen becomes economically viable at carbon prices in the range of

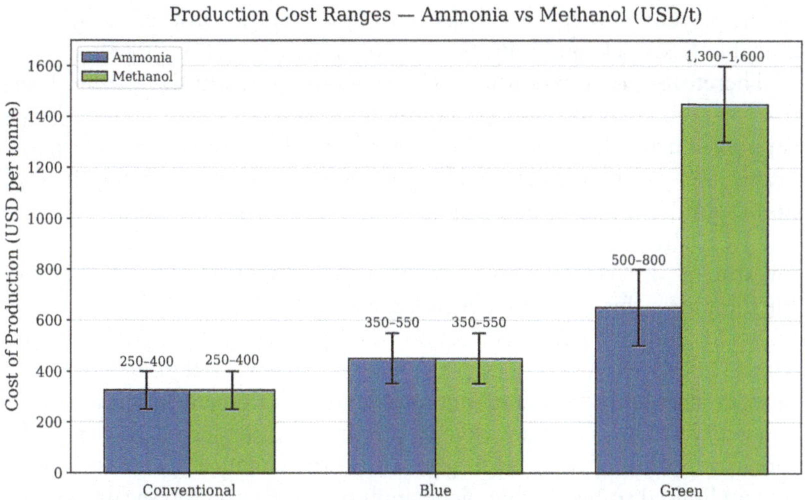


**Fig. 12.2** Typical range of production costs for conventional, blue, and green hydrogen-based chemicals. (Source: Adapted from IEA (2023), Evans et al. (2024), Fasihi and Breyer (2024), and Müller et al. (2024))

USD 50–100 per tonne of $CO_2$, whereas green hydrogen hinges on further reductions in electricity costs or additional public support to bridge its cost disadvantage (IEA, 2023). Regulatory strategies such as the US 45V tax credit and the European Union's hydrogen innovation fund are beginning to close the gap between clean and conventional hydrogen options. Crucially, the bankability of green hydrogen projects for chemicals is increasingly dictated by policy accounting rules, such as the European Union's RFNBO criteria and the US 45V guidance, which mandate hourly matching of renewable electricity and additionality. These rules determine eligibility for subsidies and the resulting carbon intensity, thereby directly impacting project design, costs, and final investment decisions.

Overall, however, despite such advances and various pilot projects around the world, green chemical production remains roughly 50–100% more costly than established processes, underlining the ongoing need for supportive policy. Blue hydrogen, when paired with efficient CCS and moderate carbon prices, approaches cost parity with established grey methods. Alternatives, such as full electrification or biomass-based routes, might present lower capital risks but are currently constrained by scale, available feedstock, and long-term supply reliability (IEA, 2023).

Therefore, the competitiveness of clean hydrogen in the chemical sector will ultimately depend on comprehensive policy action. Regulatory support—in the form of carbon pricing, direct subsidies, infrastructure grants, and green product certification—is necessary to diminish the economic gulf. Emerging demand for low-carbon fertilisers and fuels may also stimulate price premiums of 5–15%, providing further justification for investment in clean hydrogen routes (Hasanbeigi et al., 2024). Furthermore, this demand is increasingly underpinned by buyer requirements for auditable, certified carbon-intensity scores, driving the need for robust Life Cycle Assessment (LCA) and cross-border alignment of certification schemes to facilitate international trade of green chemicals. In the absence of cohesive frameworks and sustained market incentives, the widespread adoption of clean hydrogen within the chemical sector is likely to remain limited to high-value niche applications for the foreseeable future.

## Policy and Regulatory Landscape

In general, policy frameworks at both EU and national levels are increasingly targeting the integration of clean hydrogen into ammonia, methanol, and olefin production. In particular, the European Green Deal and the associated Fit for 55 package provide the foundation for these ambitions, positioning hydrogen as a 'critical enabler' of industrial decarbonisation in hard-to-abate sectors such as chemicals (European Commission, 2020; European Commission, 2023a). The 2020 EU Hydrogen Strategy explicitly identifies fertiliser and chemical production as priority end-uses for renewable hydrogen, setting the groundwork for subsequent regulatory and financial instruments (European Commission, 2020).

Consequently, significant funding from the EU Innovation Fund, among the world's largest low-carbon technology financing mechanisms, has been directed towards chemical-sector projects using hydrogen, such as the flagship 'Kairos@C' initiative (European Commission, 2022; European Commission, 2023b). Furthermore, the Important Projects of Common European Interest (IPCEI) framework has supported the integration of hydrogen into industrial processes, including ammonia and potentially methanol production, as part of broader chemical-sector decarbonisation. Under the 'Hy2Use' wave of the Important Projects of Common European Interest (IPCEI), countries including Germany, the

Netherlands, and Spain have committed substantial funding to large-scale hydrogen deployment focusing on industrial applications. Specifically, Germany has allocated up to EUR 4.6 billion for 23 hydrogen projects to support production, infrastructure, and storage (BMWK, 2023); the Netherlands provided nearly EUR 1 billion in subsidies for new electrolysis capacity and infrastructure development in 2024 (S&P Global, 2024); and Spain has committed around EUR 794 million to seven major renewable hydrogen initiatives under Hy2Use (La Moncloa, 2024).

Germany's National Hydrogen Strategy, revised in 2023, strengthens support for industrial applications by increasing the national electrolyser capacity target to 10 GW by 2030, with specific references to ammonia and methanol production as key decarbonisation priorities (BMWK, 2023). Similarly, France's updated Hydrogen Plan aims to reach 6.5 GW of installed electrolyser capacity and has identified low-carbon hydrogen integration in the petrochemical and fertiliser industries as a national objective (France Hydrogène, 2023). In the Nordics, the Nordic Hydrogen Route and Finland's 'Hydrogen Valley' initiative aim to create cross-border hydrogen corridors to supply major chemical production zones in regions such as Kokkola and Umeå (Nordic Hydrogen Route, 2024).

Outside Europe, the United States' Inflation Reduction Act (IRA) has redefined the global policy landscape by offering tax credits up to USD 3/kg for clean hydrogen production under Section 45V, depending on lifecycle emissions (US Department of Energy, 2022). In chemical applications, project economics and design are now heavily influenced by the detailed 45V rules, particularly the requirements for additionality, deliverability, and hourly matching. Several announced hydrogen hubs under the DOE's Regional Clean Hydrogen Hubs (H2Hubs) programme plan to integrate hydrogen into ammonia and methanol production, notably in the Gulf Coast and Midwest (ibid.). Similarly, Canada's Hydrogen Strategy also prioritises industrial decarbonisation, with Quebec and Alberta supporting hydrogen-based ammonia production for domestic and export markets (Government of Canada, 2020).

Regulatory instruments such as the EU Emissions Trading System (ETS) are playing an increasingly decisive role. Although most chemical products are subject to free allowances under the ETS, these are being gradually phased out under the revised directive, particularly for ammonia production (European Commission, 2025). With carbon prices fluctuating between EUR 60 and EUR 90 per tonne of $CO_2$ in 2023, the economics of clean hydrogen are becoming increasingly sensitive to policy evolution (IEEFA, 2024). In this connection, the Carbon Border Adjustment Mechanism (CBAM), which is expected to apply to ammonia imports from 2026, will further strengthen incentives for European producers to adopt clean hydrogen to maintain competitiveness (European Commission, 2024).

Certification frameworks for hydrogen are also advancing. The CertifHy scheme provides Guarantees of Origin (GoOs) for low-carbon and renewable hydrogen in Europe, enabling producers of chemicals such as ammonia and methanol to credibly demonstrate compliance with emissions standards and renewable energy targets (CertifHy, 2025). This is increasingly driven by buyer demand for verified, low-carbon products, which helps build the business case for green chemicals and necessitates cross-border alignment of certification to enable a global market. In parallel, the Renewable Energy Directive (RED II and RED III) mandates a growing share of renewable fuels of non-biological origin (RFNBOs), including green hydrogen and derived e-fuels, in industrial energy consumption (European Commission, 2025).

Nonetheless, regulatory challenges persist. Permit processes for electrolyser deployment, hydrogen storage, and grid integration are often fragmented and slow, especially in industrial clusters lacking streamlined governance frameworks (Agora Energiewende, 2022). In addition, discrepancies between national safety codes and standards for hydrogen use in chemical production—particularly concerning high-volume storage and blending into synthesis processes—create uncertainties for project developers (Calabrese et al., 2024).

Social acceptance and environmental permitting are emerging as further constraints, particularly for large-scale hydrogen production facilities co-located with chemical plants. Although because of the nascent nature of most clean hydrogen projects, communities have not yet massively raised concerns regarding land use, water consumption, and risks related to hydrogen handling and ammonia synthesis, this is likely to happen as the sector ramps up. Therefore, transparent public consultation and inclusion of hydrogen risks in Environmental Impact Assessments are becoming preconditions for project approval in several EU member states (Sala et al., 2025).

Finally, demand-side policy instruments are starting to emerge to support market creation for hydrogen-derived chemicals. Initiatives such as the European Hydrogen Bank and national clean procurement schemes aim to bridge the cost gap between fossil-based and low-carbon ammonia or methanol. The German H2Global mechanism, for example, offers long-term contracts to importers of green ammonia and methanol, providing price stability and stimulating investment in both domestic and international hydrogen supply chains (H2Global, 2025). At the same time, in general, while hydrogen integration into the chemical sector enjoys strong policy momentum, effective implementation hinges on harmonising regulatory frameworks, addressing permitting and certification barriers, and fostering predictable demand through carbon pricing and public procurement. As the policy landscape matures, ensuring consistency across jurisdictions and value chains will be critical to scaling clean hydrogen deployment in the chemical industry over the next decade.

## Case Studies and Pilot Projects

The use of clean hydrogen in the chemical industry has advanced from theoretical models to practical demonstration projects, particularly within ammonia and methanol production. These sectors represent the most promising early applications, given their established hydrogen demand and centrality in global chemical value chains. However, while several pilot and pre-commercial projects have reached operation or advanced planning stages, scaling remains constrained by high costs, infrastructure gaps, and regulatory uncertainty.

Among the most ambitious and well-developed initiatives is Saudi Arabia's NEOM Green Hydrogen Project, a collaboration between Air Products, ACWA Power, and NEOM. This globally significant project plans to produce up to 600 tonnes of green hydrogen per day through renewable-powered electrolysis, which will subsequently be converted into green ammonia for export, making it the largest facility of its kind worldwide (Air Products, 2023). At the moment, construction is underway following financial close in May 2023, with operations expected to begin by late 2026 and full production ramp-up by 2027 (NGHC, 2025). Notably, Air Products enhanced the project's long-term security by obtaining a 30-year exclusive off-take agreement for all green ammonia, with the price fixed at 2020 levels across the contract duration (Ammonia Energy Association, 2023). The project's design must navigate the challenge of aligning its massive electrolyser load with renewable power generation to meet emerging 'hourly matching' criteria for green hydrogen certification in key export markets like the European Union.

In Europe, Yara International has piloted the integration of green hydrogen into ammonia production at its Herøya plant in Porsgrunn, Norway. The project, supported by the Norwegian government and Enova, involves a 24 MW electrolyser supplied by Nel ASA and was launched in 2024 (Yara, 2024). It is expected to produce approximately 20,000 tonnes of green ammonia annually and is currently the largest project of its kind in Europe. Overall, this initiative confirms the technical and operational viability of displacing fossil-based hydrogen with renewable hydrogen in existing ammonia production, though it also underscores the need for flexible Haber-Bosch operation or significant buffer storage to manage the intermittent supply of green hydrogen, a key operational challenge for such projects.

Similarly, OCI together with Engie, through the HyNetherlands initiative, is developing a 100 MW electrolyser facility to produce renewable hydrogen for ammonia and e-methanol generation in Delfzijl/Eemshaven region in the northern Netherlands (HyNetherlands, 2025). Slated for operational launch in 2025 as a part of the first phase of a wider plan to scale electrolyser capacity to 1.85 GW by the early 2030s, the project is among the largest announced in the continent. For its e-methanol pathway, the project is sourcing biogenic $CO_2$, which is critical for achieving genuine net-zero emissions, as opposed to merely displacing them with fossil-based $CO_2$. While no delays have been announced and the initiative seems to be developing as planned, the project's long-term viability—like many large-scale hydrogen initiatives in Europe—depends heavily on timely access to public funding instruments such as the EU Innovation Fund and the European Hydrogen Bank.

In Germany, BASF inaugurated a 54 MW PEM electrolyser at its Ludwigshafen site in 2025, designed to provide low-carbon hydrogen for chemical synthesis and industrial use (BASF, 2025). The project received substantial public funding under the European Union's Important Projects of Common European Interest (IPCEI) framework. While BASF has welcomed this support, broader industry voices have raised concerns about high electricity costs and the limitations of the current EU State Aid framework, which may hinder the replication of such investments across Europe.

Iberdrola and Fertiberia, in turn, launched a joint initiative in Puertollano, Spain, to produce green hydrogen using a 20 MW electrolyser and local solar PV installed by Iberdrola, with the hydrogen then used by Fertiberia's local ammonia plant (Iberdrola, 2022). While relatively small in scale compared to NEOM, the plant has been operational since 2022, making it Iberdrola's largest green hydrogen facility for industrial use in Europe (ibid.). In addition, in 2023, Iberdrola, together with Foresa, signed a Grant Agreement with the European Climate, Infrastructure and Environment Executive Agency (CINEA) to develop a large-scale green methanol project in Begonte, Galicia (Iberdrola, 2023). Although the project is expected to become operational by 2027, the CINEA grant of EUR 122.9 million represents a fundamental step in its development (ibid.).

Beyond Europe, in Chile, HIF Global's Haru Oni pilot plant in Punta Arenas has been producing e-fuels—including e-methanol—using green hydrogen and biogenic $CO_2$ since December 2022 (HIF, 2023). While primarily aimed at e-fuels, the e-Methanol could also be used as a chemical feedstock, and this HIF's Haru Oni project represents the first operating e-fuels facility in the world. At the same time, the project highlights that $CO_2$ sourcing and logistics—initially relying on biogenic sources, with direct air capture deployment underway—are parallel challenges to hydrogen availability in scaling such systems.

As shown, these examples collectively illustrate several key themes. In particular, the early deployment of clean hydrogen in the chemical sector tends to be most viable where existing hydrogen infrastructure and demand are already in place—especially in ammonia and methanol production. While pilot and demonstration projects such as Haru Oni are demonstrating technical feasibility, efforts to scale up face significant obstacles. These include high operating costs of electrolysis-based hydrogen, exacerbated by volatile electricity prices and limited access to firm renewable power; infrastructure bottlenecks, such as grid congestion, insufficient hydrogen storage, and a lack of dedicated pipeline networks; and regulatory hurdles, including permitting delays and fragmented governance structures—particularly for cross-sector integration and renewable hydrogen certification. Moreover, the bankability of new projects is increasingly contingent on stringent policy accounting rules, such as the European Union's RFNBO and the US 45V tax credit, which mandate additionality and hourly matching of renewable power, directly influencing project design and final investment decisions (FIDs).

In addition, many pilot projects reveal the difficulty of retrofitting legacy chemical plants, which were optimised around fossil hydrogen inputs. In particular, electrolysers introduce different operating dynamics and load profiles, requiring extensive process adaptation. Similarly, as in many other sectors where clean hydrogen could potentially be applied, the economic viability of green ammonia or e-methanol hinges on carbon pricing and demand-side instruments such as quotas, mandates, or green product certification—many of which remain underdeveloped or voluntary. Furthermore, a growing buyer demand for auditable, low-carbon products is driving the need for robust Life Cycle Assessment (LCA) and cross-border alignment of certification schemes like CertifHy to enable a trusted global market for green chemicals. That is why, although pilot projects in Norway, Germany, Spain, the Netherlands, and Chile have demonstrated the technical viability of clean hydrogen integration into ammonia and methanol production, high costs, infrastructure bottlenecks, and policy uncertainty continue to limit commercial scale-up. Therefore, going forward, greater policy coherence, access to low-cost renewable electricity, and market mechanisms that reward low-carbon chemical products will be essential to unlock wider adoption of clean hydrogen across the chemical sector.

## Future Outlook and Conclusions

The chemical industry faces a particularly challenging decarbonisation journey due to its heavy reliance on fossil-based feedstocks, high-temperature heat, and complex, often continuous production processes. In this context, clean hydrogen has emerged as a central pillar in long-term decarbonisation strategies, especially for ammonia, methanol, and selected high-emitting segments of petrochemicals. Compared to sectors such as cement, where hydrogen's role is limited by process chemistry and low fuel substitution potential, the chemical sector offers a broader and more foundational application space for hydrogen, as both a fuel and a feedstock. Given the currently negligible market share of low-emissions hydrogen, the strategic, no-regret priority remains the decarbonisation of existing hydrogen demand within the industry itself. At the same time, as seen in this chapter, full integration of clean hydrogen into the chemical industry is currently facing a number of challenges, overcoming which will most likely take time. Therefore, in the short to medium term, hydrogen adoption in the chemical industry will likely focus on the substitution of grey hydrogen with low-carbon or renewable alternatives in existing processes.

This trajectory is already evident in the development of green and blue ammonia plants, where clean hydrogen is being integrated into conventional Haber-Bosch infrastructure with relatively modest technological disruption. However, for green ammonia, achieving economic utilisation rates will require solving the flexibility challenge through improved hydrogen storage or dynamic synthesis loop operation. Early flagship initiatives such as the NEOM project in Saudi Arabia or Fertiberia's collaboration with Iberdrola in Spain illustrate how hydrogen-based production can scale up where renewable energy is abundant and regulatory support is strong. These projects, unlike many of their counterparts in the cement sector, aim for commercial-scale production within this decade, providing a critical testbed for economic viability and supply chain integration.

Nonetheless, several challenges remain before hydrogen can fully transform chemical production. Key among these the most evident are the high cost of electrolysis-based hydrogen, limited infrastructure for hydrogen transport and storage, and the long asset lifecycles typical in the chemical industry, which inhibit rapid technology turnover. Additionally, co-products and process heat requirements in chemical plants often necessitate tailored integration strategies that go beyond simple fuel switching. For example, high-temperature processes like steam methane reforming and naphtha cracking may need complete redesign or electrification before hydrogen-based alternatives can be adopted at scale. It is important to underline that for olefins, the primary decarbonisation lever is process electrification; hydrogen's role is largely supplementary, for instance as a clean fuel or a potential feedstock only in specific pathways like methanol-to-olefins. These technical complexities add to the investment risk profile and contribute to the sector's cautious approach to radical change.

Looking towards the 2030s and beyond, the outlook for clean hydrogen in chemicals is considerably more optimistic than in many other hard-to-abate sectors such as cement. As the cost of renewable electricity and electrolyser technologies continues to decline, and as carbon pricing and low-carbon product certification gain momentum, the relative competitiveness of hydrogen-derived chemicals is expected to improve. In this respect, crucially, anticipated growth in global ammonia and methanol trade—driven by both traditional uses and emerging energy carriers (e.g., ammonia as a hydrogen vector or methanol as shipping fuel)—could enable first movers to capture market share and drive down costs via scale economies and learning-by-doing.

However, just like in other industries and sectors where clean hydrogen is viewed as a substitute for fossil fuels, the role of policy and regulation will be decisive. Without robust carbon pricing, procurement mandates for low-carbon chemicals, or incentives for infrastructure build-out, clean hydrogen will struggle to outcompete entrenched fossil-based pathways. The evolving regulatory accounting rules, particularly on additionality and hourly matching, will be key in determining the carbon intensity and cost of green hydrogen, thereby shaping its market penetration. In this sense, regional leadership in hydrogen adoption—particularly in the European Union, Japan, and South Korea—may create a bifurcated market in which clean hydrogen-based chemical production grows rapidly in some jurisdictions while remaining marginal elsewhere.

Nevertheless, if everything goes well, by mid-century, clean hydrogen is poised to play a key role in decarbonising large parts of the chemical sector, especially in ammonia, methanol, and potentially olefin production if electrified cracking or hydrogen-based routes become viable at scale. Unlike in the cement sector—where hydrogen's contribution is largely supplementary—hydrogen in the chemical industry may serve as a transformative vector, replacing fossil-based feedstocks altogether and enabling a fundamental shift towards circular and carbon-neutral chemical systems.

In conclusion, hydrogen does not merely represent a fuel in the chemical industry—it is an integral component of core production processes and thus offers a unique opportunity for deep decarbonisation. While its commercial deployment faces high economic and infrastructural barriers today, ongoing pilot projects, supportive policy frameworks, and falling technology costs suggest a decent medium- to long-term potential. The successful transition will depend on overcoming specific technical hurdles like flexible ammonia synthesis, securing the right $CO_2$ sources for e-methanol, and aligning with rigorous certification standards driven by buyer demand. The sector's transformation will be incremental, but potentially profound, with hydrogen forming one of the central pillars of a climate-compatible chemical economy. To unlock this future, however, policymakers must prioritise investment support, regulatory certainty, and international cooperation that will facilitate large-scale deployment and ensure that clean hydrogen can reach the tipping points necessary for widespread adoption in this sector.

## References

Agora Energiewende. (2022). *12 Insights on Hydrogen* [Online]. Retrieved July 18, 2025, from https://www.agora-energiewende.org/fileadmin/Projekte/2021/2021_11_H2_Insights/A-EW_245_H2_Insights_WEB.pdf.

Air Products. (2023). *NEOM green hydrogen complex* [Online]. Retrieved July 18, 2025, from https://www.airproducts.com/energy-transition/neom-green-hydrogen-complex.

Ammonia Energy Association. (2023). *NEOM project reaches financial close, 39 year offtake secured* [Online]. Retrieved July 19, 2025, from https://ammoniaenergy.org/articles/neom-project-reaches-financial-close-30-year-offtake-secured/.

BASF. (2025). *BASF commissions 54-megawatt water electrolyzer* [Online]. Retrieved July 19, 2025, from https://www.basf.com/global/en/media/news-releases/2025/03/p-25-046.

Bazzanella, A. M., & Ausfelder, F. (2017). *Low carbon energy and feedstock for the European chemical industry.* DECHEMA s.V.

Belmehdi, I., et al. (2024). Steam methane reforming (SMR) combined with ship based carbon capture (SBCC) for an efficient blue hydrogen production on board liquefied natural gas (LNG) carriers. *Fluid Dynamics & Materials Processing, 1*(1), 1–15.

BMWK. (2023). *Fortschreibung der Nationalen Wasserstoffstrategie* [Online]. Retrieved July 17, 2025, from https://www.bundeswirtschaftsministerium.de/Redaktion/DE/Publikationen/Energie/fortschreibung-nationale-wasserstoffstrategie.pdf?__blob=publicationFile&v=9.

Calabrese, M., et al. (2024). Hydrogen safety challenges: A comprehensive review on production, storage, transport, utilization, and CFS-based consequence and risk assessment. *Energies, 17*(6), 1–26.

CertifHy. (2025). *About us* [Online]. Retrieved July 18, 2025, from https://www.certifhy.eu/our-mission-and-vision/.

DNV. (2023). *What are the challenges when switching to hydrogen as a fuel or heating processes?* [Online]. Retrieved July 14, 2025, from https://www.industriadefuturo.pt/wp-content/uploads/2023/03/Sander-Gersen-DNV.pdf.

Energy Transitions Commission. (2021). *Making the hydrogen economy possible: Accelerating clean hydrogen in an electrified economy* [Online]. Retrieved July 13, 2025, from https://www.energy-transitions.org/publications/making-clean-hydrogen-possible/.

European Commission. (2020). *A hydrogen strategy for a climate-neutral Europe* [Online]. Retrieved July 17, 2025, from https://energy.ec.europa.eu/system/files/2020-07/hydrogen_strategy_0.pdf.

European Commission. (2022). *Kairos@C: Building strong momentum for massive decarbonisation in the EU through a unique end-to-end CCS project* [Online]. Retrieved July 17, 2025, from https://climate.ec.europa.eu/system/files/2022-07/if_pf_2022_kairos_en.pdf.

European Commission. (2023a). *Fit for 55* [Online]. Retrieved July 17, 2025, from https://www.consilium.europa.eu/en/policies/fit-for-55/.
European Commission. (2023b). *Innovation fund* [Online]. Retrieved July 17, 2025, from https://climate.ec.europa.eu/eu-action/eu-funding-climate-action/innovation-fund_en.
European Commission. (2024). *Carbon border adjustment mechanism* [Online]. Retrieved July 18, 2025, from https://taxation-customs.ec.europa.eu/carbon-border-adjustment-mechanism_en.
European Commission. (2025). *Renewable energy directive* [Online]. Retrieved July 18, 2025, from https://energy.ec.europa.eu/topics/renewable-energy/renewable-energy-directive-targets-and-rules/renewable-energy-directive_en.
Evans, T., Huyett, C., Fallurin, J., & Weiss, T. (2024). *How hydrogen could clean up the chemicals industry* [Online]. Retrieved July 16, 2025, from https://rmi.org/how-hydrogen-could-clean-up-the-chemicals-industry/.
Fasihi, M., & Breyer, C. (2024). Global production potential of green methanol based on variable renewable electricity. *Energy and Environmental Science, 17*(1), 3503–3522.
France Hydrogène. (2023). *National hydrogen strategy. Harnessing the hydrogen sector's full potential in pursuit of France's decarbonisation and reindustrialization* [Online]. Retrieved July 17, 2025, from https://www.france-hydrogene.org/app/uploads/sites/4/2023/10/France-Hydrogene_National-Hydrogen-Strategy_EN.pdf.
Government of Canada. (2020). *Hydrogen strategy for Canada* [Online]. Retrieved July 18, 2025, from https://natural-resources.canada.ca/sites/nrcan/files/environment/hydrogen/NRCan_Hydrogen%20Strategy%20for%20Canada%20Dec%2015%202200%20clean_low_accessible.pdf.
Hasanbeigi, A. (2024) *Green steel economics. Comparing economics of green H2-DRI and traditional steelmaking around the world.* SFOC.
H2Global. (2025). *Who we are* [Online]. Retrieved July 18, 2025, from https://www.h2-global.org/who-we-are.
HIF. (2023). *HIF Haru Oni* [Online]. Retrieved July 19, 2025, from https://hifglobal.com/locations/hif-haru-oni?utm.
Hydrogen Council. (2021). *Hydrogen Insights 2021* [Online]. Retrieved July 13, 2025, from https://hydrogencouncil.com/en/hydrogen-insights-2021/.
Hydrogen Council. (2024). *Hydrogen Insights 2024* [Online]. Retrieved July 16, 2025, from https://hydrogencouncil.com/wp-content/uploads/2024/09/Hydrogen-Insights-2024.pdf.
Hydrogen Europe. (2024). *Clean hydrogen monitor 2024* [Online]. Retrieved July 13, 2025, from https://hydrogeneurope.eu/wp-content/uploads/2024/11/Clean_Hydrogen_Monitor_11-2024_V2_DIGITAL_draft3-1.pdf.

Hydrogen Europe. (2025). *Hydrogen infrastructure: The recipe for a hydrogen grid plan* [Online]. Retrieved July 14, 2025, from https://hydrogeneurope.eu/wp-content/uploads/2024/10/2024.10_HE_Hydrogen-Infrastructure-Report.pdf.

HyNetherlands. (2025). *A gigawatt scale green hydrogen value chain* [Online]. Retrieved July 18, 2025, from https://www.hynetherlands.nl/.

Iberdrola. (2022). *Puertollano green hydrogen plant* [Online]. Retrieved July 19, 2025, from https://www.iberdrola.com/about-us/what-we-do/green-hydrogen/puertollano-green-hydrogen-plant#:~:text=The%20new%20plant%2C%20operational%20since,decarbonisation%20in%20the%20medium%20term.

Iberdrola. (2023). *E-methanol GREEN MEIGA Project* [Online]. Retrieved July 19, 2025, from https://www.iberdrola.com/about-us/what-we-do/green-hydrogen/green-meiga#:~:text=Iberdrola%20is%20a%20pioneer%20in,the%20chemical%20and%20maritime%20industries.

IEA. (2023). *Chemicals* [Online]. Retrieved July 13, 2025, from https://www.iea.org/energy-system/industry/chemicals.

IEA (2024) *Global Hydrogen Review 2024.* International Energy Agency.

IEEFA. (2024). *Carbon pricing in the EU* [Online]. Retrieved July 18, 2025, from https://ieefa.org/sites/default/files/2024-11/Carbon%20Pricing%20Factsheet%20Updated.pdf.

IRENA. (2021). *Innovation outlook. Renewable methanol* [Online]. Retrieved July 13, 2025, from https://www.irena.org/-/media/Files/IRENA/Agency/Publication/2021/Jan/IRENA_Innovation_Renewable_Methanol_2021.pdf.

IRENA (2023) *Global hydrogen trade to meet the 1.5°C climate goal: Technology review and cost outlook for hydrogen carriers and applications.* International Renewable Energy Agency.

Irfan, H. M., et al. (2024). Decarbonization frameworks to industrial-scale ammonia production: Techno-economic and environmental implications. *International Journal of Hydrogen Energy, 78*(1), 580–593.

Jayachandran, M., et al. (2024). Challenges and opportunities in green hydrogen adoption for decarbonizing hard-to-abate industries: A comprehensive review. *IEEE, 12*(1), 23363–23388.

La Moncloa. (2024). *Government of Spain allocates EUR 794 million to renewable hydrogen projects to advance the decarbonisation of industry* [Online]. Retrieved July 17, 2025, from https://www.lamoncloa.gob.es/lang/en/gobierno/councilministers/paginas/2024/20240709-council-press-conference.aspx#:~:text=The%20Third%20Vice%2DPresident%20of,of%20new%20'hydrogen%20valleys'.

Leeson, D., et al. (2017). A techno-economic analysis and systematic review of carbon capture and storage (CCS) applied to the iron and steel, cement, oil refining and pulp and paper industries, as well as other high purity sources. *International Journal of Greenhouse Gas Control, 61*(1), 71–84.

Material Economics. (2019). *Industrial Transformation 2050: Pathways to Net-Zero Emissions from EU Heavy Industry* [Online]. Retrieved July 13, 2025, from https://www.climate-kic.org/wp-content/uploads/2019/04/Material-Economics-Industrial-Transformation-2050.pdf.

Morales-España, G., Hernández-Serna, R., Tejada-Arango, D. A., & Weeda, M. (2024). Impact of large-scale hydrogen electrification and retrofitting of natural gas infrastructure on the European power system. *International Journal of Electrical Power & Energy Systems, 155*(B), 1–17.

Müller, M., Pfeifer, M., Holtz, D., & Müller, K. (2024). Comparison of green ammonia and green hydrogen pathways in terms of energy efficiency. *Fuel, 357*(B), 1–11.

NGHC. (2025). *World's largest green hydrogen plant reaches 80% construction completion across all sites* [Online]. Retrieved July 19, 2025, from https://nghc.com/news/worlds-largest-green-hydrogen-plant-reaches-80-construction-completion-across-all-sites/.

Nordic Hydrogen Route. (2024). *Nordic Hydrogen Route* [Online]. Retrieved July 17, 2025, from https://nordichydrogenroute.com/.

Patonia, A., & Poudineh, R. (2020). *Ammonia as a storage solution for future decarbonized energy systems.* Oxford Institute for Energy Studies.

S&P Global. (2024). *Netherlands to launch Eur1 bil hydrogen production subsidy scheme in Oct* [Online]. Retrieved July 17, 2025, from https://www.spglobal.com/commodity-insights/en/news-research/latest-news/energy-transition/082024-netherlands-to-launch-eur1-bil-hydrogen-production-subsidy-scheme-in-oct.

Sala, R., et al. (2025). Public acceptance of hydrogen technologies and hydrogen refuelling stations in Spain. *International Journal of Hydrogen Energy, 142*(1), 752–763.

Saygin, D., & Gielen, D. (2021). Zero-emission pathway for the global chemical and petrochemical sector. *Energies, 14*(1), 1–28.

US Department of Energy. (2022). *Industrial Decarbonization Roadmap* [Online]. Retrieved July 13, 2025, from https://www.energy.gov/sites/default/files/2022-09/Industrial%20Decarbonization%20Roadmap.pdf.

Yara. (2024). *Yara opens renewable hydrogen plant: 'A major milestone'* [Online]. Retrieved July 18, 2025, from https://www.yara.com/corporate-releases/yara-opens-renewable-hydrogen-plant-a-major-milestone/.

CHAPTER 13

# Hydrogen for High-Heat Processes

## Introduction

High-temperature industrial processes remain among the most persistent challenges in global decarbonisation efforts, owing to their reliance on fossil fuel combustion for sustained high grade-heat and the specific technical and economic barriers of alternative solutions. These processes—including oil refining and petrochemical steam cracking, glass melting, ceramic sintering, non-ferrous metal production, and waste incineration—collectively account for a significant share of industrial greenhouse gas (GHG) emissions (Fig. 13.1). Clean hydrogen, produced via renewable-powered electrolysis ('green') or natural gas reforming with carbon capture and storage (CCS) ('blue'), is viewed as a potentially viable alternative fuel for decarbonising these heat-intensive sectors (Saygin & Gielen, 2021; IEA, 2025). In parallel, green hydrogen is gaining traction as a feedstock substitute, particularly in refining, where its integration through electrolyser deployment can deliver direct emission reductions without fundamentally altering existing process chemistry (ibid.).

In oil refining and petrochemical steam cracking, hydrogen is already widely used as a feedstock for hydrotreating and hydrocracking, with global consumption in refineries estimated at around 40 Mt $H_2$ in 2020 (Mosca et al., 2020; IEA, 2025). Beyond its chemical role, clean hydrogen combustion could displace fossil fuels currently used to provide the high-temperature heat required for processes such as steam



A. Patonia, R. Poudineh, *Clean Hydrogen for Decarbonisation*,
https://doi.org/10.1007/978-3-032-19442-8_13

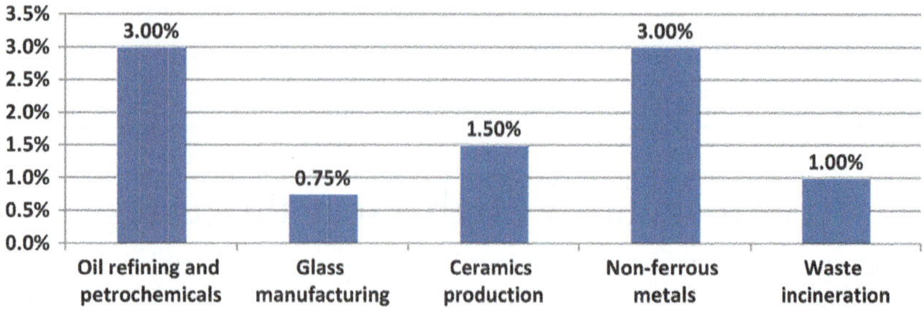


**Fig. 13.1** Estimated share of global CO2 emissions by high-heat industrial sector (%). (Source: Adapted from Saygin and Gielen (2021), European Commission (2022), and IEA (2025))

cracking—where furnaces operate at 800–900 °C to break down hydrocarbons into olefins (ExxonMobil, 2025). Pilot studies suggest that hydrogen-fired furnaces could be integrated into existing refinery and petrochemical operations, requiring modifications to burner design and heat recovery systems; however, cost and operational impacts remain key considerations (ibid.).

Glass manufacturing—responsible for approximately 0.5–1% of global $CO_2$ emissions— relies on melting furnaces operating at 1500–1600 °C (IEA, 2025; Röper et al., 2025). Hydrogen-assisted glass melting trials in Europe have shown that fossil fuel substitution is technically feasible, though altered flame characteristics and increased water vapour in the combustion gases can affect product quality and furnace lifetime (Daurer et al., 2025). Similar opportunities exist in ceramics production, which accounts for 1–2% of global emissions, primarily from the firing of kilns at 1000–1400 °C (Röper et al., 2025; Kandilli et al., 2015). Here, hydrogen combustion could fully replace natural gas, but commercial deployment remains at an early stage (ibid.).

Non-ferrous metal production—including aluminium, copper, and titanium—represents a further 2–4% of industrial $CO_2$ emissions (IEA, 2025). In aluminium remelting and casting, the EU-funded HyInHeat project has successfully demonstrated hydrogen-fuelled furnaces capable of melting scrap without compromising product quality (Speira, 2025). Similarly, hydrogen trials in copper and titanium processing are exploring its potential to replace fossil fuels in high-temperature smelting and refining (Mańkowska & Mazur, 2025; Stopić & Friedrich, 2023).

Waste incineration, which contributes roughly 1% of global emissions, also operates at sustained high temperatures of 850–1100 °C (EEA, 2024). While research in this subsector is limited, modelling suggests hydrogen combustion could be implemented in new-build plants or integrated into hybrid systems with electrified components (Butt et al., 2022).

Collectively, these sectors underscore hydrogen's potential as a clean, high-energy-density fuel for industrial heat, while also highlighting cross-cutting challenges including burner retrofitting, combustion dynamics, materials compatibility, and the high cost of clean hydrogen supply. At the same time, refinery-driven uptake illustrates how regulatory frameworks and compliance incentives can create early markets for green hydrogen, providing a pathway to scale that may accelerate cost reductions and spill over into other hard-to-abate industries (Wood Mackenzie, 2025). This chapter examines the state of play for hydrogen in high-temperature industrial processes, assessing technical readiness, pilot outcomes, cost competitiveness, and the role of supportive policy frameworks in enabling scale-up. It provides a critical comparison with electrification pathways and concludes that hydrogen's role will be complementary and targeted, rather than dominant.

This chapter proceeds as follows. Section "Hydrogen Applications in the Sector" explores the technological applications of hydrogen, detailing the sector-specific challenges and the limited potential for simple retrofits and examining the advantages and disadvantages of key decarbonisation technologies as well as their respective infrastructure requirements. Section "Economic Aspects" analyses the economic aspects, highlighting the profound cost gap. Section "Policy and Regulatory Landscape" reviews the policy landscape. Section "Case Studies and Pilot Projects" presents case studies of pioneering pilot projects. Finally, Section "Future Outlook and Conclusions" offers a future outlook, tempering expectations for hydrogen's scalability and defining its niche role within a diversified decarbonisation portfolio.

## Hydrogen Applications in the Sector

### *Technological Solutions*

In general, the technical feasibility of deploying clean hydrogen in high-heat industries depends on its capacity to provide stable combustion and uniform heat transfer across diverse applications. What differentiates these uses from hydrogen in low-heat sectors is the requirement to sustain continuous operation at extreme temperatures, often with stringent product quality specifications. This necessitates significant, and often fundamental, innovations in burner design, furnace linings, and process integration rather than straightforward retrofits.

In refineries and petrochemical plants, the transition to hydrogen centres on adapting steam crackers and process furnaces. Research shows that hydrogen-enriched flames can be stabilised through specially designed low-$NO_x$ burners, enabling partial or full substitution of conventional fuels (Kim et al., 2025). Hybrid approaches, where hydrogen is blended with natural gas, are currently seen as transitional solutions to mitigate operational risks and allow gradual infrastructure adaptation (Leichter et al., 2024; Schwarz et al., 2024).

Beyond its role as a combustion fuel, hydrogen is also an essential feedstock in hydrodesulphurisation, where it reduces the sulphur content of crude oil and intermediates. Conventionally, this hydrogen is produced from hydrocarbons via steam methane reforming (SMR), but refiners are now installing electrolysers to supply renewable hydrogen instead (Eureka, 2025; Wood Mackenzie, 2025). The underlying desulphurisation process remains unchanged, making this a 'drop-in' substitution with significant decarbonisation benefits (IEA, 2024). Crucially, Europe's oil refiners are emerging as a key demand centre for scaling green hydrogen: under EU regulations they will collectively require around 0.5 million tonnes annually by 2030, potentially replacing almost 30% of $CO_2$-emitting refinery hydrogen (Wood Mackenzie, 2025). More than USD 5 billion in low-carbon hydrogen projects has already reached final investment decision, underlining strong policy alignment and industrial momentum, and some refiners are even prepared to pay above USD 9 per kg—well above modelled project costs—reflecting the compliance value and strategic importance of renewable hydrogen in meeting RED III targets (ibid. and European Commission, 2023).

For glass production, recent demonstration trials highlight the potential for hydrogen to sustain melting conditions without major changes to furnace layout. However, hydrogen flames produce different radiative properties compared with natural gas, which influences heat distribution in the melt (Iplik et al., 2022). Oxy-fuel combustion with hydrogen has therefore gained interest, as it enhances flame luminosity and provides a more consistent heat flux to the glass bath (ibid. and Daurer et al., 2025).

In ceramics, in turn, the challenge is not the attainment of necessary kiln temperatures but the evenness of heat delivery during firing (Kandilli et al., 2015). Hydrogen's combustion characteristics can result in localised hot spots, risking product deformation or quality loss (ibid.). To counter this, experimental kilns have incorporated advanced mixing systems and staged combustion techniques that distribute thermal energy more evenly (ibid. and Norwood, 2023).

Non-ferrous metallurgy illustrates how hydrogen can be applied at different stages of the value chain. In aluminium recycling, hydrogen-fired furnaces have been successfully used for scrap remelting, while copper and titanium processes are still in experimental phases (Senkov & Froes, 1999; Mańkowska & Mazur, 2025). Adjustments in refractory materials are often necessary to withstand increased water vapour in exhaust gases, which can accelerate wear (Speira, 2025, and ibid.).

Finally, in waste management, hydrogen use is less advanced but has been modelled as an auxiliary fuel for maintaining incineration conditions (Butt et al., 2022). By partially replacing fossil-based support fuels, hydrogen could help lower the carbon footprint of plants while ensuring compliance with emission standards. Early studies indicate that its integration may be more feasible in new facilities than in retrofits, due to the need for combustion chamber redesign (ibid.).

A critical and often understated finding from pilot projects is that a full conversion to 100% hydrogen combustion is rarely a simple 'drop-in' burner retrofit. The profound differences in flame speed, radiative heat transfer, and combustion products typically necessitate a deep redesign of the combustion system, including burners, heat recovery systems, controls, and often the refractory lining, amounting to a near-rebuild of the thermal unit (Leichter et al., 2024).

In terms of technology readiness, refinery desulphurisation and hydrogen-enriched furnaces are already at TRL 6–7, with demonstrated industrial feasibility, while applications in ceramics and non-ferrous metallurgy remain closer to TRL 5–6 (Table 13.1). This level of maturity is broadly comparable to, or in some cases lower than, that of advanced electrification technologies like electric arc and plasma furnaces for similar temperature applications. The decarbonisation potential is also sector-specific: substituting grey hydrogen in refineries can virtually eliminate emissions from hydrogen supply, whereas combustion-related uses in glass or ceramics must balance emissions reductions against challenges of flame stability, $NO_x$ formation, and product quality. In any case, taken together,

**Table 13.1** Maturity and emissions reduction potential of clean hydrogen applications in high-heat industrial processes

| *Technology* | *Process type* | *Main decarbonisation agent* | *Typical emissions reduction potential (%)* | *Technology readiness level (TRL)* | *Notes* |
|---|---|---|---|---|---|
| *Oil refining -* | Hydrodesulphurisation | Green hydrogen via electrolysers | ~100 (for hydrogen source) | 6–7 | Drop-in substitution of SMR $H_2$ with renewable $H_2$; compliance with RED III drives willingness to pay > USD 9 per kg |
| | Petrochemical cracking-furnace fuel substitution (steam cracking, process heat) | Green/blue hydrogen combustion | 40–70 | 6–7 | Burner retrofits and heat flux management required; early pilots in Europe and Asia |
| *Glass manufacturing* | Melting furnaces (oxy-fuel and air-fuel combustion) | Hydrogen fuel switching | 60–90 | 6–7 | Demonstration trials show feasibility; challenges include $NO_x$ emissions and flame control |
| *Ceramics production* | Kiln firing and sintering | Hydrogen substitution in kilns | 40–80 | 5–6 | Early pilot projects; uniform heat distribution and product quality control are key issues |

| | | | | | |
|---|---|---|---|---|---|
| *Non-ferrous metal production* | Smelting, refining, and remelting | Hydrogen-fired furnaces | 50–95 | 5–6 | Aluminium remelting demonstrated at industrial scale (HyInHeat); copper/titanium trials at lab–pilot stage |
| *Waste incineration* | Auxiliary fuel for combustion | Hydrogen co-firing | 20–40 | 4–5 | Limited empirical studies; potential for hybridisation with electrification |

Source: Adapted from Senkov and Froes (1999), Kandilli et al. (2015), Mosca et al. (2020), Saygin and Gielen (2021), Butt et al. (2022), Norwood (2023), Stopić and Friedrich (2023), EEA (2024), Leichter et al. (2024), Schwarz et al. (2024), Daurer et al. (2025), ExxonMobil (2025), IEA (2025), Kim et al. (2025), Mańkowska and Mazur (2025), Röper et al. (2025), and Speira (2025)

these technological approaches demonstrate that clean hydrogen can provide the required process temperatures across all these subsectors, but only with tailored engineering solutions. This is so because each industry faces distinct technical hurdles—whether it be flame stability in crackers, glass quality in furnaces, or refractory degradation in metal smelting.

### *Advantages/Disadvantages*

The deployment of clean hydrogen in high-heat industrial processes must be evaluated not in isolation, but through a direct comparison with its primary zero-carbon competitor: direct electrification. This comparative analysis reveals a more nuanced value proposition, where hydrogen's advantages are specific to certain process conditions, and its disadvantages are often more pronounced than those of electrification.

From an environmental standpoint, the primary advantage of clean hydrogen is its capacity to serve as a zero-carbon fuel at the point of use. Combustion produces solely water vapour, eliminating direct $CO_2$ emissions from high-temperature industrial equipment such as furnaces, kilns, and crackers, which is essential for reducing emissions in major industrial sectors (IEA, 2025). This positions hydrogen as a potential solution for processes requiring intense, continuous heat above 1000 °C, particularly where the flame characteristics and reducing atmosphere of combustion are integral to the product quality, or where direct electrification faces technical barriers related to heat transfer uniformity or process chemistry. Furthermore, hydrogen combustion eliminates other harmful pollutants associated with fossil fuels, such as sulphur oxides ($SO_x$) and particulate matter (PM), contributing to improved local air quality around industrial facilities (Bazzanella & Ausfelder, 2017). However, this must be weighed against the challenge of controlling nitrogen oxide ($NO_x$) emissions, a significant local air quality disadvantage not shared by electrification.

A key operational benefit lies in hydrogen's potential for integration with existing industrial infrastructure. In many cases, such as refinery furnaces or glass melting tanks, hydrogen can be deployed through burner retrofits and system modifications rather than requiring a complete overhaul of the production process. In principle, this would allow for a more gradual and potentially cost-effective transition pathway, starting with hydrogen-natural gas blends and moving towards fully hydrogen-fired operations (Franco & Rocca, 2024). Incremental blending with natural gas offers a transitional pathway, allowing for operational experience and incremental emissions reductions. The case of hydrodesulphurisation in refineries exemplifies a near-perfect 'drop-in' advantage, where green hydrogen directly replaces grey hydrogen as a feedstock without any change to the core process chemistry, offering a 100% reduction in emissions from that of hydrogen supply (IEA, 2024) (Table 13.2).

However, the disadvantages of hydrogen are substantial, especially when compared to electrification. The well-to-wheel efficiency of green hydrogen is significantly lower than direct electrification. Accounting for electrolysis losses (~25–35%), compression/liquefaction (~10–15%), and combustion losses, the overall system efficiency for hydrogen can be below 50%, whereas direct electric heating can exceed 90%. This makes hydrogen far more energy- and resource-intensive per unit of useful heat (Energy Transitions Commission, 2021).

**Table 13.2** Emissions reduction potential, deployment barriers, and commercialisation outlook for hydrogen in high-heat processes

| *Technology* | *Deployment status* | *Key deployment barriers* | *Expected commercialisation timeline* |
|---|---|---|---|
| *Hydrogen fuel substitution* | Pilot and early demonstration | Hydrogen supply cost, $NO_x$ control, storage & distribution retrofits | Early 2030s for blends; late 2030s for 100% |
| *Electrification (resistance/ induction/ plasma)* | Commercially mature to early pilots (highly application-dependent) | Grid capacity and connection costs, power cost | Already operational for many applications; post-2035 for niche very high-temp uses |
| *Biomass/syngas* | Commercially operational in some sectors | Sustainable feedstock availability, consistent quality, emissions | Already operational but limited by feedstock |
| *CCUS retrofits* | Demonstration projects | High capture costs, $CO_2$ transport & storage infrastructure | Mid-2030s for widespread deployment |

Source: Adapted from Energy Transitions Commission (2021), Daurer et al. (2025), IEA (2024), IEA (2025), and Kim et al. (2025)

The principal economic barrier is the high cost of clean hydrogen. Green hydrogen is not expected to achieve cost parity with natural gas in most regions before 2030 without substantial policy support (IRENA, 2023). Even with carbon pricing, the levelised cost of heat for green hydrogen is typically two to three times higher than for direct electrification, where the technology is applicable (IEA, 2025).

Furthermore, hydrogen's high flame speed necessitates specially designed burners to prevent flashback, a significant safety concern, while its high adiabatic flame temperature promotes thermal $NO_x$ formation, requiring advanced, expensive combustion technologies for control. The high water vapour content in exhaust gases can also corrode standard refractory linings, necessitating costly upgrades (Kim et al., 2025; Daurer et al., 2025). Finally, hydrogen requires completely new, capital-intensive supply chains for production, storage, and distribution, alongside comprehensive safety protocols, adding complexity and cost not faced by electrification projects.

A comparative analysis of hydrogen versus electrification for high-heat processes reveals a more nuanced landscape than a simple fuel switch. The choice between them depends on a multifaceted evaluation:

- **Technology maturity:** Electrification via resistance heating is mature (TRL 9) for many applications below 1200 °C (e.g., ceramics kilns). Induction heating is also well established (TRL 8–9) in metal processing. Hydrogen combustion for high-heat is generally at TRL 5–7, making it less mature for widespread deployment. Plasma heating, for the most extreme temperatures (>1500 °C), is at a similar or lower TRL than hydrogen.
- **Efficiency and cost:** As noted, electrification's system efficiency is vastly superior, leading to a lower levelised cost of heat (LCOH) where applicable. Hydrogen's OpEx is dominated by fuel cost, while electrification's is dominated by electricity cost and potential grid connection charges. Hydrogen CapEx involves fuel supply infrastructure and combustion system retrofits/rebuilds; electrification CapEx involves new furnace/kiln assets and potentially massive grid upgrades.
- **Product quality and process envelope:** This is a critical differentiator. Electrification provides precise, uniform temperature control and a clean, oxidising atmosphere. Hydrogen combustion, by con-

trast, provides a flame with specific radiative properties and a water vapour-rich, potentially reducing atmosphere. For some processes, like certain types of glass melting or metal heat treatment, the flame atmosphere and heat transfer profile are integral to product quality and cannot be easily replicated by electric heating. In these niches, hydrogen holds a technical advantage.

- **Operational reliability:** Hydrogen's reliability is tied to a complex logistics chain (production, transport, storage), posing risks of supply disruption. Electrification's reliability is tied to grid stability and power availability. For continuous processes like glass melting, a dual-fuel hydrogen/natural gas capability can offer valuable backup, whereas a purely electric furnace is wholly dependent on the grid.
- **Safety:** Hydrogen introduces specific safety risks not present with electrification. These include its wide flammability range, low ignition energy, propensity for leakage due to small molecule size, and risk of flashback in combustion systems. Mitigation requires extensive engineering: hydrogen-specific gas detection systems, enhanced ventilation (often >30 ACH[1]), burners designed to prevent flashback, strict purging procedures before ignition and shutdown, and compliance with stringent ATEX and pressure equipment directives for all components.

In this context, the scalability of hydrogen is intrinsically linked to the parallel development of a low-carbon hydrogen supply chain. It is highly likely that regions without access to abundant low-cost renewables or without planned infrastructure for blue hydrogen production and $CO_2$ transport will face significant hurdles in securing affordable supply (Energy Transitions Commission, 2021). Consequently, while hydrogen holds targeted promise for decarbonising high-heat industries, its near-to-mid-term role is likely to be focused in specific niches: as a feedstock in refineries driven by regulation, in applications where its flame-based characteristics are essential, and in regions with strong policy incentives and cluster infrastructure. For the broader sector, a hybrid approach— combining hydrogen blending, wider adoption of electrification, biomass, and carbon capture—will likely define the decarbonisation pathway for the coming decades, with hydrogen's share growing as costs decline and technical solutions mature.

[1] ACH = Air Changes per Hour.

### *Infrastructure Requirements*

The decarbonisation of high-heat industrial processes represents one of the most formidable challenges in the net-zero transition, owing to their extreme temperature requirements and the deeply embedded nature of fossil fuel infrastructure that supports them. These sectors—including glass, ceramics, metallurgy, and refining—currently rely on extensive and optimised natural gas networks, liquefied petroleum gas (LPG) delivery systems, and fuel oil supply chains that have been developed over decades to ensure reliable, cost-effective energy delivery (Leeson et al., 2017; IEA, 2023). At the moment, this infrastructure is characterised by high-energy-density fuels delivered through pipelines, road tankers, and storage systems designed around the thermodynamic and chemical properties of hydrocarbons (ibid.).

In this context, introducing clean hydrogen as an alternative thermal fuel would necessitate substantial modifications and wholesale additions to this established infrastructure base. The core challenge stems from hydrogen's fundamental physical properties—i.e., its low volumetric energy density (approximately one-third that of natural gas at ambient conditions) and high diffusivity that require completely different approaches to transportation, storage, and combustion system design—making it a less efficient and more costly energy vector compared to electricity for delivering heat (Lipiäinen et al., 2023; Sofian et al., 2024; Mielich et al., 2025). That is why the infrastructure transformation encompasses multiple vectors: production facilities either centralised or distributed; transportation via pipelines, cryogenic tankers, or high-pressure tube trailers; storage systems as compressed gas, cryogenic liquid, or alternative carriers; and finally, site-specific modifications to burners, safety systems, and control infrastructure (Energy Transitions Commission, 2021).

In general, unsurprisingly, infrastructure requirements diverge significantly depending on the specific industrial application and geographical context. For temperature-sensitive processes such as glass melting and ceramic firing, the infrastructure must not only deliver hydrogen but also ensure extremely stable combustion characteristics to maintain product quality. This necessitates advanced burner systems, precise flow control equipment, and potentially oxy-fuel combustion units to manage flame luminosity and heat transfer properties (Daurer et al., 2025; IRENA, 2023). For metallurgical processes involving smelting and refining, in turn, the infrastructure must accommodate both the high thermal demands and the protective atmospheres required in certain applications, often requiring enhanced storage capacity and pressure management systems (Mańkowska & Mazur, 2025). Finally, in refining and petrochemical applications, where hydrogen serves dual roles as feedstock and fuel, the infrastructure must guarantee uninterrupted supply with strict purity specifications, favouring pipeline delivery or large-scale on-site production (IEA, 2024).

Alternative decarbonisation pathways for high-heat industries present substantially different infrastructure demands. Carbon capture, utilisation, and storage (CCUS) applications require $CO_2$ capture units, compression facilities, pipeline networks for transport, and access to suitable geological storage sites—infrastructure that remains largely undeveloped in most industrial regions (Leeson et al., 2017). At the same time, direct electrification through resistance or induction heating would necessitate massive grid reinforcements, high-capacity substations, and potentially dedicated renewable generation assets, creating particular challenges in industrial areas with constrained electricity infrastructure (Energy Transitions Commission, 2021). On the other hand, biomass and biogas systems require completely new supply chains for feedstock collection, processing, storage, and handling, with significant land-use implications and scalability constraints (IEA, 2023).

Comparative analysis reveals that hydrogen's infrastructure requirements are among the most capital-intensive and technically demanding of all decarbonisation options (Table 13.3). While CCUS can potentially leverage portions of existing fuel infrastructure, and electrification avoids fuel delivery systems entirely, hydrogen requires completely new production and distribution networks. Nevertheless, hydrogen potentially offers advantages in terms of technological readiness for high-temperature applications compared to electrification, and greater decarbonisation potential compared to biomass without the land-use implications (IRENA, 2023).

In general, it is currently viewed that the scalability of hydrogen infrastructure is heavily dependent on the development of industrial clusters and hydrogen hubs, where concentrated demand can justify pipeline infrastructure and shared storage facilities. The European Hydrogen Backbone initiative exemplifies this approach, proposing a transnational pipeline network connecting major industrial centres (European Hydrogen Backbone, 2025). For dispersed industrial sites, modular production or liquid organic hydrogen carriers (LOHCs) may offer alternative pathways, though at higher costs and with additional technical complexity (BNEF, 2021). This

**Table 13.3** Infrastructure requirements, scalability, adaptability, and challenges of hydrogen-based low-carbon chemical production technologies

| *Technology* | *Specific infrastructure requirements* | *Current scalability* | *Current adaptability* | *Key challenges* |
|---|---|---|---|---|
| *Hydrogen combustion* | • Dedicated hydrogen production facilities<br>• Pipeline networks or transport infrastructure<br>• High-pressure/ cryogenic storage systems<br>• Modified burners and safety equipment | Low | Limited | • High transport and storage costs<br>• Materials compatibility issues<br>• Need for completely new supply chains |
| *Hydrogen blending* | • Retrofit of existing natural gas infrastructure<br>• Hydrogen production capacity<br>• Blending stations<br>• Modified combustion systems | Moderate | High | • Limited decarbonisation potential<br>• Materials compatibility at high blend ratios<br>• Regulatory barriers |
| *CCUS retrofits* | • CO2 storage units<br>• Compression facilities<br>• Pipeline networks<br>• Geological storage sites | Moderate | Moderate | • High capital intensity<br>• Limited storage proximity<br>• Public acceptance issues |

(*continued*)

**Table 13.3** (continued)

| *Technology* | *Specific infrastructure requirements* | *Current scalability* | *Current adaptability* | *Key challenges* |
|---|---|---|---|---|
| *Direct electrification* | • Grid reinforcement<br>• High-capacity connections<br>• Renewable generation assets<br>• New furnace/ kiln sites | Very low | Very low | • Technological immaturity for high temperatures<br>• Grid capacity constraints<br>• High electricity costs |
| *Biomass/biofuels* | • Sustainable feedstock supply chains<br>• Processing facilities<br>• Storage systems<br>• Modified combustion equipment | Low-moderate | Moderate | • Feedstock availability constraints<br>• Sustainability concerns<br>• Inconsistent quality issues |
| *Ammonia combustion* | • Ammonia production facilities<br>• Storage tanks<br>• Safety systems<br>• Specialised low-$NO_x$ burners | Very low | Low | • High NOx formation<br>• Toxicity concerns<br>• Need for new safety protocols |
| *Plasma heating* | • Specialised high-voltage power supplies<br>• Advanced control systems<br>• Grid upgrades<br>• New reactor designs | Very low | Very low | • Extreme technological immaturity<br>• Very high electricity demand<br>• Limited scale |

Source: Adapted from Energy Transitions Commission (2021), IRENA (2023), IEA (2023), Lipiäinen et al. (2023), Sofian et al. (2024), Daurer et al. (2025), Mańkowska and Mazur (2025), and Mielich et al. (2025)

clustered approach contrasts with the more distributed potential of electrification, which can leverage existing, though often requiring upgrades, grid infrastructure.

In this context, while hydrogen represents a technically viable pathway for decarbonising high-heat processes, its infrastructure requirements present a major barrier to rapid deployment. The extensive new supply chains required for hydrogen, compared to the grid upgrades needed for electrification, suggest that hydrogen's role will be geographically concentrated. Furthermore, contrary to some claims, hydrogen does not hold a clear advantage in technological readiness.

Overall, there is broad agreement that hydrogen's technology readiness level (TRL) for high-heat applications is around 5–7, which is at least on par with—and in many instances lower than—electrification technologies such as resistance, induction, and plasma heating for comparable temperature requirements. Therefore, it is currently viewed that alternative options such as CCUS retrofits may offer more immediate infrastructure compatibility for cluster-based industries, while biomass co-firing may provide a transitional solution for certain applications. However, these alternatives face their own limitations regarding scalability, sustainability, and ultimate decarbonisation potential. Consequently, the decarbonisation of high-heat industries will likely proceed through a hybrid approach, combining initial hydrogen blending, targeted CCUS deployment, energy efficiency improvements, and gradual infrastructure development for pure hydrogen systems in strategic locations. This multi-vector strategy acknowledges the immense infrastructure.

## Economic Aspects

Just like in most other sectors, the economic viability of clean hydrogen as a fuel for high-heat industrial processes is fundamentally challenged by the significant cost differential with incumbent fossil fuels, a disparity driven by high production expenses and substantial capital investment requirements for retrofitting combustion systems. Unlike its role as a chemical feedstock where purity and compliance drive value, its use for thermal energy is primarily evaluated on a strict energy-equivalent cost basis, making competitiveness exceptionally difficult to achieve without robust policy mechanisms (Hydrogen Council, 2022; Sokil et al., 2025).

In general, for industrial operators, the capital expenditure (CapEx) encompasses two primary categories: the investment in hydrogen supply infrastructure and the cost of adapting thermal process units. In this context, retrofitting a natural gas-fired furnace or kiln for 100% hydrogen operation requires substantial modifications, with estimates for burner replacement, safety systems, flame monitoring, and control upgrades ranging from USD 200,000 to over USD 1 million per unit, depending on size and temperature requirements (Leichter et al., 2024; Kim et al., 2025). For a large glass melting tank or aluminium melting furnace, total retrofit costs can exceed USD 5 million, not including the necessary investments in on-site storage, vaporisation (for liquid hydrogen), and distribution piping, which can add a further USD 1–3 million (Daurer et al., 2025; Speira, 2025). It is therefore unsurprising that these figures represent a significant financial barrier, particularly for industries like ceramics and glass with high asset intensity and thin profit margins.

The dominant factor in operational expenditure (OpEx), however, is the fuel cost itself. As of mid-2024, the delivered cost of green hydrogen to an industrial site in Europe typically ranges from USD 6–10 per kilogram, while blue hydrogen would cost approximately USD 3–5 per kilogram (IEA, 2024). On an energy-equivalent basis (based on lower heating value), this equates to USD 40–67 per megawatt-hour (MWh) for green hydrogen and USD 20–33/MWh for blue hydrogen. This compares starkly with wholesale natural gas prices, which have historically fluctuated between USD 10–25/MWh in Europe, though subject to geopolitical volatility (IEA, 2023). Consequently, even with a 100% efficient burner, hydrogen's energy cost premium is currently between 200–600%, which renders it economically unfeasible for bulk heat without intervention. When compared to electrification, this cost disadvantage is exacerbated by hydrogen's lower system efficiency, meaning more primary renewable energy is required to deliver the same amount of process heat.

As seen in Fig. 13.2, the cost gap is profound. The levelised cost of heat (LCOH) for green hydrogen is currently several times higher than that of natural gas on an energy-equivalent basis. This economic reality severely constrains deployment to regions with outright bans on fossil fuel combustion or companies with binding net-zero commitments willing to absorb the cost (Wood Mackenzie, 2025).

At the moment, the pivotal lever for bridging this gap is carbon pricing. Analysis indicates that blue hydrogen could approach cost-competitiveness with conventional natural gas-fired heat at carbon prices in the range of USD 80–120 per tonne of $CO_2$, accounting for the higher efficiency of modern hydrogen burners (IEA, 2024). It should be of no surprise that

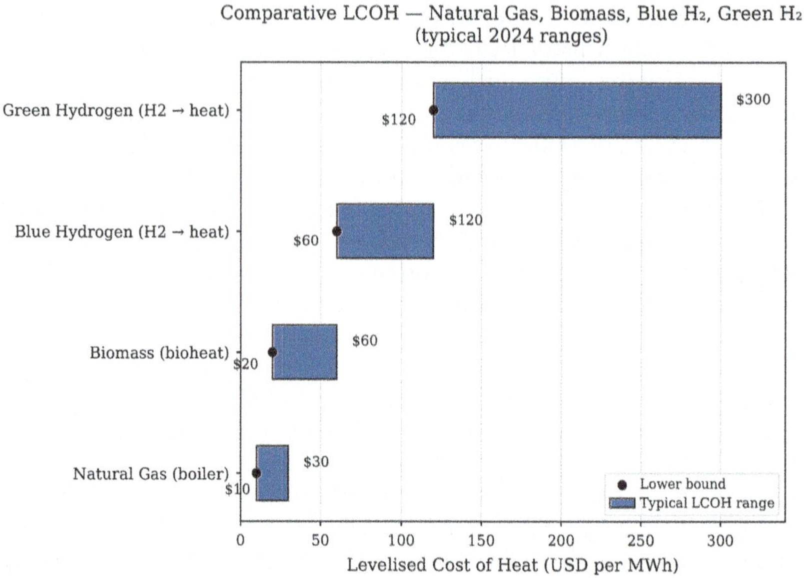


**Fig. 13.2** Comparative levelised cost of heat for key industrial high-temperature applications. (Source: Adapted from IEA (2024), BNEF (2021), and IRENA (2023))

for green hydrogen, in turn, the required carbon price to break even is substantially higher, often exceeding USD 200/tonne $CO_2$ at current technology costs, underscoring its reliance on simultaneous and dramatic reductions in renewable electricity and electrolyser capital costs (IRENA, 2023).

Beyond carbon pricing, sector-specific policy mechanisms are emerging. Contracts for Difference (CfDs), which guarantee a fixed price for clean hydrogen, are being piloted to de-risk investment in supply projects. The European Hydrogen Bank's first auction round cleared at subsidies between USD 3.0–3.5 per kilogram of hydrogen, effectively bridging a significant portion of the operational cost gap for early projects (European Commission, 2024b). Furthermore, mandates such as the United Kingdom's planned Hydrogen Levy on gas bills aim to create a dedicated revenue stream to subsidise hydrogen production, though such models risk increasing overall energy costs for industrial consumers (HM Government, 2023).

On the other hand, when compared to alternative decarbonisation pathways, hydrogen's economics still remain challenging. Electrification, where technically feasible, typically presents a significantly lower levelised cost of heat, driven by higher efficiency and the avoidance of fuel production costs, though it is hampered by grid connection costs and capacity limitations (Energy Transitions Commission, 2021). As mentioned, biomass co-firing can also offer a lower-cost transitional solution but is constrained by sustainable feedstock availability and consistent quality (IEA, 2023). Finally, CCS retrofits for existing fossil-fuel plants, while also capital-intensive, can, in principle, often provide a lower cost of abatement in the near-term for cluster-based industries, though they lock in fossil fuel dependency and face long-term storage liabilities (Global CCS Institute, 2025).

In summary, the current economic case for clean hydrogen in high-heat processes is weak without substantial and sustained policy support. Its adoption is not currently driven by market economics but by regulatory compliance, corporate strategy, and strategic government investment in early-stage technology learning. In these circumstances, the pathway to competitiveness hinges on a triad of factors: a significant decline in clean hydrogen production costs, the development of large-scale infrastructure to reduce delivery costs, and the continued strengthening of carbon pricing and sector-specific subsidies. Until this triad converges, hydrogen's role is highly likely to be limited to strategic pilots, hybrid fuel-blending applications, and niche deployments in regions with the most ambitious decarbonisation policies.

## Policy and Regulatory Landscape

The policy framework for integrating clean hydrogen into high-heat industrial processes has evolved distinctly from its application in chemical feedstocks, focusing specifically on overcoming the unique economic and technical barriers to thermal fuel substitution. Unlike the chemical sector where hydrogen can be a drop-in feedstock, its use as a combustion fuel requires a more complex regulatory approach addressing safety standards, infrastructure development, and targeted financial incentives for high-temperature applications (IRENA, 2023; HySkills, 2024).

The European Union's Industrial Carbon Management Strategy (2024) specifically identifies high-heat industries—glass, ceramics, and non-ferrous metals—as priority sectors for hydrogen-based decarbonisation, recognising the limited alternatives for achieving temperatures above 1000 °C (European Commission, 2024c). This builds upon the Net-Zero Industry Act (NZIA), which includes hydrogen technologies for industrial heat among its strategic net-zero technologies, granting them access to streamlined permitting procedures and enhanced funding opportunities (European Commission, 2024a). The Revised Energy Taxation Directive (2023) further supports this transition by proposing minimum tax rates for hydrogen used as an energy carrier, potentially improving its competitiveness against taxed fossil fuels in industrial heating (European Parliament, 2025).

Nationally, policy approaches reflect specific industrial structures. For instance, Germany's Carbon Contracts for Difference (CCfD) scheme, launched in 2024, specifically includes hydrogen-based process heat in its first auction round, offering industrial operators long-term price security for the green premium associated with hydrogen combustion (Table 13.4) (BMWK, 2023). The Netherlands' SDE++ subsidy scheme, in turn, has been expanded to include hydrogen-fired industrial boilers and furnaces, with a specific budget allocation of EUR 1.2 billion for 2024–2025

**Table 13.4** Key policy instruments supporting hydrogen in high-temperature industries

| *Policy instrument* | *Jurisdiction* | *Sector focus* | *Mechanism* | *Impact* |
|---|---|---|---|---|
| *Carbon Contracts for Difference (CCfD)* | Germany | Glass, metals | Covers cost difference between hydrogen and natural gas | Provides investment certainty for fuel switching |
| *SDE++ subsidy scheme* | Netherlands | All high-heat | Covers operational cost gap for 15 years | Enables commercial operation of H2-fired plants |
| *Hydrogen valleys programme* | Italy | Ceramics, glass | Funds integrated production-distribution-end-use | Creates cluster-based demand centres |
| *Industrial Fuel Switching Fund* | UK | Foundries, glass | Capital grants for burner retrofits and storage | Reduces upfront CapEx barrier |
| *Green public procurement* | France, Sweden | Construction materials | Premium for low-carbon glass, ceramics | Creates market pull for H2-derived products |

Source: Adapted from BMWK (2023), DESNZ (2023), Italy's Council of Ministers (2023), Regeringskansliet (2023), BMWK (2024), Government of France (2024), and Netherlands Enterprise Agency (2024)

targeting high-temperature applications (Netherlands Enterprise Agency, 2024). At the same time, Italy's National Hydrogen Strategy prioritises the decarbonisation of its glass and ceramic industrial districts through dedicated hydrogen valleys that will supply renewable hydrogen to industrial clusters (Ministero dell'Ambiente, 2024).

When it comes to the United States, its Inflation Reduction Act (IRA) has created significant transatlantic competitive pressure through its production tax credit (PTC) under Section 45V, which offers up to USD 3 per kg for clean hydrogen regardless of end-use (US Department of the Treasury, 2023). This has prompted European responses, including the European Hydrogen Bank's first auction that cleared at EUR 0.37–0.48 per kg of subsidy, though primarily for chemical applications rather than industrial heat (European Commission, 2024b). The second auction round, completed in February 2025 under the Innovation Fund's IF24 auction, awarded a total of approximately EUR 992 million to 15 renewable hydrogen projects across five countries, offering fixed premiums between EUR 0.20 and 0.60 per kg for general projects and EUR 0.45 to 1.88 per kg for maritime-focused ones (European Commission, 2025c; Frontier Economics, 2025). At the same time, while the scope now covers sectors such as transport, chemicals, methanol, and ammonia, dedicated allowances or pricing for high-temperature industrial heat applications have not been included to date (ibid.).

Regulatory barriers remain significant, particularly regarding safety standards and permitting. The absence of harmonised EU-wide standards for hydrogen storage and distribution in industrial settings creates uncertainty for operators. While the Pressure Equipment Directive (PED) has been updated to include hydrogen service, national implementation varies considerably, particularly for high-volume storage requirements in glass and metal industries (DNV, 2024). Permitting processes for electrolysers co-located with industrial facilities face delays due to unclear classification under environmental impact assessment directives, with some member states treating them as chemical plants and others as energy production facilities (Agora Industrie, 2024).

The EU Emissions Trading System (ETS) phase-out of free allowances presents both a challenge and opportunity. While high-heat industries are expected to face increased carbon costs from 2026 onward, making hydrogen more competitive, the precise timeline varies by sector. In particular, it is assumed that the glass industry will retain until 2030, while ceramics manufacturing faces full phase-out by 2027, creating uneven incentives for hydrogen adoption (European Commission, 2025b). The Carbon Border

Adjustment Mechanism (CBAM) initially covers cement and iron/steel but is expected to include glass and ceramics in its second phase, potentially creating additional drivers for hydrogen adoption in export-oriented industries (European Commission, 2025a).

Certification remains particularly challenging for thermal applications. While the CertifHy scheme provides Guarantees of Origin (GOs) for hydrogen, current frameworks do not adequately account for the emissions reduction value when hydrogen is used for high-temperature heat, as opposed to chemical feedstock use (CertifHy, 2024). The proposed Hydrogen and Gas Market Decree aims to address this by creating a separate certification system for hydrogen used in industrial combustion, but implementation is not expected before 2026 (European Hydrogen Observatory, 2025).

When it comes to social acceptance issues, for the use of clean hydrogen for high-heat processes, they are emerging differently than for chemical applications. In particular, communities near glass and ceramic plants have raised concerns about increased $NO_x$ emissions from hydrogen combustion and water usage for electrolysis, particularly in water-stressed regions like Spain and Italy (Son et al., 2023; Maketo & Ashworth, 2025). Environmental impact assessments for hydrogen projects increasingly need to address these specific concerns, with several projects in the Mediterranean region facing delays due to water resource objections (Albatayneh et al., 2025).

Overall, while the policy landscape for clean hydrogen in high-heat industries is advancing rapidly, it remains fragmented and insufficient to drive widespread adoption. The effectiveness of current measures hinges on addressing sector-specific barriers through harmonised standards, targeted financial instruments that recognise the higher cost of thermal fuel switching, and the development of certification systems that properly value decarbonised industrial heat. Therefore, as the regulatory framework matures, coherence between carbon pricing, infrastructure development, and end-use applications will be critical to realising hydrogen's potential in these hard-to-abate sectors.

Given the strategic complementarity between hydrogen and electrification, future policy must become more technology-neutral, focusing on carbon abatement costs rather than picking winners. This would create a fairer competitive landscape, allowing the most efficient solution—often electrification—to be deployed where feasible, while reserving support for hydrogen for the specific, hard-to-abate applications where it holds a technical advantage.

## Case Studies and Pilot Projects

To date, the deployment of clean hydrogen in high-heat industrial applications has progressed beyond theoretical modelling. At present, numerous pilot and demonstration projects are under way across key sectors. While most remain in the research and development phase, these initiatives provide critical insights into the technical feasibility, operational challenges, and economic realities of hydrogen integration, particularly in glass manufacturing, ceramics production, non-ferrous metals, and refinery operations.

Perhaps the most advanced deployment of clean hydrogen in high-heat applications occurs in oil refining, where, as mentioned, hydrogen could serve dual roles as feedstock and fuel. Currently running a 10 MW PEM electrolyser at the Refhyne I project, Shell plans to deploy Europe's largest PEM electrolyser with a 100 MW capacity, expected to be operational in 2027 (Reuters, 2024; Refhyne, 2025). While primarily supplying green hydrogen for hydrodesulphurisation processes, the project includes plans to demonstrate hydrogen combustion in refinery furnaces (ibid.). A critical lesson from these projects is the confirmation that deep system redesign, not simple retrofits, is required for full hydrogen conversion. Although Refhyne I has proven successful, the installation of a much larger electrolyser required substantial grid connection upgrades and integration with existing hydrogen pipeline networks, highlighting the infrastructure challenges of large-scale deployment (NS Energy, 2025).

Similarly, BP's Castellón refinery in Spain has implemented a 25 MW electrolyser facility that supplies green hydrogen for feedstock and process heat applications (BP, 2024). The project that is currently under construction will include hydrogen co-firing in fluid catalytic cracking units and reformer furnaces, demonstrating the technical feasibility of partial hydrogen substitution in complex refining processes (ibid. and Plug, 2024). The facility is expected to operate with a hybrid power supply combining grid electricity and renewable generation from photovoltaic and wind sources under a power purchase agreement with Iberdrola (ibid.).

In the glass sector, the European Union's H2GLASS project represents one of the most comprehensive demonstrations of hydrogen combustion for industrial glass melting. Launched in 2023, the project brings together

23 partners and features multiple industrial demonstrators across Europe, including key players like Steklarna Hrastnik in Slovenia and Owens Corning, aiming to develop and validate a technology stack enabling 100% hydrogen combustion in glass furnaces, while ensuring product quality and safety (H2Glass, 2025). The project addresses the significant challenges of retrofitting for hydrogen, including nitrogen oxide emissions and the distinct flame characteristics, deploying specially designed low-NOx burners and advanced heat recovery systems adapted to hydrogen's radiative properties (ibid.). With funding exceeding EUR 23 million from Horizon Europe, operational tests have reached hydrogen blends above 60%, reducing $CO_2$ emissions by more than 30% relative to traditional natural gas operations, while aiming for full decarbonisation by 2050 and acting as a pilot for multiple European glass producers (A.SPIRE, 2025). At the same time, as mentioned, it is yet to achieve operational scale with 100% clean hydrogen.

Similarly, Pilkington Glass in the United Kingdom is currently implementing a hydrogen demonstration project at its Greengate Works site in St Helens in collaboration with Progressive Energy and HyNet (Grenian Hydrogen, 2024). The project is expected to involve using green hydrogen produced onsite through electrolysis powered by renewable electricity to reduce reliance on fossil gas in float glass production (Glass Magazine, 2024). The existing flat glass furnace has been adapted to operate with a hydrogen blend, with plans to scale up to 100% hydrogen operation by around 2027, dependent on hydrogen supply infrastructure development through the HyNet cluster (Pilkington UK, 2025). This transition aims to reduce carbon emissions from the site by an estimated 15,000 tonnes annually, supporting Pilkington's sustainability targets without the need for fundamental furnace redesign (ibid.).

The ceramics industry, in turn, has made significant progress with hydrogen innovations through projects such as the ORANGE.BAT initiative based in Castellón, Spain, a major ceramics production hub (Renewable H2, 2021). This project, expected to be operational by 2028, is led by the ceramics industry consortium along with research partners including the Instituto Tecnológico de la Energía and aims to replace fossil natural gas with renewable hydrogen in combustion processes at industrial ceramic facilities (Smart Energy, 2025). The ORANGE.BAT project focuses on integrating hydrogen combustion with circular economy principles, utilising oxygen by-products and recovering heat for energy efficiency (ibid.). Among the technical challenges addressed are combustion control and heat management to achieve uniform temperature distributions critical for product quality in kilns operating around 1200 °C (ibid.). Although the project has provided essential demonstration data and shaped sector decarbonisation roadmaps, full commercial adoption still hinges on hydrogen availability and cost competitiveness.

In the aluminium industry, the EU-funded HyInHeat project is exploring the use of hydrogen as a clean fuel for melting aluminium scrap. As part of this initiative, Speira retrofitted a 1.5-tonne laboratory-scale furnace at its R&D centre in Bonn to operate on hydrogen, achieving promising results—initial tests showed no deterioration in melt quality (Speira, 2025). The process now uses an oxyfuel configuration (hydrogen burned with pure oxygen) to enhance efficiency and reduce emissions (Global Recycling, 2025). While this represents an important proof of concept in decarbonising aluminium melting, the tests remain at the R&D stage and, as of mid-2025, there is no evidence yet of scaling to other Speira facilities or commercial deployment (ibid.). Meanwhile, Speira is also investing in $H_2$-ready recycling furnace infrastructure at its Rheinwerk site, with new furnaces expected to begin production in early 2026 (Speira, 2025).

Overall, taken together, these initiatives underscore three overarching lessons. First, while the technical feasibility of integrating hydrogen into high-heat applications has been demonstrated across sectors such as refining, glass, ceramics, and aluminium, the underlying economics remain challenging without targeted policy support. In particular, current estimates suggest LCOH is still significantly higher than natural gas on an energy-equivalent basis. Second, the trials reveal that infrastructure requirements—particularly concerning large-scale electrolysers, grid connections, hydrogen storage, and distribution networks—are considerably more complex than initially anticipated, often necessitating major system upgrades before deployment. Finally, the projects demonstrate that full conversion requires significant furnace redesign to manage hydrogen's unique combustion properties, contradicting the notion of straightforward retrofits. Collectively, these findings suggest that while hydrogen is technically capable of decarbonising high-heat industrial processes, progress towards full commercialisation will depend on accelerated infrastructure investment, supportive regulatory frameworks, and sustained cost-reduction efforts.

## Future Outlook and Conclusions

The decarbonisation of high-heat industrial processes requires a pragmatic and technology-agnostic strategy. This chapter demonstrates that clean hydrogen is a technically viable alternative fuel for these sectors, but the evidence firmly positions it as a complementary solution within a broader portfolio, not a universally scalable one. Its role is most justified in specific niches where its flame-based characteristics are essential for product quality or where extreme temperatures and location-specific constraints make electrification impractical.

The near-term trajectory for hydrogen adoption will be limited and targeted. The case studies reviewed confirm that the path to 100% hydrogen combustion involves significant capital expenditure for system redesign, not simple retrofits. The economic case remains the primary obstacle; without very high carbon prices or substantial subsidies, green hydrogen cannot compete with natural gas or electrification for bulk heat. Therefore, progress will be confined to strategic pilots, regulatory-driven feedstock substitution in refineries, and low-level hydrogen blending in natural gas streams.

The medium-term outlook (2030–2040) hinges on reducing the cost of clean hydrogen and developing infrastructure, but a critical success factor will be the strategic identification of applications where hydrogen holds a definitive advantage over electrification. These are likely to be processes that require specific flame chemistry or reducing atmospheres that are difficult to replicate with electricity, those needing rapid cycling or high turndown ratios where the operational flexibility of fuel combustion is beneficial, and applications involving very high-temperature heat (>1500 °C) in geographic locations with limited grid capacity for the powerful electrical connections required by alternatives like plasma arcs.

Several formidable barriers persist. Beyond cost, the operational challenges of $NO_x$ control, refractory degradation, and complex safety management are non-trivial. The development of a dedicated hydrogen infrastructure remains a monumental task. Furthermore, the regulatory landscape must evolve to create a level playing field that rewards carbon abatement efficiency, thereby not artificially disadvantaging the often more efficient electrification route.

Looking towards 2050, a diversified, hybrid decarbonisation portfolio is inevitable. Electrification will likely form the backbone for a majority of applications where it can meet technical requirements, due to its superior efficiency and falling renewable electricity costs. Hydrogen combustion will play a targeted, yet critical, role in completing the puzzle for the hardest-to-electrify processes. Carbon capture and biomass will provide additional tools for specific contexts.

In conclusion, clean hydrogen holds targeted promise for decarbonising the most stubborn segments of industrial heat. Its potential is greatest in new-built plants designed for hydrogen from the outset and in specific process steps where its properties are uniquely beneficial. The narrative of hydrogen as a general-purpose, scalable solution for high-temperature heat is not supported by the evidence; it is a specialised tool for a specific set of problems. The pilot projects of today are laying the essential groundwork for this targeted deployment, but the transition will be a marathon, not a sprint—a necessary and challenging evolution for achieving a net-zero industrial base, best undertaken alongside a parallel and accelerated rollout of industrial electrification.

## References


A.SPIRE. (2025). *The H2GLASS Project: Decarbonising our future* [Online]. Retrieved August 31, 2025, from https://www.aspire2050.eu/success-stories/story/h2glass-project-decarbonising-our-future.

Agora Industrie. (2024). *Low-carbon hydrogen in the EU* [Online]. Retrieved August 30, 2025, from https://www.agora-energiewende.org/fileadmin/Projekte/2024/2024-11_EU_Low_Carbon_H2/A-EW_334_Low_Carbon_H2_WEB.pdf.

Albatayneh, A., et al. (2025). Water-energy nexus dilemma for hydrogen production in water-scarce regions. *Energy Nexus, 19*(1), 1–12.

Bazzanella, A., & Ausfelder, F. (2017). *Low carbon energy and feedstock for the European chemical industry*. DECHEMA.

BMWK. (2023). *The German Carbon Contracts for Difference (CCfD) scheme* [Online]. Retrieved August 30, 2025, from https://www.bundeswirtschaftsministerium.de/Redaktion/DE/Downloads/klimaschutz/introduction-ccfd_en.pdf?__blob=publicationFile&v=4.

BMWK. (2024). *National hydrogen strategy update* [Online]. Retrieved August 30, 2025, from https://www.bundeswirtschaftsministerium.de/Redaktion/EN/Hydrogen/Downloads/national-hydrogen-strategy-update.pdf?__blob=publicationFile&v=6.

BNEF. (2021). *Hydrogen economy outlook* [Online]. Retrieved August 28, 2025, from https://data.bloomberglp.com/professional/sites/24/BNEF-Hydrogen-Economy-Outlook-_Key-Messages.pdf.

BP. (2024). *BP and Iberdrola announce final investment decision for largest green hydrogen plant in Spain* [Online]. Retrieved August 31, 2025, from https://www.bp.com/en/global/corporate/news-and-insights/press-releases/bp-and-iberdrola-announce-final-investment-decision-for-largest-green-hydrogen-plant-in-spain.html.

Butt, O. M., et al. (2022). Hydrogen as potential primary energy fuel for municipal solid waste incineration for a sustainable waste management. *IEEE Access, 10*(1), 114586–114596.

CertifHy. (2024). *CertifHy. 1st EU-wide guarantee of origin for premium hydrogen* [Online]. Retrieved August 30, 2025, from https://www.certifhy.eu/wp-content/uploads/2021/10/CertifHy_folder__leaflets.pdf.

Daurer, G., et al. (2025). On the use of hydrogen in oxy-fuel glass melting furnaces: An extensive numerical study of the fuel switching effects based on coupled CFD simulations. *Fuel, 380*(1), 1–15.

DESNZ. (2023). *Industrial fuel switching programme, phase 2: Summaries of successful projects* [Online]. Retrieved August 30, 2025, from https://www.gov.uk/government/publications/industrial-fuel-switching-programme-successful-projects/industrial-fuel-switching-programme-phase-2-summaries-of-successful-projects.

DNV. (2024). *The critical role of H2 standards and guidelines in industry development* [Online]. Retrieved August 30, 2025, from https://www.dnv.com/article/the-critical-role-of-h2-standards-and-guidelines-in-industry-development/.

EEA. (2024). *Total net greenhouse gas emission trends and projections in Europe* [Online]. Retrieved August 21, 2025, from https://www.eea.europa.eu/en/analysis/indicators/total-greenhouse-gas-emission-trends.

Energy Transitions Commission. (2021). *Making the hydrogen economy possible: Accelerating clean hydrogen in an electrified economy* [Online]. Retrieved August 26, 2025, from https://www.energy-transitions.org/publications/making-clean-hydrogen-possible/.

Eureka. (2025). *Hydrotreating vs. hydreodesulfurization (HDS): Key differences and applications* [Online]. Retrieved August 26, 2025, from https://eureka.patsnap.com/article/hydrotreating-vs-hydrodesulfurization-hds-key-differences-and-applications.

European Commission. (2022). *The role of hydrogen in energy decarbonisation scenarios. Views on 2030 and 2050.* Publications Office of the European Union.

European Commission. (2023). *Renewable Energy Directive* [Online]. Retrieved August 26, 2025, from https://energy.ec.europa.eu/topics/renewable-energy/renewable-energy-directive-targets-and-rules/renewable-energy-directive_en.

European Commission. (2024a). *EU Net-Zero Industry Act* [Online]. Retrieved August 30, 2025, from https://eur-lex.europa.eu/legal-content/PL/ALL/?uri=LEGISSUM:4781345.

European Commission. (2024b). *European Hydrogen Bank* [Online]. Retrieved August 29, 2025, from https://energy.ec.europa.eu/topics/eus-energy-system/hydrogen/european-hydrogen-bank_en.

European Commission. (2024c). *Towards an ambitious industrial carbon management for the EU* [Online]. Retrieved August 29, 2025, from https://data.consilium.europa.eu/doc/document/ST-6306-2024-INIT/en/pdf.

European Commission. (2025a). *CBAM guidance and legislation* [Online]. Retrieved August 30, 2025, from https://taxation-customs.ec.europa.eu/carbon-border-adjustment-mechanism/cbam-guidance-and-legislation_en.

European Commission. (2025b). *Free allocation* [Online]. Retrieved August 30, 2025, from https://climate.ec.europa.eu/eu-action/carbon-markets/eu-emissions-trading-system-eu-ets/free-allocation_en.

European Commission. (2025c). *IF24 auction* [Online]. Retrieved August 30, 2025, from https://climate.ec.europa.eu/eu-action/eu-funding-climate-action/innovation-fund/calls-proposals/if24-auction_en?utm.

European Hydrogen Backbone. (2025). *The European Hydrogen Backbone (EHB) initiative* [Online]. Retrieved August 28, 2025, from https://ehb.eu/.

European Hydrogen Observatory. (2025). *Hydrogen and decarbonised gas market package* [Online]. Retrieved August 30, 2025, from https://observatory.clean-hydrogen.europa.eu/eu-policy/hydrogen-and-decarbonised-gas-market-package.

European Parliament. (2025). *Revision of the Energy Taxation Directive (ETD) – Q2 2021* [Online]. Retrieved August 30, 2025, from https://www.europarl.europa.eu/legislative-train/carriage/revision-of-the-energy-taxation-directive/report?sid=9301.

ExxonMobil. (2025). *Baytown breakthrough: Our next-generation hydrogen burner can help decarbonise a key industry* [Online]. Retrieved August 19, 2025, from https://corporate.exxonmobil.com/what-we-do/delivering-industrial-solutions/hydrogen/baytown-hydrogen-burner-decarbonize-industry.

Franco, A., & Rocca, M. (2024). Industrial decarbonisation through blended combustion of natural gas and hydrogen. *Hydrogen, 5*(3), 519–539.

Frontier Economics. (2025). *Results of EU hydrogen bank auction announced* [Online]. Retrieved August 30, 2025, from https://climate.ec.europa.eu/eu-action/eu-funding-climate-action/innovation-fund/calls-proposals/if24-auction_en?utm.

Glass Magazine. (2024). *NSG Group plans hydrogen plant in UK* [Online]. Retrieved August 31, 2025, from https://www.glassmagazine.com/news/2024/nsg-group-plans-hydrogen-plant-uk.

Global CCS Institute. (2025). *Global status of CCS 2024* [Online]. Retrieved August 29, 2025, from https://www.globalccsinstitute.com/resources/global-status-report/.

Global Recycling. (2025). *Successful resting of a hydrogen-powered melting furnace* [Online]. Retrieved August 31, 2025, from https://global-recycling.info/archives/10498?utm.

Government of France. (2024). *Le Plan national pour des achats durables 2022–2025* [Online]. Retrieved August 30, 2025, from https://achats-durables.gouv.fr/plan-national-achats-durables-2022-2025-422.

Grenian Hydrogen. (2024). *St. Helens* [Online]. Retrieved August 31, 2025, from https://grenianhydrogen.com/st-helens/.

H2Glass. (2025). *Who we are* [Online]. Retrieved August 31, 2025, from https://h2-glass.eu/who-we-are/.

HM Government. (2023). *Hydrogen strategy update to the market: August 2023* [Online]. Retrieved August 29, 2025, from https://assets.publishing.service.gov.uk/media/67571058f1e6b277c4f79a76/hydrogen-strategy-update-to-the-market-august-2023.pdf.

Hydrogen Council. (2022). *Global hydrogen flows* [Online]. Retrieved August 27, 2025, from https://hydrogencouncil.com/wp-content/uploads/2022/10/Global-Hydrogen-Flows.pdf.

HySkills. (2024). *Module 2. Hydrogen safety, risks, standards & regulation* [Online]. Retrieved August 29, 2025, from https://ec.europa.eu/programmes/erasmus-plus/project-result-content/05decaf7-fd4c-460d-ac1c-3192c50da206/HySkills-Unit-2_Hydrogen-Safety-Risk-Standards-Regulation.pdf.

IEA. (2023). *Net zero roadmap: A global pathway to keep the 1.5 °C goal in reach* [Online]. Retrieved August 27, 2025, from https://www.iea.org/reports/net-zero-roadmap-a-global-pathway-to-keep-the-15-0c-goal-in-reach.

IEA. (2024). *Global hydrogen review 2024* [Online]. Retrieved August 26, 2025, from https://www.iea.org/reports/global-hydrogen-review-2024.

IEA. (2025). *Policy toolbox for industrial decarbonisation* [Online]. Retrieved August 19, 2025, from https://www.iea.org/reports/policy-toolbox-for-industrial-decarbonisation.

Iplik, E., Adendorff, M., & Muren, D. (2022). Hydrogen oxyfuel combustion for energy-intensive industries. In *Clean energy technologies – Hydrogen and gasification processes*. IntechOpen.

IRENA. (2023). *Global hydrogen trade to meet the 1.5 °C climate goal: Part III: Green hydrogen cost and potential* [Online]. Retrieved August 29, 2025, from https://irena.org/-/media/Files/IRENA/Agency/Publication/2022/May/IRENA_Global_Hydrogen_Trade_Costs_2022.pdf.

Italy's Council of Ministers. (2023). *Piano Nazionale di Ripresa e Resilienza* [Online]. Retrieved August 30, 2025, from https://www.governo.it/sites/governo.it/files/PNRR.pdf.

Kandilli, C., Ayna, O. M., & Sahin, M. (2015). Evaluation of the performance of a hydrogen enriched combustion system for ceramic sector. *International Journal of Hydrogen Energy, 40*(34), 11195–11206.

Kim, Y. B., Sohn, C. B., & Jeong, Y. S. (2025). Development of a low-NOx hydrogen combustion burner with an oblong flame port and orthogonal fuel-air injection. *Applied Thermal Engineering, 279*(C), 1–11.

Leeson, D., et al. (2017). A techno-economic analysis and systematic review of carbon capture and storage (CCS) applied to the iron and steel, cement, oil refining and pulp and paper industries, as well as other high purity sources. *International Journal of Greenhouse Gas Control, 61*(1), 71–84.

Leichter, J., Giese, A., & Wieland, C. (2024). Electrification or hydrogen? The challenge of decarbonizing industrial (high-temperature) process heat. *J, 7*(4), 439–456.

Lipiäinen, S., Lipiäinen, K., Ahola, A., & Vakkilainen, E. (2023). Use of existing gas infrastructure in European hydrogen economy. *International Journal of Hydrogen Energy, 48*(80), 31317–31329.

Maketo, L., & Ashworth, P. (2025). Social acceptance of green hydrogen in European Union and the United Kingdom: A systematic review. *Renewable and Sustainable Energy Reviews, 218*(1), 1–10.

Mańkowska, E., & Mazur, M. (2025). Hydrogen gas sensing performance of p-type copper and titanium mixed oxides: Influence of the elemental composition and the annealing temperature. *International Journal of Hydrogen Energy, 144*(1), 292–302.

Mielich, T., et al. (2025). Europe's way from natural gas to green hydrogen: Modeling and simulation of the transforming European gas transport infrastructure. *International Journal of Hydrogen Energy, 135*(1), 156–171.

Ministero dell'Ambiente. (2024). *Strategia Nazionale Idrogeno* [Online]. Retrieved August 30, 2025, from https://www.mase.gov.it/portale/sites/default/files/Strategia%20Nazionale%20Idrogeno.pdf.

Mosca, L., et al. (2020). Hydrogen in chemical and petrochemical industry. In *Current trends and future developments on (bio-) membranes. New perspectives on hydrogen production, separation, and utilization* (pp. 387–410). Elsevier.

Netherlands Enterprise Agency. (2024). *SDE++ 2024. Stimulation of sustainable energy production and climate transition* [Online]. Retrieved August 30, 2025, from https://english.rvo.nl/sites/default/files/2024-09/Brochure_SDE_English_20240906.pdf.

Norwood, A. (2023). *Hydrogen firing: UK's Lucideon works with ceramics industry on hydrogen-firing trials* [Online]. Retrieved August 25, 2025, from https://

bulletin.ceramics.org/article/hydrogen-firing-uks-lucideon-works-with-ceramics-industry-on-hydrogen-firing-trials/.

NS Energy. (2025). *REFHYNE 2 PEM hydrogen electrolyser, Germany* [Online]. Retrieved August 31, 2025, from https://www.nsenergybusiness.com/projects/refhyne-2-germany/.

Pilkington UK. (2025). *Pilkington UK opens new glass production line in St Helens* [Online]. Retrieved August 31, 2025, from https://www.pilkington.com/en-gb/uk/news-insights/latest/pilkington-uk-opens-new-glass-production-line-in-st-helens.

Plug. (2024). *Plug contracts with bp and Iberdrola Joint Ventur to supply 25 MW of PEM electrolyzers for bp's Castellon Refinery Project in Valencia, Spain* [Online]. Retrieved August 31, 2025, from https://www.ir.plugpower.com/press-releases/news-details/2024/Plug-Contracts-with-bp-and-Iberdrola-Joint-Venture-to-Supply-25-MW-of-PEM-Electrolyzers-for-bps-Casteln-Refinery-Project-in-Valencia-Spain/default.aspx.

Refhyne. (2025). *REFHYNE 2* [Online]. Retrieved August 31, 2025, from https://www.refhyne.eu/refhyne-2/.

Regeringskansliet. (2023). *Regeringens klimatpolitik* [Online]. Retrieved August 30, 2025, from https://www.regeringen.se/regeringens-politik/regeringens-klimatpolitik/.

Renewable H2. (2021). *Major European ceramics industry makes giant leap* [Online]. Retrieved August 31, 2025, from https://renewableh2.eu/stories/major-ceramics-industry-makes-giants-leap/.

Reuters. (2024). *Shell to build renewable hydrogen electrolyser in Germany* [Online]. Retrieved August 31, 2025, from https://www.reuters.com/business/energy/shell-build-renewable-hydrogen-electrolyser-germany-2024-07-25/.

Röper, K., Kunz, N., & Gast, L. (2025). Renewable hydrogen in industrial production: A bibliometric analysis of current and future applications. *International Journal of Hydrogen Energy, 98*(1), 687–696.

Saygin, D., & Gielen, D. (2021). Zero-emission pathway for the global chemical and petrochemical sector. *Energies, 14*(13), 1–28.

Schwarz, S., et al. (2024). Experimental investigation of hydrogen enriched natural gas combustion with a focus on nitrogen oxide formation on a semi-industrial scale. *International Journal of Hydrogen Energy, 63*(1), 173–183.

Senkov, O., & Froes, F. H. (1999). Thermohydrogen processing of titanium alloys. *International Journal of Hydrogen Energy, 24*(6), 565–576.

Smart Energy. (2025). *ORANGE.BAT expected to start operation in 2025* [Online]. Retrieved August 30, 2025, from https://www.smartenergy.net/orange-bat-expected-to-start-operation-in-2025/.

Sofian, M., et al. (2024). A review on hydrogen blending in gas network: Insight into safety, corrosion, embrittlement, coatings and liners, and bibliometric analysis. *International Journal of Hydrogen Energy, 60*(1), 867–889.

Sokil, O., et al. (2025). Hydrogen for heating: Technologies, challenges, and opportunities. *Open Research Europe, 5*(143), 1–21.

Son, W., Lee, S., & Woo, J. (2023). Community acceptance of hydrogen power plant projects: The case of South Korea. *Renewable and Sustainable Energy Reviews, 187*(1), 1–11.

Speira. (2025). *Speira advances decarbonisation with hydrogen technology* [Online]. Retrieved August 21, 2025, from https://www.speira.com/newsroom/press/speira-advances-decarbonisation-with-hydrogen-technology/.

Stopić, S., & Friedrich, B. G. (2023). Formation and application of hydrogen in non-ferrous metallurgy. *Military Technical Courier, 71*(3), 783–796.

US Department of the Treasury. (2023). *U.S. Department of the Treasury releases final rules for Clean Hydrogen Production Tax Credit* [Online]. Retrieved August 30, 2025, from https://home.treasury.gov/news/press-releases/jy2768.

Wood Mackenzie. (2025). *European refiners may hold the key to scaling green hydrogen* [Online]. Retrieved August 26, 2025, from https://www.woodmac.com/press-releases/european-refiners-may-hold-the-key-to-scaling-green-hydrogen/.

CHAPTER 14

# Conclusions

## The Central Thesis and the Core Problem

The global energy transition is not merely a substitution of fuels but a reconfiguration of the material, economic, and institutional foundations of modern civilisation. At its core lies a question that has animated this book: *What is the realistic role of hydrogen in that reconfiguration?* For decades, hydrogen has been portrayed alternately as a panacea for decarbonisation and as a distraction from more immediate solutions. The central problem addressed in this volume is how to distinguish between these two narratives—to separate the conditions under which hydrogen genuinely adds value from those where it merely recycles old expectations under new slogans.

The book's central thesis is that hydrogen occupies a selective but indispensable role in the emerging low-carbon economy. It is not a universal energy vector but a precision tool—essential in some sectors, marginal in others, and counterproductive in a few. For example, cement production is a domain where hydrogen's physical limits and costs make its role marginal compared with material substitution and carbon capture-based approaches. Hydrogen's value arises not from its ubiquity but from its specificity: its ability to decarbonise industrial and chemical processes that electricity alone cannot reach, to provide seasonal storage and system balancing, and to anchor new industrial linkages between energy



A. Patonia, R. Poudineh, *Clean Hydrogen for Decarbonisation*,
https://doi.org/10.1007/978-3-032-19442-8_14

and materials. In this sense, hydrogen is best understood not as a competing energy system but as a complementary infrastructure—one that, under the right conditions, underpins, extends, and stabilises electrification.[1]

At the same time, the hydrogen transition exposes deep economic and governance tensions within the broader energy transformation. The molecule itself is simple, but the system required to produce, transport, and use it cleanly is complex and capital-intensive. The central challenge, therefore, is not technological discovery but institutional design: how to allocate cost, risk, and responsibility across public and private actors in a domain where market signals alone are insufficient to achieve economically coherent decarbonisation. Hydrogen sits at the intersection of energy, industry, and climate policy—demanding a level of coordination that few policy frameworks have yet achieved.

The argument advanced throughout this book is that hydrogen's success depends less on intrinsic technological promise than on contextual fit. Where renewable electricity is abundant and cheap, where industrial heat or feedstock substitution is genuinely required, and where supportive governance frameworks exist, hydrogen can thrive. Where these conditions are absent, it will struggle. The book has therefore treated hydrogen not as an isolated technology but as an integrated system component—its viability determined by interactions among energy markets, industrial structure, infrastructure geography, and policy design.

By tracing hydrogen's potential across power systems, heavy industry, transport, and international trade, the book has shown that hydrogen is both a technical solution and a social choice. It carries the imprint of political ambition, industrial strategy, and public narrative. Its deployment will shape not only emission trajectories but also patterns of industrial competitiveness, trade dependency, and geopolitical influence. In that sense, hydrogen is as much a lens on the future political economy of energy as it is a decarbonisation pathway.

Ultimately, the core message that emerges is one of disciplined optimism. Hydrogen will matter profoundly, but only where it is applied judiciously, with transparency about costs, trade-offs, and system

[1] Two cautions follow from this synthesis. First, because much of the institutional detail in this book is drawn from Europe (and especially the United Kingdom), readers should treat the analysis of policy design as illustrative rather than universally representative; conditions in other major markets can differ materially. Second, hydrogen leakage should be viewed as a climate-governance constraint as well as a safety issue: credible deployment at scale requires measurement, verification, and mitigation practices that prevent indirect warming impacts from eroding decarbonisation gains.

boundaries. The hydrogen economy will not materialise through aspiration alone—it must be built through selectivity, coordination, and evidence-based governance. The challenge, therefore, is not to decide whether hydrogen is 'good' or 'bad', but to determine where, when, and how it contributes most effectively to the collective project of decarbonisation. Clean hydrogen will not be the 'next oil': it will be an important, but bounded and specialised, connective infrastructure for a decarbonised industrial system.

## Synthesis of Key Findings

Hydrogen's value emerges not from its novelty but from its systemic positioning within the broader decarbonisation landscape. Across sectors, a recurring pattern becomes evident: hydrogen is most effective where direct electrification reaches its physical or chemical limits. This includes processes requiring chemical reduction on very high temperatures—steelmaking, ammonia synthesis, methanol production, and some long-duration storage applications—where hydrogen provides molecular functions that electricity cannot practically substitute. In such contexts—steelmaking, ammonia, methanol, or long-duration storage—hydrogen substitutes not merely as a fuel but as a molecular enabler of processes that demand chemical reduction or high-temperature combustion. These are the domains where hydrogen can 'win': where it provides unique functionality that electrons cannot replicate, and where it can be integrated into industrial value chains that already consume or handle hydrogen.

The analysis demonstrates that hydrogen's strongest near-term foothold lies in industrial applications that already rely on grey hydrogen or fossil feedstocks. In these sectors, substitution with clean hydrogen entails continuity rather than disruption. The transition is technologically tractable because process chemistry remains largely intact; what changes is the carbon intensity of input molecules. This applies most clearly to ammonia, methanol, and refining, which together account for over 80% of today's global hydrogen use. Here, the path to decarbonisation is evolutionary: existing assets can be retrofitted, supply chains are familiar, and the product remains fungible in global trade. These conditions make the chemical industry not only hydrogen's first large-scale market but also the institutional laboratory for the hydrogen economy's industrial organisation.

Beyond feedstock substitution, hydrogen may also 'win' as a flexibility mechanism within increasingly renewable power systems. Its ability to convert surplus electricity into storable chemical energy can create an interface between variable renewable generation and continuous industrial demand. Hydrogen thus can act as a temporal and spatial buffer—absorbing electricity when it is abundant and releasing energy or industrial feedstock when required. In regions such as Northern Europe or coastal China, where renewable curtailment is rising, hydrogen can provide a means of system balancing that extends the utility of electricity infrastructure rather than competing with it.

However, hydrogen's potential advantage diminishes in applications where direct electrification or other less complex decarbonisation options are technically feasible and economically superior. In sectors such as short-haul transport, residential heating, or moderate-temperature industrial processes, electrification through heat pumps or electric furnaces delivers higher efficiency, lower infrastructure cost, and faster scalability. The cement chapter illustrates this clearly: while hydrogen can, in principle, reduce combustion-related emissions, it cannot address the dominant process $CO_2$ from calcination, so its role in cement decarbonisation is limited to material substitution, clinker reduction, or CCUS. The book's cross-sectoral analysis thus reveals a clear efficiency hierarchy: electrons should be used directly whenever possible, and hydrogen should be reserved for sectors that cannot function without its molecular properties. Treating hydrogen as a universal substitute for fossil energy risks both economic inefficiency and policy misallocation.

The evidence also shows that hydrogen's deployment is most credible when it is clustered rather than diffuse. Hydrogen's high transport and storage costs make standalone projects prohibitively expensive, whereas industrial clusters—integrating production, storage, and multiple end-uses—can exploit economies of scale and cross-sectoral synergies. The emergence of such clusters around refineries, ports, and heavy industrial zones (e.g., the North Sea, Gulf Coast, and Japanese coastal complexes) represents not just an engineering solution but a governance innovation: hydrogen becomes viable when it is embedded within coordinated regional ecosystems.

Yet hydrogen remains contentious in several domains. The first point of contention is its economic competitiveness. Despite rapid cost declines in renewables and electrolysers, green hydrogen remains at least two to four times more expensive than grey hydrogen, and even blue hydrogen faces uncertain cost trajectories due to carbon capture efficiency and methane leakage. The second is system efficiency: when converted, compressed, or transported, hydrogen loses significant energy—raising questions about opportunity costs in an energy-constrained world. The third concerns resource dependencies—notably the large volumes of water and critical minerals, among others, required for electrolysis and the remaining parts of the value chain. Collectively, these challenges frame hydrogen not as an inevitable transition vector but as a conditional opportunity, whose viability hinges on concurrent progress in infrastructure, policy, and markets.

Hydrogen's contested nature is also political. The molecule has become a symbol of industrial renewal, invoked to justify investment and policy support across widely divergent national contexts. At times hydrogen's symbolism has been caricatured as the 'new oil'; this rhetoric can misdirect if not tethered to technical and economic reality. For some countries, hydrogen represents technological leadership and export potential; for others, it is a hedge against stranded fossil assets. This duality has produced a spectrum of hydrogen visions—from pragmatic industrial decarbonisation to geopolitical projection. The analytical implication is that hydrogen is as much a policy artefact as a technological one. Its adoption depends not solely on cost curves but on narratives, alliances, and the institutional capacity to translate ambition into delivery.

At the same time, a set of foundational enablers consistently recurs across successful hydrogen pathways. The first is abundant low-cost renewable electricity, without which no green hydrogen can exist. The second is infrastructure integration—pipelines, storage, and port facilities that allow hydrogen and its derivatives to move economically between production and demand centres. The third is policy architecture: stable carbon pricing, risk mitigation instruments, and public–private partnerships that de-risk early investments and signal long-term commitment. The fourth is standards and certification, which establish credibility and traceability in international trade. Together, these enablers constitute the institutional scaffolding of a viable hydrogen economy.

A cross-cutting insight is that hydrogen development follows a sequenced logic of diffusion. It begins with local substitution in existing grey hydrogen markets, expands through industrial clusters where scale and co-location minimise cost, and only later transitions to global trade in hydrogen carriers such as ammonia or methanol. This sequencing—local substitution, cluster growth, then selective international trade—is critical to avoid overextension and public disillusionment. The evidence suggests that hydrogen transitions succeed when they proceed incrementally and are spatially concentrated and policy-coordinated, rather than through broad, undifferentiated deployment.

Finally, the book reveals a deeper systemic pattern: hydrogen's rise signals not merely the diversification of energy vectors but the recomposition of the industrial economy itself. In chemicals and steel, hydrogen substitutes for fossil carbon as the fundamental input to material production. In power systems, it links electrons to molecules; in trade, it redefines comparative advantage around renewable endowment rather than hydrocarbon reserves. The cumulative picture is one of industrial evolution rather than technological revolution—a transformation that maintains continuity with the fossil era's infrastructures and supply chains, but reorients them towards a post-carbon equilibrium. Hydrogen thus stands at the intersection of continuity and change: the medium through which the old industrial order adapts to the physical and moral imperatives of a decarbonised world.

## Navigating the Primary Challenges and Trade-Offs

The transition to a hydrogen-based industrial system is neither automatic nor assured. While the technological feasibility of clean hydrogen is well established, the economic, infrastructural, and resource preconditions for large-scale deployment remain deeply constraining. The most fundamental challenge is cost: clean hydrogen—whether produced through electrolysis or with carbon capture—remains substantially more expensive than its fossil counterpart. Even under optimistic assumptions of falling renewable and electrolyser costs, production prices are unlikely to reach parity with grey hydrogen without strong carbon pricing or long-term subsidy mechanisms. This raises a systemic trade-off between climate ambition and fiscal realism. Governments must determine how much public support can be justified to bridge the cost gap, and for how long, before technological learning and market maturity take over.

The infrastructure deficit compounds this cost barrier. Hydrogen is a physically demanding molecule—difficult to transport, store, and handle safely. The existing energy infrastructure, optimised for liquid hydrocarbons and natural gas, cannot be repurposed without significant modification. Dedicated hydrogen pipelines, storage caverns, port terminals, and conversion facilities must be built almost from scratch, requiring multibillion-dollar investment and long lead times. This infrastructure must also be regionally coordinated: isolated facilities cannot achieve scale economies or system efficiency. The challenge is not merely financial but institutional—how to align investment across energy, industry, and transport systems that have historically been governed separately. The hydrogen economy thus tests the capacity of states and markets to plan collectively across sectors, a competence largely eroded in liberalised energy systems.

A parallel challenge lies in the regulatory and policy architecture required to orchestrate this transition. The current policy landscape is fragmented: divergent definitions of 'low-carbon hydrogen', inconsistent certification schemes, and varying treatment of blue and green hydrogen complicate trade and investment. Moreover, the temporal mismatch between rapid policy ambition and slow infrastructure delivery creates uncertainty for investors. Even within advanced economies, permitting procedures and grid access delays have stalled flagship projects. Without coherent regulation—covering emissions accounting, safety standards, and long-term pricing mechanisms—the hydrogen sector risks evolving into a patchwork of uncoordinated national initiatives rather than a unified global market. The trade-off here is between policy precision and policy speed: over-regulation may deter innovation, while weak governance invites inefficiency and reputational risk.

Resource constraints add a further layer of complexity. Water consumption for electrolysis—at least nine litres per kilogram of hydrogen—appears modest in isolation but becomes significant at scale, especially in arid regions where many renewable energy hubs are located. Competing demands for water in agriculture and human consumption raise ethical and logistical dilemmas. Similarly, the critical minerals required for electrolysers, fuel cells, and storage systems—nickel, platinum group metals, and rare earth elements—pose supply chain vulnerabilities. Their extraction is geographically concentrated and environmentally intensive, risking a new form of dependency reminiscent of the fossil age. Thus, decarbonisation through hydrogen may inadvertently shift the world's material dependencies rather than eliminate them.

These material and economic constraints translate into a broader political economy dilemma. The hydrogen transition redistributes costs and benefits unevenly across sectors, regions, and social groups. Industrialised economies with high technological capacity can capture the value-added segments of the supply chain, while resource-rich but developing regions risk becoming exporters of low-cost renewable energy or hydrogen intermediates with limited domestic industrialisation. Within nations, the costs of hydrogen infrastructure—borne by taxpayers and consumers—may exceed the visible benefits for years. Managing this asymmetry will require deliberate policy instruments to ensure a just and geographically balanced transition, avoiding the perception that hydrogen is a project for industrial incumbents rather than for society as a whole.

Finally, the hydrogen economy faces an unavoidable temporal trade-off. Rapid deployment can accelerate cost reduction through learning and scale effects, but premature investment in immature technologies or poorly sited infrastructure risks locking in inefficiency and stranded assets. Conversely, waiting for perfect economics may delay decarbonisation beyond climate-relevant timelines. The strategic challenge is to calibrate the pace of transition—to deploy fast enough to learn, but selectively enough to avoid waste. The cement sector again demonstrates this temporal and technical boundary: acting too fast to substitute hydrogen for all fuel needs risks wasted investment where other decarbonisation levers are more effective. In this sense, the hydrogen transition exemplifies the broader condition of the energy transition itself: it is a managed experiment in which uncertainty, coordination, and timing determine success as much as technology or cost.

## Pathways to Implementation: A Call to Action

The empirical and conceptual analysis across this book makes clear that the success of the hydrogen transition depends not on technological breakthroughs alone but on the strategic coordination of multiple policy, industrial, and financial systems. The immediate task for policymakers is to move from vision statements to institutional delivery—translating national hydrogen strategies into credible, bankable, and regionally integrated projects. This requires aligning energy, industrial, and environmental policies around shared objectives. Hydrogen should not be treated as a standalone sector but as an infrastructure of infrastructures, linking electricity markets, heavy industry, and cross-border trade. Establishing clear governance frameworks—defining roles for the state, private sector, and public financiers—is essential to avoid duplication, subsidy overlap, and policy volatility that could undermine investor confidence.

For policymakers, the priority must be to create durable economic signals that close the cost gap between clean and fossil-based hydrogen. Instruments such as Carbon Contracts for Difference (CCfDs) in the way the applied in the electricity sector may not be sufficient to lower the cost and increase the scale. Support mechanisms should be targeted to sectors and projects where hydrogen has a clear comparative advantage, rather than broad-based subsidies that risk misallocating public funds. At the same time, carbon pricing should be progressively strengthened and broadened to internalise emissions across sectors, thereby making fossil alternatives less competitive over time. Policymakers must also invest in regulatory harmonisation and certification, ensuring that definitions of 'green' or 'low-carbon' hydrogen are transparent, interoperable, and internationally recognised. Without credible standards, markets will fragment, and the environmental legitimacy of hydrogen will erode.

For industry, the imperative is to redefine competitiveness in systemic rather than sectoral terms. The transition to clean hydrogen is not a race to produce the cheapest molecule but to build the most efficient and integrated value chains. Companies should prioritise participation in industrial clusters, where shared infrastructure and symbiotic energy flows can reduce costs and risk. Early collaboration between energy producers, equipment manufacturers, and end-users will be decisive in establishing economies of scale. Industrial players need to reconsider their investment approaches, seeing decarbonisation not merely as a compliance expense but as a strategic opportunity to maintain long-term market access in an economy where carbon intensity increasingly shapes competitive advantage.

For investors and financial institutions, the challenge is to extend time horizons and redefine risk metrics. Hydrogen projects, like other capital-intensive infrastructure, require long-term policy stability and patient capital. Traditional project finance models are ill suited to the early stages of hydrogen deployment, where revenues depend on uncertain policy frameworks. Novel financial tools —like blended finance, green bonds, and public–private risk-sharing mechanisms—can help reduce initial risks while encouraging private sector engagement. Engaging institutional investors, sovereign wealth funds, and development banks may be essential to ensure industrial resilience, job creation, and energy security.

Cross-sectoral coordination will also be critical. The deployment of hydrogen infrastructure intersects with electricity system planning, water management, and land-use policy. Governments must therefore establish integrated planning authorities or cross-ministerial task forces to align these domains. The same applies internationally: no single country can construct the hydrogen economy in isolation. Cross-border pipeline projects, maritime ammonia corridors, and certification partnerships must become central pillars of foreign and trade policy. Hydrogen thus demands a new form of cooperative industrial diplomacy—one that treats decarbonisation as a shared economic endeavour rather than a zero-sum competition.

Finally, all stakeholders must recognise that implementation will succeed only if accompanied by social legitimacy and transparency. Public trust can be eroded by unrealistic expectations, opaque subsidies, or local environmental trade-offs. Governments and firms must therefore communicate hydrogen's benefits and limits candidly—acknowledging that it is neither a miracle solution nor a marginal technology, but a targeted instrument in a wider portfolio of transition tools. The path forward requires not ideological enthusiasm but institutional discipline: choosing applications that deliver genuine system value, sequencing deployment according to regional strengths, and maintaining accountability for outcomes. Only through such disciplined pragmatism can hydrogen evolve from promise to practice—becoming a cornerstone, rather than a casualty, of the energy transition.

## Avenues for Future Research

While this book has aimed to clarify hydrogen's role within the broader low-carbon transition, it has also revealed the depth of what remains uncertain. A key avenue for future research is the comprehensive integration of hydrogen across power systems, industrial sectors, and transportation networks. Current modelling frameworks often treat hydrogen as an isolated vector, with limited attention to the operational and institutional feedbacks between power systems, industrial demand, and infrastructure geography. New analytical tools are needed to capture these cross-sectoral linkages—how hydrogen interacts with grid balancing, renewable curtailment, and industrial clustering. Understanding these dynamic interdependencies will be essential for designing efficient investment sequences and avoiding overcapacity or stranded assets.

A second line of inquiry relates to governance and policy design. The emergence of hydrogen challenges the conventional division between energy and industrial policy, requiring hybrid institutions capable of coordinating markets, technology development, and infrastructure planning. Yet the optimal balance between market mechanisms and strategic state intervention remains unclear. Comparative studies of national hydrogen strategies could help identify which combinations of instruments—such as carbon pricing, subsidies, and public procurement—produce the most effective outcomes under varying political and economic conditions. Future work should also explore new governance models for transnational hydrogen trade, including certification systems, carbon border adjustments, and mechanisms for equitable value sharing between exporting and importing regions.

A third domain of uncertainty lies in resource and environmental constraints. The large-scale production of hydrogen will entail, among others, substantial demand for land, water, and critical minerals. Although these challenges are acknowledged, their cumulative impacts on ecosystems, supply chains, and local communities are poorly quantified. Further research is needed to assess the environmental lifecycle of hydrogen technologies—including the embedded carbon in electrolyser manufacturing, the ecological costs of metal extraction, and the implications of water stress in renewable-rich but arid regions. Addressing these externalities requires interdisciplinary methods that bridge engineering, environmental science, and political ecology, moving beyond the techno-economic metrics that dominate current debates.

Finally, the social and geopolitical dimensions of the hydrogen transition remain largely underexplored. Hydrogen will reshape industrial geography, trade dependencies, and patterns of political influence, yet its implications for global governance and development equity are only beginning to be understood. How will hydrogen trade alter relationships between the Global North and South? What new forms of interdependence, vulnerability, or cooperation might emerge? And at the domestic level, how can public acceptance, labour market transitions, and regional disparities be managed in a hydrogen-based industrial transformation? These questions point to the need for a new interdisciplinary research agenda that situates hydrogen not only as an energy technology but as a driver of systemic economic and geopolitical change.

## Concluding Vision

Hydrogen is the medium through which energy and industry converge—the link between electrons and molecules, between renewable resources and human-made systems of production. If deployed judiciously, it can anchor a new industrial equilibrium: one that reconciles economic growth with planetary boundaries, and technological progress with environmental responsibility. Yet the emergence of a hydrogen economy will not unfold automatically or evenly. It will depend on collective intelligence, institutional coordination, and political courage. The challenge is to move beyond the rhetoric of technological salvation towards a disciplined realism that recognises both potential and limits. Hydrogen will succeed only where it is applied with precision—where its use complements, rather than competes with, electrification and efficiency. The task for the coming decades is therefore one of strategic selectivity: to prioritise applications that deliver genuine system value, to design policies that distribute costs and benefits fairly, and to build the infrastructure that transforms isolated projects into coherent industrial systems. This is not the work of a single technology or sector but of an entire social contract—between governments willing to plan, industries willing to adapt, and societies willing to invest in the long term.

The horizon that this book envisions is neither utopian nor fatalistic. It is one of governed transformation—a transition guided by evidence, grounded in material realism, and informed by a shared understanding of interdependence. Hydrogen offers the means to reindustrialise economies on sustainable foundations, to forge new partnerships between energy producers and consumers, and to restore a sense of strategic purpose to industrial policy. But it will also test the integrity of our institutions: their capacity to coordinate across borders, sectors, and generations. The emergence of a hydrogen-based industrial system will therefore be a measure not only of technological innovation but of collective governance competence in an age of ecological constraint.

Clean hydrogen will not be the 'next oil'. It will not recreate the scale or the geopolitics of hydrocarbons. Instead, where it is most effective, it can act as the connective tissue of a decarbonised industrial economy—modest in scale, decisive in impact, and indispensable where no other option performs as well.

The manufacturer's authorised representative in the EU is Springer Nature Customer Service Centre GmbH, Europaplatz 3, 69115 Heidelberg, Germany. If you have any concerns regarding our products, please contact ProductSafety@springernature.com

Printed and bound by CPI Group (UK) Ltd, Croydon, CR0 4YY
22/09/2026
02220956-0003